A BIBLIOGRAPHY OF ANANDA KENTISH COOMARASWAMY

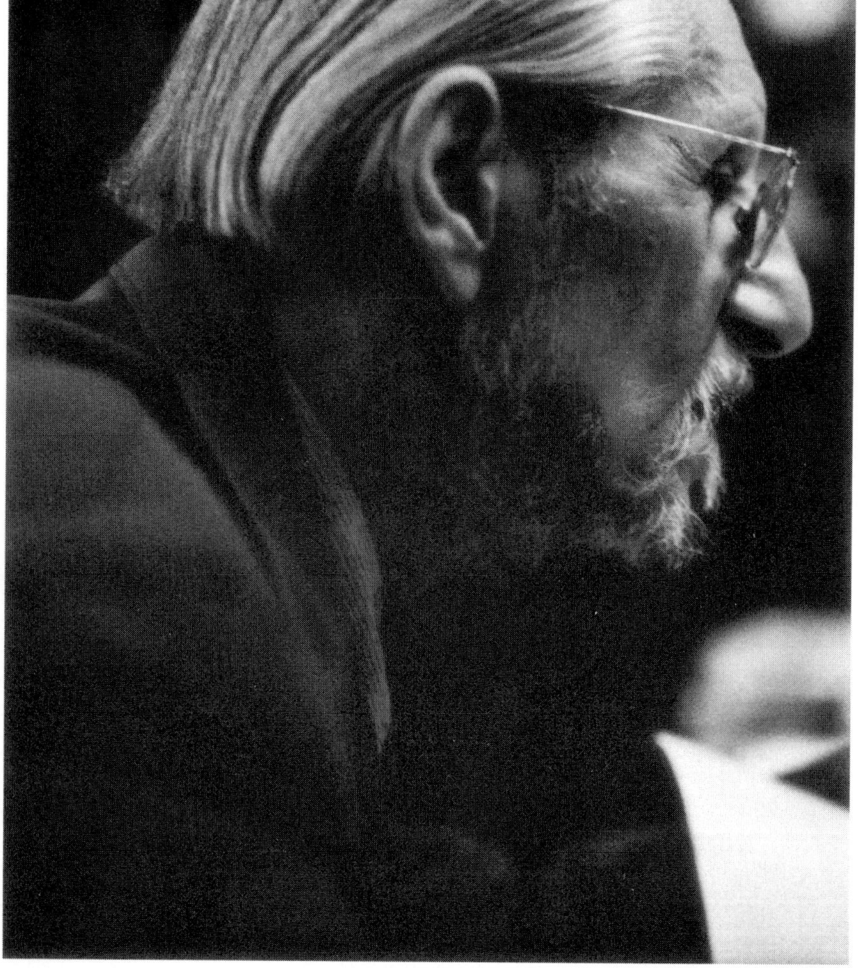

A BIBLIOGRAPHY OF ANANDA KENTISH COOMARASWAMY

by

JAMES S. CROUCH

INDIRA GANDHI NATIONAL CENTRE FOR THE ARTS
NEW DELHI

MANOHAR
2002

First published 2002

ISBN 81-7304-428-7

Published by
Indira Gandhi National Centre for the Arts,
Janpath, New Delhi
in association with
Ajay Kumar Jain for
Manohar Publishers & Distributors
4753/23 Ansari Road, Daryaganj
New Delhi 110002

Printed at

Lordson Publishers Pvt. Ltd.
Delhi 110007

To

H. A. I. GOONETILEKE

Contents

Introductory Note

This bibliography is a revision and expansion of my "Ananda Coomaraswamy in Ceylon: A Bibliography", which appeared in the *Ceylon Journal of Historical and Social Studies*, Peradeniya, for July/December 1973 (but not published until December 1974). The aim of the present undertaking has been to record everything that issued from Ananda K. Coomaraswamy's pen that was published in order to present as true a picture as possible of his life's work. Omissions are through want of information, or my failure to locate files of periodicals and newspapers, and are not intentional. Some bibliographical data are lacking for the relatively few periodical contributions I have been able to see only as clippings.

It has been said that the bibliographer's first duty is to make his bibliography useful; that ideally a bibliography should supply "the greatest number of wants with the least expense of time and effort on the part of the user" (Louis Nicholas Feipel). I have endeavoured throughout to satisfy this dictum.

While other bibliographies, catalogues, indexes, etc., have been consulted in the course of the preparation of the present work, no item has been included merely on the authority of other bibliographers. The existence of every item (unless otherwise noted) has been verified by the compiler through personal inspection. The descriptions of Coomaraswamy's books, and books containing contributions by him, are based upon actual sightings of the books themselves (with additional information supplied from other sources). The principle of personal verification has also been followed with Coomaraswamy's periodical contributions, which have, in almost every instance, been examined *in situ*.

Although most of the bibliographical and other conventions adopted in this book will be self-evident, the following explanations might be helpful, firstly to do with matters which affect the entire book, then with particular sections:

The bibliography is arranged in five sections, and chronologically within the sections (except for Section E, which is arranged in alphabetical order of authors).

The *annotations* are purely descriptive and informative and contain no critical or evaluative comment (though this rule has been somewhat relaxed in Section E). While annotations are called for in the first instance when titles do not clearly or accurately reflect the content, my annotations are further designed to give a detailed and fairly complete account of the entire substance and scope of Coomaraswamy's *oeuvre*. In preparing them I have found that direct quotation of Coomaraswamy's words is often preferable to a paraphrase, as his own declarations of intent are so well formulated that it would be difficult or impossible to put them in other words. Since Coomaraswamy's writings concerning the island of *Ceylon* precede that country's change of name (to Sri Lanka on 22 May 1972), this use has been retained in my annotations. *Dates* are not quoted but transposed to a standard form, e.g. 21 April 1942. A date given in square brackets has been supplied by the compiler, having been established on external evidence; the portion of the date that is conjectural or dubious being followed by a question mark. The term *plates* refers to illustrative matter in books and periodicals printed separately from the text and occupying only one side of a leaf (usually of special paper). As a general rule, when plates are printed on both sides of a leaf this is noted, as it is also when they are not included in the page count but have their own numbering (or are unnumbered). When plates are inserted before or after the text their location is indicated. Plates are printed in black-and-white unless otherwise described. Time at the compiler's disposal was insufficient to pursue with any thoroughness the *translations* into foreign languages of Coomaraswamy's writings. Other translations doubtless exist; I include only those of which I have definite knowledge. It may be assumed, in the entries for Coomaraswamy's books, that the language of the translation is that of the given place of publication.

Section A: The entries in this section are devoted to Coomaraswamy's own books. In the description of books I have tried to conform to the method formulated by Donald Gallup in his remarkable work *Ezra Pound: A Bibliography* (Charlottesville: University Press of Virginia [1983]). With Mr Gallup's permission I quote his explanation of this descriptive method, which accounts for all leaves, instead of only the numbered pages of the text: "The general rule is that when the unnumbered printed preliminary leaves count up (as pages) to the first numbered page of the book, these leaves are not specified in the collation. When they do *not* count up, they *are* specified: *e.g.* 1 blank leaf, 3 leaves, 9-29 pp., because here the *printed* preliminary material counts up to only six pages. When the first numbered page is the verso of a leaf unnumbered on the recto, the number of the recto is supplied in square brackets: *e.g.* 1 blank leaf, 3 leaves, [9]-29 pp., thus indicating that 10 is the first page numbered. The collation '29 pp.' alone indicates that the preliminary material counts up to the first numbered page and that the text ends on a page numbered 29 (page [30], being blank, is not specified). The collation '29, [1] pp.', on the other hand, indicates either that the text ends on the unnumbered page [30], or that a colophon, an index, or some other printed material appears on that page. '29 pp., 1 leaf' indicates that the text ends on page 29, page [30] is blank, and additional material not a continuation of the text appears on a final unnumbered leaf, either recto or verso or both being printed."

First editions (i.e. the first impression of the first printing) of books by Coomaraswamy are described in some detail. As a general rule, impressions and editions subsequent to the first have been ignored unless substantive correction or revision has taken place, or when new prefaces or other additional matter has been incorporated. Whenever possible I have supplied the exact date of publication and the number of copies printed. The title-pages of Coomaraswamy's books are transcribed verbatim and in their entirety, though no attempt has been made to indicate variations in type face, size, or capitalization;

the end of each line is marked by an upright rule. The dimensions of books are of the original covers measured in centimeters, height before width, and include the bulge of the spine and projection of the covers beyond the edges of the leaves. In the descriptions of Coomaraswamy's books it may be assumed that all edges are trimmed and plain unless otherwise stated. Dust-jackets have been recorded when I have encountered them.

Reviews of Coomaraswamy's books are listed chronologically (as part of the entry for the book). I record only those reviews that I have definite information about; others certainly exist.

Section B: This section deals with Coomaraswamy's contributions to books, i.e. items published for the first time or in book form for the first time. The descriptive method for books has been much simplified, as its presence in this case does not serve a really useful purpose.

Section C: The arrangement of Coomaraswamy's periodical contributions is chronological; those dated by the whole year only precede those dated by month, etc.; those of the same date are listed alphabetically. Individual pieces within the same issue of a periodical are listed in the order in which they appear in the periodical. As a rule only first periodical appearances have been listed, of contributions not already printed in books. Subsequent periodical appearances are not allocated a separate entry but are noted as part of the entry for the first appearance. Contributions are listed in the index under both title and periodical. The language in which a contribution is printed has been specified when it is not that of, or apparent from, the title. The initial definite articles in English titles of periodicals have been omitted. Offprints have been recorded (as part of the entry for the periodical contribution) when I have come across them and when they have been given their own pagination and wrappers, as these are likely to be mistaken for separate pamphlet publications.

Sections D and E: These sections employ the same descriptive methods as for Sections B and C. Section D calls, I think, for no special comment. Section E which forms an appendix to the bibliography is a list of selected writings *about* Coomaraswamy, selectively annotated. The entries are arranged in alphabetical order of writers. When there is more than one work by a writer these are listed in chronological order of publication. The book reviews in Section A are not repeated, except for a few which have some particular significance.

Unfortunately the opportunities for error in a book of this sort are abundant. I shall be grateful to anyone who cares to take the trouble to inform me of errors, and omissions, here or anywhere else in the bibliography. It is a matter for regret that only three months were available to me for research in England and America, as this was insufficient time to locate and inspect copies of *every* edition, impression, and reprint of books by Coomaraswamy. Lacunae, particularly in Section A, should be understood in the light of this statement.

INTRODUCTORY NOTE

The *terminus ad quem* for the collection of material for inclusion in this bibliography was December 1992, although it has been found possible to admit some of the more important publications that appeared after that date.

For convenience, Ananda Kentish Coomaraswamy will be referred to throughout the bibliography by his initials AKC.

The frontispiece to this book shows Coomaraswamy in the Summer of 1947 in his office at the Museum of Fine Arts, Boston, two weeks before his death, photographed by Dorothy Norman and reproduced here by courtesy of the Philadelphia Museum of Art.

Acknowledgements

Most bibliographies are based to a large extent upon the labours of others; the present work is no exception. The main foundation upon which this bibliography has been built is the check-list of Coomaraswamy's writings instigated by the late Richard Ettinghausen and compiled by Helen E. Ladd (with assistance from Coomaraswamy), which was printed in *Ars Islamica*, Ann Arbor, in 1942. My debt to Miss Ladd's pioneering work is great, and I acknowledge it with gratitude. At an early stage in my undertaking Roger Lipsey in New York kindly sent me a private list that the late Doña Luisa Coomaraswamy had prepared of her husband's work. I am grateful to Mr Lipsey for this and for other help over the years. I have also profited from Coomaraswamy's own lists of his publications compiled between 1917 and 1947 for inclusion in the *Annual Reports* of the Museum of Fine Arts, Boston, and the extraordinary and—it must be said—demanding productions of the late S. Durai Raja Singam, doyen of Coomaraswamy *aficionados*, in particular his *Ananda Kentish Coomaraswamy: A Bibliographical Record* (Kuala Lumpur, 1981-84).

I am deeply indebted to the former Librarian of the University of Sri Lanka at Peradeniya, H.A.I. Goonetileke (to whom this book is dedicated), for his encouragement and guidance at a crucial period in the preparation of the present work, and for generously granting me access in 1973 to the Library's then uncatalogued D.P.E. Hettiaratchi Collection of Ceyloniana, with its fabulously rich component of Coomaraswamy material. In Greenwich (Connecticut) in 1991 I was privileged to examine copies of books, papers, and correspondence by Coomaraswamy, in the possession of his son and literary executor, Rama P. Coomaraswamy, M.D. He has gone out of his way to help me at all stages of my work, with information about his father's writings and by taking the trouble to obtain materials that might be of use to me. I wish to record my gratitude for his kindness and for his long-standing belief in my work which has helped sustain me throughout this difficult undertaking.

I am grateful to the following libraries, institutions, and individual members of their staffs for the cheerful and unfailing assistance they have rendered:

In America: Albright-Knox Art Gallery, Buffalo (Douglas G. Schultz); American Oriental Society, New Haven (Ferris J. Stephens); Boston Public Library, Boston (Theresa Cederholm, Natalie Palme Breed); Catholic University of America, the John K. Mullen of Denver Memorial Library, Washington, D.C.; Cleveland Museum of Art, Cleveland; College of Notre Dame of Maryland, Baltimore (Sister M. John de Matha Bersch); Freer Gallery of Art Library at the Arthur M. Sackler Gallery, Washington, D.C. (Kathryn Phillips); Harvard University, the Widener Library and the Hilles Library, Cambridge; Jewish Theological Seminary of

America, New York (Jessica Feingold); Library of Congress, Washington, D.C.; Minneapolis Public Library and Information Center, Minneapolis (Michael F. Winter); Museum of Fine Arts, Boston, the William Morris Hunt Memorial Library (Nancy S. Allen, D.F. Dwyer); New York Public Library, and the New York Public Library for the Performing Arts at Lincoln Center, New York; Princeton University, the Marquand (Art) Library and the Firestone Library, Princeton (Jean F. Preston, Ann Van Arsdale, Stephen Ferguson and The Ananda Coomaraswamy Papers in the Department of Rare Books and Special Collections); Princeton University Press, Princeton (William McGuire); Seattle Public Library, Seattle (Patricia Tyler); Union Theological Seminary, New York; University of California at Berkeley, the General Library and the Graduate Theological Union Library; University of Hawaii at Manoa, the Thomas Hale Hamilton Library, Honolulu; University of Minnesota, Minneapolis (Henry Scholberg and the Ames Library of South Asia); Worcester Art Museum, Worcester (Charlene Key Sokal).

In Australia: Australian National University Library, Canberra; National Library of Australia, Canberra (H.L. White); Royal Geographical Society of Australasia, Adelaide (D.J. Evans); State Library of New South Wales, Sydney (Judith Hunter); State Library of Queensland, Brisbane (E.G. Heap, M.F. Lynch, J.L. McCann); State Library of South Australia, Adelaide (R.K. Olding); State Library of Victoria, Melbourne (Dianne Reilly, Gail Schmidt); University of Adelaide, the Barr Smith Library, Adelaide; University of Melbourne, the Baillieu Library, Melbourne (Patrick Singleton); University of Queensland Library, St Lucia (Jean Keating, S.J. Routh); University of Sydney, the Fisher Library, Sydney (Margaret Lundie).

In England: The British Library, Department of Printed Books, London; Cambridge University Library, Cambridge; India Office Library and Records, London (Catherine R. Pickett, A. Potts); Royal Asiatic Society, London (Jill Davies, V. Nielsen); Royal Society for India, Pakistan, and Sri Lanka, London (Aileen M. Armstrong); University of London Library, Senate House and the School of Oriental and African Studies Library, London; Victoria and Albert Museum, the National Art Library, London (John P. Harthan); Wycliffe College Library, Stonehouse (Fr G.E. Andow, Noel W. Johnston).

In India: Adyar Library and Research Centre, Madras; American Institute of Indian Studies, Varanasi; The Asiatic Society Library, Calcutta; Bombay University Library, Fort Campus, Bombay; India International Centre Library, New Delhi; Karnatak University Library, Dharwar (K.S. Deshpande); National Archives of India, New Delhi (J.C. Srivastava); National Library of India, Calcutta (Kalpana Das Gupta); National Museum Library, New Delhi; Ramakrishna Mission Institute of Culture Library, Calcutta; University of Madras Library, Madras.

In Sri Lanka: Department of National Archives, Colombo and Gangodawila (Harischandra de Silva); National Museum Library, Colombo (Vijita de Silva and the H.C.P. Bell Collection); University of Sri Lanka Library, Peradeniya (H.A.I. Goonetileke and the Muhandiram D.P.E. Hettiaratchi Collection).

My thanks are due to the following people who have contributed information, supplied copies of books, or helped in other ways: the late S. Arasaratnam; Jonathan and Erica Bader; Greg Bailey; Senake Bandaranayake; Cecil Bethell; the late John Cage; Pramod Chandra; the late F. Clive-Ross; Nicholas Daniels; Klára Doroszlay; John Dunham; Eithne Eastman; Harriet Edquist; Fr Ian Herring; R. Gordon Heyzer; K.C. Kamaliah; Lester Kanefsky; Brian Keeble; Richard Kelly; Kurt F. Leidecker; the late Hazel McCrea; Colin McDowell; Michael Meister; David Miller; the late Donovan Moldrich; Tambyah Nadaraja; the late Swami Narikutti; Kenneth (Harry) S. Oldmeadow; the late Marco Pallis; Roger N. Parisious; Whitall N. Perry; George Pollard; Derek John de Solla Price; Airavathan Ranganathan; Keith Richmond; Arnold Rood; the late James Rutnam; Paul Schroeder; Walter Shewring; Michael Stevenson; the late Harold Stewart; Peter Stewart; Graeme Vanderstoel; James R. W[illegible]more; Ken White; Scott Whittaker; Sarathchandra Wickramasuriya.

And finally, I wish to express my thanks to the Indira Gandhi National Centre for the Arts, New Delhi, in particular Dr Kapila Vatsyayan and Dr Lalit M. Gujral, for their patient co-operation and for making available the necessary funds for me to visit various libraries in India in 1992, thereby enabling me to bring this work to its present stage of completion.

Melbourne, Australia
June 1999

J. S. C.

A. Books and Pamphlets by Ananda K. Coomaraswamy

A. Books and Pamphlets

A1 REPORT ON THORIANITE AND THORITE [1904]

First edition:

REPORT ON THORIANITE AND THORITE, BY MR. ANANDA K. COOMARASWAMY, | B.Sc., DIRECTOR, MINERALOGICAL SURVEY, CEYLON [Colombo: Government Printing Office]

5 pp., 2 text illus. (incl. map). 33 x 20.5 cm. (approx.). Title-leaf and last leaf serve as wrappers. Wire-stitched(?).

Contents: Report on Thorianite and Thorite [dated Kandy, 3 Aug. 1904, with a "Postscript", dated Kandy, 1 Nov. 1904]—Report on the Occurrence of Thorium-bearing Minerals in Ceylon [by Wyndham R. Dunstan, dated 31 Mar. 1904].

Notes: An expansion and revision of the report given in C42—pp. E6-E9.

A second printing, not so identified, was issued in January 1905; the contents, pagination, and size are identical with those of the first edition.

A2 SOME KANDYAN CRAFTS [1905]

First edition:

SOME KANDYAN CRAFTS. A LECTURE GIVEN | IN THE TOWN HALL, KANDY, NOVEMBER 14, | 1904. BY ANANDA K. COOMARASWAMY, B.Sc. [Kandy: Printed for the author at the Industrial School]

1 leaf, 23, [1] pp., 1 blank leaf. 21.5 x 16.9 cm. Limp brown paper wrappers with, on front, white paper label lettered in black; sewn.

Colophon (page [24]): 300 copies printed at the Industrial School, Kandy and finished on the 20th day of January 1905. To be had from the Author, at Rock House, Kandy, price 50 cents.

Notes: On the traditional methods and implements of the village craftsman, as these are employed in pottery, iron smelting, steel making, weaving, and embroidery; together with suggestions for the encouragement and preservation of these crafts. Technical craft terms are printed in Sinhalese script with English equivalents. An epigraph comprising a quotation, printed in 11 lines, from "Art and Industry in the Fourteenth Century", by William Morris, appears on verso of the title-leaf. A list of errata is printed in 4 lines on page 23. Two printed announcements (handbills?) of this lecture are reproduced in *Coomaraswamy 3: His Life and Work*, by Roger Lipsey ([1977])—B94a—p. [27]. Lipsey's caption erroneously dates these announcements "ca. 1906".

A3 BORROWED PLUMES [1905]

First edition:

BORROWED PLUMES: BY | A. K. COOMARASWAMY. [Kandy: Printed for the author at the Industrial School]

7, [1] pp. 20.5 x 16.1 cm. Title-leaf and the last leaf serve as wrappers; sewn.

Colophon (page [8]): 100 copies printed for the Author at the Industrial School, Kandy and finished on the 26th day of January 1905.

Notes: A plea for the retention of native apparel in Ceylon, taking the form of a meditation upon seeing an ill-dressed mother and child on the pilgrims' track from Ratnapura to Adam's Peak. AKC also gives his impressions of an old *vihāra* and *chena* cultivation, along with other aspects of Ceylonese rural life. Quotations from Pindar and from Walter Crane appear as epigraphs on page [2].

Translation: A note printed in *Ceylon National Review*, Colombo, I. 2 (July 1906), Supplement, p. [5], refers to a Sinhala translation issued in Ceylon between January and April 1905 (not sighted by the compiler).

A4 AN OPEN LETTER TO THE KANDYAN CHIEFS [1905]

a. *First edition:*

AN OPEN LETTER TO THE KANDYAN CHIEFS. | BY ANANDA K. COOMARASWAMY. [Kandy: Printed for the author at the Industrial School]

14, [1] pp., 1 text illus. 20.7 x 16.3 cm. Limp olive green paper wrappers with, on front, white paper label lettered in black; sewn.

Colophon (page [15]): 350 copies printed for the Writer, at the Industrial School, Kandy and finished the 15th day of April, 1905.

Notes: An appeal (somewhat after the manner of William Morris's Society for the Protection of Ancient Buildings) for the better preservation of Buddhist buildings in Ceylon, with particular reference to those of the 17th and 18th centuries; incorporating a description of the wall-paintings in the Degaldoruvā Vihāra (pp. 6-9). A reprint of "An Open Letter to the Kandyan Chiefs: An Expert on Kandyan Architecture and Painting in the Days of Old", in *Ceylon Observer*, Colombo, for 17 Feb. 1905—C46, with additionally a prefatory note printed in 21 lines (p. 2), and a text illustration (p. 13).

b. *New edition* (1957):

AN OPEN LETTER | TO THE | KANDYAN CHIEFS | BY | ANANDA K. COOMARASWAMY | [*ornament*] | Published by the Arts Council of Ceylon | [*swelled rule*] | 1957

1 leaf, 7 pp. 24.5 x 14 cm. Limp light green paper wrappers lettered in brown and black. Front wrapper serves in place of title-leaf; wire-stitched.

Notes: Contents identical with the first edition, except for slight changes, and the omission of the text illustration. Re-issued by the same publisher in 1983.

A5 REPORT ON THE OCCURRENCE OF CASSITERITE [1905]

First edition:

REPORT ON THE OCCURRENCE OF | CASSITERITE (OXIDE OF TIN) | IN CEYLON. BY ANANDA K. COOMARASWAMY, B.Sc., DIRECTOR, | MINERALOGICAL SURVEY. [Colombo: Government Printing Office]

3 pp. 22.2 x 14 cm. (approx.). Title-leaf and the last leaf serve as wrappers; wire-stitched (?).

Published 31 May 1905; number of copies unknown.

Contents: Report on the Occurrence of Cassiterite (Oxide of Tin) in Ceylon [dated Ratnapura, 18 Mar. 1905]—Additional Report on an Occurrence of Cassiterite [by James Parsons, dated Ratnapura, 9 Apr. 1905]—Report on Cassiterite from Ceylon [by Wyndham R. Dunstan].

Note: AKC's portion of this pamphlet was first printed as "Tin in Ceylon", in *Ceylon Observer*, Colombo, for 24 March 1905—C50.

A6 VOLUSPA [1905]

a. *First edition:*

VOLUSPA. [Kandy: Printed for the author at the Industrial School]

12 pp. 9.1 x 5.7 cm. Limp olive green or brown paper wrappers with, on front, white paper label lettered in black; sewn.

Colophon (page 12)*:* Done into English out of the Icelandic of the Elder Edda by Ananda K. Coomaraswamy. 40 copies printed at the Kandy Industrial School and finished the 28th day of August 1905.

b. *Second edition* ([1909])*:*

VÖLUSPA: DONE INTO ENGLISH OUT OF | THE ICELANDIC OF THE ELDER EDDA, | BY ANANDA K. COOMARASWAMY [*two leaf ornaments.* Broad Campden, Gloucestershire: Essex House Press]

3 blank leaves, 1 leaf, 5-29 pp., 3 blank leaves. 20 x 13.6 cm. Limp light grey paper wrappers lettered on the front in black: VÖLUSPA.; sewn; edges untrimmed.

Colophon (page 29): Printed at the Essex House Press, in the Norman Chapel at Broad Campden. Sold at the Essex House Press, and by David Nutt, Long Acre, London. January, 1909. Of One Hundred Copies printed, this is No. [*number written in. Publisher's device, i.e. a pink, printed below*] (One copy was printed on vellum, and this was not for sale.)

Contents: Foreword—Argument—Völuspa.

Notes: The translation was considerably revised by AKC for this edition; there is additionally a foreword (p. 5), and a synopsis of the poem (pp. 6-7). "The present translation of Völuspa, the 'Sibyl's Saying', is made from the text of Codex Regius, as edited by Dr. Ferdinand Detter (Vienna, 1899), and Detter and Heinzel (Leipzig, 1903), without rearrangement of the text, or the elimination of additions or interpolations. . . . The translator is very greatly indebted to Professor J. Lawrence, Litt.D., of Tokyo University, and to Mr. Eirikr Magnusson, M.A., of Cambridge, for many suggestions and revisions." ("Foreword").

Review: Albany F. Major, *Folklore*, London, XX. (1909) 366.

A7 THE PROSELYTE [1906]

First edition:

THE PROSELYTE. [Colombo: Printed privately for gratis distribution by the author]

Fly-sheet, printed on recto and verso. 25.2 x 18.9 cm.

Colophon (page [2]): 50 copies printed for the author, Colombo, April 1906.

Notes: A one-act play concerning the distress of an old Kandyan chief, Pindeniya, and his wife (they are Buddhist), on discovering that their daughter, Kirimenika, while away at mission school, has been converted to Christianity, persuaded to adopt European dress, and christened "Alice".

An epigraph, quoting Matt. X. 34-5, is printed on page [1].

Whether this play was ever performed, or even intended to be performed, is not known.

A8 TWO ADDRESSES 1906

First edition:

TWO ADDRESSES | BY | ANANDA K. COOMARASWAMY, D.Sc. | [*Ornamental rule*] | PRINTED BY THE COLOMBO APOTHECARIES CO., LTD. | 1906.

23 pp. 18.1 x 12 cm. Limp white paper wrappers lettered in black; sewn.

Published Summer 1906; number of copies unknown.

Contents: Foreword [dated Madugoda, 9 July 1906]—I. [AKC's reply at a public reception held in his honour at the Hindu College Hall, Jaffna, on 4 June 1906]—II. [An excerpt from AKC's lecture, "The Anglicization of India", given at Jaffna, 5 June 1906]—Appendix [an excerpt from *India and Its Problems*, by W.S. Lilly].

Note: The first of these addresses is reprinted, with minor alterations, from *Ceylon Observer*, Colombo, for 7 June 1906—C114; the second, which concerns Christian missionary activity, is printed here for the first time.

Review: Central Hindu College Magazine, Benares, N.S. VI. 10 (1 Oct. 1906) 262-3.

Translation: Tamil, Jaffna: Navalar Press, 1906 (the first address only).

A9 HANDBOOK TO THE EXHIBITION OF ARTS & CRAFTS . . . 1906

First edition:

HANDBOOK | TO THE | EXHIBITION OF ARTS & CRAFTS | IN CONNECTION WITH THE | CEYLON RUBBER EXHIBITION. | [*Ornament*] | COLOMBO: | H.M. RICHARDS, ACTING GOVERNMENT PRINTER, CEYLON. | [*Rule*] | 1906.

38 pp., IV numbered pls. 25.8 x 15.8 cm. Stiff mauve paper wrappers printed in black, blue, and dark blue, with title on front lettered as above, then additionally: PERADENIYA, SEPT. 13 TO 27, 1906. | . . . UNDER THE AUSPICES OF THE CEYLON | AGRICULTURAL SOCIETY. | . . . BY | ANANDA K. COOMARASWAMY, D.Sc., | DIRECTOR OF MINERALOGICAL SURVEY. | . . . PRICE 25 CENTS.; sewn.

Published September 1906 at 25 cents; number of copies unknown.

Contents: Preface—Arts and Crafts: 1. Manufacture of Iron and Steel—2. Weaving—3. Embroidery—4. Dyeing—5. Mat Weaving by Kinnaras—8. [*sic*; chapters 8, 9 and 10 are printed out of order] Paper and Tinder—9. Pottery—10. Lacwork—6. Grass and Palm Leaf Plaiting—7. Lace—11. Painting—12. Gold and Silver—13. Brass, Bronze, and Iron—14. Woodwork—15. Ivory Work.

Notes: "The main idea has been to exhibit craftsmen actually at work, but specimens of good old and new work are also shown. This book does not pretend to an exhaustive treatment of the subject; having been compiled at short notice on purpose for the Exhibition . . . the writer has in hand, and now in an advanced state, a larger work on the Arts and Crafts of the Sinhalese [i.e. *Mediaeval Sinhalese Art* ([1908])—A14a], in which the whole subject will be treated at length" ("Preface", p. [3]). In some copies a "Correction" slip to the chapter on painting is inserted at page 32. Chapters 4, 5, 8, 10, and 11 were reprinted, in revised and expanded form, as "Notes on Painting, Dyeing, Lacwork, Dumbara Mats, and Paper in Ceylon", in *Journal of the Royal Asiatic Society (Ceylon Branch)*, Colombo (1907)—C134.

A10 THE DEEPER MEANING OF THE STRUGGLE [1907]

First edition:

THE DEEPER MEANING OF THE | STRUGGLE. | BY ANANDA K. COOMARASWAMY. [Broad Campden, Gloucestershire: Essex House Press]

26 pp., 1 blank leaf. 22.7 x 15 cm. Limp grey or buff paper wrappers lettered in black on front; sewn; fore and bottom edges untrimmed.

Colophon (page 26)*:* Printed and sold by Ananda K. Coomaraswamy at the Essex House Press in the Norman Chapel at Broad Campden, Gloucestershire. One thousand and seventy five copies printed, and finished on the 5th day of November, 1907. Of seventy five copies on fine paper, this is No. [*number written in. Publisher's device, i.e. two trees intertwined, printed below*]

Contents: The Deeper Meaning of the Struggle—Mata Bharata—India: A Nation.

Notes: This pamphlet is concerned with the conflict between the ideals of British imperialism and those of Indian nationalism: "Imperialism involves the subordination of many nationalities to one [while] nationalism is inseparable from the idea of Internationalism . . . we believe that every nation has its own part to play in the long tale of human progress, and that nations, which are not free to develope [*sic*] their own individuality and own character, are also unable to make the contribution to the sum of human culture which the world has a right to expect of them" (pp. 4, 5). "Mata Bharata" is an allegory of the history of India's relations with Britain; "India: A Nation", incorporates "Credo", by Shiv Naryen, and the song "Bande Mataram" ("Hail! Motherland"), by Bankim Chandra Chatterji.

The pamphlet's title is borrowed from that of William Morris's letter to the *Daily Chronicle* on the English miners' strike of 1893.

The Deeper Meaning of the Struggle was the first publication to be issued by the Essex House Press, after AKC became its proprietor and director. In all, eleven of his titles were to appear under this imprint. Essex House was a private press established in 1898 by the English architect and designer C.R. Ashbee, as an additional activity of the Guild of Handicraft. The Press took its name from Essex House in Mile End Road, London, to which in 1891 Ashbee had moved the Guild.

Ashbee's express purpose was to perpetuate the standard and emulate the style of William Morris's Kelmscott Press. He acquired the plant (but not the blocks and type) used by Morris. AKC purchased the Press from the Guild and from 1907 until its demise in 1911 it was under his direction. AKC housed the plant in a building known as the Norman Chapel, at Broad Campden, Gloucestershire; the Chapel also served as his private residence. For further on the history of the Press, and AKC's association with Ashbee, see E39.

The contents of this pamphlet were reprinted to form the first three chapters of *Essays in National Idealism* ([1909?])—A18a, and, omitting "Mata Bharata" and with other changes, as "The 'New Birth' in India: 'A Living Movement'", in *Hindustan Review*, Allahabad, for August 1908—C185.

Review: Modern Review, Calcutta, IV. 3 (Sept. 1908) 271-2.

A11 NĒTRA MAṄGALYA [1908]

First edition:

NĒTRA MAṄGALYA, OR CEREMONY OF PAINTING | THE EYES OF IMAGES, AS PERFORMED BY CRAFTSMEN IN CEYLON. | BY ANANDA K. COOMARASWAMY, D.Sc. [Broad Campden, Gloucestershire: Essex House Press]

7, [1] pp. 36 x 27 cm. Unbound sheets; edges untrimmed.

Colophon (page [8]): Extract from 'Mediaeval Sinhalese Art'. Twenty-five copies printed, the eleventh day of January, nineteen hundred and eight. Essex House Press, Broad Campden.

Notes: An advance printing (for private circulation only) of "Appendix to Chapter III.II" in *Mediaeval Sinhalese Art* ([1908])—A14a—pp. 70-5.

A detailed account of the ceremony, and how it shows (1) "the craftsman in his sacerdotal capacity", and (2) "the relation between him and his patron". The eye-painting is reserved for a suitably auspicious occasion, as "some idea of danger . . . appears to attach to this consecration of the image, whereby it is made a medium between the worshipper and his god" (p. 3). AKC gives reasons for regarding Nētra Maṅgalya as being of Hindu origin rather than Buddhist.

A12 THE AIMS OF INDIAN ART [1908]

First edition:

THE AIMS OF INDIAN ART [*ornament*] | BY ANANDA K. COOMARASWAMY, D.Sc. [Broad Campden, Gloucestershire: Essex House Press]

1 leaf, 1 blank leaf, 1 leaf, 23 pp., incl. frontis., 1 text illus., 2 blank leaves. 25.5 x 18 cm. Limp grey paper wrappers lettered in black on front; sewn; top edges roughly trimmed, fore and bottom edges untrimmed.

Colophon (page 23): Two hundred and seventy-five copies printed at the Essex House Press, in the Norman Chapel at Broad Campden, and finished the 29th day of May, 1908. [*Publisher's device, i.e. two trees intertwined, printed below*]

Notes: Fifty copies of this pamphlet were printed on hand-made paper and two on vellum (the latter not for sale); these special copies were published simultaneously with those on ordinary paper. The former are bound in grey paper boards, with cream cloth back; they are otherwise identical with the ordinary paper copies. Those on vellum have not been sighted by the compiler.

On the traditional Indian artist's depiction of "the sphere of ideal forms", contrasting this with the Western (post-Renaissance) artist's imitation of phenomenal appearance: highlighting the Indian artist's method of visualization through the contemplation of mental images, and his requisite adherence to canonical prescription. AKC quotes extensively from the *Śilpa Sastras*, the *Śukranītisāra* of Śukrācārya, and the *Memorials of Edward Burne-Jones*.

Reviews: Burlington Magazine, London, XIV. 68 (Nov. 1908) 115; Sister Nivedita, *Modern Review*, Calcutta, X. 2. (Aug. 1911) 214-16.

Translation: Tamil, Madras: Meykandan Press (for the Indian Society of Oriental Art), 1914.

A13 THE INFLUENCE OF GREEK ON INDIAN ART [1908]

a. *First edition, first impression:*

THE INFLUENCE OF GREEK ON INDIAN ART | BY ANANDA K. COOMARASWAMY, D.Sc. [Broad Campden, Gloucestershire: Essex House Press]

1 leaf, 7 pp., 1 blank leaf. 35.6 x 27 cm. Limp grey paper wrappers lettered in black on front; sewn; edges untrimmed.

Colophon (page 7)*:* Seventy-five copies printed at the Essex House Press, in the Norman Chapel at Broad Campden, Gloucestershire, and finished July 31st, 1908. Advance copies of a paper read at the Oriental Congress, Copenhagen, August, 1908.

b. *Second impression (revised text):*

6, [1] pp. 33.5 x 25.5 cm. Limp grey paper wrappers lettered in black on front; sewn; edges untrimmed.

Colophon (page [7])*:* Read at the Fifteenth International Oriental Congress, Copenhagen, August, 1908. Fifty copies printed at the Essex House Press, in the Norman Chapel at Broad Campden, Gloucestershire, and finished October 2nd, 1908. (Revised Edition.)

Notes: This essay, in its revised form, appears as "Appendix to Chapter XVII" in *Mediaeval Sinhalese Art* ([1908])—A14a—pp. 256-61.

AKC says the Greek influence, as expounded by Albert Grünwedel and other scholars, is "magnified out of all proportion", and "ultimately neither very profound nor very important". AKC highlights (1) the "fundamental difference in the spirit and aims of Classic Greek and true Indian art", and (2) the fact that India possessed its own schools of sculpture long before the Gandhāra period.

For AKC's reading of this paper, see *Actes du quinzième congrès international des orientalistes, session de Copenhague, 1908* (Copenhagen: Imprimerie Graebe, 1909), pp. 53-6.

Reviews: E.B. Havell, *Modern Review*, Calcutta, IV. 4 (Oct. 1908) 277-80; Sister Nivedita, *Modern Review*, Calcutta, X. 2 (Aug. 1911) 214-16.

A14 MEDIAEVAL SINHALESE ART [1908]

a. *First edition:*

MEDIAEVAL SINHALESE ART [*ornament*] | BY ANANDA K. COOMARASWAMY, D.Sc., FELLOW OF UNIVERSITY | COLLEGE, LONDON. [*Ornament*] BEING A

MONOGRAPH ON MEDIAEVAL | SINHALESE ARTS AND CRAFTS, MAINLY AS SURVIVING IN THE | EIGHTEENTH CENTURY, WITH AN ACCOUNT OF THE STRUCTURE | OF SOCIETY AND THE STATUS OF THE CRAFTSMEN. [*Ornament.* Broad Campden, Gloucestershire: Essex House Press]

3 blank leaves, xvi pp., 1 leaf, 340 pp., 55 pls., incl. frontis., 1 leaf, 3 blank leaves. 35.4 x 27 cm. Grey paper boards lettered in black on front cover: MEDIAEVAL SINHALESE ART; canvas back, with white paper label lettered in black: MEDIAEVAL | SINHALESE | ART | BY | ANANDA K. | COOMARA- | SWAMY.; endpapers (paste-downs only).

Colophon (recto of leaf following Plate LIII)*:* Four hundred and twenty-five copies printed under the care of the Author at the Essex House Press in the Norman Chapel at Broad Campden, Gloucestershire. Begun September, 1907, and finished December, 1908. [*Number written in. Publisher's device.*]

Dedication (page [iii])*:* . . . To E[thel]. M[ary]. C[oomaraswamy (i.e. Mrs AKC)]. my comrade in this undertaking.

Contents: Foreword—List of Illustrations in the Text—I. The Sinhalese People—II. Social Economy of the Kandyan Sinhalese in the Eighteenth Century—Appendices to Chap. II. (Education. Books.)—III. Particular Account of the Artificers—Appendices to Chap. III. (Teaching of Drawing. Nētra Maṅgalya. Artificer Tenant Holdings. Vihāra Grants. Viśvakarma.)—IV. Elements of Sinhalese Design and Ornament—Appendix to Chap. IV. (The Rūpāvaliya.)—V. Architecture—Appendix to Chap. V. (Māyāmataya.)—VI. Woodwork—VII. Stonework—VIII. Figure Sculpture—Appendix to Chap. VIII. (Sāriputra.)—IX. Painting—Appendices to Chap IX. (Paper Manuscripts. How to Prepare Colours. How to Make Glue.)—X. Ivory, Bone, Horn and Shell—XI. Metal Work: Iron, Brass, Copper and Bronze; Gold and Silver; Jewellery—XII. Lac-Work—XIII. Earthenware—Appendix to Chap. XIII. (Potter's Song.)—XIV. Weaving—XV. Embroidery—Appendix to Chap. XV. (Revival of Sinhalese Embroidery.)—XVI. Mat Weaving and Dyeing—Appendices to Chap. XVI. (Kinnaraya's Song. Pannan Katura)—XVII. History of Sinhalese Art—Appendix to Chap. XVII. (The Influence of Greek on Indian Art.)—Appendix I. The Kandyan Art Association—Appendix II. Addenda and Corrigenda—Glossary and Index—Errata—Postscript—Description of Plates—Plates.

Notes: Twenty-five of the 425 copies of this book were printed on hand-made paper. Size, title-page, contents, and pagination are identical with those printed on ordinary paper.

"This book is a record of the work and the life of the craftsmen in a feudal society not unlike that of Early Mediaeval Europe. . . . Sinhalese art is essentially Indian, but possesses this especial interest, that it is in many ways of an earlier character . . . than any Indian art surviving on the mainland so late as the beginning of the nineteenth century . . . This book is not primarily intended as a work of scholarship, but is written first of all for the Sinhalese people, as a memorial of a period which at present they are not willing to understand" ("Foreword", pp. v, vi).

"It is of interest to record . . . that this book has been printed by hand, upon the press used by William Morris for printing the Kelmscott Chaucer". The publisher's device (or pressmark), which is printed as a part of the colophon, was specially drawn for the book by C.R. Ashbee, and "represents, in a design based on a Sinhalese painting, the gathering of flowers from the tree of Eastern art, and records the history of the Press on which the book has been printed" ("Foreword", pp. ix, x).

The frontispiece (Plate I), and Plates XVII-XX, XXIV, XXX-XXXI, XXXIV, are coloured. Although the last plate is numbered LIII, there are within the sequence two supplementary plates: VIIIa and XLIIIa. Most of the photographs reproduced in the plates were taken by Ethel Mary Coomaraswamy. There are 153 text illustrations, and these (unless otherwise stated in the captions) are drawn by AKC. Figure 69, on page 111, is rubricated.

Reviews: Journal of the Ceylon University Association, Colombo, II. 6 (Jan./Feb. 1909) 115-17, 146; Laurence Housman, *Manchester Guardian*, Manchester (3 Feb. 1909) 5; *Times Literary Supplement*, London, 376 (25 Mar. 1909) 116; E.B. Havell, *Hindustan Review*, Allahabad, XX. 119 (July 1909) 81-4; Sister Nivedita, *Modern Review*, Calcutta, VI. 1 (July 1909) 64-7; C.G.S., *Nature*, London, LXXXI. 2,071 (8 July 1909) 39-40; C.J. Herringham, *Burlington Magazine*, London, XV. 77 (Aug. 1909) 317-19; Roger Fry, *Quarterly Review*, London, CCXII. 422 (Jan. 1910) 225-39; John H. Marshall, *Journal of the Royal Asiatic Society*, London (1911) 839-43.

b. *Second edition* ([1956]):

[*Ornament*] Ananda K. Coomaraswamy | MEDIAEVAL SINHALESE ART | BEING A MONOGRAPH ON MEDIAEVAL SINHALESE | ARTS AND CRAFTS, MAINLY AS SURVIVING IN | THE EIGHTEENTH CENTURY, WITH AN ACCOUNT OF | THE STRUCTURE OF SOCIETY AND THE STATUS | OF THE CRAFTSMEN | Second Edition, incorporating | the author's corrections | [New York] Pantheon Books

xvi, 344 pp., 55 pls.(on 28 leaves). 28.6 x 22.3 cm. Green cloth boards with black cloth back lettered in gold on spine; end-papers. Beige dust-jacket printed in brown.

Published late 1956 at $12.50; number of copies unknown.

Note: "Published . . . with the patronage of the Government of Ceylon" (*verso of title-leaf*). Substantially a reprint by offset of the first edition, save for the inclusion of a new and revised list of "Errata and Additional Addenda", which occupies pp. 315-21. The eight coloured plates and coloured frontispiece of the first edition are reproduced in black-and-white halftones; the frontispiece has been moved to the back, where it appears as Plate I, facing page 344.

Reviews: William E. Ward, *Artibus Asiae*, Ascona, XX. 2/3 (1957) 216; Stella Kramrisch, *Journal of Asian Studies*, Ann Arbor, XVI. 3 (May 1957) 466-7.

Translation: Sinhala, Colombo: Government Press (for the Department of Cultural Affairs), 1962.

A15 THE TWO PAINTERS [1908]

First edition:

THE TWO PAINTERS [*ornament*] | BY A. K. COOMARASWAMY. [Broad Campden, Gloucestershire: Essex House Press]

20 pp. 12.8 x 9.2 cm. (leaves); sewn; edges untrimmed.

Colophon (page 20): Printed at the Essex House Press in the Norman Chapel at Broad Campden, and finished the 16th day of December, 1908. Thirty copies. Not for sale. One copy on vellum.

Notes: No copies of this book in the original binding, nor the copy printed on vellum, have been sighted by the compiler.

An allegory of the traditional idea of the union of wisdom and method in the production of a work of art.

Reproduced, in facsimile (but omitting the title-page), in *Ananda Coomaraswamy—the Bridge Builder; a Study of a Scholar-Colossus*, by S. Durai Raja Singam (1977)—B94—pp.[608-9].

A16 THE INDIAN CRAFTSMAN 1909

a. *First edition:*

[*Within double rule border, in two rectangles formed by double rules, separated by a larger central rectangle; in upper rectangle:*] THE INDIAN CRAFTS- | MAN: BY ANANDA K. COOMARASWAMY, D.SC. | Author of "Mediaeval Sinhalese Art." | [*In lower rectangle:*] PROBSTHAIN & CO., | 41, GREAT RUSSELL ST., LONDON, W.C. | 1909

3 leaves, v-xv, [1], 130 pp., 2 leaves. 19.6 x 13.6 cm. Dark blue cloth boards stamped in gold on front within rising sun device: PROBSTHAIN'S ORIENTAL SERIES and across the spine: THE | INDIAN | CRAFTSMAN | A.K. COOMARA- | SWAMY | PROBSTHAIN | & CO.; end-papers; fore and bottom edges untrimmed.

Published April 1909 at 3*s*. 6*d*.; number of copies unknown.

Contents: [List of] Appendices—Foreword [by C.R. Ashbee]—I. The Village Craftsman [from C171, expanded]—II. The Craft Guilds of the Great Cities [from C171, expanded]—III. The Feudal Craftsman in India and Ceylon [C177, expanded]—IV. Standard and Regulation [from C189, expanded]—V. Religious Ideas in Craftsmanship [from C189, expanded]—VI. Education [from Cl89, expanded]—List of Appendices—APPENDICES: I. Sir George Birdwood on the Indian Village Potter—II. Sir George Birdwood on Machinery and Handicraft in India—III. William Morris on Commercial War—IV. E.B. Havell on Craftsmanship and Culture—V. E.B. Havell on the Official Suppression of Indian Craftsmanship at the Present Day—VI. Lafcadio Hearn on Craft Gods in Ceylon—VII. Lafcadio Hearn on Craft Guilds in Japan—VIII. Ser Marco Polo on Craft Guilds in China—IX. Bhikku P.C. Jinavar avamsa on Craftsmen of Siam—X. Municipal Institutions in Ancient India [by R.C. Shashi]—XI. Books Recommended to the Reader.

Note: Epigrams excerpted from the *Laws of Manu*, Homer's *Odyssey*, and *Ecclesiasticus* are printed on page [xvi].

Reviews: Manchester Guardian, Manchester, 19,577 (7 May 1909) 4; E.B. Havell,

Hindustan Review, Allahabad, XX. 120 (Aug. 1909) 209-12; *South Asian Review*, London, XXIX. 3 (1910) 427; *Studio*, London, XLIX. 203 (Feb. 1910) 80.

b. *Second edition (first Indian edition;* [1989]):

THE INDIAN CRAFTSMAN | Ananda K. Coomaraswamy | with a foreword by | Alvin C. Moore Jr. | [*Publisher's device*] | Munshiram Manoharlal | Publishers Pvt. Ltd. [New Delhi]

1 blank leaf, xiv, 95 pp. 22.3 x 14.6 cm. Olive green cloth boards lettered in white down the spine; end-papers. White dust-jacket printed in light grey and red.

Published in 1989; number of copies unknown.

Notes: The contents of this edition are identical with those of A16a, except for a new foreword, by Alvin C. Moore Jr. (pp. [vii]-xiv), which replaces that of C.R. Ashbee, the addition of an index, minor alterations and corrections to the text, and the omission of the epigrams.

The "Bibliography" (p.[89]), which in the first edition is called "Appendix XI. Books Recommended to the Reader", omits the entries for John Ruskin's *Unto This Last* and "The Nature of Gothic". A footnote that belongs to page [76] is printed on page [89].

A17 THE MESSAGE OF THE EAST [1909]

First edition:

THE | MESSAGE OF THE EAST | BY | ANANDA K. COOMARASWAMY, D.Sc. | MADRAS | GANESH & CO., PUBLISHERS

3 leaves, 50 pp., incl. frontis. (photo port. of AKC), 5 leaves (publishers' advertisements). 18.3 x 12.3 cm. Stiff brown, or mauve, paper wrappers lettered on front in dark blue: THE | MESSAGE OF THE EAST | A.K. COOMARASAWMY [*sic*]; end-papers.

Published Summer 1909; number of copies unknown.

Contents: The Message of the East I—[The Message of the East] II—[The Message of the East] III [i.e. C201, 208, and 214]—The Art and Swadeshi ["Art and Svadeshi"].

Reviews: Statesman, Calcutta (23 Sept. 1909); Chuni Lal Mukerji, *Modern Review*, Calcutta, VII. 1 (Jan. 1910) 89-90.

A18 ESSAYS IN NATIONAL IDEALISM [1909?]

a. *First edition:*

ESSAYS IN NATIONAL | IDEALISM: BY ANANDA K. | COOMARASWAMY, D.Sc. [Colombo: Colombo Apothecaries Co., Ltd.]

2 leaves, ix, 206 pp., VI numbered pls., 1 text illus. 22.4 x 14.4 cm. Grey paper boards lettered in black on front, with blue cloth back; end-papers.

Published December 1909(?) at 2 rupees, 50 cents; number of copies unknown.

Contents: Preface—I. The Deeper Meaning of the Struggle—II. Indian Nationality ["India: A Nation"]—III. Mata Bharata [preceding three chapters reprinted from A10]—IV. The Aims and Methods of Indian Art [A12, expanded and revised]—V. Art and Yoga in India—VI. The Influence of Modern Europe on Indian Art [C149 and C150, revised]—VII. Art of the East and of the West—VIII. The Influence of Greek on Indian Art [A13b, condensed and revised]—IX. Education in India—X. Memory in Education—XI. Christian Missions in India [C194 and C197]—XII. Swadeshi [C143, expanded and revised]—XIII. Indian Music [from C162, with additions]—XIV. Music and Education in India [from C162, with additions]—XV. Gramophones—and Why Not?

Notes: The "Preface" is dated: Campden [Gloucestershire], December 1909.

"These essays represent an endeavour towards an explanation of the true significance of the national movement in India. . . . this struggle is much more than a political conflict. It is a struggle for spiritual and mental freedom from the domination of an alien ideal. . . . it may appear strange that . . . so much space should be given to art, so little said of politics. It is because nations are made by artists and by poets, not by traders and politicians. . . . The causes which have led to the degeneration of Indian art, and prevent its revival, are identical with those that prevent the recovery of her political efficiency" ("Preface", pp. [i], ii, iii).

An epigram from *The Pilgrims of Hope*, by William Morris, is printed on verso of the 2nd leaf. In all copies examined a slip containing "Errata" printed in three lines and a "Postscript" (i.e. acknowledgements) printed in four lines, is inserted at page [i].

An Indian reprint (hardbound) of A18a was produced by offset in 1981 in New Delhi by Munshiram Manoharlal Publishers Pvt., Ltd. This reprint does not include the list of errata.

Reviews: F. J. Payne, *Buddhist Review*, London, II. (1910) 229-32; *Ceylon National Review*, Colombo, III. 9 (Mar. 1910) 200; [Sister] N[ivedita]., *Modern Review*, Calcutta, VIII. 3 (Sept. 1910) 336-7.

b. *Second edition* ([1910]):

ESSAYS | IN | NATIONAL IDEALISM | BY | ANANDA K. COOMARASWAMY, D.Sc. | POPULAR EDITION | [*decorative rule*] | PRICE: ONE RUPEE. | G. A. NATESAN AND CO. | MADRAS.

3 leaves, ix, 213, [1] pp., 9 leaves, 6 pls. 18.4 x 12.4 cm. Limp tan paper wrappers lettered in black.

Published in 1910 at 1 rupee; number of copies unknown.

Note: This has additionally a "Preface to the Second Edition", page ix, which reads: "In this edition a few minor alterations and corrections are embodied"; page [214] contains a list of other books by AKC; this is followed by 9 leaves of publishers' advertisements; otherwise the contents are identical with those of the first edition.

A19 THE ORIENTAL VIEW OF WOMAN [1910]

First edition:

THE ORIENTAL VIEW | OF WOMAN [*two leaf ornaments*] | BY A.K. COOMARASWAMY, D.SC. [Broad Campden, Gloucestershire: Essex House Press]

2 blank leaves, 1 leaf, 7-23 pp., 2 blank leaves. 15 x 10.8 cm. Limp grey paper wrappers lettered in black on front: THE ORIENTAL [*ornament*] | VIEW OF WOMAN; sewn; top edges roughly trimmed, other edges untrimmed.

Colophon (page 23)*:* One hundred and twenty-five copies printed at the Essex House Press in the Norman Chapel at Broad Campden, August, 1910. Sold at the Essex House Press, and by Messrs. Probsthain & Co., 41, Great Russell Street, London. The Essay originally appeared in *Votes for Women*, May 13th, 1910.

Notes: A reprint, in a slightly expanded form, of C245.

Twenty-five of the 125 copies of this pamphlet were printed on hand-made paper. Size, title-page, contents, and pagination are identical with those printed on ordinary paper.

All examined copies of this pamphlet have "Women" (for "Woman") in the heading printed on the first page of the text (i.e. page 7).

A20 DOMESTIC HANDICRAFT AND CULTURE [1910]

First edition:

DOMESTIC HANDICRAFT | AND CULTURE: A LECTURE | READ BEFORE THE ASSOCIATION OF | TEACHERS OF DOMESTIC SCIENCE, | MAY 28TH, 1910. BY ANANDA | K. COOMARASWAMY, D.SC. [Broad Campden, Gloucestershire: Essex House Press]

2 blank leaves, 1 leaf, 7-35 pp., 2 blank leaves. 15.8 x 12.3 cm. (wrappers); 15 x 11.2 cm. (leaves). Limp grey paper wrappers lettered in black on front; sewn; edges untrimmed.

Colophon (page 35)*:* One hundred and twenty-five copies printed at the Essex House Press in the Norman Chapel at Broad Campden, September, 1910. This is No. [*number written in*].

Notes: A reprint of C246.

Twenty-five of the 125 copies of this pamphlet were printed on hand-made paper. Size, title-page, contents, and pagination are identical with those printed on ordinary paper.

A21 SELECTED EXAMPLES OF INDIAN ART [1910]

First edition:

SELECTED EXAMPLES | OF INDIAN ART [*three leaf ornaments*] | BY ANANDA K. COOMARASWAMY, D.Sc. [Broad Campden, Gloucestershire: Essex House Press]

1 blank leaf, vii, 19, [1] pp., XL numbered pls. (all have protective tissue with descriptive letterpress; plates I, II, VII, VIII, XII, and XV are coloured). 36 x 27.5 cm. Portfolio. Grey paper boards with canvas back and ties, enclosing brochure of text, and plates (unbound).

Colophon (page [20]): Four hundred and twenty-five copies printed at the Essex House Press in the Norman Chapel at Broad Campden, Gloucestershire, September, 1910. Sold at the Essex House Press, and by Mr. Bernard Quaritch, Grafton Street, London. This is No. [*number written in*].

Contents: Introduction—List of Plates—Description of Plates—[Plates].

Notes: Twenty-five of the 425 copies of this portfolio were printed on hand-made paper. They are otherwise identical with those on ordinary paper.

"The forty-two [*sic*] plates . . . are intended to provide for schools and colleges in India, Museums and Libraries and private individuals, a convenient series of more adequate reproductions of Indian sculpture and painting than those at present available elsewhere" ("Introduction", p. v). The plates comprise reproductions of Rājput, Mughal, and Modern schools, and sculpture from India, Ceylon, Java, and Nepal. AKC appends a note on page vi concerning the colour plates: ". . . I, II, VII, and XII have been very carefully reproduced for me by Messrs. Griggs of Peckham. As many as forty-five printings were made in the case of Plate II. Plate VIII is a six colour print by the Medici Society. Plate XV is a Chromoxylograph by the Kokka Co. of Japan." In all examined copies of this portfolio Plate XXXV is misnumbered XXII.

An "Errata" slip, printed in 11 lines, is tipped in at page v, in some copies at page [20]. In later copies this slip is accompanied by a "Corrigenda" slip, printed in 10 lines, dated 1 January 1913.

An Indian reprint (hardbound) was produced by offset in 1971 in New Delhi by Today & Tomorrow's Printers & Publishers. This reprint retains the coloured plates. The misnumbering of Plate XXXV in the first edition has been corrected (by hand). There are no other corrections; the "Errata" and "Corrigenda" slips are not included.

Reviews: W.H. J[ames]. W[eale]., *Burlington Magazine*, London, XVIII. 95 (Feb. 1911) 296; Sister Nivedita, *Modern Review*, Calcutta., X. 2 (Aug. 1911) 214-16.

A22 INDIAN DRAWINGS [1910]

First edition:

INDIAN DRAWINGS | BY ANANDA K. COOMARASWAMY, D.Sc. [Broad Campden, Gloucestershire: Printed for the India Society by Essex House Press]

3 blank leaves, vii, 32 pp., 25 text illus., XXIX numbered pls. (autotype reproductions; each with a leaf of protective tissue containing descriptive letterpress in red), 3 blank leaves. 28.8 x 22.4 cm. Grey paper boards lettered in black on front; canvas back with white paper label lettered in black; end-papers (paste-downs only, i.e. the leaves of first and last signatures).

Colophon (page 32): Printed for the India Society, London, at the Essex House Press, in the Norman Chapel, at Broad Campden, and finished October, 1910. Issued to members of the India Society, 1910, and sold at the Essex House Press, Campden, and by Messrs. Probsthain, 41, Great Russell Street, London. Four hundred copies, of which this is No. [*number written in*].

Dedication (page [iii]): To E.B. H[avell]., W[illiam]. R[othenstein]., C[hristiana]. J. H[erringham]., G[aganendra]. N[ath]. T[agore].

Contents: Foreword—[Text]—[Plates].

Notes: "The first book ever published on India's graphic arts" (Andrew Topsfield, *Times Literary Supplement*, London, 4,169 (25 Feb. 1983), p. 179).

"The main purpose of this book has been to put before those who love art some examples of the achievement of Indian artists, in one particular direction, and I do not doubt that . . . the actual reproductions will be welcomed as a revelation of an exquisite but hitherto almost unknown art. But I also trust that the growing recognition of the value of Indian aesthetic, of which the demand for such books as this is itself sufficient evidence, may react beneficially upon the methods of teaching accepted by Indian educationalists, and may contribute toward a more intimate relation of this teaching to the traditional culture of a country that has given beauty to the world in so full a measure" (p. 31). AKC draws attention to the characteristic identity of Oriental draughtsmanship; notes the parallel that Indian work offers in spirit and technique to the Italian primitives; describes the actual working methods of Indian artists; and discusses in detail the various schools of drawing represented in the plates: Mughal (pp. 10-20), Rājput (pp. 20-7), the Tanjore school and the Buddhist school (pp. 27-31).

"The text figures [are] mostly outline tracings of my own from photographs of the originals" (p. vii).

Later copies have an "Addenda and Corrigenda" slip, printed in 10 lines, tipped in at page 32.

AKC co-founded the India Society, with E.B. Havell and William Rothenstein, early in 1910. He resigned from the Executive Committee in 1916. See also E108 *n*.

An Indian reprint of this book (hardbound) was produced by offset in 1979 in New Delhi by Bharatiya Publishing House. This omits the dedication leaf, and the protective tissues, of the first edition. The descriptive letterpress contained on the tissues has been transferred to rectos of leaves containing the plates. The "Addenda and Corrigenda" slip is reproduced on page [33].

Reviews: Studio, London, LIII. 220 (July 1911) 170-1; Sister Nivedita, *Modern Review*, Calcutta, X. 2 (Aug. 1911) 214-16; Laurence Binyon, *Journal of the Royal Asiatic Society*, London (1913) 491-5.

A23 SWADESHI, TRUE & FALSE [1910?]

First edition:

SWADESHI, TRUE & FALSE | BY | DR. ANANIA [*sic*] K. COOMARASWAMY | Arts Section, U[nited]. P[rovinces]. Exhibition, Allahabad. [Madras: The Guardian Press]

11 pp. 21.6 x 13.8 cm. (leaves). Sewn?

Published probably December 1910; number of copies unknown.

Notes: Reprinted in *Art and Swadeshi* ([1912])—A25, with the addition of a footnote: Read at the 5th Annual Industrial Conference, Allahabad, 1910.

The above description is based on the sole copy of this pamphlet sighted by the compiler (April 1991), in the possession of Dr Rama P. Coomaraswamy, Greenwich, Conn. No title-page (as such) or wrappers present. Transcription of title is taken from the chapter-style heading on the first page of the text.

On the nature and causes, both internal and external, of the decay of India's industrial arts. AKC is critical of the Swadeshi movement for its failure to take a constructive attitude toward preservation of traditional Indian methods of manufacture. (AKC was Officer in Charge of the Courts of Fine Arts, Wood, Stone, and Metal at the United Provinces Exhibition at Allahabad, 1 December 1910 to 28 February 1911.)

A24 BURNING AND MELTING [1912]

First edition:

[*In red:*] BURNING AND MELTING | [*in black:*] BEING THE SŪZ-U-GUDĀZ OF MU- | HAMMAD RIZĀ NAU'Ī OF KHABŪ- | SHĀN TRANSLATED INTO ENGLISH | BY MIRZA Y. DAWUD OF PERSIA | AND ANANDA K. COOMARASWAMY | OF CEYLON [London: Old Bourne Press]

2 blank leaves, 65, [1] pp., 1 blank leaf, 3 unnumbered collotype pls. (each with a leaf of protective tissue). 22.2 x 13.9 cm. Scarlet silk boards lettered in black on front; end-papers (paste-downs only).

Colophon (page [66]): Four hundred and five copies printed at the Old Bourne Press, 15 Holborn. Sold by Ananda K. Coomaraswamy: and by Messrs. Luzac, 46 Great Russell Street, London. Finished May, 1912. This is No. [*number written in*]

Contents: Foreword—Praise of God—Praise of Muhammad—Commands of Prince Dāniyāl—I. Of the Reign of Akbar—II. The Desire of the Lovers—III. The Troubled Lover Reveals the Secret of His Heart to His Father—IV. The Maiden Desires to be Burned with Her Beloved—V. Akbar Pādshāh Summons the Maiden to Comfort Her—VI. The King Allows the Maiden's Desire—VII. Entering of the Maiden into the Fire—VIII. Prince Dāniyāl Approaches the Fire and Would Urge the Maiden to Come Out from It—Notes.

Notes: A 16th century poem "on the true and tragical event of a lovely Hindu princess, who . . . became a Sati, that is, burned herself on the funeral pyre with her deceased husband . . . The purpose of this English rendering is to make real to those to whom they have been incredible, the perfection of the Indian woman's ideal, and the unifying truth of the religion of Love in whatever form it appears. . . . this little book is of profound interest as a contribution to our knowledge of the psychology of the Musulman rulers of Northern India in the time of great Akbar, towards Hindus and the Hindu faith" ("Foreword", pp. 4, 6, 12).

In all copies examined an erratum slip is tipped in at page 3, which reads as follows: ". . . P. 3, 1.6 for 1506 read 1606".

Reviews: Athenaeum, London (27 July 1912) 85; J. Sarkar, *Modern Review*, Calcutta, XIII. 3 (Mar. 1913) 346-7.

A25 ART AND SWADESHI [1912]

a. *First edition:*

ART AND SWADESHI | BY | ANANDA K. COOMARASWAMY, D.Sc. | MADRAS | GANESH & CO., PUBLISHERS

4 leaves, 150, [1] pp., 1 blank leaf, XVIII numbered pls. (each with blank leaf of protective tissue). 18.4 x 12.4 cm. Stiff tan paper wrappers lettered in black on front and down the spine; end-papers.

Published Summer 1912; number of copies unknown.

Contents: List of Illustrations—I. Art and Swadeshi—II. Swadeshi, True and False—III. Domestic Handicraft and Culture—IV. The International Congress of Applied Chemistry 1901: and Aniline Dyes—V. The Function of Schools of Art in India: A Reply to Mr. Cecil Burns—VI. On the Study of Indian Art—VII. Facial Expression in Indian Sculpture—VIII. On Mughal and Rajput Painting—IX. Night Effects in Indian Pictures—X. Song-Words of a Panjabi Singer—XI. Poems of Rabindranath Tagore [C270, 272, expanded]—XII. The Modern School of Indian Painting [C299]—XIII. Education in Ceylon.

Notes: "Facial Expression in Indian Sculpture" and "Education in Ceylon" (proposing an alternative to the form of English education which ignores the intellectual inheritance of the Ceylonese—an excerpt from AKC's speech as Chairman at the Annual Ceylon Dinner, London, in December 1911), are both printed here for the first time. Chapter IV is called "Chemistry and Dyes" in the list of contents (i.e. recto of third leaf). "Poems of Rabindranath Tagore" comprises (1) eleven poems translated from the Bengali, of which AKC says "some are based on versions supplied to me by Mr. A[jit]. K[umar]. Chakravarti, others on translations given to me by the author himself" (p. 126), (2) an appreciation of Tagore, (3) a short biography of him—reprinted in B10, and (4) some comments on the revival of a national literature in India.

A list of "Corrigenda" is printed, in 11 lines, on page [151].

Reviews: Indian Review, Madras, XIII. 8 (Aug. 1912) 672; "Pol", *Modern Review*, Calcutta, XII. 3 (Sept. 1912) 307; Ezra Pound, *Poetry*, Chicago, II. 6 (Sept. 1913) 226-7.

b. *New edition* ([1994]):

ART AND SWADESHI | ANANDA K. COOMARASWAMY | [*publisher's device*] | [New Delhi] MUNSHIRAM MANOHARLAL | PUBLISHERS PVT LTD

1 leaf, vi, 144 pp., XVIII numbered pls. (tipped in; also counted as pages). 22 x 14.6 cm. Dark blue cloth boards stamped in gold down the spine; end-papers. White dust-jacket printed in blue and black.

Note: Contents as in A25a save for the addition of an index, which occupies pages 141-4, and the correction of misprints.

A26 INDIAN DRAWINGS: SECOND SERIES, CHIEFLY RĀJPUT [1912]

First edition:

INDIAN DRAWINGS: | SECOND SERIES, CHIEFLY RĀJPUT | BY ANANDA K. COOMARASWAMY. [London: Printed for the India Society by the Old Bourne Press]

1 blank leaf, 2 leaves, 7-34 pp., 16 text illus., XXVI numbered pls. (autotype reproductions, each with leaf of protective tissue containing descriptive letterpress in red), 1 blank leaf. 28.8 x 22.4 cm. Grey paper boards lettered in black on front; canvas back with white paper label lettered in black; end-papers.

Colophon (page 33): Printed for the India Society, London, at the Old Bourne Press, 15 Holborn, London, and finished July, 1912. Issued to members of the India Society, 1912, and sold by the author, and by Messrs. Probsthain, 41 Great Russell Street, London. Four hundred and five copies, of which this is No. [*number written in*]

Dedication (page [5]): To R[atan]. D[evī, i.e. Mrs AKC].

Contents: Chap. I. Introduction—Chap. II. Paper Stencils—Chap. III. Description of the Drawings: 1. Jaipur Cartoons, 2. Pahāṛī Drawings, 3. Rājput Portraits, 4. Animals—Chap. IV. Mughal Drawings—Addenda and Corrigenda to Indian Drawings, First Series [i.e. A22]—Addenda and Corrigenda to the Present Volume.

Notes: As the singularity and importance of the Rājput schools was not fully realized by AKC at the time that the first series of *Indian Drawings*—A22—was assembled, the present work is therefore "intended as complementary and supplementary" (p. 7). Chap. I discusses the differentiation of Rājput from other Hindu painting, and from Mughal work, describes the materials and methods employed by Rājput draughtsmen, considers the matter of superscriptions, and comments on the folk-element in the drawings. Chap. II argues that the art of stencil cutting is really a branch of the art of drawing.

"Addenda and Corrigenda to Indian Drawings, First Series", printed in 21 lines on page

34, reproduces, in a revised and expanded form, the slip tipped in at page 32 of A22. "Addenda and Corrigenda to the Present Volume", is printed in 8 lines, the first line on page 34, the remainder on a slip tipped in at that page. (A further addendum is printed in *Rupam*, Calcutta, for January 1929—C534.)

The title on front cover and spine has Roman numeral "II" in place of the words "Second Series".

An Indian reprint of this book (hardbound) was produced by offset in 1979 in New Delhi by Bharatiya Publishing House. This omits the dedication, and the protective tissues, of the first edition. The descriptive letterpress contained on the tissues has been transferred to rectos of leaves containing the plates. The two lists of addenda and corrigenda are retained; that which was printed on a slip in the first edition has been transferred to the recto of a leaf following page 34.

Reviews: O.C. Gangoly, *Modern Review*, Calcutta, XII. 6 (Dec. 1912) 675-6; Laurence Binyon, *Journal of the Royal Asiatic Society*, London (1913) 491-5.

A27 THIRTY SONGS FROM THE PANJAB AND KASHMĪR [1913]

a. *First edition:*

[*In red:*] THIRTY SONGS FROM THE PANJAB AND KASHMĪR: | [*in black:*] RECORDED BY RATAN DEVĪ WITH INTRODUCTION | AND TRANSLATIONS BY ANANDA K. COOMARASWAMY | AND A FOREWORD BY RABINDRANATH TAGORE. [London: Printed for the authors by the Old Bourne Press]

3 blank leaves, 1 leaf, vii, 76, [1] pp., incl. music, II numbered pls. (incl. frontis., each with leaf of protective tissue containing descriptive letterpress in red), 4 blank leaves. 27.8 x 21.8 cm. Grey paper boards lettered in black on front: THIRTY INDIAN SONGS; canvas back with white paper label lettered up the spine in black as on front cover; end-papers (paste-downs only).

Published February 1913 at 10*s.* 6*d.*; 405 copies printed.

Colophon (page [77]): Four hundred and five copies printed for the authors at the Old Bourne Press, and published February, 1913. Sold by Messrs. Luzac, 46 Great Russell Street, and by Novello & Co., Ltd., 160 Wardour Street, London.

Dedication (page iii): To Nārada [i.e. AKC's elder son].

Contents: Foreword [by Rabindranath Tagore]—Part I. Classic Rāgs—Part II. Kāshmīrī Songs, A. Music of the Paṇḍits, B. Cradle Songs of the Paṇḍitānīs, C. Songs of Four Tailor Boys, D. Minstrel Songs—Appendix I. Songs of a Delhi Minstrel—Appendix II. [Verses of a Kashmir court singer].

Notes: This book is a revision, with additions, of "Song-Words of a Panjabi Singer", in *Art and Swadeshi* ([1912])—A25a, but omitting the third, thirteenth, and twenty-first of the songs translated there. In the main, the additional material comprises (1) Punjabi, Urdu, and Hindi texts of the songs, (2) music (in staff notation), and (3) new songs. The songs in Part I were collected in 1911 by AKC and Ratan Devī (i.e. Mrs AKC) from the repertoire of Abdul Rahīm, a contemporary *ustād* of Kapurthala. A photo portrait of this singer is reproduced as the frontispiece to the book. The Kāshmīrī songs in Part II, and the songs in the appendices, were taken down from the performances of other Indian singers. AKC's English versions in Part I were prepared with the assistance of Paira Mall. Part I includes notes on the gestures used by Indian singers to accompany song (pp. 4-5), critical comments (by Ratan Devī) on the voice production of Indian singers (pp. 5-6), and thoughts on the future of Indian music (p. 6).

"[We] will be more than glad if [this book] should be the means of introducing even one Western musician to a new world of art, still more if they might lead any Indian or English educationist in India to a knowledge of one of the many sides of Indian life ignored in every existing scheme of Indian education" (p. 6).

An American reprint of this book was produced by offset in 1979 in West Newfield, Maine, by Longwood Press (not sighted by the compiler).

Reviews: Athenaeum, London (22 Feb. 1913) 227; *Times Literary Supplement*, London, 582 (6 Mar. 1913) 98; L.A., *Manchester Guardian*, Manchester, 20,812 (21 Apr. 1913) 5; *Indian Review*, Madras, XIV. 5 (May 1913) 415; U.R., *Modern Review*, Calcutta, XIV. 2 (Aug. 1913) 230; C.R.H., *Theosophist*, Madras, XXXV. 3 (Dec. 1913) [453].

b. *New edition* (1994):

THIRTY SONGS FROM THE | PANJAB AND KĀSHMĪR | RATAN DEVĪ | ANANDA K. COOMARASWAMY | New Edition | Revised and Enlarged | Edited by | PREMLATA [*sic*] SHARMA | Foreword by | KAPILA VATSYAYAN | [*in one line: publishers' devices*] | INDIRA GANDHI NATIONAL CENTRE FOR THE ARTS | NEW DELHI | STERLING PUBLISHERS PRIVATE LIMITED, NEW DELHI | 1994

xv, 177 pp., incl. music, II numbered pls., 1 blank leaf. 28.2 x 22.2 cm. Black-grained red imitation leather boards stamped in gold down the spine; end-papers. White dust-jacket printed in ochre and brown.

Published Summer 1994 at 500 rupees; number of copies unknown.

Contents: Foreword [by Kapila Vatsyayan]—PART I [photographic reprint of the text and plates of the first edition to page 76, with:] PART II: Editor's Introduction—Appendix: List of Notated Items with Indication of Musical Genres—Devanāgarī Transcription of Text and Music, Hindi Translation of Song-Texts and Hindi Notes with their English Translation—Select Bibliography.

Notes: For this new edition the letterpress on the protective tissues has been transferred to the plates themselves; the colophon of the first edition has been omitted; the original title-page is reproduced on the half-title leaf. Preserves the original dedication page and the "Foreword" by Tagore.

A28 THE ARTS & CRAFTS OF INDIA & CEYLON 1913

First edition:

THE | ARTS & CRAFTS OF | INDIA & CEYLON | BY | ANANDA K. COOMARASWAMY | D.SC. (LONDON), F.L.S., F.G.S., M.R.A.S., | FELLOW OF UNIVERSITY COLLEGE, LONDON | AUTHOR OF MEDIAEVAL SINHALESE ART; THE | INDIAN CRAFTSMAN; ESSAYS IN NATIONAL | IDEALISM; INDIAN DRAWINGS; ETC. | CONTAINING | TWO HUNDRED & TWENTY-FIVE ILLUSTRATIONS | T.N. FOULIS | LONDON & EDINBURGH | 1913

1 blank leaf, 3 leaves, v-xxi, [1], 255, [1] pp., incl. coloured frontis. (tipped in, with blank leaf of protective tissue), 28 text illus., 52 pls. (containing 197 illus.). 20 x 15.2 cm. Tan cloth boards stamped in gold on front cover (with a design of Gaja-Lakṣmī incorporating the title, within single rule border), and across the spine; end-papers; top edges gilt, other edges untrimmed. Grey dust-jacket printed in black with, on front, a coloured reproduction of *Head of Krishna* pasted down within single rule border.

Published November 1913 at 6*s*.; number of copies unknown.

Contents: Preface—List of Illustrations—PART ONE, HINDU AND BUDDHIST ART: Chap. I. Indian Character and History—Chap. II. Sculpture—Chap. III. Painting—Chap. IV. Architecture—Chap. V. Metal Work, Enamels, and Jewellery—Chap. VI. Woodwork—Chap. VII. Ivory—Chap. VIII. Stone, Earthenware, Gesso, Lac—Chap. IX. Textiles, Embroidery, Costume, Etc.—PART TWO, MUGHAL ART: Chap. X. Architecture—Chap. XI. Mughal Painting and Calligraphy—Chap. XII. Of the Minor Mughal Arts—Chief Publications on the Subject of this Volume.

Notes: This book was issued in the publisher's "The World of Art Series".

"The value of a small book must depend on its suggestiveness rather than its completeness . . . The scope of the book is indicated in its title. Ceylon, from the standpoint of ethnology and culture, is an integral part of India. I have passed beyond the Indian boundary only to include the sculpture of Java and Cambodia [and] the art of Nepal" ("Preface", pp. v-vi).

An American reprint of this book (hardbound and paperbound) was produced by offset in 1964 in New York by Farrar, Straus & Company, with additionally an "Introduction (1963)", by Doña Luisa Coomaraswamy (i.e. Mrs AKC), and an index. An Indian reprint was produced by offset, without these additions, in 1971 in New Delhi by Today & Tomorrow's Printers & Publishers.

Reviews: Mukandi Lal, *Oxford Indian Magazine*, London (1914) 104-6; Yakub Hasan, *Indian Review*, Madras, XV. 1 (Jan. 1914) 38-9; [Edward Gordon Craig], *Mask*, Florence, VI. 3 (Jan. 1914) 270-2; *Manchester Guardian*, Manchester, 21,064 (10 Feb. 1914) 6; Anthony M. Ludovici, *New Age*, London, XIV. 21 (26 Mar. 1914) 665-6; A.J.W., *Theosophist*, Madras, XXXV. 8 (May 1914) 299-300; O.C. Gangoly, *Modern Review*, Calcutta, XVI. 1 (July 1914) 105-6; *Times Literary Supplement*, London (9 July 1914) 333; F. R. G., *Burlington Magazine*, London, XXV. 137 (Aug. 1914) 308-9; George Sarton, *Isis*, Wondelgem-lez-Gand, Belgium, II. 6 (Sept. 1919) 404-7; Hugo Munsterberg, *Literature East & West*, Austin, Tex., VIII. (1964) 153; John T. Hatfield, *Journal of the History of Philosophy*, Clarmont, Calif., IV. (Apr. 1966) 182.

Translations: French, Brussels & Paris: Vromant et Cie, 1924. Spanish, Madrid: M. Aguilar Editor, 1934(?).

A29 MYTHS OF THE HINDUS & BUDDHISTS 1913

a. First edition, first impression:

[*In brown:*] MYTHS OF THE | HINDUS & BUDDHISTS | [*in black:*] BY | THE SISTER NIVEDITA | (MARGARET E. NOBLE) | OF RĀMAKRISHNA-VIVEKĀNANDA | AND | ANANDA K. COOMARASWAMY | WITH THIRTY-TWO ILLUSTRATIONS IN | COLOUR BY INDIAN ARTISTS UNDER THE | SUPERVISION OF | ABANINDRO NĀTH TAGORE C.I.E. | [*In brown: ornament*] | [*in black:*] LONDON | GEORGE G. HARRAP & COMPANY | 3 PORTSMOUTH STREET KINGSWAY W.C. | 1913

3 leaves, v-xii, 399, [1] pp., XXXII numbered pls. (coloured; incl. frontis.; each with protective tissue containing descriptive letterpress), 1 blank leaf. 24 x 17 cm. Dark blue cloth boards stamped in gold on the front cover and across the spine; end-papers; top edges gilt, other edges roughly trimmed.

Published November 1913 at 15*s*.; number of copies unknown.

Contents: Preface—[List of] Illustrations—Chap. I. Mythology of the Indo-Aryan Races—Chap. II. The Rāmāyana—Chap. III. The Mahābhārata—Chap. IV. Krishna—Chap. V. Buddha—Chap. VI. Shiva—Chap. VII. Other Stories from the Purānas, Epics, and Vedas—Chap. VIII. Conclusion: Summary of Indian Theology.

Notes: "Sister Nivedita's untimely death in [October] 1911 has made it necessary that the present work should be completed by another hand . . . [AKC is responsible for pages v-vii, 6-14, 23-117, 186-90, 217-90, 295-339, 342-78, 389-[400], i.e. more than two-thirds of the whole]. My aim has been to relate [the myths] in a manner as close to the original as possible, but usually much condensed . . . The stories . . . include very much of which a knowledge is absolutely essential for every foreigner who proposes in any way to co-operate with the Indian people for the attainment of their desired ends—nowhere more clearly formulated than in mythology and art. Amongst these are, I hope, to be included not only such avowed lovers of Indian ideals as was Nivedita herself, but also civil servants and missionaries. The Indian myths here retold include almost all those which are commonly illustrated in Indian sculpture and painting. Finally, they include much that must very soon be recognized as belonging not only to India, but to the whole world . . ." ("Preface", pp. v, vi-vii).

The plates comprise reproductions of paintings executed specially for the book by Abanindranath Tagore, Nandalal Bose, and others of the Calcutta school.

An American reprint (paperbound) was produced by offset from A29a in 1967 in New York by Dover Publications, Inc. The title-page transposes the authors' names; the plates are reproduced in black-and-white halftones.

Excerpts from pages 345-52 were printed, as "Yama and the Princess: A Hindu Love

Story", in *Argosy*, London, XI. 10 (Oct. 1950) 89-94, and excerpts from Chapter II were printed, under the heading "Ramayana", in *The Hamish Hamilton Book of Goblins*, edited by Alan Garner (London: Hamish Hamilton, 1969), pp. 134-73.

Reviews: Dial, New York, LVII. (1914) 81; W.G. Tinckom Fernandez, *Nation*, New York, XCIX. (1914) 717; K., *Theosophist*, Madras, XXXV. 4 (Feb. 1914) 768; Maung Tin, *Journal of the Burma Research Society*, Rangoon, V.1 (1915) 36-7; Permeswar Lall, *Hindustan Review*, Allahabad, XXXI. 185 (Jan. 1915) 72-80; O.C. Gangoly, *Modern Review*, Calcutta, XVII. 3 (Mar. 1915) 315-17; S.R.C., *Theosophist*, Madras, XXXVI. 2 (Apr. 1915) 83-6.

b. *Second impression* (1914):

Title-page as in the first impression save for publication date (1914).

Note: Contents, pagination, and size are identical with those of A29a, except for the addition, on pages 401-[426], of a combined "Glossary & Index". The plates in this impression are unnumbered, and without protective tissues (the letterpress has been transferred to the plates themselves).

c. *American issue* (1914):

Title-page as in A29a save for the imprint: NEW YORK | HENRY HOLT & COMPANY | 1914

Note: This issue uses the sheets of A29a; it does not contain the "Glossary & Index" that was printed with the second impression.

A30 BRONZES FROM CEYLON, CHIEFLY IN THE COLOMBO MUSEUM 1914

First edition:

MEMOIRS | OF THE | COLOMBO MUSEUM | EDITED BY | JOSEPH PEARSON, D.SC., F.L.S. | DIRECTOR OF THE COLOMBO MUSEUM | SERIES A. NO. 1 | BRONZES FROM CEYLON, CHIEFLY | IN THE COLOMBO MUSEUM | BY | ANANDA K. COOMARASWAMY, D.SC. | FELLOW OF UNIVERSITY COLLEGE, LONDON | WITH TWENTY-EIGHT PLATES | CEYLON | PRINTED FOR THE COLOMBO MUSEUM [by Horace Hart, printer to the University, Oxford] | 1914

31 pp., XXVIII numbered pls. (containing 189 illus., each plate has a leaf of protective tissue and a leaf containing descriptive letterpress). 33.7 x 26.3 cm. Limp light grey paper wrappers lettered in black on front; fore and bottom edges untrimmed.

Published late in 1914; number of copies unknown.

Contents: Preface [by Joseph Pearson]—Ceylonese Bronzes Chiefly in the Colombo Museum: Introduction—List of Hindu Figures Illustrated—List of Buddhist Figures Illustrated—List of Animal Figures and Minor Metal Objects Illustrated—Plates.

Notes: "The present work, in the hundred and sixty-seven figures of Pls. I-XXIV, illustrates all the Ceylonese bronzes, and the one or two Indian examples, in the Colombo Museum collection, together with some specimens on loan. In the twenty-two figures of Pls. XXV-XXVIII are given almost all the old Ceylonese bronzes in the British Museum, the Indian Museum at South Kensington, and the collection of the present writer . . . in the title of this monograph, the term bronze is used in a wide sense to indicate all metal images and minor metal-work . . . a short introduction [discusses] the archaeological and aesthetic significance of the specimens. This introduction falls into the following sections: 1. Buddhist bronzes of Anurādhapura, and a few others; also Kandyan Buddhist art, posterior to the 16th century. 2. The Hindū images of Polonnāruva" ("Introduction", pp. [5]-6).

An errata slip is inserted at p. [4].

An exact reprint (entirely reset) of this book (hardbound) was issued in 1978 [i.e. 1979] in Colombo by the Department of National Museums.

Reviews: Ceylon Antiquary, Colombo, I. 1 (July 1915) 70; X., *Burlington Magazine*, London, XXVII. 150 (Sept. 1915) 243; L.D. Barnett, *Journal of the Royal Asiatic Society*, London (1916) 174-7.

A31 VIŚVAKARMĀ 1914

First edition in this form:

VIŚVAKARMĀ: EXAMPLES OF INDIAN ARCHI- | TECTURE, SCULPTURE, PAINTING, HANDICRAFT, CHOSEN BY | ANANDA K. COOMARASWAMY, D.SC. [*Ornament*] FIRST SERIES: ONE | HUNDRED EXAMPLES OF INDIAN SCULPTURE: WITH AN IN- | TRODUCTION BY ERIC GILL. | Sold by Messrs. Luzac, 46 Great Russell Street, London, W.C.: Otto Harrassowitz, | Querstrasse, Leipzig: and Messrs. Taraporevala, Medows Street, Bombay. | 1914.

1 blank leaf, 30, [1] pp., C numbered pls., followed by 3 pls. additional to the sequence: LXXIA, LXXIIA, LXXIIIA, 1 blank leaf. 27 x 21.5 cm.(leaves).

Published November 1914; 500 copies printed.

Contents: Preface [by Eric Gill]—List of Plates: Buddhas and Bodhisattvas—Brahmanical Divinities—Men, Women and Nagas—Animals, Including Animal Avatars—Editorial Note—Plates.

Notes: This book was originally issued in eight parts, as follows: Part I (July 1912), Part II (Oct. 1912), Part III (Jan. 1913), Part IV (Apr. 1913), Part V (July 1913), Part VI (Oct. 1913), Part VII (June 1914), and Part VIII (Nov. 1914); these each have limp green paper wrappers lettered in black on the front cover, and measure 27.8 x 22.6 cm. The eight parts collected form the first volume of an intended series, of which no more were published.

"The present series is mainly . . . for those who are interested as artists in Indian art. The illustrations have in no case been selected soley for archaeological interest. . . . One thousand copies of the whole edition have been printed, of which five hundred have been prepared for sale in parts, the remainder in one volume" ("Editorial Note", p. [31]). A quotation from the *Mahābhārata*, I. 2592, is printed on the verso of the title-leaf.

No copy of this book in the original binding has been sighted by the compiler.

An Indian reprint of this book (hardbound) was produced by offset from the first edition in 1978 in New Delhi by Munshiram Manoharlal Publishers Pvt., Ltd.

Reviews: O.C. G[angoly]., *Modern Review*, Calcutta, XII. 6 (Dec. 1912) 676; *South Asian Review*, London, I. 4 (1913) 427; *Athenaeum*, London (17 May 1913) 549; O.C. G[angoly]., *Modern Review*, Calcutta, XIV. 1 (July 1913) 112; *South Asian Review*, London, V. 4 (1914) 522; [Edward Gordon Craig], *Mask*, Florence, VI. 3 (Jan. 1914) 272; O.C. G[angoly]., *Modern Review*, Calcutta, XV. 1 (Jan. 1914) 108, and XVII. 2 (Feb. 1915) 214-15; Johan van Manen, *Theosophist*, Madras, XXXVI. 2 (May 1915) 187-8; George Sarton, *Isis*, Wondelgem-lez-Gand, Belgium, II. 6 (Sept. 1919) 403-4.

A32 VIDYĀPATI: BANGĪYA PADĀBALI SONGS OF THE LOVE OF RĀDHĀ AND KRISHNA 1915

First edition:

[*In red:*] VIDYĀPATI: BANGĪYA PADĀBALI | [*in black:*] SONGS OF THE LOVE OF RĀDHĀ AND KRISHNA TRANS- | LATED INTO ENGLISH BY ANANDA COOMARASWAMY AND | ARUN SEN WITH INTRODUCTION AND NOTES AND ILLUS- | TRATIONS FROM INDIAN PAINTINGS | LONDON: THE OLD BOURNE PRESS, | 15 HOLBORN, E.C. | 1915.

1 blank leaf, xi, [1] pp., 1 blank leaf, 3-191, [1] pp., 11 pls. (black-and-white, tipped in on leaves facing pp. 3, 19, 27, 33, 43, 63, 71, 77, 95, 115, 151; each has a leaf of protective tissue containing descriptive letterpress in red), 2 blank leaves. 26.5 x 22.2 cm. Limp tan paper wrappers lettered in red on front cover; edges roughly trimmed.

Published February 1915 at 10*s*. 6*d*.; 353 copies printed.

Colophon (page [192]): . . . Of this edition of VIDYĀPATI three hundred fifty and [*sic*] copies have been printed, and three on handmade paper.

Contents: Introduction—Krishna Pūrbbarāga [The First Passion of Krishna]—Rādhā Bayahsandi [The Growing-up of Rādhā]—Rādhā Pūrbbarāga [The First Passion of Rādhā]—Sakhi-Shikshā-Bacanādi [The Counsel of Girl-friends]— Prathama Milna [First Meetings]—Abhisāra [Radha's Going-forth to Visit Krishna]—Vasanta Līlā [Dalliance in Spring]—Māna [Wilfulness]—Mānānte Milna [Reunion after Wilfulness]—Ākshepa Anuyoga O Viraha [Reproaches, Lack and Longing]—Punarmilna O Rasodgāra [Reunion and the Flow of Nectar]—Notes: Dramatis Personae—Elucidations—Birds, Flowers and Trees [i.e. a glossary]—Illustrations [i.e. a descriptive list]—[Five Bengali song] Texts.

Notes: These songs of the 14th century Maithilī poet Vidyāpati are numbered I-CXXXVIII and grouped within eleven sections. The plates comprise reproductions of Rājput miniatures, mainly selected from the Kāngrā school.

In a letter to William Rothenstein, 5 Jan. 1915, AKC writes, concerning Vidyāpati: "I think that sort of literature is of value to modern Europe quite apart from the mysticism—as an education in love: also to remind us that Muhammad could have been perfectly sincere when he said 'Three things he had loved, Perfume, Women and Prayer, but the last most!'. Kabir is a prophet. But Vidyapati is an artist and seems to me to carry out the Kabir doctrine of seeing the physical and spiritual as one thing" (*Selected Letters of Ananda K. Coomaraswamy* (1988)—A89—p. 376).

A list of corrigenda is printed in six lines on page [192].

An Indian reprint of this book (hardbound) was produced by offset from the first edition in 1979 in Delhi by Bharatiya Publishing House. This omits the protective tissues (the letterpress has been transferred to the plates themselves), and the colophon.

Reviews: S[ureshchandra Banerjee]., *Modern Review*, Calcutta, XVII. 4 (Apr. 1915) 488; Kundan Lall, *Hindustan Review*, Allahabad, XXXI. 188 (Apr. 1915) 435-7; *Athenaeum*, London, 4,562 (3 Apr. 1915) 312; *Indian Review*, Madras, XVI. 5 (May 1915) 445; D.M.C., *Commonweal*, Madras, IV. (13 Aug. 1915) 126; *New Age*, London, XVII. 16 (19 Aug. 1915) 388; *Quest*, London (Oct. 1915) [180]-182.

A33 THE TAKING OF TOLL 1915

First edition:

[*In red:*] THE TAKING OF TOLL | [*in black:*] BEING THE DĀNA LĪLĀ OF RĀJENDRA | TRANSLATED INTO ENGLISH BY ANANDA | COOMARASWAMY WITH AN INTRODUCTION | AND NOTES AND A WOODCUT BY ERIC GILL | THE OLD BOURNE PRESS | LONDON | 1915

v, [1] pp., 1 leaf, 5, [3] pp., incl. frontis., 1 text illus. 27.3 x 21.1 cm. Limp tan paper wrappers lettered on front in red; wire-stitched.

Published July 1915 at 2*s.* 6*d.*; number of copies unknown.

Contents: Introduction—The Taking of Toll—Elucidations.

Notes: "An episode (not in the *Bhāgavata Purāṇa*), known as the *Dāna Līlā*, depicts *Kṛṣṇa* as keeper of the ferry on the Jamnā, which the milkmaids must cross when they take their milk and curds to sell in Mathurā. He demands from them a fee, which at first they refuse, but at last acknowledge him as lord of all that they are or possess; they remain with him all night and again take part in the *Rāsa Maṇḍala*" (*Catalogue of the Indian Collections in the Museum of Fine Arts, Boston Part V Rājput Painting* (1926)—A49—p. 58).

The woodcut by Eric Gill is reproduced as the frontispiece; a reproduction of an Indian drawing is printed on page [8].

Review: Bharadwaja, *Modern Review*, Calcutta, XVIII. 6 (Dec. 1915) 675-6.

A34 RAJPUT PAINTING 1916

a. *First edition:*

[*In red:*] RAJPUT PAINTING | [*in black:*] BEING AN ACCOUNT OF THE HINDU PAINTINGS OF | RAJASTHAN AND THE PANJAB HIMALAYAS | FROM THE SIXTEENTH TO THE NINETEENTH CENTURY | DESCRIBED IN THEIR RELATION TO CONTEMPORARY THOUGHT | WITH TEXTS AND TRANSLATIONS | BY | [*in red:*] ANANDA COOMARASWAMY | [*in black:*] D.SC. LONDON; FELLOW OF UNIVERSITY COLLEGE, LONDON; HON. CORRESPONDENT ARCHAEOLOGICAL | SURVEY OF INDIA; AUTHOR OF 'MEDIAEVAL SINHALESE ART' | 'INDIAN DRAWINGS' AND 'THE ARTS AND CRAFTS OF INDIA AND CEYLON' | VOLUME I. TEXT [-VOLUME II. PLATES] | HUMPHREY MILFORD | OXFORD UNIVERSITY PRESS | LONDON EDINBURGH GLASGOW NEW YORK TORONTO | MELBOURNE BOMBAY MADRAS CALCUTTA | 1916

Volume I: 4 leaves, [1]-83, [1]pp., incl. 1 table, 1 map, and 12 text illus.; *volume II:* vii pp., LXXVII numbered pls. (tipped in, each with leaf of protective tissue containing on the verso descriptive letterpress; plates I, II, IX, XVI, XXI, LI, LIII are coloured), 1 blank leaf. 37.7 x 28 cm. Tan cloth boards stamped in gold on front: RAJPUT PAINTING | [*ornament*], and across spine: [*double rule*] | RAJPUT | PAINTING | ANANDA | COOMARA- | SWAMY | [*ornament*] | TEXT [-*volume II:* PLATES] | MILFORD | [*double rule*]; end-papers.

Published January 1916 at 105*s.*; 525 copies printed.

Colophon (in volume I, p. [84]): Five hundred and twenty-five copies of this edition have been printed, of which three copies only are on hand-made paper.

Contents: Volume I. Acknowledgement—Note on Pronunciation—List of Illustrations in the Text—Introduction—PART I. THE RĀJPUT SCHOOLS: Chap. I. Rājasthānī—Chap. II. Pahāṛī: A. Jammu; B. Kāngṛā—PART II. SUBJECT-MATTER OF RĀJPUT PAINTINGS: Chap. I. The Krishna Līlā —Appendix: The Cult of Śrī Nātha-Jī—Chap. II. Sṛṅgāra: The Eight Nāyakās; The Nāyakā as Svakīyā, Parakīyā or Sāmānyā; Viraha; Saṃyoga—Chap. III. Śiva and Pārvatī—Chap. IV. The Epics: The *Rāmāyaṇa*; The *Mahābhārata*—Chap. V. Ballad and Romance—Chap. VI. Rāgmālās—Chap. VII. Seasons, Animals, Landscape—Chap. VIII. Portraiture—PART III. ALLIED ARTS AND THE PRESENT DAY: Chap. I. Allied Arts—Chap. II. To-day and To-morrow; volume II. List of Plates—[Plates].

Notes: "No separate work on Rājput painting has yet been published, and no contributions to its study have been made by other investigators; this is, therefore, a pioneer work . . ." (p. 6).

"I desire to express my thanks here to H.H. the Mahārājā Gaekwar of Baroda, and to the Under-Secretary of the State for India, representing the India Office, for grants, respectively of Rs. 1,000 and of £75, toward the cost of publication of *Rājput Painting*. I also wish to acknowledge my debt to Mr. Mukandi Lāl for constant assistance in the interpretation of Hindī texts . . ." ("Acknowledgement", *recto of first leaf following title-leaf*).

An American reprint of this book (the two volumes in one, hardbound) was produced by offset from the first edition in New York in 1975 by Hacker Art Books, with the colour plates reproduced in black-and-white halftones.

Reviews: Times Literary Supplement, London, 739 (16 Mar. 1916) 127; Therese Muir Mackenzie, *Ladies' Field*, London (25 Mar. 1916) 136-7; *Athenaeum*, London, 4,604 (Apr. 1916) 204-5; Raphael Petrucci, *Burlington Magazine*, London, XXIX. 158 (May 1916) 74-9; Laurence Binyon, *Hindustan Review*, Allahabad, XXXIV. 203 (July 1916) [81]-86; F.J. Mather, *Nation*, New York, CIII. (13 July 1916) 45; H.A.R., *Journal of the Royal Asiatic Society*, London (1918) 338-40; E. Blochet, *Gazette des Beaux-Arts*, Paris (Jan./ Mar. 1918) [108]-114; Michael Meister, *Journal of the American Oriental Society*, New Haven, XCIX. 3 (July/Sept. 1979) 524-5.

b. *Second (offset) edition* ([1977]):

Title page as in A34a except for: FOREWORD BY | KARL J. KHANDALAVALA | Bar-at-Law | CHAIRMAN, PRINCE OF WALES MUSEUM, BOMBAY, and the imprint: MOTILAL BANARSIDASS | DELHI :: VARANASI :: PATNA

Volume I: 16 pp., 2 leaves, [1]-83 pp., incl. frontis.; *volume II:* 1 leaf, vii pp., LXXVII numbered pls. (each with leaf of protective tissue containing descriptive letterpress; plates I, II, IX, XVI, XXI, LI, LIII are coloured). 37.4 x 25.7 cm. White cloth boards lettered on front in red, with reproduction of a line drawing of two Rājput musicians printed in brown, and on the spine; decorated end-papers.

Published in 1977; number of copies unknown.

Contents: Volume I. Foreword [by Karl J. Khandalavala], pp. [5]-13 (first count)—List of Plates, pp. [14]-16 (first count)—[pp. [1]-83 (second count) a reprint by offset of the text in A34a]; volume II. [a reprint by offset of the text and plates in A34a].

Notes: The "List of Plates", in Volume I, is in the main a revision by Karl J. Khandalavala of AKC's dating and ascriptions of provenance (AKC's original list is preserved in Volume II). "Motilal Banarsidass and the present editor were both in complete agreement that neither Coomaraswamy's text nor his notes . . . should be altered but that a separate Foreword with revised notes, to indicate the progress made in the study of Rajput painting, should be included" ("Foreword", p. [5]).

The frontispiece is a reproduction of a photograph of AKC by Doña Luisa Coomaraswamy (i.e. Mrs AKC).

Review: T.K. Mahadevan, *Indian & Foreign Review*, New Delhi, XIV. 24 (1 Oct. 1977) 20-1.

A35 BUDDHA AND THE GOSPEL OF BUDDHISM 1916

a. *First edition, first impression:*

[*In brown:*] BUDDHA AND THE | GOSPEL OF BUDDHISM | [*in black:*] BY | ANANDA COOMARASWAMY D.SC. | AUTHOR OF "ARTS AND CRAFTS OF INDIA

AND CEYLON" "RAJPUT | PAINTING" AND "ESSAYS IN NATIONAL IDEALISM" JOINT-AUTHOR | OF "MYTHS OF THE HINDUS AND BUDDHISTS" | WITH ILLUSTRATIONS IN COLOUR BY | ABANINDRO NĀTH TAGORE C.I.E. | & NANDA LĀL BOSE | AND THIRTY-TWO REPRODUCTIONS IN | BLACK AND WHITE FROM PHOTOGRAPHS | [*in brown: ornament (encircled lotus)*] | [*in black:*] LONDON | GEORGE G. HARRAP & COMPANY | 2 & 3 PORTSMOUTH STREET KINGSWAY W.C. | MCMXVI

1 blank leaf, 3 leaves, v-viii, 369, [1] pp., VIII numbered pls. (coloured, incl. frontis., each with leaf of protective tissue containing descriptive letterpress) and 32 black-and-white halftone pls. lettered A-H, J-U, W-Z, and AA-HH, 1 blank leaf. Black cloth boards stamped in gold on front cover (with: ANANDA COOMARASWAMY, in blind), and across the spine with a design of Dharmacakra and Umbrella of Lordship combined stamped in olive green with, at base: HARRAP, in blind; end-papers; edges roughly trimmed.

Published November 1916 at 15*s*.; number of copies unknown.

Dedication (verso of title-leaf): To A.E. [i.e. George William Russell?]

Contents: Preface—List of Plates—List of Plates in Colour—Quotations—PART I: THE LIFE OF THE BUDDHA—PART II: THE GOSPEL OF EARLY BUDDHISM: I. Dhamma, the Doctrine and Discipline—II. Samsāra and Kamma (Karma)—III. Buddhist Heavens and How to Reach Them—IV. Nibbāna—V. Ethics—VI. Conscience—VII. Spiritual Exercises—VIII. Consolation—IX. The Order—X. Tolerance—XI. Women—XII. Early Buddhism and Nature—XIII. Buddhist Pessimism—XIV. A Buddhist Emperor—PART III: CONTEMPORARY SYSTEMS: I. The Vedānta—II. Sāmkhya—III. Yoga—IV. Buddhism and Brāhmanism—PART IV: THE MAHĀYĀNA: I. Beginnings of the Mahāyāna—II. System of the Mahāyāna—III. Ch'an, or Zen Buddhism—PART V: BUDDHIST ART: I. Buddhist Literature—II. Sculpture and Painting—Bibliography of Works Consulted by the Author—Glossary—Index.

Reviews: R.F.J., *Journal of the North-China Branch of the Royal Asiatic Society*, Shanghai, XLVIII. (1917) 198-203; T.W. R[hys].-D[avids]., *Manchester Guardian*, Manchester, 21,971 (6 Jan. 1917) 5; A. Worsley, *Hindustan Review*, Allahabad, XXXVI. 215 (July 1917) 76-81; W.D.S.B., *Theosophist*, Madras, XXXVIII. 2 (Aug. 1917) 575-7; *South Asia Review*, London, XIV. (1918) 520; W. Printz, *Zeitschrift der Deutschen Morgenlandischen Gesellschaft*, Leipzig, LXXXII. (1928) cols. 238-9; H. Zimmer, *Orientalistische Literaturzeitung*, Leipzig, XXXIV. (1931) cols. 1082-3.

b. *American issue* (1916):

Title-page as for A35a save for the publishers' imprint: NEW YORK | G. P. PUTNAM'S SONS | 1916

Published November 1916 at $3.75; number of copies unknown.

Note: This issue uses the sheets of A35a; an errata slip is tipped in at the title-page or in some copies at page 203.

Reviews: Dial, New York, LXII. 741 (3 May 1917) 405; *New York Times Book Review*,

New York (23 Sept. 1917) 357; Irving Babbitt, *Nation*, New York, CV. 2,729 (18 Oct. 1917) 424-8.

c. *Indian edition* ([1956]):

BUDDHA | AND THE GOSPEL OF | BUDDHISM | ANANDA COOMARASWAMY | [*publisher's device*] | ASIA PUBLISHING HOUSE | BOMBAY • CALCUTTA • NEW DELHI • MADRAS

xii, 2 leaves, 370 pp., 1 blank leaf, 24 black-and-white plates lettered A-H, J-U, W-Z. 22.4 x 14.5 cm. Maroon cloth boards, lettered down the spine in black; end-papers.

Published in 1956; number of copies unknown.

Notes: The text of this edition, entirely reset, is identical with that of A35a save for some corrections of misprints. The colour plates are omitted, and there is a reduction in the number of black-and-white plates.

An Indian reprint (hardbound) was produced by offset from A35a in New Delhi in 1972 by Munshiram Manoharlal.

d. *New (offset) edition* ([1964]):

Ananda K. Coomaraswamy | Buddha and the | Gospel of | Buddhism | Revised by DOÑA LUISA | COOMARASWAMY [*design within circle of Dharmacakra supported by lotus*] | HARPER TORCHBOOKS [*publishers' device*] | THE CLOISTER LIBRARY | Harper & Row, Publishers | New York, Evanston, and London

vii, [1] pp., 3 leaves, 9-369, [1] pp., incl. frontis., 42 pls. lettered A-Pa-b, Qa-b, R-Xa-b, Y-Za-b, and AA-CCa-d, DD-HH, JJ-LL, 6 leaves (i.e. publishers' advertisements). 20.2 x 13.5 cm. Heavy white paper wrappers printed in brown and yellow.

Published late 1964 at $2.45; number of copies unknown.

Notes: This edition is a reprint by offset of the text of A35a with misprints corrected and incorporating revisions by Doña Luisa Coomaraswamy (these are fairly easily detected as they are in slightly lighter type than the original); a note by Doña Luisa Coomaraswamy (dated 1964) printed in five lines on page [viii]; additional footnotes on pages 31, 35, 205, 210, 213, 223, 225, 230, 268, 269, 272, 274, 297, 298 (those on pages 205 and 223 are signed: I.B.H., i.e. Isaline Blew Horner); the omission of the colour plates; the original black-and-white plates replaced by other photographs of the same subjects or by photographs of other examples of the same subjects; the captions to the plates expanded; and the addition of five entirely new plates (A, B, C, I, and S) , and a new frontispiece.

Simultaneously with this new edition, an American reprint (hardbound) was produced by offset from A35a in New York by University Books, Inc., with additionally a "New Introduction", by Arnold Kunst, and an "Introduction", by John C. Wilson. The colour plates of the first edition are omitted, and the black-and-white plates are reduced in number.

Reviews: Marco Pallis, *Tomorrow*, London, XII. 3 (Summer 1964) 245; Arnold L. Green, *Journal of Asian Studies*, Ann Arbor, XXIV. 3 (May 1965) 547; W. L. King, *Journal for the Scientific Study of Religion*, Washington, D.C., V. (Spring 1966) 332-3; *Pacific Affairs*, Vancouver, XL. (1967) 170.

A36 THE MIRROR OF GESTURE 1917

a. *First edition:*

THE MIRROR OF GESTURE | BEING THE ABHINAYA DARPAṆA | OF NANDIKEŚVARA | TRANSLATED INTO ENGLISH | BY | ANANDA COOMARASWAMY | AND | GOPALA KRISTNAYYA DUGGIRALA | WITH INTRODUCTION AND | ILLUSTRATIONS | [*publisher's device*] | CAMBRIDGE | HARVARD UNIVERSITY PRESS | LONDON: HUMPHREY MILFORD | OXFORD UNIVERSITY PRESS | 1917

1 blank leaf, vii, 52 pp., 1 leaf, XV numbered pls., 1 blank leaf. 24.8 x 16.6 cm. Dark green cloth boards lettered in black down the spine on white paper label: [*ornament, thin-thick vertical rule*] The Mirror of Gesture • Coomaraswamy [*thick-thin vertical rule, ornament*]; end-papers; top edges roughly trimmed, other edges untrimmed.

Published March 1917 at $1.50; number of copies unknown.

Dedication (page [iii]): Inscribed by the translators with affectionate greeting to all actors and actresses

Contents: List of Plates—The Mirror of Gesture: Introduction—The Indian Editor's Preface [i.e. by Maḍābhūshi Tiruvenkaṭa of Niḍāmangalam]—Invocation—Dialogue of Indra and Nandikeśvara—Nāṭya, Nṛtta and Nṛtya—The Audience, Ministers, Stage, Danseuse, Bells, Dancer, Inner and Outer Life of the Danseuse, Vulgar Dancing, The Course of the Dance—Gesture—Nine Movements of the Head—Eight Glances—Forty-four Glances—Six Movements of the Brows—Lives of the Hands—Twenty-eight Single Hands—Twenty-four Combined Hands—Twenty-six Combined Hands—Hands Denoting Relationships—Hands Denoting Devas—Hands Denoting the Nine Planets—Hands Denoting the Avatars of Vishnu—Hands Denoting the Four Castes—Hands Denoting Famous Emperors—Hands Denoting the Seven Oceans—Hands Denoting Famous Rivers—Hands Denoting the Upper and Lower Worlds—Hands Denoting Trees—Hands Denoting Animals—Hands Denoting Flying Creatures—Hands Denoting Water Creatures—Colophon—[List of] Works of Comparison and Reference—Plates.

Notes: This translation by AKC and Duggirāla Gopālakrishnāyya of Nandikeśvara's treatise (of AD 13th century, or earlier) on Indian dramatic technique "is based upon a Nāgarī transcript of the second Telugu edition of the 'Abhinaya Darpaṇa' . . . published under the editorship of the late Tiruvenkaṭācāri of Niḍāmangalam" ("Introduction", p. 10).

An Indian reprint (hardbound) was produced by offset from the first edition in July 1970 in New Delhi by Munshiram Manoharlal Publishers Pvt. Ltd.

Reviews: L. D. Barnett, *Journal of the Royal Asiatic Society*, London (1917) 627-8; Sheldon Cheney, *Theatre Arts Magazine*, New York, I. (1917) 146; *Times Literary Supplement*, London, 797 (26 Apr. 1917) 199; James H. Cousins, *Commonweal*, Madras, VII. (8 June 1917) 450; *Nation*, New York, CIV. 2,711 (14 June 1917) 716; O[rdhendra]. C[oomar]. G[angoly]., *Modern Review*, Calcutta, XXII. 4 (Oct. 1917) 436-7; H[arold]. H. C[hild]., *Burlington Magazine*, London, XXXI. 177 (Dec. 1917) 246; [Edward Gordon Craig?], *Mask*, Florence, VIII. 12 ([Apr. 1919]) 52.

b. *Second edition* (1936):

THE MIRROR OF GESTURE | BEING THE ABHINAYA DARPAṆA | OF NANDIKEŚVARA | Translated into English by | ANANDA K. COOMARASWAMY | and | DUGGIRĀLA GOPĀLAKRISHNĀYYA | With Introduction and | Illustrations | E. WEYHE • NEW YORK • 1936

1 blank leaf, 9-81 pp., 1 leaf, XX numbered pls., 1 blank leaf. 24.3 x 16.4 cm. Dark blue cloth boards stamped in gold up the spine: The Mirror of Gesture • Coomaraswamy; endpapers; fore edges untrimmed, bottom edges roughly trimmed.

Published late 1936 at $5.00; number of copies unknown.

Contents: List of Plates—Preface to the Second Edition—Introduction—The Indian Editor's Preface—Invocation—Dialogue of Indra and Nandikeśvara—Nāṭya, Nṛtta, and Nṛtya—The Audience, Ministers, Stage, Danseuse, Bells, Dancer, Inner and Outer Life of the Danseuse, Vulgar Dancing, The Course of the Dance—Gesture—Nine Movements of the Head—Twenty-four Movements of the Head—Eight Glances—Forty-four Glances—Six Movements of the Brows—Four Necks—Lives of the Hands—Twenty-eight Single Hands—Twenty-four Combined Hands[I]—Twenty-four Combined Hands [II]—Hands Denoting Relationships—Hands Denoting Devas—Hands Denoting the Nine Planets—Hands Denoting the Avatars of Vishnu—Hands Denoting the Four Castes—Hands Denoting Famous Emperors—Hands Denoting the Seven Oceans—Hands Denoting Famous Rivers—Hands Denoting the Upper and Lower Worlds—Hands Denoting Trees—Hands Denoting Animals—Hands Denoting Flying Creatures—Hands Denoting Water Creatures—Colophon—Appendix: Positions and Movements of the Feet and Legs—Bibliography—Plates.

Note: For this edition AKC has revised the translation in the light of Manomohan Ghosh's 1934 edition and translation of the *Abhinaya Darpaṇa*. There is additionally a "Preface to the Second Edition", by AKC (dated Boston, June 1936), which includes an appreciation and an account of the life of Duggirāla Gopālakrishnāyya, who had died between the publication of the two editions. This preface occupies pages 9-13. The introduction to the first edition has been retained. The appendix comprises some verses not included in the Telugu edition upon which the translation of the first edition of this book was based. Five new plates have been added (X-XIV), and the bibliography has been augmented. The dedication of the first edition has been retained.

Reviews: René Guénon, *Études Traditionnelles*, Paris, XLI. 204 (Dec. 1936) [474]; E. H. Johnston, *Journal of the Royal Asiatic Society*, London (1937) 527; Dorothy Coit, *Theatre Arts Monthly*, New York, XXI. 2 (Feb. 1937) 155-7; S.K. De, *Oriental Literary Digest*, Poona, I. 3 (Sept. 1937) cols. 1-3.

A37 INDIAN ART 1918

First edition:

[*Within single rule border:*] HANDBOOK | OF | THE MUSEUM OF FINE ARTS | BOSTON | [*design comprising an outline plan of the Museum incorporating words giving names and disposition of the separate galleries, etc.*] | INDIAN ART | [Boston: Museum of Fine Arts, Boston] 1918

20 pp., incl. frontis. and 10 unnumbered pls. (i.e. pp. 10-20). 16.3 x 11.8 cm. Limp grey paper wrappers lettered on front in black as above (front wrapper serves as title-page) and with publisher's device printed on the verso of back wrapper; sewn.

Published in 1918; number of copies unknown.

Contents: Indian Art—Bibliography—[Plates].

Note: The text of this pamphlet is signed (on page 9): A.K.C. Probably the same as B15.

A38 THE DANCE OF ŚIVA 1918

a. *First edition:*

THE DANCE OF ŚIVA | FOURTEEN INDIAN ESSAYS | BY | ANANDA COOMARASWAMY | [*publisher's device*] | THE SUNWISE TURN, INC. | 2 EAST 31ST STREET | NEW YORK | 1918

1 blank leaf, 4 leaves, 139, [1] pp., incl. frontis., XXVII numbered pls. 25.2 x 16.8 cm. Dark green cloth boards lettered in black down the spine on white paper label: [*ornament, thin-thick vertical rule*] The Dance of Śiva | FOURTEEN INDIAN ESSAYS [*to the right of these two lines:*] By Ananda Coomaraswamy [*thick-thin vertical rule, ornament*]; end-papers; edges untrimmed.

Published June 1918 at $2.50; number of copies unknown.

Contents: List of Plates—What Has India Contributed to Human Welfare?—Hindu View of Art: I. History of Aesthetic [from C347]—Hindu View of Art: II. Theory of Beauty [from C347]—That Beauty Is a State—Buddhist Primitives [C360 and 363, combined]—The Dance of Śiva—Indian Images with Many Arms [C305, revised and reduced]—Indian Music [C380, with addenda]—Status of Indian Women [formerly "Sati: A Vindication of the Hindu Woman", revised]—Sahaja—Intellectual Fraternity—Cosmopolitan View of Nietzsche—Young India [C386 and 389, combined]—Individuality, Autonomy and Function—[Acknowledgements].

Notes: The following essays are apparently printed here for the first time: "Sahaja", "Cosmopolitan View of Nietzsche", and "Individuality, Autonomy and Function". The other essays, with the exception of "The Dance of Śiva", and "Intellectual Fraternity", are printed here for the first time in book-form.

Plate XVI is a reproduction of a photograph of Ratan Devī (i.e. Mrs AKC) by Arnold Genthe.

Reviews: Museum of Fine Arts Bulletin, Boston, XVI. 96 (Aug. 1918) 63; *Times Literary Supplement*, London, 864 (8 Aug. 1918) 370; A.J. Penty, *New Age*, London, XXIII. 17 (22 Aug. 1918) 273-4; Eric Gill, *Burlington Magazine*, London, XXXIII. 187 (Oct. 1918) 123-5; *Nation*, New York, CVII. 2,784 (9 Nov. 1918) 560; Maheshchandra Ghose, *Modern*

Review, Calcutta, XXV. 1 (Jan. 1919) 70; A. de L., *Theosophist*, Madras, XL. 1 (Jan. 1919) 403-5; A Mourner Clad in Green (i.e. Aleister Crowley), *Equinox*, Detroit, III. 1 (Mar. 1919) 292-4; [Harold A. Loeb], *Broom*, Rome, II. 1 (Apr. 1922) 94-5.

Translations: French, Paris: F. Rieder et Cie, 1922 (by Madeleine Rolland, with an introduction by Romain Rolland); Plan-de-la-Tour: Editions d'Aujourd'hui, 1984; Spanish, Madrid: Ediciones Siruela, 1996 (by Eva Fernández del Campo; the second, third, fourth, fifth, sixth, seventh, and eighth of the essays only).

b. *Second edition* (1924):

THE DANCE OF ŚIVA | FOURTEEN INDIAN ESSAYS | BY | ANANDA COOMARASWAMY | WITH INTRODUCTORY PREFACE | BY | ROMAIN ROLLAND | [*publisher's device*] | THE SUNWISE TURN, INC. | 51 EAST 44TH STREET | NEW YORK | 1924

1 blank leaf, 4 leaves, vi pp., 1 blank leaf, 139, [1] pp., 2 blank leaves, incl. frontis., XXVII numbered pls. 24.5 x 16.5 cm. Black cloth boards stamped in gold on front cover within thick-thin rule frame: THE DANCE OF ŚIVA | COOMARASWAMY, and across the spine (some copies were also issued in a binding almost identical with the first edition); end-papers; edges untrimmed.

Published late in 1924 at $3.00; number of copies unknown.

Notes: The contents of this second edition are identical with those of A38a save for the addition, on pages [i]-vi, of a "Foreword" (called "Introductory Preface" on title-page), by Romain Rolland, which is a reprint in English of his introduction to the 1922 French translation of this book.

This second edition was also published in London (using the American sheets?) by Simpkin, Marshall, Hamilton, Kent in 1924.

An Indian reprint (hardbound) of A38b, entirely reset, was published in 1948 in Bombay by Asia Publishing House. In this reprint the plates are gathered between pages 100 and 101; the footnotes are printed as endnotes (pages [187]-196); and a publisher's note, signed P.S. Jayasinghe, is printed in six lines on page 12. Rolland's "Foreword" is printed on pages [5]-11.

An American reprint (paperbound) of A38b was produced by offset in 1985 in New York by Dover Publications, Inc. For this reprint the original subtitle has been replaced with: *Essays on Indian Art and Culture*. Rolland's "Foreword" occupies pages [xi]-xvi.

Reviews: Hindustan Review, Allahabad, XLVIII. 285 (July 1925) 459; *Saturday Review of Literature*, New York, II. (6 Feb. 1926) 547; Henri Peyre, *Dial*, New York, LXXXIV. 5 (May 1928) 377; Alain Daniélou, *Visva-Bharati Quarterly*, Calcutta, N.S. XIV. 3 (Nov. 1948/Jan. 1949) [225]-226; Shankar Mokashi-Punekar, *Journal of the Karnatak University*, Dharwar, XII. (1968) 76-91.

c. *Third edition, revised and corrected* (1957):

THE DANCE OF | SHIVA | Revised Edition | FOURTEEN INDIAN ESSAYS | [*ornament*] | Ananda K. Coomaraswamy | [*publisher's device*] | THE NOONDAY PRESS | NEW YORK | 1957

6 leaves, incl. frontis., 16 pls. (containing 36 numbered illus.), [3]-182 pp., 1 blank leaf. 21.6 x 14.7 cm. Grey and white striped paper boards with black cloth back stamped in gold across the spine with publisher's device in blind; end-papers; top edges stained yellow.

Published in 1957 at $4.50; number of copies unknown.

Notes: "This book . . . was revised by the author shortly before his death in 1947. It is the only authorized edition now in print" (*verso of the title-leaf*).

The revisions are slight; the only substantial change is the addition of a new sentence concerning "reincarnation", page 12, lines 24-8. A sentence containing a statement on slavery in India, that occurs in A38a on page 108, is omitted; the misprints in A38a are corrected.

The illustrations in the first edition are retained, except for those on plates XV and XVI; there are four new illustrations (i.e. 18, 22, 23, 31). The frontispiece is a reproduction of a drawing, by Nathan Gluck, of Śiva as Naṭarāja.

This edition was also published (hardbound) in 1958 in London by Peter Owen, using the American sheets (the title-leaf is a cancel). An Indian reprint (hardbound) was produced by offset from A38c in 1982 in New Delhi by Sagar Publications.

A39 PRAYERS AND EPIGRAMS [1918]

First edition:

[*In black:*] Prayers and Epigrams | By Ananda Coomaraswamy | [*in blue and red: publisher's device.* New York: The Sunwise Turn, Inc.]

2 leaves, 1 text illus. 11 x 8.4 cm. Limp white paper wrappers lettered on front as above (front wrapper serves as title-page), with a colophon lettered in black on verso of back wrapper; sewn; edges untrimmed.

Privately printed and distributed gratis for Christmas 1918; 100 copies printed.

Colophon (verso back wrapper): One hundred copies printed, Xmas 1918

Contents: Body and Soul—Beauté de ma Belle—Epigrams.

Note: The poems "Body and Soul" and "Beauté de ma Belle" were reprinted in *Three Poems* (1920)—A41; the second of the three epigrams was printed simultaneously, as "Severe Consolation", in *Youth*, Cambridge, Mass., for December 1918—C402.

A40 SPIRIT AND FLESH 1918

First edition:

SPIRIT AND FLESH BY ANANDA K. COOMARASWAMY. DITCHLING, SUSSEX: S. DOMINIC'S PRESS, 1918.

4 pp., 1 text illus. Wrappers.

Privately printed and distributed gratis for Christmas 1918; 50 copies printed.

Notes: This pamphlet comprises a poem by AKC, with a wood-engraving by Eric Gill. No copy has been sighted by the compiler.

A41 THREE POEMS 1920

First edition:

[*In black:*] THREE POEMS | BY | ANANDA COOMARASWAMY | with a woodcut by | ERIC GILL | [*in red: wood-engraving "Welsh Dragon", by Eric Gill*] | [*in black: rule*] | PRINTED AT S. DOMINIC'S PRESS, DITCHLING, SUSSEX. | A.D. MCMXX.

8 pp. (incl. wrappers), 3 text illus. 25.4 x 17.8 cm. White paper wrappers (front wrapper serves as title-page); sewn.

Published early in 1920; number of copies unknown.

Contents: New England Woods—Body and Soul—Beauté de ma Belle.

Notes: In addition to the wood-engraving by Eric Gill on the front wrapper there are two further wood-engravings by him on pages 2 and [7].

The poem "New England Woods" is reprinted from *Modern School*, Ferrer Colony, Stelton, N.J., for August 1919—C413, and the poems, "Body and Soul" and "Beauté de ma Belle", are from *Prayers and Epigrams* ([1918])—A39.

Reviews: Times Literary Supplement, London, 954 (29 Apr. 1920) 274; *Athenaeum*, London, 4,697 (7 May 1920) 621.

A42 TWENTY-EIGHT DRAWINGS 1920

First edition:

TWENTY-EIGHT DRAWINGS | BY | ANANDA COOMARASWAMY | SUNWISE TURN, NEW YORK | 1920

1 blank leaf, 2 leaves, 28 numbered pls. (on 14 leaves), 1 blank leaf. 32 x 23.7 cm. Limp olive green gold-flecked paper wrappers with, on front, white paper label lettered in black; end-papers (paste-downs only); stabbed and tied with white thread.

Published August 1920 at $7.50; 250 copies printed (of which 222 were for sale).

Contents: List of Drawings—1. Leaning Back—2. Abandon—3. Relaxation—4. Diver—5. Movement—6. Bending—7. Movement—8. Portrait—9. Portrait—10. In the Bath—11. Invitation—12. Intension—13. Peace—14. Extension—15. Sleep—16. Memory—17. In the Bath—18. Grief—19. Relaxation—20. Looking Up—21. Looking Down—22. Extension—23. Extension—24. Extension—25. Back—26. Back—27. Memory—28. Extension.

Note: This book comprises reproductions of 24 brush drawings and 4 chalk drawings (i.e. plates 2, 3, 7, and 12) by AKC of female nudes. These are printed, in brown, on both sides of double leaves of rice paper folded Japanese style.

A43 PORTFOLIO OF INDIAN ART 1923

First edition:

MUSEUM OF FINE ARTS, BOSTON | PORTFOLIO | OF | INDIAN ART | OBJECTS SELECTED FROM THE COLLECTIONS | OF THE MUSEUM | WITH A DESCRIPTIVE TEXT BY | ANANDA K. COOMARASWAMY, D.Sc., LONDON | KEEPER OF INDIAN AND MUHAMMADAN ART | AT THE MUSEUM | [*Museum's device*] | E. WEYHE, NEW YORK; PAUL GEUTHNER, PARIS | MARTINUS NIJHOFF, THE HAGUE; MARUZEN CO., LTD., TOKYO | D.B. TARAPOREVALA SONS & CO., BOMBAY | 1923

110 leaves, CVIII numbered pls. (in monochrome heliotype; XV, XXXIII, LXVIII, and LXXXIX are coloured), measuring 29.2 x 21.6 cm., unbound in a grey linen board portfolio, measuring 29.4 x 22 cm., lined with grey-and-white marbled paper and stamped in gold on front: PORTFOLIO OF | INDIAN ART | COOMARASWAMY | MUSEUM OF | FINE ARTS [*ornaments*] | BOSTON, U.S.A.

Published 5 July 1923 at $35.00; 500 copies printed.

Note: Each plate is accompanied by a leaf containing descriptive letterpress; there is also a leaf containing a "List of Plates", and an errata slip (laid in).

Reviews: Victor Goloubew, *Bulletin de l'École Française d'Extrême-Orient*, Hanoi, XXIII. (1923) 454-6; *Museum of Fine Arts Bulletin*, Boston, XXI. 126 (Aug. 1923) 54, and XXII. 130 (Apr. 1924) 13; *Times Literary Supplement*, London, 1,137 (1 Nov. 1923) 721; T. Grahame Bailey, *Journal of the Royal Asiatic Society*, London (1924) 285; Atul Bose, *Year Book of Oriental Art and Culture*, London, I. (1924/25) 130-4; *Rupam*, Calcutta, 17 (Jan. 1924) 52-3; Maurice S. Dimand, *Art Bulletin*, New York, VII. 1 (Sept. 1924) 30-2.

A44 CATALOGUE OF THE INDIAN COLLECTIONS IN THE MUSEUM OF FINE ARTS, BOSTON . . . [PART I GENERAL INTRODUCTION . . . PART II SCULPTURE] 1923

First edition:

CATALOGUE | OF THE | INDIAN COLLECTIONS | IN THE | MUSEUM OF FINE ARTS, BOSTON [*on recto of leaf following title-leaf:* . . . PART I | GENERAL

A. BOOKS AND PAMPHLETS

INTRODUCTION . . . PART II | SCULPTURE] | BY | ANANDA K. COOMARASWAMY D.Sc. (LOND.) | KEEPER OF INDIAN AND MUHAMMADAN ART | IN THE MUSEUM *[publisher's (i.e. Museum's) device]* | MUSEUM OF FINE ARTS, BOSTON 1923

Part I: 5 leaves, 3-53, [1] pp., 1 blank leaf; *part II:* 4 leaves, 3-149, [1] pp., 11 text illus., LXXXVI numbered pls. (containing 209 illus.). 30 x 22 cm. Light brown paper boards, dark brown cloth back with white paper label printed in black; end-papers.

Published 7 August 1923 at $2.25 (Part I), $6.25 (Part II), $7.75 (the two parts bound together); 625 copies printed.

Contents: Part I. [Preface]—GENERAL INTRODUCTION: Vedic Period—Upaniṣads—Sannyasa and Yoga—Buddhism—Jainism—Brāhmaṇical Theism (Hinduism)—Tāntrik Systems—The Epics and Purāṇas—Drama—Aesthetic—Short Chronology—Bibliography; part II. SCULPTURE: History of Indian Sculpture—Hindu Mythology—Buddhist Mythology—Jaina Mythology—The Use of Images—Iconography—Indian Sculptors—Bibliography—List of Sculptures: Śuṅga, Kuṣāna and Late Āndhra—Gupta—Early and Mid-Mediaeval—Late Mediaeval and Modern—Mughal—List of Donors of Sculptures—Index of Deities Represented—Index of Registry Numbers—[Plates].

Notes: "The [Indian] collections as now existing are mainly the gift of Dr. Denman W. Ross, including a large number from the 'Ross Collection', and also the greater part of the 'Coomaraswamy Collection' of paintings and bronzes, presented to the Museum by Dr. Ross in 1917" *(recto of third leaf following title-leaf)*.

Parts I and II of the *Catalogue* were first issued as separate volumes, but later could also be purchased bound together. Publication of the entire *Catalogue*, comprising five parts (i.e. A44, 47, 49, 53), was concluded in 1930.

A catalogue of the Museum's Buddhist paintings, in collaboration with John Ellerton Lodge, to have been Part III of the series and announced as "planned" (in *Museum of Fine Arts Bulletin*, Boston, for October 1923, p. 66), and a "catalogue of Persian and Arabic painting and calligraphy" in the Museum collections, begun by AKC, and so referred to by him in Part VI of the *Catalogue*, p. 32, were not published. The Museum's *Handbook* (1935), p. 179, further states that other parts of the *Catalogue of the Indian Collections* "will deal with Jewelry, Textiles, and Minor Arts"; but these parts also did not materialize.

An Indian reprint (hardbound) was produced by offset in 1978 in Delhi by Bharatiya Publishing House.

Reviews: Victor Goloubew, *Bulletin de l'École Française d'Extrême-Orient*, Hanoi, XXIII. (1923) 454-6; *Hindustan Review*, Allahabad, XLVII. 278 (Oct. 1923) 105; *Times Literary Supplement*, London, 1,137 (1 Nov. 1923) 721; G[eorge]. S[arton]., *Isis*, Brussels, VI. 1 (1924) 73-4; T. Grahame Bailey, *Journal of the Royal Asiatic Society*, London (1924) 285; *Museum of Fine Arts Bulletin*, Boston, XXII. 130 (Apr. 1924) 13; S.M. Edwardes, *Indian Antiquary*, Bombay, LIII. (Aug. 1924) 184; Maurice S. Dimand, *Art Bulletin*, New York, VII. 1 (Sept. 1924) 30-2; Atul Bose, *Year Book of Oriental Art and Culture*, London, I. (1924/25) 130-4; J. Charpentier, *Bulletin of the School of Oriental Studies*, London, IV. (1926/27) 861-2.

Translation: Paris: Éditions Bossard, 1926. This comprises excerpts only, adapted and translated by Jean Buhot (and revised by AKC), with the title: *Pour comprendre l'Art Hindou.*

A45 INTRODUCTION TO INDIAN ART 1923

a. *First edition:*

INTRODUCTION TO INDIAN ART | BY | ANANDA K. COOMARASWAMY | CONTAINING | THIRTY-FOUR ILLUSTRATIONS | THEOSOPHICAL PUBLISHING HOUSE | ADYAR MADRAS INDIA | 1923

xi, 141, [1] pp., XVI numbered pls. (containing 35 black-and-white numbered illus.), 1 blank leaf. 16.6 x 12.5 cm. Light blue cloth boards with, on front, in upper left quarter, within blind stamped thick-thin rule border, white paper label, pasted over blind stamped panel, printed in black, within thin rule border on three sides, on the left, vertically downwards: THE ASIAN [*in centre: design of elephant's head; on the right vertically downwards:*] LIBRARY [*below:*] INTRODUCTION | TO INDIAN ART [*the preceding four words underscored*] | ANANDA K. COOMARASWAMY, and with white paper label on spine, lettered in black: INTRO- | DUCTION | TO | INDIAN | ART | [*rule*] | Ananda | K. Coo- | mara- | swamy; end-papers.

Published late in 1923; number of copies unknown.

Contents: Introduction—List of Illustrations—Sect. 1. Vedic Origins—Sect. 2. Pre-Mauryan Sculpture—Sect. 3. The Great Enlightenment—Sect. 4. Early Buddhist Art: Maurya, Ṣunga and Early Āndhra—Sect. 5. Development of Devotional Theism—Sect. 6. Kuṣāṇ and Later Āndhra Period—Sect. 7. The Gupta Period—Sect. 8. Early Mediaeval—Sect. 9. Mediaeval Sculpture 850-1200—Sect. 10. Southern India 10th-18th Century—Sect. 11. Further India and Indonesia—Sect. 12. Mediaeval Buddhist Painting—Sect. 13. Jain Painting—Sect. 14. Rajput Painting—Appendix: Bibliographies.

Notes: "The subject of Mughal painting lies outside the scope of the present volume" (p. 127).

The "List of Illustrations" (pp. ix-x) omits a description for illustration 13: the description given for 13 is that of illustration 14. The sequence is further disturbed by two illustrations (on Plates XV and XVI) being given the same number: 32. Thus the list numbers (and the descriptions) 14 to 31 do not correspond to the numbers (and illustrations) on the plates, and there are 35 illustrations, not 34 (as stated on the title-page and called for by the count in the "List of Illustrations").

Reviews: F.L. Woodward, *Theosophist*, Madras, XLV. 1 (Feb. 1924) 700; *Modern Review*, Calcutta, XXXV. 3 (Mar. 1924) 323-4; B.N. Treasurywalla, *Rupam*, Calcutta, 18 (Apr. 1924) 91-3; *Hindustan Review*, Allahabad, XLVIII. 284 (Apr. 1925) 345-6.

b. *Second edition* (1956):

INTRODUCTION TO INDIAN ART | BY | ANANDA COOMARASWAMY | EDITED BY MULK RAJ ANAND | THE THEOSOPHICAL PUBLISHING HOUSE, ADYAR | 1956

viii, [1], 122 pp., tipped in frontis. (coloured), 72 text illus., 12 numbered black-and-white pls. 24 x 17 cm. (approx.).

Published in 1956; number of copies unknown.

Contents: Editor's Preface—List of Illustrations—Sect. I. Indo-Sumerian—Sect. 2. Dravidians and Aryans—[Sect. 3-12 are a reprint of Sect. 1-10 of A45a]—Sect. 13. Architecture under Mussalman Rule—[Sect. 14-16 are a reprint of Sect. 11-13 of A45a]—Sect. 17. Moghul Painting—[Sect. 18 is a reprint of Sect. 14 of A45a]—Sect. 19. Sikh Painting—Sect. 20. Modern Indian Painting—Bibliography [a reprint of that in A45a].

Notes: "I happened to come across . . . *Introduction to Indian Art* . . . it was flawed by the omission of any mention of Muhammadan Architecture and Moghul Painting . . . I expressed the hope that [AKC] would one day revise the small book . . ., but he excused himself on the plea of lack of time and suggested that I should do this if I was very keen, as also I might translate [Heinrich] Zimmer's *Kunstform und Yoga im indischen Kultbild*, which had just then come out [i.e. in 1926] and which he thought very highly of . . . [T]he book is being issued, almost exactly as it was originally written by Dr. Coomaraswamy, except for some additional sections. Three of these have been culled from Dr. Coomaraswamy's inimitable writings, namely, Indo-Sumerian, Dravidian and Aryan, and Moghul Painting; while three essays have been written by me, variously on Architecture under Mussalman Rule, Sikh Painting and Modern Painting . . . As all the original illustrations were impossible to obtain, I have substituted different ones here and there, keeping Dr. Coomaraswamy's intentions in mind as faithfully as I could. . . . I wish to record my gratitude to Dr. H[ermann]. Goetz for incidental advice. Also, I want to thank Mr. Gobhai and Miss D. Sahiar for the pen and ink drawings . . ." ("Editor's Preface", pp. [iii]-iv).

The additional Sections 1 and 2 are reprinted from *History of Indian and Indonesian Art* (1927)—A50—pp. 3-6; the additional Section 17 is from *Catalogue of the Indian Collections in the Museum of Fine Arts, Boston Part VI Mughal Painting* (1930)—A53—pp. 3-13.

This edition does not contain the introduction by AKC.

The compiler has been unable to see a copy of A45b in the original binding.

c. *Third edition* ([1969]):

[*Facing pages, on left, in red: device incorporating publisher's name*] | [*on right, in black:*] INTRODUCTION TO | [*in red:*] INDIAN ART | [*in black:*] BY | ANANDA K. COOMARASWAMY | Edited by | MRS ANANDA K. COOMARASWAMY | WITH FORTY-FOUR ILLUSTRATIONS | MUNSHIRAM MANOHARLAL, DELHI

7 leaves, 104, [1] pp., 32 pls. on 16 leaves (containing 44 numbered black-and-white illus.). 23.3 x 15.6 cm. Brown cloth boards printed in gold down the spine; end-papers.

Published February 1969; number of copies unknown.

Contents: List of Illustrations—Abbreviations—Introduction—1. Indo-Sumerian—2. Dravidians and Aryans—3. The Śaiśunaga-Nanda Period (642-320 B.C.)—[Chap. 4-17 are a reprint of Sect. 1-14 of the first edition]—18. Understanding Indian Art—Supplementary Bibliography—Notes on Illustrations—Index—Illustrations.

Note: In this edition the following material is additional to that in A45a: chapters 1-3, reprinted from *History of Indian and Indonesian Art* (1927)—A50—pp. 3-14; chapter 18, a reprint of "Understanding the Art of India"—C671; "Notes on Illustrations", excerpted variously from the descriptive lists in A50, and in *Catalogue of the Indian Collections in the Museum of Fine Arts, Boston* (1923-30)—A44, 47, 49, 53; an index; and illustrations 1-9.

A46 THE TREATISE OF AL-JAZARĪ ON AUTOMATA 1924

First edition:

MUSEUM OF FINE ARTS, BOSTON | COMMUNICATIONS TO THE TRUSTEES, VI | [*thick-thin rule*] | THE TREATISE OF AL-JAZARĪ | ON AUTOMATA | LEAVES FROM A MANUSCRIPT OF THE KITĀB FĪ MA'ARIFAT | AL-ḤIYAL AL HANDASIYA IN THE MUSEUM OF | FINE ARTS, BOSTON, AND ELSEWHERE | BY | ANANDA K. COOMARASWAMY, D.Sc. (LOND.) | KEEPER OF INDIAN AND MUHAMMADAN ART | IN THE MUSEUM | [*publisher's (i.e. Museum's) device*] | BOSTON | MCMXXIV

1 blank leaf, 4 leaves, 21 pp., 1 blank leaf, 1 text illus., VIII numbered heliotype pls. (laid in a folded sheet, of which page [1] contains printed matter). 31.5 x 22.5 cm. Stiff dark green paper wrappers with, on front, white paper label lettered in black within ornamental rule border; end-papers (paste-downs only); sewn.

Published June 1924 at $2.25; number of copies unknown.

Contents: I. Introduction—II. Al-Jazarī's "Book of the Knowledge of Ingenious Geometrical (Mechanical) Devices"—III. Other Manuscripts—IV. Dating of the Leaves in the Museum and Elsewhere —V. Detailed Description of the Six Leaves in the Museum of Fine Arts and of Two Others—VI. Bibliography and List of Abbreviations—[Descriptive list of] Plates—[Plates].

Note: AKC describes and illustrates eight leaves from the manuscript of a 13th century Arabian craftsman, on water-clocks and other automatic contrivances. Six of these leaves are at Boston; of the others, one belongs to the Fogg Art Museum, and one to Paul J. Sachs.

Reviews: S. de R., *Gazette des Beaux-Arts*, Paris, XII. (1924) 123; E. Wiedemann, *Islam*, Berlin, XV. (1924) 158-9; *Times Literary Supplement*, London, 1,181 (4 Sept. 1924) 541.

A47 CATALOGUE OF THE INDIAN COLLECTIONS IN THE MUSEUM OF FINE ARTS, BOSTON . . . [PART IV JAINA PAINTINGS AND MANUSCRIPTS] 1924

First edition:

CATALOGUE | OF THE | INDIAN COLLECTIONS | IN THE | MUSEUM OF FINE ARTS, BOSTON [*on recto of leaf following title-leaf:* . . . PART IV | JAINA PAINTINGS AND MANUSCRIPTS] | BY | ANANDA K. COOMARASWAMY, D.Sc. (LOND.) | KEEPER OF INDIAN AND MUHAMMADAN ART | IN THE MUSEUM | [*publisher's (i.e. Museum's) device*] | MUSEUM OF FINE ARTS, BOSTON | 1924

4 leaves, 3-74 pp., 2 leaves, XXXIX numbered pls. (containing 84 illus.). 30 x 22 cm. Light brown paper boards, dark brown cloth back with white paper label printed in black; end-papers.

Published December 1924 at $3.75; number of copies unknown.

Contents: INTRODUCTION: Jainism—Life of Mahāvīra and Other Jinas—Summary of the Story of Kālakācārya—Summary of the Story of Śālibhadra—Jaina Cosmology—Jaina Literature—Jaina Painting—Bibliography of Jainism—LIST OF MANUSCRIPTS AND PAINTINGS: Manuscripts—Jinas—Miscellaneous Drawings—APPENDIX: List of Donors—Index of Registry Numbers—PLATES.

Note: An Indian reprint (hardbound) was produced by offset in 1978 in Delhi by Bharatiya Publishing House.

Reviews: R.C. Temple, *Indian Antiquary*, Bombay, LV. (1925) 40; *South Asian Review*, London, XXI. 4 (1925) 340; *Hindustan Review*, Allahabad, XLVIII. 283 (Jan. 1925) 210; G., *Rupam*, Calcutta, 21 (Jan. 1925) 33-4; S.P., *Burlington Magazine*, London, LI. 293 (Aug. 1927) 99.

A48 BIBLIOGRAPHIES OF INDIAN ART 1925

First edition:

MUSEUM OF FINE ARTS, BOSTON | [*rule*] | BIBLIOGRAPHIES OF | INDIAN ART | BY | ANANDA K. COOMARASWAMY, D.Sc. (LOND.) | KEEPER OF INDIAN AND MUHAMMADAN ART | IN THE MUSEUM | [*publisher's (i.e. Museum's) device*] | BOSTON, MASSACHUSETTS | 1925

v, 54 pp. 29.8 x 22.2 cm. Stiff brown paper wrappers printed in black on front within thick-thin rule border; end-papers.

Published 15 October 1925 at $2.75; 350 copies printed.

Contents: Preface (dated Boston, 1 Aug. 1925)—I. General; List of Journals and Indices to Journals: Bibliographies—II. Sculpture—III. Painting: 1. Buddhist, Jaina, and Hindu; 2. Mughal—IV. Textiles—V. Other Minor Arts—VI. Index of Places, Technical Terms and Indian Texts named in Book Titles.

Note: This bibliography, comprising 935 entries, "is partly reprinted with additions from [the bibliographies contained in] parts I, II, and IV of the *Catalogue of the Indian Collections in the Museum of Fine Arts* [A44, 47] . . . The General Bibliography covers the whole-cultural environment in which the art of India has arisen . . . also included [are] . . . some of the more important works on architecture for which no separate volume of the Catalogue and consequently no bibliography is contemplated. Included under sculpture are a few of the more important works on coins" ("Preface", p. iii). AKC's intention, expressed *ibidem*, to issue continuous revisions of this bibliography, was never realized. AKC has provided some of the entries with annotations, for these see pages 9-10, 16-18, 20, 22-43.

Reviews: L.D. Barnett, *Journal of the Royal Asiatic Society*, London (1926) 766; W. Printz, *Zeitschrift der Deutschen Morgenländischen Gesellschaft*, Leipzig, V. (1926) 216-17; G., *Rupam*, Calcutta, 25 (Jan. 1926) 25; *Hindustan Review*, Allahabad, L. 291 (Jan. 1927) 170; S.M. Edwardes, *Indian Antiquary*, Bombay, LVI. (Mar. 1927) 58-9.

A49 CATALOGUE OF THE INDIAN COLLECTIONS IN THE MUSEUM OF FINE ARTS, BOSTON PART V RĀJPUT PAINTING 1926

First edition:

CATALOGUE | OF THE | INDIAN COLLECTIONS | IN THE | MUSEUM OF FINE ARTS, BOSTON | PART V | RĀJPUT PAINTING | BY | ANANDA K. COOMARASWAMY, D.Sc. (LOND.) | KEEPER OF INDIAN AND MUHAMMADAN ART | IN THE MUSEUM | *[Museum's device]* | PUBLISHED FOR THE | MUSEUM OF FINE ARTS, BOSTON | BY THE | HARVARD UNIVERSITY PRESS | CAMBRIDGE, MASS. | 1926

7 leaves, 3-271, [1] pp., 1 leaf, incl. map, and frontis. (coloured and with protective tissue), 4 text illus., CXXXI numbered pls. (on 66 leaves, containing 265 black-and-white half-tone illus.), 1 blank leaf. 30 x 22 cm. Light brown paper boards, dark brown cloth back with white paper label printed in black; end-papers.

Published December 1926 at $18.00; number of copies unknown.

Contents: [Prefatory note (dated Boston, 1 Aug. 1926)]—INTRODUCTION: Schools of Rājput Painting—Rājput Painting: Technique—Costume and Other Accessories in Rājput Painting—Ancient Motifs in Rājput Painting—LIST OF PAINTINGS: 1. Early Schools mainly before 1630—2. Later Schools, after 1630 and mainly late Eighteenth Century—Bibliography—[List of] Abbreviations—[Scheme of] Transliteration—List of Donors—Index of Deities and Persons Represented—Index of Registry Numbers—PLATES.

Notes: "The collection of Rājput paintings includes the greater part of the Coomaraswamy, now Ross-Coomaraswamy Collection, given to the Museum by Dr. Denman W. Ross in 1917. . . . The collection as a whole is undoubtedly the largest and most representative in the world. Since my 'Rājput Painting' appeared, in 1916 [—A34a], the main outlines of our knowledge have not been greatly modified, but additional information has accumulated, mainly through the studies of Dr. Hermann Goetz, . . . this information has been as far as possible incorporated in the present volume, particularly in the section on costume" (*prefatory note, recto of leaf following title-leaf*).

The "List of Paintings" (which occupies pp. 69-253) is descriptive and incorporates texts of inscriptions, e.g. Rāgmālā poems, etc., found on the paintings, with AKC's translations of these into English. The "Bibliography" (pp. 254-64) is of the whole of Indian painting and is annotated. The frontispiece is also reproduced as Plate XVIII.

An Indian reprint (hardbound) was produced by offset in 1981 in Delhi by Bharatiya Publishing House. This reprint does not include the frontispiece.

Reviews: Rupam, Calcutta, 29 (Jan. 1927) 31-3; *Saturday Review of Literature*, New York (19 Mar. 1927) 661; L. D. Barnett, *Journal of the Royal Asiatic Society*, London (Oct. 1927) 873-4.

A50 HISTORY OF INDIAN AND INDONESIAN ART 1927

First edition:

[*In black:*] HISTORY OF | INDIAN AND INDONESIAN ART | [*thick-thin rule*] | BY | ANANDA K. COOMARASWAMY | KEEPER OF INDIAN AND MUHAMMADAN ART | IN THE MUSEUM OF FINE ARTS, BOSTON, U.S.A. | [*In brown: reproduction of a drawing (by Stella Bloch?) of Śiva as Naṭarāja*] | [*in black:*] WITH 400 ILLUSTRATIONS | ON 128 PLATES AND 9 MAPS | [*at left:*] LEIPZIG | KARL W. HIERSEMANN | [*in centre:*] LONDON | EDWARD GOLDSTON | 1927 | [*at right:*] NEW YORK | E. WEYHE

4 leaves, 295 pp., incl. 9 maps, CXXVIII numbered pls. (on 64 leaves, containing 400 black-and-white halftone illus.). 29.2 x 21.2 cm. Green cloth boards stamped in gold, on front cover with ornamental border, and on spine with a black and brown leather label stamped in gold; end-papers.

Published April 1927, simultaneously with copies for sale in Germany (in a translation by Hermann Goetz), in Great Britain, and in the U.S.A., at $17.50 (50*s*.); number of copies unknown.

Dedication (verso of title-leaf): Dedicated to S.B. [i.e. Stella Bloch? (Mrs AKC)].

Contents: List of Museums in which Indian Art is Represented—Preface [dated Boston, 15 May 1926]—Part I: Pre-Maurya—Part II: Maurya, Śuṅga, Early Āndhra and Scytho-Parthian (Kṣatrapa)—Part III: Kuṣāna, Later Āndhra and Gupta—Part IV: Early Mediaeval, Mediaeval, Rājput Painting and Later Arts and Crafts—Part V: Kaśmīr, Nepal, Tibet,

Chinese Turkistān, and the Far East—Part VI: Farther India, Indonesia and Ceylon—Bibliography—Description of the Plates—Maps—Index—[Plates].

Notes: "I am very grateful to Miss Mary Fairbank[s] for her assistance in reading the first proof, to Dr. Hermann Goetz in Berlin both for his translation and a final revision, to Dr. Wilhelm Olbrich in Leipzig for reading all intermediate proofs and revising the index. Attention may be called to some special features of the present volume. The latest available information regarding Indo-Sumerian finds is embodied; the early architecture as represented in reliefs and on coins has been rather fully illustrated; the origin of the Buddha image is discussed in some detail; a synthetic survey of Farther Indian and Indonesian arts is for the first time attempted. Space did not permit a treatment of Musalman art in India, . . . It may be remarked that the author has personally visited, often on several occasions, most of the sites and museums referred to" ("Preface", p. 2).

The "Bibliography" (which occupies pages 214-28) comprises 632 items. Sixty of the illustrations are reproduced from AKC's "own negatives" (these illustrations are identified in the "Preface").

An American reprint (paperbound) was produced by offset in 1965 in New York by Dover Publications, Inc., and an Indian reprint (hardbound) was produced by offset in July 1972 in New Delhi by Munshiram Manoharlal.

Reviews: Journal of Indian History, Madras, VI. 2 (Aug. 1927) 209-14; *Luzac's Oriental List*, London, XXXVIII. (Apr./June 1927) 72-3; "Plotinus", *Rupam*, Calcutta, 31 (July 1927) 74-80; W. Perceval Yetts, *Journal of the Royal Asiatic Society*, London (July 1927) 644-5; S.P., *Burlington Magazine*, London, LI. 293 (Aug. 1927) 99; *Times Literary Supplement*, London, 1,334 (25 Aug. 1927) 573; Ernst Diez, *Saturday Review of Literature*, New York, IV. (3 Sept. 1927) 89; W. Norman Brown, *New York Herald Tribune*, New York (20 Nov. 1927) 25; Betty Heimann, *Orientalistische Literaturzeitung*, Berlin, 8/9 (1928) cols. 666-71; Alfred Salmony, *Artibus Asiae*, Hellerau-Dresden, III. (1928) 74-5; *Hindustan Review*, Allahabad, LI. 295 (Jan. 1928) 182; W. Norman Brown, *Nation*, New York, CXXVI. 3,266 (8 Feb. 1928) 166-7; Paul Pelliot, *T'oung Pao*, Leiden, XXVI. (1929) [379]-388.

A51 YAKṢAS 1928

a. *First edition:*

SMITHSONIAN MISCELLANEOUS COLLECTIONS | VOLUME 80, NUMBER 6 | YAKṢAS | (WITH 23 PLATES) | BY | ANANDA K. COOMARASWAMY | Keeper of Indian, Persian, and Muhammadan Art | Museum of Fine Arts, Boston | [*publisher's (i.e. Smithsonian Institution's) device*] | (Publication 2926) | CITY OF WASHINGTON | PUBLISHED BY THE SMITHSONIAN INSTITUTION | MAY 8, 1928

1 leaf, 43 pp., 23 numbered pls. (on 12 leaves, containing 55 illus.). 24.5 x 16.2 cm. Buff

paper wrappers lettered in black on front exactly as title-page, within thick-thin rule border; edges roughly trimmed.

Published 8 May 1928; number of copies unknown.

Contents: 1. Introduction—2. Yakṣas and Yakṣattva ("Geni-hood")—3. Yakṣas as Tutelary Deities (Patron Saints) and Guardian Angels—4. Shrines and Temples (*Cāitya, Āyatana*)—5. Worship (*Pūjā*) in Yakṣa Shrines—6. Yakṣa Worship a Bhakti Cult—7. Yakṣa Sources in Buddhist Iconography—8. Woman and Tree Motif—Conclusion—Explanation of Plates—Appendix—[Plates].

Notes: In this book AKC gathers material from literary and monumental sources in an attempt to demonstrate the antiquity and popularity of Yakṣa worship (a phase of non- and pre-Aryan Indian "animism"), to establish the habitat and general character of the Yakṣa and Yakṣī types, and to indicate the significance of Yakṣas in religious history and in the iconographic evolution of Indian art. Addenda to this is printed with *Yakṣas Part II* (1931)—A54a—pp. 1-12.

An Indian reprint (hardbound) was produced by offset in August 1971 in New Delhi by Munshiram Manoharlal (together with *Yakṣas Part II* (1931)—A54a—in a single volume with the title: *Yakṣas*).

Reviews: Jean Buhot, *Revue des Arts Asiatiques*, Paris, V. (1928) 115; K. N. C., *Modern Review*, Calcutta, XLIV. 5 (Nov. 1928) 549-50; Sten Konow, *Acta Orientalia*, Lund, VII. 1 (1929) 78-80; L. de la Vallée Poussin, *Muséon*, Louvain (1929) 320; W.F. Stutterheim, *Djawa*, Weltevreden, IX. (1929) 203; W. Norman Brown, *Journal of the American Oriental Society*, New Haven, LI. 3 (1931) 286-8; L.D. Barnett, *Journal of the Royal Asiatic Society*, London (1932) 421-4.

b. *New edition, with Yakṣas Part II* (1993)*:*

ANANDA K. | COOMARASWAMY | *[rule]* | Yakṣas | Essays in the | Water Cosmology | New Edition | Revised and Enlarged | Edited by | PAUL SCHROEDER | Foreword by | KAPILA VATSYAYAN | *[arranged in one line: publishers' devices]* | INDIRA GANDHI NATIONAL CENTRE FOR THE ARTS, NEW DELHI | OXFORD UNIVERSITY PRESS | DELHI BOMBAY CALCUTTA MADRAS | 1993

xvii, [1], 339 pp., incl. 73 pls. (occupying pp. [259-331], and containing 212 illus.). 24.3 x 16 cm. Black-grained red imitation leather boards stamped in gold down the spine; end-papers. White dust-jacket printed in beige, ochre, and black.

Published in 1993 at 500 rupees; number of copies unknown.

Contents: Foreword [by Kapila Vatsyayan]—Editor's Note—Acknowledgements—Abbreviations—Introduction [by AKC]—PART I. YAKṢAS: 1. The Yakṣa of the Vedas and Upaniṣads—2. Māra-Kāmadeva, and the Buddha—3. Kubera Vaiśravaṇa and Others—4. Naigameṣa, Gaṇeśa, Hayagrīva, Assamukhī, and Kuvaṇṇā—5. Yakṣas as Tutelary Deities, Patron Saints, and Guardian Angels—6. Yakṣattva as a Station in the Cycle of Birth and Rebirth—7. Shrines and Temples: Cāitya, Āyatana—8. Worship (Pūjā, Bali-Karaṇa, Vandana) in Yakṣa Shrines—9. Woman and Tree—10. Yakṣa Sources in Buddhist Iconography—PART II. THE WATER COSMOLOGY: 11. The Source of Life in the

Waters—12. The Water Cosmology in the Literature—13. Varuṇa—14. The Grail Motif—15. The Makara—16. The Lotus—17. The Vase of Plenty, or Full Vessel—18. Bowls on Figure-Pedestals—19. River Goddesses and Nymphs—PART III. WHAT ARE THE WATERS?: 20. The Cult of Life: What Are the Waters?—Bibliography—Explanation of Plates—[Plates]—Index.

Notes: "The new introductory material, revised chapters, and addition of a complete 'Appendix' (included here as Part 3) leave no doubt that Coomaraswamy intended to publish this work whole. After 50 years this is now possible. . . . The illustrations and their descriptions have been left unchanged from the original publication. . . . The texts of all revisions which are included in this edition are housed in the collections of Princeton University's library" ("Editor's Note", pp. [xiii], xiv).

"The first four chapters have been entirely rewritten . . . The remainder of the text has been more or less rearranged, new references have been added, and some matter has been eliminated" ("Introduction", p. 4).

The first chapter reprints C735 in a revised form.

The subtitle of this new edition was devised by Kapila Vatsyayan; it "reminds us that Coomaraswamy's concern was directed both to 'water' and 'the Waters', whose source is the 'center without a place'" ("Editor's Note", p. xv).

"*Yakṣas* is the sixth in the series of the Collected Works of A.K. Coomaraswamy in the IGNCA's publication programme" (*front flap of dust-jacket*).

A52 LES MINIATURES ORIENTALES 1929

First edition:

ARS ASIATICA | ÉTUDES ET DOCUMENTS PUBLIÉS PAR VICTOR GOLOUBEW | SOUS LE PATRONAGE DE L'ÉCOLE FRANÇAISE D'EXTRÊME-ORIENT | [*short rule*] | XIII | LES MINIATURES ORIENTALES | DE LA | COLLECTION GOLOUBEW | AU MUSEUM OF FINE ARTS DE BOSTON | PAR | ANANDA K. COOMARASWAMY | CONSERVATEUR DES COLLECTIONS INDIENNES ET MUSULMANES AU MUSEUM OF FINE ARTS DE BOSTON | AVEC UN AVANT-PROPOS DE VICTOR GOLOUBEW | MEMBRE DE L'ÉCOLE FRANÇAISE D'EXTRÊME-ORIENT | [*short rule*] | PARIS ET BRUXELLES | LES ÉDITIONS G. VAN OEST | [*short rule*] | 1929

1 blank leaf, 111 pp., 2 leaves, LXXXVIII numbered pls. (on 88 leaves, containing 181 illus.), 1 blank leaf. 35 x 27.1 cm. (approx.). Heavy buff paper wrappers (?).

Colophon (recto of second leaf following page 111): ACHEVÉ D'IMPRIMER LE DIX FÉVRIER MIL NEUF CENT VINGT-NEUF PAR L'IMPRIMERIE PROTAT FRÈRES A MACON, POUR LES ÉDITIONS G. VAN OEST A PARIS ET BRUXELLES. PLANCHES HORS TEXTE EN HÉLIOTYPIE DE L. MAROTTE A PARIS.

Contents: Avant-propos [by Victor Goloubew]—[Note, by AKC]—Notices des Planches:

Mésopotamie ('Abbāssides) avant 1258 de notre ère; Mongols (1258-1380 ap. J.-C.) et Timourides (1380-1502 ap. J.-C.); Ṣafivides (1502-1722 ap. J.-C.); Turquie; Les Mogols (XVIe-XVIIIe siècle)—Bibliographie de la Miniature Persane, Turque et Mogole—Index des Auteurs, des Textes et des Personnages Légendaires ou Historiques—Index des Noms d'Artistes—Table des Planches—[Plates].

Notes: "Les miniatures reproduites dans ce livre ont été réunies par moi au cours des années 1908-11. Quelques-unes d'entre elles figurèrent à l'exposition des arts musulmans à Munich, en 1910. La collection entière a été présentée au public parisien en mai 1912, dans une salle du Pavillon de Marsan. Elle appartient depuis 1914 au Musée des Beaux-Arts de Boston, dont les *Trustees* ont bien voulu autoriser, sur la demande de mon ami Ananda Coomaraswamy, la présente publication" ("Avant-propos", p. [5]).

"L'auteur désire exprimer sa reconnaisance à M. N. N. Martinovitch, professeur à l'Université de Columbia, New York, qui a blen voulu se charger de déchiffrer toutes les inscriptions arabes et la plupart des textes persans. Il adresse également ses remerciements à MM. les *Trustees* du Museum of Fine Arts de Boston pour l'autorisation de faire paraître cet ouvrage au dehors. Toutes le pièces énumerées ici figureront dans le catalogue des miniatures persanes et turques et dans le catalogue des miniatures mogoles que prépare le Musée" (*Note*, p. [12]).

The compiler has not been able to see a copy of this book in the original binding.

Reviews: L. Bouvat, *Journal Asiatique*, Paris, CCXVII. (1929) 170-1; Hermann Goetz, *Orientalistische Literaturzeitung*, Leipzig, XXXV. (1929) cols. 42-3; *Indian Art and Letters*, London, N.S. IV. (1929) 147; Ivan Stchoukine, *Revue des Arts Asiatiques*, Paris, VI. (1929) 56-7; J. V. S. Wilkinson, *Journal of the Royal Asiatic Society*, London (1929) 882-3; O. C. G[angoly]., *Rupam*, Calcutta, 38/39 (Apr./July 1929) 92-4; *Apollo*, London, X. (Aug. 1929) 111-12; T.W. A[rnold]., *Burlington Magazine*, London, LV. (29 Aug. 1929) 98-9.

A53 CATALOGUE OF THE INDIAN COLLECTIONS IN THE MUSEUM OF FINE ARTS, BOSTON PART VI MUGHAL PAINTING 1930

First edition:

CATALOGUE | OF THE | INDIAN COLLECTIONS | IN THE | MUSEUM OF FINE ARTS, BOSTON | PART VI | MUGHAL PAINTING | BY | ANANDA K. COOMARASWAMY, D.SC. (LOND.) | KEEPER OF INDIAN, PERSIAN, AND MUHAMMADAN ART | IN THE MUSEUM | [*Museum's device*] | PUBLISHED FOR THE | MUSEUM OF FINE ARTS, BOSTON | BY THE | HARVARD UNIVERSITY PRESS | CAMBRIDGE, MASS. | 1930

1 blank leaf, 6 leaves (incl. tipped in coloured frontis., with leaf of protective tissue

containing descriptive letterpress on the verso), 3-114 pp., 1 leaf, LXXIV numbered pls. (on 74 leaves, containing 145 illus.). 30 x 22 cm. Light brown paper boards, dark brown cloth back with white paper label printed in black; end-papers.

Published April 1930 at $10.25; number of copies unknown.

Contents: Introduction—LIST OF PAINTINGS: School of Akbar (1556-1605); Early Illustrations of Hindu Subjects; School of Jahāngīr; School of Shāh Jahān (1628-1657); School of Aurangzīb (1658-1706); Late Mughal; Patna; Flowers and Floral Designs; Sīmurgh; Architectural Drawings; Dakhanī School; Tañjore School; Gaṛhwāl—Bibliography of Persian and Mughal Painting—Index of Donors—Index of Persons—Index of Registry Numbers—PLATES.

Notes: The frontispiece is also reproduced as Plates IV (detail) and V.

An Indian reprint (hardbound) was produced by offset in 1981 in Delhi by Bharatiya Publishing House. This reprint does not include the frontispiece.

Reviews: [Sten Konow], *Acta Orientalia*, Lund, IX. (1930) 80; S. R[einach]., *Revue Archéologique*, Paris, 5me Sér. XVIII. (1930) 188; J[ean]. B[uhot]., *Revue des Arts Asiatiques*, Paris, VI. 4 (1930) 265; *Bulletin of the Museum of Fine Arts*, Boston, XXVIII. 166 (Apr. 1930) 39; A.W.K., *Art News*, New York, XXVIII. (24 May 1930) 8; M.S. Dimand, *International Studio*, New York, XCVII. (Oct. 1930) 74; Emmy Wellesz, *Wiener Beiträge zur Kunst- und Kulturgeschichte*, Vienna, V. (1931) 71-2; J.V.S. Wilkinson, *Journal of the Royal Asiatic Society*, London (Jan. 1931) 234-5; Alvan Clark Eastman, *Parnassus*, New York, III. 2 (Feb. 1931) 36-7; N.N. Martinovitch, *Journal of the American Oriental Society*, New Haven, LI. 1 (Mar. 1931) 71-3; C.E.A.W. Oldham, *Indian Antiquary*, Bombay, LX. (May 1931) 98-9; *South Asian Review*, London, XXVIII. 4 (1932) 358; Ivan Stchoukine, *Journal Asiatique*, Paris, CCXX. (Jan./Mar. 1932) 181-6.

A54 YAKṢAS PART II 1931

a. *First edition:*

SMITHSONIAN INSTITUTION | FREER GALLERY OF ART | YAKṢAS | PART II | (WITH 50 PLATES) | BY | ANANDA K. COOMARASWAMY | Keeper of Indian, Persian, and Muhammadan Art | Museum of Fine Arts, Boston | [*publisher's (i.e. Smithsonian Institution's) device*] | (PUBLICATION 3059) | WASHINGTON, D.C. | MAY 19, 1931

1 leaf, 84 pp., 50 numbered pls. (on 25 leaves, containing 156 illus.), 1 blank leaf. 24.5 x 16.4 cm. Buff paper wrappers lettered in black on front exactly as title-page, within thick-thin rule border; edges roughly trimmed.

Published 19 May 1931; number of copies unknown.

Contents: 1. ADDENDA TO YAKṢAS, PART I—2. THE WATER COSMOLOGY: Introduction; 1. The Water Cosmology in the Literature; 2. Varuṇa; 3. The Grail Motif;

4. The Makara; 5. The Lotus; 6. Vases of Plenty or Brimming Vessels; 7. Bowls on Figure-Pedestals; 8. River Goddesses and Nymphs—Explanation of Plates—[Plates].

Notes: This treatise argues that the Indian Yakṣas and Yakṣis, though vegetal divinities and of terrestrial habitat, are almost invariably accompanied by vehicles or supports representing mythical aqueous animals, and that this provides part of the evidence available for the view that these genii are primarily connected with the life-giving Waters, and only secondarily with vegetation. AKC discusses further the water cosmology of early Indian religion and as it is reflected in the Indian iconography. In addition, AKC's thesis serves to substantiate his claim that "hitherto, a concentration of attention upon the sectarian, theistic art of India . . . and upon stylistic development in connection with the cult image only, has obscured the fact that quantitatively speaking, Indian art is to a greater extent than has been supposed, an illustration of Vedic ideas" (p. 16).

"Nearly all of the drawings [in the present volume] have been made by Mr. Sunchiro Tomita" (p. 72).

An Indian reprint (hardbound) was produced by offset in August 1971 in New Delhi by Munshiram Manoharlal (together with *Yakṣas* (1928)—A51a—in a single volume with the title: *Yakṣas*).

Reviews: Jean Buhot, *Bulletin de l'Association Française des Amis de l'Orient*, Paris, XI. (1931) 52; *Nature*, London (11 July 1931) 71; W. Norman Brown, *Journal of the American Oriental Society*, New Haven, LI. 3 (Sept. 1931) 286-8; L. D. Barnett, *Journal of the Royal Asiatic Society*, London (1932) 421-4; Paul Pelliot, *T'oung Pao*, Leiden, XXIX. (1932) 162-3; *Sociology and Social Research*, Los Angeles, XVII. (1933) 475.

b. *New edition, with Yakṣas* (1993):

For description see under *Yakṣas* (1928)—A51b.

A55 INTRODUCTION TO THE ART OF EASTERN ASIA [1932]

First edition:

INTRODUCTION TO THE ART | OF | EASTERN ASIA | BY | ANANDA K. COOMARASWAMY | MUSEUM OF FINE ARTS, BOSTON | Reprinted from The Open Court, March, 1932 [Chicago: The Open Court Publishing Company]

2 leaves, 42 pp., 1 blank leaf, 17 text illus. (incl. one printed on front wrapper). 23.7 x 15.7 cm. Stiff buff paper wrappers lettered on front in brown, with reproduction of a photograph of a Japanese swordguard; wire-stitched.

Published April or May 1932 at 50¢; number of copies unknown.

Contents: List of Illustrations—Introduction to the Art of Eastern Asia—Bibliography.

Note: A reprint, in an expanded form, of C628a. New paragraphs are incorporated on pages 1-2, 4, 11-13, 17, 25-6, 34-5, and six new illustrations are added, on front wrapper, and on pages 9, 20, 22, 27, 30. The bibliography is slightly augmented.

A56 THE TRANSFORMATION OF NATURE IN ART 1934

a. *First edition:*

THE TRANSFORMATION | OF NATURE IN ART | BY | ANANDA K. COOMARASWAMY | [*publisher's device*] | HARVARD UNIVERSITY PRESS | CAMBRIDGE, MASSACHUSETTS | [*on facing page:* LONDON: HUMPHREY MILFORD | OXFORD UNIVERSITY PRESS] 1934

1 blank leaf, 4 leaves, [3]-245 pp., 1 blank leaf. 21.8 x 15.2 cm. Shiny black cloth boards with, on front, a single-rule blind stamped border, and on the spine a white paper label printed in black; end-papers; top edges gilt, other edges roughly trimmed.

Published February 1934 at $3.00 (12*s*. 6*d*.); number of copies unknown.

Contents: I. The Theory of Art in Asia—II. Meister Eckhart's View of Art—III. Reactions to Art in India—IV. Aesthetic of the Śukranītisāra—V. Parokṣa—VI. Ābhāsa [C634, revised and expanded]—VII. The Origin and Use of Images in India [C548, revised and expanded]—Notes—Sanskrit Glossary—List of Chinese Characters—Bibliography.

Notes: On page 238 AKC points out that "Introduction to the Art of Eastern Asia"—C628a—is "partly identical with the present text" (i.e. *The Transformation of Nature in Art*).

Chapter V, which, along with Chapters I and II, is printed here for the first time, discusses (1) the Sanskrit term of Hindu metaphysic that denotes the angelic, or purely intelligible, level of reference, (2) the nature of symbols and the distinction of "symbol" from "sign", and (3) suggestions for desirable English renderings of *parokṣa.*

The bibliography, which occupies pages [237]-245, comprises 189 items.

Reviews: A[nne]. W[ebb]. K[arnaghan]., *Bulletin of the Museum of Fine Arts*, Boston, XXXII. 189 (Feb. 1934) 16-17; *Art News*, New York, XXXII. (10 Feb. 1934) 10; James W. Lane, *New York Times Book Review*, New York (11 Mar. 1934) 12; *Art Digest*, New York, VIII. (15 Apr. 1934) 22; Philip Henderson, *New Britain*, London, II. 5 (16 May 1934) 780-1; *Times Literary Supplement*, London (31 May 1934) 387; Bernard Lemann, *American Magazine of Art*, New York, XXVII. (June 1934) 347-8; J.P. Hogan, *Aryan Path*, Bombay, V. 6 (June 1934) 387-8; W. Norman Brown, *Journal of the American Oriental Society*, New Haven, LIV. 2 (June 1934) 216-18; Charles L. Fabri, *Journal of the Indian Society of Oriental Art*, Calcutta, II. 1 (June 1934) [63]-65; Thomas Munro, *Art Bulletin*, New York, XVI. 4 (Dec. 1934) 397-8; K. de B. Codrington, *Burlington Magazine*, London, LXV. 381 (Dec. 1934) 298; Otto Fischer, *Artibus Asiae*, Ascona, V. (1935) 334-6; *Isis*, Cambridge, Mass., XXIII. (1935) 475; Geraldine Carr, *Personalist*, Los Angeles, XVI. (1935) 90; H.C.E. Zacharias, *Blackfriars*, Oxford, XVI. 179 (Feb. 1935) 146-8; A.C. Banerji,

Modern Review, Calcutta, LVII. 2 (Feb. 1935) 220; *Parnassus*, New York, VII. (Feb. 1935) 26; A.F. Kindersley, *Journal of the Central Asian Society*, London, XXII. (Oct. 1935) 672; Golapchandra Raychandhuri, *Indian Culture*, Calcutta, III. 2 (Aug. 1936) [391].

b. *Second edition* (1935):

[*Title-page as in first edition, except at bottom:*] 1935

Pagination, size, and binding as for A56a. Buff dust-jacket printed in black.

Published in 1935; number of copies unknown.

Notes: In this second edition the only significant change is the revision made to passages concerning *sādṛśya* on pages 12-14 and 183-4. The bibliography is slightly augmented; some misprints remain uncorrected.

An American reprint (paperbound) was produced by offset in 1956 in New York by Dover Publications, and an Indian reprint (hardbound) was produced by offset in August 1974 in New Delhi by Munshiram Manoharlal.

Chapter I was reprinted, omitting the notes, in *Aesthetics Today*, edited by Morris H. Philipson (New York: Meridian Books, Inc., 1961), pp. [33]-63.

Translation: Milan: Rusconi, 1975.

A57 A NEW APPROACH TO THE VEDAS 1933 [*i.e.* 1934?]

a. *First edition:*

A NEW APPROACH | TO THE VEDAS | AN ESSAY IN | TRANSLATION AND EXEGESIS | BY | ANANDA K. COOMARASWAMY | [*publishers' device*] | LONDON | LUZAC & CO. | 46 GREAT RUSSELL STREET, W.C. 1 | 1933 [*i.e.* 1934?]

ix, 116 pp., 1 diagram, 1 blank leaf. 21.1 x 14.2 cm. Grey paper wrappers lettered on front in black within triple-rule border, and up the spine.

Published April 1934? at 5*s*.; number of copies unknown.

Contents: Introduction [dated Museum of Fine Arts, Boston, December 1932]—I. Bṛhadāraṇyaka Upaniṣad, I, 2—II. Portions of the Maitri Upaniṣad—III. Three Vedic Hymns—Notes—Appendix [on the Supernal Sun].

Notes: AKC describes this book as "an essay in the exposition of Vedic ideas by means of a translation and a commentary in which the resources of the other forms of the universal tradition are taken for granted. . . . As regards the commentary: here I have simply used the resources of Vedic and Christian scriptures side by side . . . each illuminates the other. And that is in itself an important contribution to understanding . . . Whatever may be asserted or denied with respect to the 'value' of the Vedas, this at least is certain, that their fundamental doctrines are by no means singular" ("Introduction", pp. viii, ix).

The translations included in this book are almost identical with those of "Versions from the Vedas"—C638.

An Indian reprint (hardbound) was produced by offset in 1985 in Delhi by Aparna Publications.

Reviews: C.A.F. Rhys Davids, *Philosophy*, Cambridge, England, IX. (1934) 502; A[nne]. W[ebb]. K[arnaghan]., *Bulletin of the Museum of Fine Arts*, Boston, XXXII. 189 (Feb. 1934) 16-17; *Hindustan Review*, Allahabad, LXVI. 357 (Nov. 1934) 331; S.M. Katre, *Annals of the Bhandarkar Research Institute*, Poona, XVI. 3/4 (1934/35) 320-1; Walther Wüst, *Orientalistische Literaturzeitung*, Berlin, X. (1935), cols. 640-2; T.N. Siqueira, *New Review*, Calcutta, I. (May 1935) 506-7; V.S.R., *Vedanta Kesari*, Madras, XXII. 4 (Aug. 1935) 158; J.C. Tavadia, *Journal of the K.R. Cama Oriental Institute*, Bombay, XXXI. (1937) 185-7.

b. *New edition, with The Ṛg Veda as Land-Náma-Bók* (1976):

THE VEDAS | ESSAYS IN TRANSLATION | AND EXEGESIS | BY | ANANDA K. COOMARASWAMY | Reprint Edition with Corrections | of "A New Approach to the Vedas" (1933) | and "The Ṛg Veda as Land-Náma-Bók" (1935) | [Beckenham, England] PROLOGOS BOOKS | 1976

xv, 160 pp., 3 text illus., 1 diagram. 19.8 x 13.3 cm. Stiff white paper wrappers printed in black with, on front, a reproduction in black-and-white halftones of a painting from a MS. of the *Kalpa Sūtra*, and on the back a review (in French) by René Guénon of *The Ṛg Veda as Land-Náma-Bók.*

Published 10 September 1976 at £4.50; number of copies unknown.

Dedication (page [v]): This Edition Dedicated in Remembrance to René Guénon

Notes: This book comprises a reprint by offset of *A New Approach to the Vedas* and *The Ṛg Veda as Land-Náma-Bók* (1935)—A61a—these occupy pages xi-xv, 1-116, and pages [117]-159, respectively, with the addition of a "Preface", occupying pages ix-x, excerpted from "The Vedanta and Western Tradition"—C729 *n.*, and a list of "Corrections and Additions" to both *A New Approach to the Vedas* and *The Ṛg Veda as Land-Náma-Bók*, printed in 18 lines on page xv; page 160 is blank.

An unknown number of copies (about 20?) of this edition were bound in red cloth boards, stamped in gold on the spine. The title-page, contents, and pagination are identical with the paperbound copies except for two of the three illustrations (that accompany *The Ṛg Veda as Land-Náma-Bók*) which in these copies are printed in colour and tipped in. None of these hardbound copies have been sighted by the compiler.

A58 THE DARKER SIDE OF DAWN 1935

First edition:

SMITHSONIAN MISCELLANEOUS COLLECTIONS | VOLUME 94, NUMBER 1 | THE DARKER SIDE OF DAWN | BY | ANANDA K. COOMARASWAMY | Fellow for Research in Indian, Persian and Muhammadan Art | Museum of

Fine Arts, Boston | [*publisher's device*] | (PUBLICATION 3304) | CITY OF WASHINGTON | PUBLISHED BY THE SMITHSONIAN INSTITUTION | APRIL 17, 1935

1 leaf, 18 pp. 24.5 x 16.3 cm. Buff paper wrappers lettered in black on front within thick-thin rule border; edges untrimmed; sewn.

Published 17 April 1935 at 10¢; number of copies unknown.

Contents: Introduction—The Darker Side of Dawn—Notes.

Notes: This paper was read by AKC on 24 April 1935 at the 147th Meeting of the American Oriental Society held at the University of Michigan, Ann Arbor.

"An exposition of the duality of deity particularly the [Indian] solar deity Sūrya, or Agni and the feminine counterpart, Ūṣas or Dawn, together with a statement of their metaphysical implications" (Alvan Clark Eastman). The thesis is supported by evidence cited from the Ṛg Veda as well as from later Indian classical literature. AKC intended that this work be read in conjunction with his "Angel and Titan: An Essay in Vedic Ontology" (1935)—C680.

Reviews: René Guénon, *Le Voile d'Isis*, Paris, XL. 187 (July 1935) 305; Alvan Clark Eastman, *Indian Historical Quarterly*, Calcutta, XI. 3 (Sept. 1935) [588]-593.

Translation: See *La Doctrine du Sacrifice* ([1978])—A84.

A59 LA SCULPTURE DE BODHGAYĀ 1935

First edition:

ARS ASIATICA | ÉTUDES ET DOCUMENTS PUBLIÉS SOUS LA DIRECTION DE M. VICTOR GOLOUBEW | ET SOUS LE PATRONAGE DE L'ÉCOLE FRANÇAISE D'EXTRÊME-ORIENT | [*short rule*] | XVIII | LA SCULPTURE | DE | BODHGAYĀ | PAR | ANANDA K. COOMARASWAMY | "FELLOW FOR RESEARCH IN INDIAN, PERSIAN AND MUHAMMADAN ART" | AU MUSEUM OF FINE ARTS DE BOSTON | [*short rule*] | PARIS | LES ÉDITIONS D'ART ET D'HISTOIRE | [*short rule*] | 1935

2 leaves, [1]-72, [1] pp., 16 text illus., 1 blank leaf, 1 fold. map, LX numbered pls. (on 60 leaves, containing 142 illus.). 35 x 26.5 cm. Grey paper wrappers folded over stiff white blanks, lettered on front: [*in gold:*] ARS ASIATICA | [*in black: reproduction of a drawing of a relief illustrated on Plate LI, "Adoration d'un Arbre Sacre"*] | [*in gold:*] LA SCULPTURE DE BODHGAYĀ | PAR ANANDA K. COOMARASWAMY, and across the spine: [*in black: thick-thin rule*] | [*in gold:*] ARS | ASIA- | TICA | [*in black: rule*] | XVIII | [rule] | [*in gold:*] PARIS | LES ÉDITIONS | D'ART | ET D'HISTOIRE | 1935 | [*in black: thin-thick rule*]; edges untrimmed.

Published 10 May 1935 at 300 francs; number of copies unknown.

Colophon (page [73]): ACHEVÉ D'IMPRIMER LE DIX MAI MIL NEUF CENT TRENTE-CINQ PAR L'IMPRIMERIE PROTAT FRÉRES A MACON POUR LES ÉDITIONS D'ART ET D'HISTOIRE A PARIS. PLANCHES HORS TEXTE EN HÉLIOTYPIE DE FAUCHEUX ET FILS A CHELLES.

Contents: I. Historique de L'Enceinte de Bodhgayā—II. L'Architecture—III. Scènes des Incarnations passées et Dernières du Bouddha—IV. Sujets non exclusivement Bouddhiques—V. Les Inscriptions—Bibliographie—Table des Planches—Table des figures dans le texte—Plans—Table des Matières—Planches.

Reviews: J. Bacot, *Journal des Savants*, Paris (1935) 279; O. Fischer, *Artibus Asiae*, Ascona, V. (1935) 336; R. P. B[edford]., *Connoisseur*, London, XCVI. (Nov. 1935) 300; C. E. A. W. Oldham, *Journal of the Royal Asiatic Society*, London (1936) 672-6; K. de B. Codrington, *Burlington Magazine*, London, LXVIII. 397 (Apr. 1936) 201-2; W. Norman Brown, *Journal of the American Oriental Society*, New Haven, LVII. 1 (Mar. 1937) 115-17.

A60 ELEMENTS OF BUDDHIST ICONOGRAPHY 1935

First edition:

ELEMENTS OF | BUDDHIST ICONOGRAPHY | BY | ANANDA K. COOMARASWAMY | [*publisher's device*] | CAMBRIDGE, MASSACHUSETTS | HARVARD UNIVERSITY PRESS | [*on facing page:* LONDON: HUMPHREY MILFORD | OXFORD UNIVERSITY PRESS] 1935

5 leaves, 3-195 pp., 1 leaf, XV numbered pls. (on 15 leaves, containing 44 illus., with descriptive letterpress on versos of plates and on verso of leaf following page 195. 30.4 x 21.9 cm. Green cloth boards stamped in gold on front, within blind stamped single rule border, and down the spine; end-papers.

Published July 1935 at $3.50 (15*s*.); number of copies unknown.

Contents: Foreword [by Walter Eugene Clark, dated Harvard University, 27 June 1934]—Part I. Tree of Life, Earth-Lotus, and Word-Wheel—Part II. The Place of the Lotus-Throne—Notes—Supplementary Notes and Descriptions—Plates.

Notes: An expansion of lectures given by AKC at the Museum of Fine Arts, Boston, and at the Fogg Art Museum, Cambridge, Mass., in the Spring of 1933.

In this study—published under the auspices of the Harvard-Yenching Institute—AKC marshals literary evidence from canonical texts to support his central argument "that the Buddha, humanly presented, is in fact connatural with the Vedic Agni, and that Buddhist symbolism, far from being an isolated language, is proper to the one great tradition which has persisted from the Vedic or a pre-Vedic period until now'' (p. 59).

An Indian reprint (hardbound) was produced by offset in 1972 in New Delhi by Munshiram Manoharlal.

Reviews: J.B., *Bulletin Amis de l'Orient*, Paris, XIX. (1935) 52; J.B., *Revue des Arts Asiatiques*, Paris, IX. (1935) 235; *American Magazine of Art*, New York, XXVIII. (Nov.

1935) 692; Helen B. Chapin, *Art Bulletin*, New York, XVII. 4 (Dec. 1935) 513-14; Otto Fischer, *Artibus Asiae*, Ascona, VI. (1936) 157-8; R. Heine-Geldern, *Weiner Beitrage zur Kunst und Kulturgeschte Asiens*, Vienna, X. (1936) 68; P. Mus, *Bulletin de l'École Française d'Extrême-Orient*, Hanoi, XXXV. (1936) 391-7; Wilhelm Printz, *Zeitschrift der Deutschen Morgenlandischen Gesellschaft*, Leipzig, XV. 90 (1936) 502; F. Otto Schrader, *Orientalistische Literaturzeitung*, Berlin, XXXIX. (1936), cols. 258-61; D.C. Sircar, *Indian Culture*, Calcutta, II. 4 (1936) 831; E.J. Thomas, *Journal of the Royal Asiatic Society*, London (1936) 297-9; L.P. Roberts, *Brooklyn Museum Quarterly*, New York, XXIII. (Jan. 1936) 50-1; A.P. McMahon, *Parnassus*, New York, VIII. (Feb. 1936) 35-6; *Times Literary Supplement*, London, 1,776 (15 Feb. 1936) 140; K. de B. Codrington, *Burlington Magazine*, London, LXVIII. 397 (Apr. 1936) 201-2; Beni Madhav Barua, *Journal of the Indian Society of Oriental Art*, Calcutta, IV. 1 (June 1936) 84; René Guénon, *Études Traditionnelles*, Paris, XLI. 199 (July 1936) 281-2; P. Mus, *Journal Asiatique*, Paris, CCXXVIII. (Oct./Dec. 1936) 631-5; E. Waldschmidt, *Ostasiatische Zeitschrift*, Berlin & Leipzig, N.S. XIII. (Jan. 1937) 43-4; W. Norman Brown, *Journal of the American Oriental Society*, New Haven, LVII. 1 (Mar. 1937) 115-17; Mircea Eliade, *Zalmoxis*, Bucharest & Paris, I. (1938) 226-49.

A61 THE ṚG VEDA AS LAND-NÁMA-BÓK 1935

a. *First edition:*

THE ṚG VEDA AS | LAND-NÁMA-BÓK | By | ANANDA K. COOMARASWAMY | LONDON | LUZAC & CO. | 46 GREAT RUSSELL STREET, W.C.1 | 1935

1 blank leaf, viii, 39 pp., 1 blank leaf, 3 numbered pls. (measuring approx. 11 x 8 cm. and tipped in on pp. vi, 6, 18). 21.3 x 14.2 cm. Grey paper wrappers lettered in black on front, within triple rule border, and up the spine.

Published July 1935 at 3*s.* 6*d.*; number of copies unknown.

Dedication (page [v]): Dedicated to Walter Andrae . . . and to Carl Anders Scharbau . . .

Contents: Introduction—The Ṛg Veda as Land-Náma-Bók: Ārya, Arya—Carṣaṇi and Kṛṣṭi—Nau—Pañca Janāḥ, Carṣaṇayaḥ, or Kṛṣṭayaḥ—Sarasvatī—Setu—Vāpa-Maṅgala—Viśa, Viśpati—Yajña—Yama as Viśpati—Conclusion—Notes.

Notes: This volume comprises an examination and analysis of the meanings of a number of frequently recurring and characteristic Vedic words in connection with rites associated with the occupation of territories.

The title alludes to the Icelandic "Book of the Taking of Land", which is compared here, in certain respects, with the Ṛg Veda.

AKC takes the view that "dans tous les écrits traditionnels de cette sorte, ce qui est décrit en réalité est le manifestation même des êtres à l'origine et leur établissement dans un monde désigné symboliquement comme une 'terre', de sorte que les allusions géographiques et historiques, s'il y en a, n'ont elles-mêmes qu'une valeur de symbole et d'analogie, comme tout événement peut l'avoir effectivement en raison des correspondances macrocosmiques et microcosmiques" (René Guénon).

An Indian reprint (hardbound) was produced by offset in 1980 in Delhi by Bharatiya Publishing House.

Reviews: René Guénon, *Le Voile d'Isis*, Paris, XL. 190 (Oct. 1935) [420]; *Indian Review*, Madras, XXXVI. 10 (Oct. 1935) 690; P. Johanns, *New Review*, Calcutta, II. (Oct. 1935) 398-9; *Man in India*, Ranchi, XVI. (1936) 94; *The Kashmir Times*, Srinagar, III. 6 (11 Feb. 1936) 2; P. Masson-Oursel, *Journal Asiatique*, Paris, CCXXVIII. (Oct./Dec. 1936) 635; P. Thieme, *Orientalistische Literaturzeitung*, Leipzig, I. (1937), cols. 42-4; Walther Wüst, *Deutsche Literaturzeitung*, Berlin, II. 10 (Jan. 1937), cols. 48-52; *Vedanta Kesari*, Madras, XXV. 1 (May 1938) 36; Mircea Eliade, *Zalmoxis*, Paris & Bucharest, II. 1 (1939) 168-9.

b. *New edition, with A New Approach to the Vedas* (1976)*:*

For description see A57b.

Note: In this new edition the tipped in plates are reproduced by offset as text illustrations (see also the note above concerning the hardbound copies of A57b).

A62 PATRON AND ARTIST PRE-RENAISSANCE AND MODERN 1936

First edition:

[*Three ornamental rules*] | Patron and Artist | Pre-Renaissance and Modern | BY | A.K. COOMARASWAMY | AND | A. GRAHAM CAREY | [*three short ornamental rules*] | WHEATON COLLEGE PRESS | NORTON, MASSACHUSETTS | 1936 | [*three ornamental rules*]

1 blank leaf, 7-69 pp., 1 text illus. (on p. 45), 1 blank leaf. 20.3 x 13.7 cm. Grey marbled paper boards lettered in black on front cover, with black cloth back; end-papers.

Published Summer 1936 at $1.00; number of copies unknown.

Contents: Preface [by Esther Isabel Seaver, dated Wheaton College, May 1936]—The Normal View of Art [by AKC, pp. 7-38]—Liberty and Discipline in the Four Artistic Essentials [by A. Graham Carey, pp. 39-69].

Notes: "During February of the current year [i.e. 26-29 February 1936] the Department of Art and the Art Club of Wheaton College sponsored a conference on the subject dealt with in this volume and the papers published here were first read at those meetings" ("Preface" p. [5]).

AKC's paper is divided into six sections: I. Introduction—II. The Abnormal View—III. Patron and Artist—IV. The Normal View of Art—V. Beauty—VI. Truth.

Reviews: Eric Gill, *Blackfriars*, Oxford, XVII. 200 (Nov. 1936) 842-6; René Guénon, *Études Traditionnelles*, Paris, XLI. 204 (Dec. 1936) [474]-475; H.R.W., *Apollo*, London, XXVII. 158 (Feb. 1938) 100; Vincent O'Connor, *Art Notes*, London, II. 2 (Nov./Dec. 1938) 29-30; *Modern Review*, Calcutta, LXVII. 4 (Apr. 1940) 455-6.

A63 IS ART A SUPERSTITION, OR A WAY OF LIFE? 1937

First edition:

IS ART A SUPERSTITION, | OR A WAY OF LIFE? | LECTURE | GIVEN AT THE METROPOLITAN MUSEUM | OF ART, NEW YORK, IN APRIL 1937 | BY DR. ANANDA K. COOMARASWAMY | *[ornament]* | PUBLISHED BY JOHN STEVENS | 29 THAMES STREET, NEWPORT, | RHODE ISLAND. MDCCCCXXXVII

1 blank leaf, 1 leaf, 23 pp., 2 leaves. 23.1 x 16.4 cm. Stiff blue paper wrappers lettered on front in black exactly as for title-page; fore edges untrimmed; wire-stitched.

Published probably late Summer 1937 at 50¢; 400 copies printed.

Colophon (recto of second leaf following page 23): Four hundred copies of this book were printed by the Ward Printing Company Newport Rhode Island

Notes: "Under present circumstances, . . . art is by and large a luxury: a luxury that few can afford, and one that need not be overmuch lamented by those who cannot afford to buy. This same 'art' was once the principle of knowledge by which the means of life were produced, and the physical and spiritual needs of man were provided for. . . . To resume all that has been said in a single statement,—Art *is* a superstition: art *was* a way of life" (p. 23).

Reprinted, with additionally a postscript replying to a review by Richard Florsheim of *Is Art a Superstition, or a Way of Life?*, as Chapter III of *Why Exhibit Works of Art?* (1943)—A67—pp. 61-88.

Reviews: René Guénon, *Études Traditionnelles*, Paris, XLII. 216 (Dec. 1937) [436]; Richard Florsheim, *Art Bulletin*, New York, XX. 1 (Mar. 1938) 126-7.

A64 ASIATIC ART 1938

First edition:

THE NEW ORIENT | *[calligraphic ornament]* | ASIATIC ART | BY | ANANDA K. COOMARASWAMY | MUSEUM OF FINE ARTS, BOSTON | THE NEW ORIENT SOCIETY OF AMERICA | [Chicago] 1938 cover-title, 2 leaves, [3]-15, [1] pp., 3 pls. (incl. frontis.). 24.1 x 15.9 cm. (wrappers); 23.5 x 15.4 cm. (leaves). Stiff blue paper wrappers with on front title-page (as above) lettered in dark blue; wire-stitched.

Published May 1938; number of copies unknown.

Note: This pamphlet was reprinted, omitting the plates, in *On the Traditional Doctrine of Art* ([1977])—A83—pp. 5-[17].

Review: René Guénon, *Études Traditionnelles*, Paris, XLIII. 226 (Oct. 1938) [371].

Translation: In *Être: Approches de la non-dualité*, Paris, X. 2 (1982) 5-17, as "L'Art asiatique".

A65 THE CHRISTIAN AND ORIENTAL OR TRUE PHILOSOPHY OF ART 1939

First edition:

THE CHRISTIAN AND ORIENTAL | OR TRUE PHILOSOPHY OF ART | A LECTURE | GIVEN AT BOSTON COLLEGE, NEWTON | MASSACHUSETTS, IN MARCH, 1939, BY | DR. ANANDA K. COOMARASWAMY | *[publisher's device]* | PUBLISHED BY JOHN STEVENS | 29 THAMES STREET, NEWPORT, | RHODE ISLAND. MDCCCCXXXIX

1 blank leaf, 2 leaves, 3-38, [1] pp., incl. frontis. 23.3 x 16.5 cm. Stiff ochre paper wrappers printed in black on front (exactly as title-page); fore edges untrimmed; wire-stitched.

Published Summer 1939; 400 copies printed.

Colophon (page [39])*:* Four hundred copies of this book were printed by the Ward Printing Company Newport Rhode Island

Notes: AKC's lecture was first given in early 1939 at the George Walter Vincent Smith Art Gallery, Hartford, Connecticut, and later, in March, at Boston College, Newton, Massachusetts. The lecture is printed here "with minor emendations by the author" (p.[2]). The frontispiece (p.[1]) is a reproduction of a wood-engraving by Eric Gill. A "Short Bibliography for the Philosophy of Medieval and Oriental Art", which comprises 52 items, occupies pages 37-8.

This pamphlet was reprinted as Chapter II of *Why Exhibit Works of Art?* (1943)—A67, with an augmented bibliography (still further addenda is printed in *Figures of Speech or Figures of Thought* (1946)—A71—p. 68); and, in a revised and expanded version, as "Art, Man and Manufacture", in *Our Emergent Civilization*, edited by Ruth Nanda Anshen (1947)—B76.

Reviews: A.P. McMahon, *Parnassus*, New York, XII. (Oct. 1939) 31; René Guénon, *Études Traditionnelles*, Paris, XLV. 241 (Jan. 1940) [31]-32; Herbert Read, *New English Weekly*, London, XVII. 12 (11 July 1940) 143-4.

A66 SPIRITUAL AUTHORITY AND TEMPORAL POWER IN THE INDIAN THEORY OF GOVERNMENT 1942

a. *First edition:*

Spiritual Authority and Temporal Power | in the | Indian Theory of Government | BY | ANANDA K. COOMARASWAMY | Museum of Fine Arts, Boston | AMERICAN ORIENTAL SOCIETY | NEW HAVEN, CONNECTICUT | 1942 [*on facing page:*] AMERICAN ORIENTAL | SERIES | VOLUME 22 | EDITOR | ZELLIG S. HARRIS | ASSOCIATE EDITORS | MURRAY B. EMENEAU GEORGE A. KENNEDY | AMERICAN ORIENTAL SOCIETY | NEW HAVEN, CONNECTICUT | 1942

1 blank leaf, 3 leaves, 87 pp., 1 blank leaf, incl. frontis. 25.4 x 17.6 cm. Terracotta paper wrappers printed in black on front (exactly as title-page), and down the spine.

Published June 1942 at $1.75; about 500 copies printed.

Notes: A detailed analysis and explication, based chiefly on the Brāhmaṇas and Ṛgveda, of the Oriental and traditional relation of the Priest to the King. AKC demonstrates the metaphysical implications of their complementarism, together with a discussion of the cosmic and political aspects of the science of government (with comparisons made to Platonic and other Western conceptions of government), and concluding with an examination of the traditional doctrine of government in its self-referent application. "The application is to the 'King', the 'man of action' and 'artist' in any domain whatever; there is nothing that can be truly and well done or made except by the man in whom the marriage of the Sacerdotium and the Regnum has been consummated, nor can any peace be made except by those who have made their peace with themselves" (p. 87).

Footnote 41, which occupies pages 53-60, comprises a discussion of the ritual chant (*sāman*) and of the purpose of speech.

"The author and the Society wish to thank Mr. Chauncy Stillman for his contribution toward the publication of this volume" (*verso of the title-leaf*) .

An American reprint (softbound) was produced by offset in 1967 in New York by Kraus Reprint Corporation, and an Indian reprint (hardbound) was produced by offset in 1978 in New Delhi by Munshiram Manoharlal Pvt. Ltd.

Reviews: Lee Bowen, *Speculum*, Cambridge, Mass., XVII. 3 (July 1942) 418-20; Walter Sandelius, *American Political Science Review*, Madison, XXXVI. (Dec. 1942) 1192-5; *Thought*, Bronx, XVII. (Dec. 1942) 735; Kenneth P. Landon, *Journal of Philosophy*, New York, XL. 4 (18 Feb. 1943) 110-11; Walter Shewring, *Blackfriars*, Oxford, XXIV. 276 (Mar. 1943) 99-101; Heinrich Zimmer, *Review of Religion*, New York, VII. 3 (Mar. 1943) 275-8; V.R.R. Dikshitar, *Aryan Path*, Bombay, XIV. 9 (Sept. 1943) 428; René Guénon, *Études Traditionnelles*, Paris, XLVII. 253 (Aug. 1946) 339-41; Mircea Eliade, *Critique*, Paris, XXXV. (1949) 342-9.

b. *New edition* (*French;* 1985)*:*

Ananda K. Coomaraswamy | Autorité Spirituelle | et | Pouvoir Temporel | dans la perspective indienne du gouvernement | AVEC UN

INDEX | Traduit de l'anglais par | MICHEL BOUTET | [*reproduction of a Late Antique roundel depicting the anointing of a king*] | ARCHÈ | MILANO | 1985

156, [1] pp., 1 blank leaf, incl. frontis. 22 x 15.2 cm. Stiff ochre paper wrappers printed in black, and in black-and-white halftones, on front (exactly as title-page), and on back cover and up the spine; top and bottom edges untrimmed.

Published in 1985; 500 copies printed.

Colophon (page [6]): Il a été tiré de cet ouvrage 500 exemplaires sur papier Arcoprint Avorio constituant l'édition originale.

Notes: The contents of this new edition in French are identical with that of A66a, save for the addition of an index, and AKC's corrigenda and addenda (introduced within square brackets on pages 8, 16, 17, 21, 33, 35, 39, 41, 58, 59, 66, 92, 103). The translator has contributed a number of footnotes; these are signed: N.d.T. "La présente traduction a valeur d'édition *ne varietur* d'*Autorité spirituelle et pouvoir temporel dans la perspective indienne du gouvernement* puisqu'elle tient compte des corrections et additions apportées par Coomaraswamy en vue d'une édition définitive. L'éditeur remercie le fils de l'auteur, le docteur Rama P. Coomaraswamy, qui très aimablement lui a donné copie de ces corrections et additions. . . ." ("Note de l'éditeur", p.[7]).

A67 WHY EXHIBIT WORKS OF ART? 1943

First edition:

WHY EXHIBIT | WORKS OF ART? | [*On front wrapper:* Collected Essays on the traditional or "normal" view | of Art] By | ANANDA K. COOMARASWAMY | [*publishers' device*] | LONDON | LUZAC & CO. | 46 GREAT RUSSELL STREET, W.C. 1 | 1943

148 pp., 2 text illus. 21.4 x 14.1 cm. Buff paper wrappers printed in black on front exactly as title-page, within thick-thin rule border (with additionally a sub-title, as above, and, in most copies sighted, a slip pasted down, measuring 2.6 x 6.5 cm., containing within a single rule border a eulogy printed in 4 lines, excerpted from Eric Gill's *Autobiography*, p. 174), and up the spine.

Published May 1943 at 6*s*.; number of copies unknown.

Contents: I. Why Exhibit Works of Art?—II. The Christian and Oriental, or True, Philosophy of Art [A65, expanded]—III. Is Art a Superstition, or a Way of Life?—Postscript: Note on a Review by Richard Florsheim of *Is Art a Superstition or a Way of Life?*—IV. What Is the Use of Art, Anyway?—V. Beauty and Truth [from "Mediaeval Aesthetic II. St. Thomas Aquinas on Dionysius, and a Note on the Relation of Beauty to Truth"—C731]—VI. The Nature of Mediaeval Art—VII. The Traditional Conception of Ideal Portraiture [C757, revised and expanded]—VIII. The Nature of "Folklore" and "Popular Art" [C694, revised and expanded]—IX. Beauty of Mathematics: A Review [C787]—Acknowledgements—[List of works] By the Same Author.

Notes: None of the essays printed here appear for the first time.

Chapter II has as an appendix, occupying pages 59-60, a "Short Bibliography for the Philosophy of Mediaeval and Oriental Art".

"This book has not been copyrighted; quotations, long or short, may be made without express permission" (*verso of the title-leaf*).

An American reprint (softbound) was produced by offset in 1956 in New York by Dover Publications Inc., and an Indian reprint (hardbound) was produced by offset in 1974 in New Delhi by Munshiram Manoharlal Publishers Pvt. Ltd.; both reprints are re-titled: *Christian and Oriental Philosophy of Art.*

Reviews: Walter Shewring, *Weekly Review*, London (27 May 1943) 101-2; Herbert Read, *Listener*, London, XXX. 759 (29 July 1943) 132; Elizabeth Milne, *Dublin Magazine*, Dublin, N.S. XVIII. 3 (July/Sept. 1943) 79-80; Bernard Kelly, *Blackfriars*, Oxford, XXIV. 282 (Sept. 1943) [345]-348; E.I. Watkin, *Dublin Review*, London, CCXII. 427 (Oct. 1943) 194-5; Hugh I'Anson Fausset, *Aryan Path*, Bombay, XIV. 11 (Nov. 1943) 518-19; Helmut Kuhn, *Journal of Philosophy*, New York, XLI. 4 (17 Feb. 1944) 104-7; John A. Pope, *Review of Religion*, New York, VIII. 3 (Mar. 1944) 314-19; *Studio*, London, XXVII. (Apr. 1944) 136; Iredell Jenkins, *Modern Schoolman*, St. Louis, XXI. 4 (May 1944) 240-2; Earl of Listowel, *Philosophy*, London, XIX. 73 (July 1944) 176; Douglas Cooper, *Burlington Magazine*, London, LXXXVII. 512 (Nov. 1945) 286; René Guénon, *Études Traditionnelles*, Paris, XLVII. 252 (June/July 1946) [287]-289; S. S[rikantaya]., *Quarterly Journal of the Mythic Society*, Bangalore, XXXVII. 1 (July 1946) 52-3; Katharine Gilbert, *Art Bulletin*, New York, XXX. 2 (June 1948) 157-9; Anthony M. Ludovici, *New English Weekly*, London, XXIV. 6 (25 Nov. 1948) 49.

Translations: Milan: Rusconi, 1977; Madrid: Taurus, 1980; Puiseaux: Éditions Pardès, 1990; Athens: Pemptoussia Books, 1994 (omitting Chapter I).

A68 HINDUISM AND BUDDHISM [1943]

a. *First edition, first impression:*

HINDUISM | and | BUDDHISM | By | ANANDA K. COOMARASWAMY | Museum of Fine Arts, Boston | PHILOSOPHICAL LIBRARY | NEW YORK

1 blank leaf, 4 leaves, 3-86 pp., 1 blank leaf. 23.4 x 15.8 cm. Orange cloth boards stamped in blue on front cover and down the spine; end-papers; top edges stained blue.

Published Summer 1943 at $1.75; number of copies unknown.

Contents: I. HINDUISM: Introduction—The Myth—The Way of Works—The Social Order—Notes to Hinduism—II. BUDDHISM: Introduction—The Myth—The Doctrine—Notes to Buddhism.

Notes: This book is based upon two lectures that were given by AKC at the Jewish Theological Seminary of America's Institute for Religious Studies, in New York, on 10 and 17 February 1942. AKC presents a general account of the two traditions, drawing parallels to Platonic and to Christian texts. His central thesis seeks to demonstrate that

Buddhism has an intrinsically orthodox position in relation to Hinduism.

Endnotes 150 and 154, which should have appeared on pages 41 and 42, have been omitted.

An epigraph comprising a quotation from Meister Eckhart is printed in seven lines on page [2].

An American reprint (hardbound) was produced by offset in 1971 in Westport, Conn., by Greenwood Press, and an Indian reprint (hardbound) was produced by offset in 1975 in New Delhi by Munshiram Manoharlal Publishers Pvt. Ltd.

Reviews: Ralph T. Flewelling, *Personalist*, Los Angeles, XXIV. (1943) 419; Fred D. Gealy, *Southwest Review*, Dallas, XXVIII. (1943) 445; J.J. Rolbiecki, *New Scholasticism*, Washington, D.C., XVII. (July 1943) 298-9; Howard C. Hollis, *Journal of Aesthetics and Art Criticism*, New York, II. 8 (Fall 1943) 89-91; Lucian Scherman, *Journal of the American Oriental Society*, New Haven, LXIII. (Oct. 1943) 241-62; Kenneth P. Landon, *Journal of Philosophy*, New York, XL. 26 (23 Dec. 1943) 723-4; I.B. Horner, *Indian Art and Letters*, London, N.S. XVIII. 1 (1944) 61-2; Bertram Morris, *Philosophical Review*, Ithaca, LIII. (1944) 605; *Modern Schoolman*, St. Louis, XXI. (Jan. 1944) 126-7; M. Hiriyanna, *Aryan Path*, Bombay, XV. 2 (Feb. 1944) [76]-77; Murray Fowler, *Review of Religion*, New York, VIII. 3 (Mar. 1944) 281-4; L. Yeddanapalli, *Thought*, Bronx, XIX. (Mar. 1944) 172-3; Walter Eugene Clark, *Harvard Journal of Asiatic Studies*, Cambridge, Mass., VIII. (1944/45) 63-70; *Ethics*, Chicago, LV. (1945) 324; *Mind Digest*, York, Penn., (Feb. 1946) 92; Sidney L. Gulick, *Personalist*, Los Angeles, XXVII. (July 1946) 306-13; René Guénon, *Études Traditionnelles*, Paris, XLVII. 253 (Aug. 1946) [337]-339 and LI. 282 (Mar. 1950) [95]; Louis Renou, *Critique*, Paris, III. 18 (Nov. 1947) 473-5.

Translations: Paris: Gallimard [1949] (with the notes brought forward from the end of each section to the actual pages to which they refer); Milan: Rusconi, 1973.

b. *Later impressions:*

Title-page and collation as in first impression. These later impressions—not identified as such—were bound in blue (or light blue) paper boards with publisher's device stamped in light blue (or dark blue) on front cover, and lettered down the spine; they measure 21.3 x 14.3 (or 19.1 x 12.1) cm. In these copies the top edges are not stained; the two endnotes omitted in the first impression have not been restored.

A69 RECOLLECTION, INDIAN AND PLATONIC AND ON THE ONE AND ONLY TRANSMIGRANT 1944

First edition:

SUPPLEMENT | TO THE | JOURNAL | OF THE | AMERICAN ORIENTAL SOCIETY | EDITOR | ZELLIG S. HARRIS | University of Pennsylvania | ASSOCIATE EDITORS | *[at left:]* MURRAY B. EMENEAU | University of California *[at right:]* GEORGE A. KENNEDY | Yale University | *[in centre: short rule]* | *[at left:]* NUMBER 3 *[at right:]* APRIL-JUNE 1944 | *[in centre:*

short rule] | RECOLLECTION, INDIAN AND PLATONIC | AND | ON THE ONE AND ONLY TRANSMIGRANT | BY | ANANDA K. COOMARASWAMY | Museum of Fine Arts, Boston | CONTENTS | Recollection, Indian and Platonic [*leaders*] 1 | On the One and Only Transmigrant [*leaders*] 19 | [*ornamental rule*] | PUBLISHED BY THE AMERICAN ORIENTAL SOCIETY | 20 Hopkins Place, Baltimore - 1, Maryland | Entered as second-class matter, March 1, 1937, at the post office at Baltimore, Maryland, | under the Act of August 24, 1912. Published quarterly.

cover-title, 43 pp., 2 blank leaves. 22.9 x 15.4 cm. Buff paper wrappers printed in black; wire-stitched.

Published as a supplement to, and issued with, the *Journal of the American Oriental Society*, LXIV. 2 (Apr./June 1944); number of copies unknown.

Notes: In the first paper, which occupies pages 1-18, AKC draws on Indian and Platonic texts to argue that the doctrine "we call 'learning' is really a 'remembering', and that our 'knowledge' is by participation in the Omniscience of an immanent spiritual principle . . . Our main object [is] to call attention both to the importance and to the universality of the doctrine of Recollection, and to bring out that it is only one of the many consistent features of a philosophy that is essentially the same in Plato and in the Vedanta" (pp. 1, 18). In the second paper, which occupies pages 19-43, the distinction of reincarnation from transmigration is explained, and documentary evidence is introduced to support the argument that the notion of the Lord as the only Transmigrant is by no means an exclusively Indian doctrine. "In 'Recollection, Indian and Platonic', we have shown that timeless omnipresence and providential omiscience [*sic*] are interdependent and inseparable notions. The related thesis of ['On the One and Only Transmigrant'] is that the omnipresent omniscient is 'the only transmigrant' and that in the last analysis this 'transmigration' is nothing but his knowledge of himself expressed in terms of a duration" (p. 20).

Both papers were reprinted, incorporating addenda, but omitting the abstract that prefaces the second paper, in *Coomaraswamy 2: Selected Papers, Metaphysics* ([1977])—A82—pp. 49-65 and 66-87, respectively. "On the One and Only Transmigrant', was also reprinted, in a reduced form, in *Indian Review,* Madras, XLVI. 12 (Dec. 1945) 669-75.

Reviews: K.P. L[andon]., *Journal of Philosophy*, New York, XLII. 6 (15 Mar. 1945) 165; *Modern Schoolman*, St. Louis, XXII. (Mar. 1945) 181-2; John Clark Archer, *Review of Religion*, New York, X. 3 (Mar. 1946) [308]-310.

A70 THE RELIGIOUS BASIS OF THE FORMS OF INDIAN SOCIETY . . . INDIAN CULTURE AND ENGLISH INFLUENCE . . . EAST AND WEST 1946

a. *First edition:*

THE RELIGIOUS BASIS OF THE FORMS | OF INDIAN SOCIETY | An Address to the Student's Religious Association [at the University of Michigan],

| Ann Arbor, January 1946 | INDIAN CULTURE AND ENGLISH | INFLUENCE | An Address to Indian Students and Their Friends, | Massachusetts Institute of Technology, January 1944 | and | EAST AND WEST | by | ANANDA K. COOMARASWAMY | ORIENTALIA | 47 WEST 47TH STREET, NEW YORK | 1946

1 leaf, 51 pp., 1 blank leaf. 22.8 x 15.3 cm. Stiff brown paper wrappers printed in black; wire-stitched.

Published Spring 1946; number of copies unknown.

Contents: I. The Religious Basis of the Forms of Indian Society—Notes—II. Indian Culture and English Influence—III. East and West.

Note: The two addresses are printed here for the first time.

Reviews: John J. Honigmann, *Psychiatry*, Baltimore, IX. (1946) 285-6; V. Raghavan, *Journal of Oriental Research*, Madras, XV. 4 (June 1946) 189-90; J[oseph]. Dalby, *New English Weekly*, London, XXX. 5 (14 Nov. 1946) 44-5; Bernard Kelly, *Blackfriars*, Oxford, XXVII. 320 (Nov. 1946) 437-9; René Guénon, *Études Traditionnelles*, Paris, XLVII. 256 (Dec. 1946) 460-2; Ralph T. Flewelling, *Personalist*, Los Angeles, XXVIII. (1947) 221; Philip Mairet, *Aryan Path*, Bombay, XVIII. 2 (Feb. 1947) 82-3; George W. Briggs, *Review of Religion*, New York, XI. 3 (Mar. 1947) 317-18.

b. *Sri Lankan edition* ([1947]):

EAST AND WEST | AND OTHER ESSAYS | By | ANANDA K. COOMARASWAMY | [*publisher's device*] | OLA BOOKS, LTD., | COLOMBO, CEYLON

3 leaves, 66 pp. 18.6 x 12.3 cm. White (?) paper wrappers printed in green (?); wire-stitched.

Note: The contents of this edition are identical with those of A70a, save that the three essays are arranged in a different order, as follows: I. East and West—II. The Religious Basis of the Forms of Indian Society—III. Indian Culture and English Influence; the endnotes to "The Religious Basis of the Forms of Indian Society" are printed as footnotes.

A71 FIGURES OF SPEECH OR FIGURES OF THOUGHT 1946

First edition:

FIGURES OF SPEECH | OR | FIGURES OF THOUGHT | COLLECTED ESSAYS ON THE TRADITIONAL OR | "NORMAL" VIEW OF ART | SECOND SERIES | By | ANANDA K. COOMARASWAMY | [*publishers' device*] | LONDON | LUZAC & CO. | 46 GREAT RUSSELL STREET, W.C.1 | 1946

256 pp., 2 unnumbered pls. (facing pp. 145, 226). 21.2 x 14 cm. Stiff green or light blue paper wrappers printed in black, on front (exactly as title-page) within thick-thin rule border, and up the spine.

Published June 1946 at 10*s*. 6*d*.; number of copies unknown.

Contents: Author's Preface [dated Boston, 22 August 1945]—Chap. I. "A Figure of Speech, or a Figure of Thought?"—Chap. II. The Mediaeval Theory of Beauty [C669 and 731, combined and revised]—Chap. III. Ornament [C763]—Chap. IV. Ars Sine Scientia Nihil—Chap. V. The Meeting of Eyes—Chap. VI. Shaker Furniture [from C755]—Chap. VII. Literary Symbolism [B60, expanded]—Chap. VIII. Intention—Chap. IX. Imitation, Expression, and Participation—Chap. X. The Intellectual Operation in Indian Art—Chap. XI. The Nature of Buddhist Art—Chap. XII. *Saṁvega*, "Aesthetic Shock"—Chap. XIII. An Early Passage on Indian Painting—Chap. XIV. Some References to Pictorial Relief—Chap. XV. Primitive Mentality—Chap. XVI. Notes on "Savage" Art [from C755]—Chap. XVII. Symptom, Diagnosis, and Regimen—Chap. XVIII. Walter Andrae: On the Life of Symbols [C668].

Notes: "With the exception of the first, the . . . chapters [in this book] are revised versions of essays that have appeared in various Journals, chiefly American . . . This is not a systematic treatise: each of the . . . chapters deals with some particular aspect or application of the traditional theory of art, and is complete in itself . . . But if not systematic, the subject matter of the whole is consistently one and the same, and no other than that of my *Why Exhibit Works of Art?* and *Transformation of Nature in Art*: and I think I may say that whoever makes use of these three books *and* of the sources referred to in them will have a fairly complete view of the doctrine about art that the greater part of mankind has accepted from prehistoric times until yesterday" ("Author's Preface", p. 5).

In Chapter I (the only essay that is printed here for the first time; the title is derived from Quintilian) AKC presents his thesis of art as a rhetorical activity ("rhetoric" carrying here the Platonic meaning of giving effectiveness to Truth), as distinct from the modern notion of art as nothing more than an aesthetic pursuit. AKC proposes the abandonment of the term "aesthetic" altogether in any discussion of the traditional arts. The argument is based on Plato's doctrine of art, with parallels drawn from Oriental sources.

AKC intended the title of this book to be question-marked (following his penchant, beginning in the late 1930s, for titles cast in the form of rhetorical questions, e.g. A63, 67, and C887); but in this instance the printer, for whatever reason, has failed to comply with his wishes.

"No rights reserved. Quotations of reasonable length may be made without written permission" (*verso of the title-leaf*).

Two epigrams, comprising quotations from the anthropologists Margaret Mead and Raymond Firth, are printed on page 8.

Save for the "Author's Preface", and Chapters XIII, XIV, XVI, XVIII, the contents of this book, in most cases incorporating addenda, were reprinted in *Coomaraswamy 1: Selected Papers, Traditional Art and Symbolism* ([1977])—A82. Chapter I was also reprinted, in two instalments, in *Studies in Comparative Religion*, Bedfont, Middx., VI. 1 (Winter 1972), pp. 43-61, and 2 (Spring 1972), pp. 104-12.

An Indian reprint of this book (hardbound) was produced by offset in New Delhi in 1981 by Munshiram Manoharlal Publishers Pvt. Ltd.

Reviews: Maurice Collis, *Observer*, London (21 July 1946) 2; Geoffrey Grigson, *Spectator*, London, CLXXVII. 6,174 (25 Oct. 1946) 428, 430; René Guénon, *Études Traditionnelles*,

Paris, XLVII. 256 (Dec. 1946) [458]-460; Hugh I'Anson Fausset, *Aryan Path*, Bombay, XVIII. 2 (Feb. 1947) 81-2; Victor Rienaecker, *Journal of the Royal Asiatic Society*, London (Apr. 1947) 126-7; P. Samarao, *Prabuddha Bharata*, Calcutta, LII. 4 (Apr. 1947) [183]-184; *Times Literary Supplement*, London, 2,359 (19 Apr. 1947) 180, 183; George Every, *New English Weekly*, London, XXXI. 4 (8 May 1947) 34-5; Bernard Kelly, *Blackfriars*, Oxford, XXVIII. 328 (July 1947) 331-3; Arthur Szathmary, *Review of Religion*, New York, XII. 1 (Nov. 1947) 87-9; Katharine Gilbert, *Art Bulletin*, New York, XXX. 2 (June 1948) 157-9; *Wind and the Rain*, London, V. 1 (Summer 1948) 63-4.

A72 AM I MY BROTHER'S KEEPER? [1947]

a. *First edition:*

Am I My | Brother's Keeper? | By ANANDA K. COOMARASWAMY | With an Introduction by Robert Allerton Parker | AN ASIA PRESS BOOK | THE JOHN DAY COMPANY, NEW YORK

xiii pp., 1 leaf, 110 pp., 1 blank leaf. 19.4 x 13.5 cm. Brown cloth boards lettered in silver down the spine; end-papers. Beige dust-jacket printed in black, with on back a portrait photograph of AKC, and a quotation from *Autobiography*, by Eric Gill.

Published early in 1947 at $2.25; number of copies unknown.

Contents: Introduction [by Robert Allerton Parker, dated New York, March 1946]—I. Am I My Brother's Keeper?—II. The Bugbear of Literacy—III. Paths That Lead to the Same Summit—IV. Eastern Wisdom and Western Knowledge—V. East and West [C860]—VI. "Spiritual Paternity" and the "Puppet Complex"—VII. Gradation, Evolution, and Reincarnation.

Notes: "The essays in this volume [none of which appear here for the first time] have been slightly revised, and notes have been added" ("Acknowledgements", p. [iv]).

A wood-engraving by Eric Gill, with the caption: "Progress", is reproduced on verso of leaf following page xiii.

An American reprint (hardbound) was produced by offset in 1967 in Freeport (New York) by Books for Libraries Press.

Reviews: Ernestine Evans, *New York Herald Tribune Weekly Book Review*, New York (16 Mar. 1947), Sect. VII, p. 2; Eleanor M. Hough, *Aryan Path*, Bombay, XVIII. 9 (Sept. 1947) 411; Walter Shewring, *Blackfriars*, Oxford, XXVIII. 331 (Oct. 1947) 481-2; R.O. Winstedt, *Journal of the Royal Asiatic Society*, London (Dec. 1947) 231-2; René Guénon, *Études Traditionnelles*, Paris, XLIX. 266 (Mar. 1948) [84]-85; *Catholic Art Quarterly*, Collegeville, Minn., XI. (Easter 1948) 109-10; W.H. Sheldon, *Review of Religion*, New York, XII. 4 (May 1948) 421-8; *Wind and the Rain*, London, V. 1 (Summer 1948) 63-4; *Eastern World*, London, IV. 3 (1950) 21; *Dublin Magazine*, Dublin, N.S. XXV. 2 (Apr./June 1950) 63.

Translation: Milan: Rusconi, 1975.

b. *First English edition* ([1949]):

The Bugbear | of Literacy | By | ANANDA K. COOMARASWAMY | With an Introduction by Robert Allerton Parker | London | DENNIS DOBSON LTD.

xiv, 130 pp. 19 x 12.6 cm. Blue cloth boards stamped in red and gold on spine, with publisher's device blind stamped in lower right-hand corner of back cover; end-papers. Beige dust-jacket printed in red and black.

Published November 1949 at 7*s*. 6*d*.; number of copies unknown.

Note: The contents of this edition are identical with those of A72a save for the incorporation of corrections and additions (mainly to the notes); these occur on pages 3, 17-18, 20-2, 25, 38, 41, 44, 59, 60, 61, 65, 88-9, 91, 109, 119, 120, 129-30.

c. *New (offset) edition* ([1979]):

THE BUGBEAR OF | LITERACY | ANANDA K. COOMARASWAMY | With an Introduction by Robert Allerton Parker | PERENNIAL BOOKS LTD | Pates Manor, Bedfont, Middlesex

150 pp., 1 blank leaf. Stiff white paper wrappers printed in Prussian blue, red, and ochre.

Published in 1979 at £3.25; number of copies unknown.

Notes: Pages [7]-124 are a reprint by offset of pages vii-xviii, 1-110 of A72a, with the addition of a new concluding essay, "The Bugbear of Democracy, Freedom and Equality"—C900, occupying pages [125]-150, which is published here for the first time in book form.

This edition does not include the additions and corrections in A72b.

A73 TIME AND ETERNITY 1947

a. *First edition:*

ANANDA K. COOMARASWAMY | TIME AND ETERNITY | [*publisher's device (design of ouroboros)*] | MCMXLVII | [*rule*] | ARTIBUS ASIAE PUBLISHERS ASCONA (SWITZERLAND)

1 blank leaf, 3 leaves, 140 pp. 21 x 15.3 cm. Plum cloth boards stamped in gold, on front: ARTIBUS ASIAE | SUPPLEMENTUM OCTAVUM | [*short rule*] | [*publisher's device (design of ouroboros)*], and up the spine; end-papers. White dust-jacket printed in black with, on front, a reproduction of a photograph of AKC by Doña Luisa (Mrs A.K.) Coomaraswamy.

Published 22 August 1947 at 20 SFrs ($4.80); number of copies unknown.

Contents: List of Abbreviations—Time and Eternity: Introduction—I. Hinduism—II. Buddhism—III. Greece—IV. Islām—V. Christian and Modern.

Notes: A documented exposition of the metaphysical relationship between time and eternity, with special attention given to the doctrine which "contrasts time as a continuum with the eternity that is not in time" (p. 3), and further, this doctrine as it has been enunciated with fundamental agreement among the various traditions.

"Artibus Asiae | curat editionem Alfred Salmony | Supplementum VIII | Published under the patronage of the | China-Institute—Berne" (*recto of leaf preceding title-leaf*).

This book is replete with misprints, including repetition and transposition of lines, e.g. on page 71 what should have been the last line of the text has been printed as line 5, and the lines at the top of page 91 are a repetition of lines 15-17.

The blurb on the front and back flaps of the dust-jacket was written specially for this purpose by AKC.

An Indian reprint (hardbound) was produced by offset in 1988 in New Delhi by Munshiram Manoharlal Publishers Pvt. Ltd.

Reviews: Murray Fowler, *Artibus Asiae*, Ascona, X. 3 (1947) 249-[250]; *Wind and the Rain*, London, V. 1 (Summer 1948) 63-4; K.J. Spalding, *Oriental Art*, London, I. 2 (Autumn 1948) 95-6; René Guénon, *Études Traditionnelles*, Paris, XLIX. 272 (Dec. 1948) 370-1; *Eastern World*, London, III. 6 (1949) 18; Neville Whymant, *United Asia*, Bombay, I. 8 (Mar. 1949) 198; Murray Fowler, *Journal of the American Oriental Society*, New Haven, LXIX. 2 (Apr./June 1949) 109; Joseph Katz, *Review of Religion*, New York, XIII. 4 (May 1949) 435-6.

b. *Second edition (Indian;* 1989)*:*

ANANDA K. COOMARASWAMY | [*swelled rule*] | TIME | AND | ETERNITY | [*design of Viṣṇu reposing on Ananta*] | [*quotation in one line*] | SELECT BOOKS BANGALORE | 1989

2 leaves, vi pp., 1 leaf, 99 pp. 21.9 x 14.3 cm. Tan paper wrappers, printed in dark brown on front and down the spine, folded over stiff white blanks; end-papers.

Published in 1989; number of copies unknown.

Notes: The contents of this edition are identical with those of A73a save for the correction of misprints, and the incorporation of AKC's additions and revisions, and the addition of a "Foreword" by William Stoddart, pages [i]-iii, and a "Preface" by K.K.S. Murthy and K.N. Iengar, pages [v]-vi. The footnotes in the first edition have here been printed as endnotes.

An Indian reprint (hardbound) of A73b was produced by offset in 1990 in New Delhi by the Indira Gandhi National Centre for the Arts. This omits the "Foreword" and "Preface" of A73b, replacing the former with a new foreword by Kapila Vatsyayan, pages [vi]-viii. An index has been provided.

Translations: Paris: Dervy-Livres [1976]; Madrid: Taurus, 1980. These translations incorporate the corrections, revisions, and additions (but not the "Foreword" and "Preface") that were later published in A73b.

A74 THE LIVING THOUGHTS OF GOTAMA THE BUDDHA [1948, *i.e.* 1949]

First edition:

THE LIVING THOUGHTS OF | GOTAMA THE BUDDHA | PRESENTED BY | ANANDA K. COOMARASWAMY | AND | I.B. HORNER | *[publishers' device]* | CASSELL | AND COMPANY, LIMITED | LONDON, TORONTO, MELBOURNE | AND SYDNEY

x, 224 pp., incl. frontis., 1 blank leaf. 19.2 x 13 cm. Red cloth boards stamped in gold across the spine; top edges stained red; end-papers. White dust-jacket printed in blue and black.

Published February 1949 at 6*s*; number of copies unknown.

Contents: Abbreviations—Pronunciations—Life of the Buddha—The Buddhist Doctrine—Extracts from the Buddhist Doctrine: Chapter I. Introductory—Chapter II. The Founder and the Arahants—Chapter III. Training—Chapter IV. Relations with Others—Chapter V. Evolution—Chapter VI. The Teaching—Chapter VII. Transcendent.

Notes: This book is number 26 in the publisher's series "The Living Thoughts Library", edited by Alfred O. Mendel.

Isaline Blew Horner has commented elsewhere on this collaboration with AKC: "Coomaraswamy wrote the Introductions [i.e. "Life of the Buddha" and "The Buddhist Doctrine"], we both chose which passages we wished to include, and in the main I translated them . . . he did not live to see the proofs" ("An Appreciation of a Pali Buddhist Scholar"—E83, p. 133).

The blurb on the front flap of the dust-jacket is signed: *The Editors* (i.e. AKC and I.B. Horner).

An Indian reprint (hardbound) was produced by offset in 1982 in New Delhi by Munshiram Manoharlal Publishers Pvt. Ltd.

Reviews: Clifford Bax, *Aryan Path*, Bombay, XX. 6 (June 1949) 276; René Guénon, *Études Traditionnelles*, Paris, L. 277 (July/Aug. 1949) 234-5; *Dublin Magazine*, Dublin, N.S. XXIV. 3 (July/Sept. 1949) 72-3; R.J. Jackson, *Eastern World*, London, III. 8 (Aug. 1949) 20.

Translations: Paris: Correa [1949]; Sao Paulo: Livraria Martins Editora, 1952; Puisseaux (France): Éditions Pardès, 1987.

A75 LA SCULPTURE DE BHARHUT 1956

First edition:

MINISTÈRE DE L'ÉDUCATION NATIONALE | ANNALES DU MUSÉE GUIMET | BIBLIOTHÈQUE D'ART. NOUVELLE SÉRIE: VI | *[rule]* | LA SCULPTURE | DE | BHARHUT | PAR | ANANDA K. COOMARASWAMY | TRADUCTION DE JEAN BUHOT

| 1956 | VANOEST | ÉDITIONS D'ART ET D'HISTOIRE | 3 ET 5, RUE DU PETIT-PONT, V^e | PARIS

97 pp., 2 leaves, 1 blank leaf, LI numbered pls. (on 26 leaves, containing 169 illus.). 30.3 x 22.5 cm. Buff paper wrappers printed in dark green.

Published 14 December 1956; number of copies unknown.

Colophon (verso 2nd leaf following page 97): ACHEVÉ D'IMPRIMER SUR LES PRESSES DE PROTAT FRERES, MACON LE QUATORZE DÉCEMBRE 1956 DÉPOT LÉGAL Ier TRIMESTRE 1957 N[os] D'ORDRE IMPRIMEUR: 5283; ÉDITEUR: 30

Contents: Chap. I. Historique—Chap. II. L'Iconographie du Bouddha a Bharhut—Planches [i.e. a descriptive list]—Plans—Liste de Abréviations Utilisées—Planches.

Note: "Du fait de la mort de son auteur, puis de celle de son traducteur, la parution de cet ouvrage a subi quelque retard. Certains détails ne sont donc plus tout à fait à jour, mais nous sommes efforces d'y remédier dans la mesure du possible" (p. [7], footnote 2).

A76 COOMARASWAMIANA 1960

First edition in this form:

[*Within ornamental border:*] COOMARASWAMIANA | [*photograph of AKC*] | Dr. Ananda K. Coomaraswamy | [*photograph of display of books and pamphlets*] | Edited by S. Durai Raja Singam, | Kuantan, Malaya. | 1960 (Edition of 100 copies) | [*outside border:*] Duplicated by KWOK YOKE WENG, 22, Arcade, Singapore.

cover title, [256] pp. 25.6 x 20.8 cm. Buff paper wrappers printed in black; wire-stitched.

Published in 1960; 100 copies printed.

Contents: 1. Borrowed Plumes—2. The Oriental View of Woman—3. Broadcast: Dialogue between Madam [*sic*] La Meri and Dr. Ananda Coomaraswamy—4. Domestic Handicraft and Culture—5. Foreword to "The Gesture Language of the Hindu Dance"—6. A Book Review of "The Gesture Language of the Hindu Dance"—7. Mahatma [B48]—8. Paintings by Rabindranath Tagore [B33]—9. The Appreciation of the Unfamiliar Arts—10. Unexplored Kandyan Literature—11. Sri Ramakrishna & Religious Tolerance—12. The Bee-song of Sur Das—13. The Indian Doctrine of Man's Last End—14. Paths That Lead to the Same Summit—15. Vegetarianism in Ceylon—16. Ragmala Poems—17. Todi Ragini [C475]—18. America and India—19. Education in India [B56]—20. Indonesian and Further Indian Art.

Notes: Title is taken from front wrapper; spine adds: Vol. I, but no further volumes were issued. Originally published as a series of 20 pamphlets reproduced from typewriting and issued from October 1957 to July/August 1959, with the series title: Writing and Speeches of Dr. Ananda K. Coomaraswamy. For publication in the present form the pamphlets have been bound together, with the original pagination and title-pages retained; the pages of this book are therefore not continuously numbered.

The only item printed here for the first time is "Broadcast: Dialogue between Madam [*sic*] La Meri [i.e pseud. of Russell Meriwether Hughes] and Dr. Ananda Coomaraswamy" (pp. [33-45]), which dialogue concerns the Indian dance with reference to the traditional doctrine of art. The broadcast had been given in New York on 26 April 1943, under the auspices of the East & West Association.

A77 THE ORIGIN OF THE BUDDHA IMAGE [1972]

First edition:

THE ORIGIN OF | THE BUDDHA IMAGE | BY | ANANDA K. COOMARASWAMY | [*publisher's device*] | Munshiram Manoharlal | Publishers Pvt. Ltd. [New Delhi]

3 leaves, 42 pp., 12 pls. (incl. frontis., on 7 leaves, containing 73 illus.). 28.7 x 21.9 cm. Navy blue cloth boards printed in green and red, and lettered in white across front cover and down the spine; end-papers. White dust-jacket printed in blue, red, and black.

Published in 1972 at 40 rupees; number of copies unknown.

Note: A reprint by offset of C505, incorporating the corrigenda.

A78 LETTERS OF ANANDA COOMARASWAMY 1972

First edition:

[*Within border comprising repeated word:* COOMARASWAMIANA:] LETTERS | OF | ANANDA | COOMARASWAMY | EDITED BY: | S. DURAI RAJA SINGAM | [Petaling Jaya, Malaysia] 1972

cover title, 28 pp. 20.8 x 16 cm. Yellow paper wrappers printed in black; wire-stitched.

Distributed gratis beginning 1972; 30 copies printed.

Notes: This pamphlet, privately printed (reproduced from typewriting) for gratis distribution by the editor to his family and friends, comprises 19 letters to S. Durai Raja Singam, and to his son Gandhikijai Singam, reprinted from *Letters of the Great* ([1954])—B86, with additionally a telegram from AKC to S. Durai Raja Singam, dated 13 October 1946.

"From Ananda Coomaraswamy to S. Durai Raja Singam. (N.B. Not for Publication (Private) 30 copies done.)" (*verso front wrapper*).

A79 THE FLOOD IN HINDU TRADITION [1972?]

First edition:

The Flood | in | Hindu Tradition | by | A.K. COOMARASWAMY | PRINTED BY PEMBRIDGE DESIGN STUDIO LIMITED | LONDON

2 leaves, 15 pp., incl. frontis. 23.1 x 15.8 cm. Buff paper wrappers, folded over stiff white blanks, printed in black on front; sewn.

Published probably in 1972; number of copies unknown.

Notes: "This essay, never before published, is drawn from the two-volume *Selected Writings of Ananda K. Coomaraswamy* [i.e. *Coomaraswamy: Selected Papers* ([1977])—A82], edited by Roger Lipsey, to be published in Bollingen Series by Princeton University Press. It is printed by arrangement with Princeton University Press and Rama P. Coomaraswamy, M.D., Literary Executor of the Coomaraswamy Estate" (*verso title-leaf*) .

"The primary object of the present note is to present the Indian Flood Legend as a special case of the Patriarchal Voyage (*pitṛyāna*), and at the same time in coherent and intelligible relation with other fundamental conceptions of Vedic cosmology and eschatology. Some analogies with other traditional aspects of the Flood Legend are incidentally noted" (p. 1).

A80 WHO IS 'SATAN' AND WHERE IS 'HELL'? [1974?]

First edition:

Who is | 'SATAN' | and | where is | 'HELL'? | by | A.K. Coomaraswamy | PUBLISHED AND PRINTED | BY PEMBRIDGE STUDIO LIMITED LONDON

2 leaves, 18 pp., incl. frontis., 1 blank leaf. 23 x 15.1 cm. Grey paper wrappers, folded over stiff white blanks, printed in black on front; sewn.

Published probably in 1974; number of copies unknown.

Note: A reprint, for the first time in pamphlet form, of C887.

A81 EARLY INDIAN ARCHITECTURE: PALACES [1975]

First edition:

EARLY | INDIAN | ARCHITECTURE: | PALACES | by | Ananda K. Coomaraswamy | [*publisher's device*] | Munshiram Manoharlal | Publishers Pvt. Ltd. [New Delhi]

2 leaves, 17 pp., 1 leaf, 20 pls. (on 10 leaves, containing 84 illus.). 28.5 x 22.3 cm. Navy

blue cloth boards lettered in yellow across front cover and down the spine; end-papers. White dust-jacket printed in yellow and black.

Published in 1975 at 60 rupees; number of copies unknown.

Note: A reprint by offset of C597.

A82 COOMARASWAMY 1[-2]: SELECTED PAPERS . . . [1977]

First edition:

[*In black: ornamental rule*] | [*in red:*] Coomaraswamy | [*in black: rule*] | 1[-2]: SELECTED PAPERS | TRADITIONAL ART | AND SYMBOLISM [-METAPHYSICS] | EDITED BY | Roger Lipsey | [*device*] | BOLLINGEN SERIES LXXXIX | PRINCETON UNIVERSITY PRESS [Princeton] | [*ornamental rule*]

Volume 1: 1 blank leaf, xxxviii, 580 pp., incl. frontis., 8 text illus., 14 pls. (also counted as pages, containing 29 illus.), 1 leaf, 1 blank leaf; *volume 2:* 1 blank leaf, xxvi, 470 pp., incl. frontis., 1 leaf, 2 blank leaves. 24.3 x 16.2 cm. Red cloth boards stamped in gold and red on spine; end-papers. White dust-jacket printed in black, red, and grey.

Published Autumn 1977 at $50.00 the set, $30.00 singly; number of copies unknown.

Contents: Volume 1. Editor's Note—List of Illustrations—List of Abbreviations and Short Titles—List of Works by A.K. Coomaraswamy Cited in These Volumes—Introduction, by Roger Lipsey—THE INDIAN TEMPLE: An Indian Temple: The Kandarya Mahadeo—SYNOPTIC ESSAYS: A Figure of Speech or a Figure of Thought? ["'A Figure of Speech, or a Figure of Thought?'"]—The Philosophy of Mediaeval and Oriental Art—The Part of Art in Indian Life—Introduction to the Art of Eastern Asia—INDIAN ART AND AESTHETICS: The Intellectual Operation in Indian Art—The Nature of Buddhist Art—*Saṃvega*: Aesthetic Shock—MEDIAEVAL ART AND AESTHETICS: The Mediaeval Theory of Beauty—*Ars sine scientia nihil*—The Meeting of Eyes—FURTHER STUDIES: Ornament [C763]—Shaker Furniture—Note on the Philosophy of Persian Art—Intention—Imitation, Expression, and Participation—Primitive Mentality—Chinese Painting at Boston—Symptom, Diagnosis, and Regimen—TRADITIONAL SYMBOLISM: METHODOLOGY: Literary Symbolism—The Rape of a Nāgī: An Indian Gupta Seal [C708 and 714]—Walter Andrae's *Die ionische Säule: Bauform oder Symbol?*: A Review [C670]—TRADITIONAL SYMBOLISM: FOUR STUDIES: On the Loathly Bride—*Le Corps parsemé d'yeux*—The Inverted Tree—The Sea—TRADITIONAL SYMBOLISM: THE SUNDOOR AND RELATED MOTIFS: The Symbolism of the Dome ["Symbolism of the Dome"]—Appendix: Pāli *kaṇṇikā*: Circular Roof-plate [C584]—*Svayamātṛṇṇā*: Janua Coeli—Symplegades—General Index—Index of Greek Terms—Index of Sanskrit and Pāli Terms; volume 2. Editor's Note—List of Abbreviations and Short Titles—List of Works by A.K. Coomaraswamy Cited in These Volumes—INTRODUCTORY ESSAYS: The Vedānta and Western Tradition—Who Is "Satan" and Where Is "Hell"?—Śrī Ramakrishna and Religious Tolerance—The "E" at Delphi—THE MAJOR ESSAYS: Recollection, Indian and Platonic [from A69]—On the One and Only Transmigrant [from

A69]—*Ākiṃcañña*: Self-Naughting—*Ātmayajña*: Self-Sacrifice—*Līlā*—Play and Seriousness—Measures of Fire—Vedic "Monotheism" [C687]—Vedic Exemplarism—The Vedic Doctrine of "Silence"—*Manas*—*Kha* and Other Words Denoting "Zero", in Connection with the Indian Metaphysics of Space ["*Kha* and Other Words Denoting 'Zero' in Connection with the Metaphysics of Space"]—The Tantric Doctrine of Divine Biunity—Two Passages in Dante's *Paradiso*—*Nirukta=Hermeneia* [C696 and 702]—Some Pāli Words—UNPUBLISHED WORKS: On the Indian and Traditional Psychology, or Rather Pneumatology—*Mahā Puruṣa*: "Supreme Identity"—Bhakta Aspects of the Ātman Doctrine—The Flood in Hindu Tradition—Does "Socrates Is Old" Imply That "Socrates Is"?—The Meaning of Death—THE SEVENTIETH BIRTHDAY ADDRESS ["Dr. Coomaraswamy's Talk at His Boston Dinner"]—General Index—Index of Greek Terms—Index of Sanskrit and Pāli Terms.

Notes: These two volumes, the eighty-ninth in a Series sponsored by Bollingen Foundation, collect 56 essays written between 1932 and 1947 (one other essay, "Pāli *kaṇṇikā*: Circular Roof-plate", from 1930, is printed as an appendix in volume 1). Twenty-nine of the essays are printed here for the first time in book-form. Fourteen essays, in volume 1, had been collected earlier in *Figures of Speech or Figures of Thought* (1946)—A71. Of the six essays printed in volume 2 under the heading "Unpublished Works", only the first, second, third, and fifth, are in fact printed here for the first time. Concerning the title "Bhakta Aspects of the Ātman Doctrine", Whitall N. Perry has remarked that the first word "should presumably read 'Bhakti'" (in *Studies in Comparative Religion*, Bedfont, Middx., XI. 4 (Autumn 1977), p. 211). An excerpt from a letter by AKC to Walter Shewring, 4 March 1936, is printed with the "Editor's Note", page vii (in both volumes).

"Coomaraswamy's addenda to the essays have been a matter of interest to scholars and friends. He kept desk copies of his published works and added notes to them over the years . . . After his death . . . his widow, Doña Luisa . . . determined to incorporate these addenda into the essays. . . . [In 1952, she] successfully applied for a Bollingen Fellowship to carry on this work. . . . In due course the editors of Bollingen Series made a place in the program for a publication of selected writings. Mrs. Coomaraswamy's death in 1971 [*sic*, for October 1969] left the project still incomplete and requiring redirection. . . . In reformulating the editorial task, I found it appropriate to include no addenda other than those which are genuinely finished paragraphs or clear references; with regret, I eschewed a great many addenda . . . This policy makes the essays less rich in addenda than was expected by scholars and friends close to the project. With few exceptions, addenda have been placed in footnotes, and in all cases . . . enclosed in brackets [ ] to distinguish them from the text as Coomaraswamy published it" ("Editor's Note", pp. v, vi, in both volumes).

The frontispieces reproduce photographs of AKC by Doña Luisa Coomaraswamy.

A paperbound edition was issued by Princeton University Press in 1986 (vol. 1) and 1987 (vol. 2). In 1997, a selection of essays, drawn from both volumes, was also published by Princeton University Press, as *The Door in the Sky: Coomaraswamy on Myth and Meaning*—A95.

Bollingen Series LXXXIX is completed by a third volume: a biography of AKC, by Roger Lipsey. For description of this, and of the material by AKC that it contains, see B94a.

Reviews: Whitall N. Perry, *Studies in Comparative Religion*, Bedfont, Middx., XI. 4 (Autumn 1977) 205-20; Patricia R. Hausman, *Library Journal*, New York, CII. 17 (1 Oct. 1977) 2067-8; John Kenneth Galbraith, *New York Times*, New York (12 Mar. 1978) Sect.

VII, pp. 14, 32; Herbert A. Kenny, *Boston Sunday Globe*, Boston (12 Mar. 1978) A16; Schuyler Cammann, *Parabola*, New York, III. 2 (May 1978) 84-91; Kathleen Raine, *The Times*, London (18 May 1978) 22; *Burlington Magazine*, London, CXX. 906 (Sept. 1978) 632; Martin Green, *Worldview*, New York (Sept. 1978) 49-50; A. Ranganathan, *Indian Review*, Madras, LXXIV. 6 (Sept. 1978) 59-60; Mahrukh Tarapor, *Journal of the Royal Society of Arts*, London, CXXVI. 5,268 (Nov. 1978) 769-70; J.C. Wright, *Bulletin of the School of Oriental and African Studies*, London, XLII. 2 (1979) 391-2; Philip Rawson, *New York Review of Books*, New York, XXVI. 2 (22 Feb. 1979) 15-17; Joseph Rykwert, *Religion*, London, IX. (Spring 1979) 104-15; Huston Smith, *Philosophy East and West*, Honolulu, XXIX. 3 (July 1979) [347]-356; Adrian Cunningham, *Tablet*, London, CCXXXIII. 7,259 (25 Aug. 1979) 825; Jim C. Masselos, *South Asia*, Nedlands, Western Australia, N.S. II. 1/2 (Mar./Sept. 1979) 163-5; Donald B. Kuspit, *Art Bulletin*, New York, LXI. 3 (Sept. 1979) 501-4; Mircea Eliade, *History of Religions*, Chicago, XIX. 2 (Nov. 1979) 167-76; Michael W. Meister, *Journal of the American Oriental Society*, New Haven, C. 2 (Apr./June 1980) 153-4; B.D.H. Miller, *Oriental Art*, London, N.S. XXVI. 2 (Summer 1980) 221; S.H. Nasr, *Temenos*, London, 2 (1982) 252-9; Partha Mitter, *Asian Studies Association of Australia Review*, Canberra, VII. 3 (Apr. 1984) 48-51; Herbert A. Kenny, *National Review*, New York, XXXVIII. 14 (1 Aug. 1986) 44.

A83 ON THE TRADITIONAL DOCTRINE OF ART [1977]

First edition:

[*In black:*] A.K. Coomaraswamy | On the | Traditional Doctrine of | Art | [*in red: ornament*] | [*in black:*] Golgonooza Press [Ipswich, Suffolk]

1 blank leaf, 24, [1] pp., 1 blank leaf. 22.7 x 15.2 cm. Heavy cream paper wrappers printed on front in black and red; sewn.

Published in 1977 at £1.00; number of copies unknown.

Contents: Foreword [B55]—Asiatic Art [A64]—Athena & Hephaistos—Notes.

Note: Nothing is printed here for the first time. The decorations on the front wrapper and on the title-page are rubricated wood block impressions reproduced from *The Arts & Crafts of India & Ceylon* (1913)—A28—pp. 171, 200.

Reviews: Kathleen Raine, *The Times*, London (18 May 1978) 22; David Lake, *Studies in Comparative Religion*, Bedfont, Middx., XIII. 3/4 (Summer/Autumn 1979) 244.

A84 LA DOCTRINE DU SACRIFICE [1978]

First edition:

COLLECTION “MYSTIQUES ET RELIGIONS” | ANANDA K. COOMARASWAMY | LA | DOCTRINE | DU | SACRIFICE | Textes réunis | et traduits de l’anglais par

| Gérard Leconte | [*device*] | DERVY-LIVRES | 6, rue de Savoie | PARIS-VIe

1 blank leaf, 4 leaves, [7]-243 pp., 4 pls. (on 2 leaves), 2 leaves. 24 x 16.1 cm. Heavy terracotta paper wrappers printed on front in green and black, and in black up the spine.

Published 16 January 1978 at 68 francs; number of copies unknown.

Contents: Introduction [by Gérard Leconte]—Sommaire—Liste des Abréviations—I. Anges et Titans—II. La Face obscure de l'Aurore—III. Sire Gauvain et le Chevalier Vert: Indra et Namuci—IV. L'Epouse hideuse—V. Les Magiciens sans tête et l'Acte de Vérité—VI. Le Rapt d'une Nâgî—VII. Sarpabandha—VIII. Atmayajña: le sacrifice de soi.

Note: Collects eight articles—C680, A58, C831, 854, 845, 708 and 714 combined, 806, 789, respectively—not previously in French translation, which investigate myths and extricate, mainly from the Vedic and Celtic tradition, motifs of which the sense is that sacrifice is a necessary condition of the possibility of purification, whether it be access to sovereignty, to liberation, or to divinity.

A85 SOURCES OF WISDOM [1981]

First edition:

SOURCES | OF | WISDOM | ANANDA K. COOMARASWAMY | MINISTRY OF CULTURAL AFFAIRS | SRI LANKA [Colombo]

4 leaves, 231 pp., incl. frontis. 21 x 13.8 cm. Heavy white paper wrappers printed in blue, yellow, black, and red.

Published Summer 1981; number of copies unknown.

Contents: Preface [by E.L.B. Hurulle]—Introduction [by Rama P. Coomaraswamy]—The Farewell Dinner—For What Heritage and to Whom Are the English-speaking Peoples Responsible?—Indian Culture and English Influence—What Is Civilization?—The Religious Basis of the Forms of Indian Society—Buddhism—Understanding the Art of India [C658]—Some Sources of Buddhist Iconography—Gradation, Evolution and Reincarnation—The Indian Doctrine of Man's Last End—The Common Wisdom of the World—Art, Man and Manufacture—The Renaissance of Indian Culture—Selected Bibliography.

Notes: Nothing of AKC's is printed here for the first time.

"[A] collection of essays [from the period 1934 to 1947], selected by the author's son, Dr. Rama P. Coomaraswamy, which is representative of the later work of his distinguished father. . . . Some extra references and English translations of words in [Sanskrit,] Latin, Greek, French, German and Italian have been provided in footnotes enclosed in square brackets" ("Preface", p. 3).

A86 SYMBOLISM OF INDIAN ARCHITECTURE 1983

First edition:

[*In black:*] A.K. COOMARASWAMY | [*in red:*] Symbolism of Indian Architecture | [*in black:*] Introduction | by | PRAMOD CHANDRA | [*in red: ornament*] | [*in black:*] The Historical Research Documentation Programme | Jaipur | 1983

6 leaves, [3]-80 pp. 25.3 x 18.8 cm. Light brown cloth boards lettered in dark brown down the spine, with an ornament printed in dark brown on front cover; end-papers. White dust-jacket printed in red and black.

Published in 1983 at 80 rupees; number of copies unknown.

Contents: Publisher's Note—Abbreviations—Introduction [by Pramod Chandra]—Part I. Architectural Representation of the World Creation—Part II. Meaningfulness of the Traditional Arts—Part III. World Roof and Its Eye—References—A Bibliography of Coomaraswamy's Works on Indian Architecture—Index.

Notes: "[O]riginally published . . . as 'Symbolism of the Dome' [C732]. We have changed the title [and] have inserted a suitable title to each of its three parts; these parts were not entitled in the original article. We have also added Sanskrit equivalents in Devanagari script to make it more useful. An Introduction . . . [an Index] and a Bibliography . . . have also been given" ("Publisher's Note", *recto of third leaf*) .

The footnotes accompanying the original publication of C732 are printed here as endnotes under the heading "References".

The dust-jacket (only) carries a subtitle: *The Skambha and the Stūpa.*

Review: John Irwin, *Journal of the American Oriental Society*, New Haven, CV. 1 (1985) 177-8.

A87 L'ARBRE INVERSÉ 1984

First edition:

Ananda K. Coomaraswamy | L'Arbre Inversé | Traduit de l'anglais | par | Gérard Leconte | [*device*] | ARCHÈ | MILANO | 1984

1 blank leaf, 2 leaves, 7-58 pp., 1 leaf. 22 x 15.1 cm. Heavy white paper wrappers printed in black on front, and up the spine; top and bottom edges roughly trimmed.

Published in 1984 at 57 francs; number of copies unknown.

Contents: Avant-propos [by Gérard Leconte]—Liste des Abréviations—[L'Arbre Inversé].

Notes: Issued as number 12 in the publisher's series "Cahiers de l'Unicorne".

A translation of "The Inverted Tree" (1938)—C741—from the version that was printed in A82.

A88 FUNDAMENTALS OF INDIAN ART 1985

First edition:

[*In black:*] COOMARASWAMY 4-VOLUME SERIES | [*in red:*] Fundamentals of Indian Art | [*in black:*] A.K. COOMARASWAMY | [*portrait of AKC*] | Vol I | (Themes & Concepts) | INTRODUCTION | by | S. DURAI RAJA SINGAM | [*in red: device*] | [*in black:*] The Historical Research Documentation Programme | JAIPUR | 1985

xix, 103 pp. 25 x 19 cm. Ochre paper boards with beige cloth back, printed in brown on front; end-papers. White dust-jacket printed in red and black.

Published in May 1985 at 100 rupees; number of copies unknown.

Dedication (page [v])*:* . . . To Dr. S. Durai Raja Singam His Sincerest Biographer.

Contents: Introduction [by S. Durai Raja Singam]—1. The Aims of Indian Art—2. The Art of Asia (Asiatic Art: India) ["Asiatic Art—1. India"]—3. Pali Kannika: Circular Roof-Plate—4. Votive Sculptures of Ancestors and Donors in Indian Art [B35]—5. Understanding the Art of India [C671]—6. What Is Common to Indian and Chinese Art?—7. The Intellectual Operation in Indian Art—8. An Approach to Indian Art—9. Is Art a Superstition or a Way of Life?—Appendix: AKC's Rejoinder ["Note on a Review by Richard Florsheim of *Is Art a Superstition or a Way of Life?*"]—Index.

Notes: Nothing of AKC's is printed here for the first time. The essays which appear as chapters 2 and 6 are printed here for the first time in book-form.

This volume is the first of the publisher's projected series, of which no more were published.

A89 SELECTED LETTERS 1988

First edition:

SELECTED LETTERS OF | Ananda K. Coomaraswamy | Edited by | ALVIN MOORE, JR. | and | RAMA POONAMBULAM [*sic*] COOMARASWAMY | INDIRA GANDHI NATIONAL CENTRE FOR THE ARTS | OXFORD UNIVERSITY PRESS | DELHI BOMBAY CALCUTTA MADRAS | 1988

xxxiii, 479 pp., 1 blank leaf, 8 unnumbered pls. (incl. frontis.). 24.6 x 16.4 cm. Cinnamon hand-spun khadi cloth boards, stamped in gold down the spine, with publishers' devices at base; end-papers. White dust-jacket printed in brown, black, and beige, with reproduction of a drawing of AKC by Gaganendranath Tagore on the front, and again on the back, but reduced and reversed out.

Published 12 December 1988 at 250 rupees; number of copies unknown.

Contents: [List of] Illustrations—Foreword [by Whitall N. Perry]—Preface—Acknowledgements [including a note by Kapila Vatsyayan]—Introduction [by Alvin

Moore, Jr. and Rama Ponnambalam Coomaraswamy]—The Letters—Farewell Address ["Dr. Coomaraswamy's Talk at His Boston Dinner"]—Editors' Note—Bibliographic Appendix—Index to Letters [i.e. names of recipients]—General Index: The Man from His Letters.

Notes: This book comprises 348 letters, written between 15 September 1910 and 8 September 1947, arranged thematically. A letter from AKC to Eric Gill, 12 February [1938], is reproduced in facsimile of AKC's autograph facing page 208 but not otherwise printed in the book. Some of the items by AKC included here are not strictly speaking letters, these are as follows: "Note on a Review by Richard Florsheim of *Is Art a Superstition or Way of Life?*", pp. 47-8; message sent to International Festival (1947), Michigan State College, pp. 55-6; note on René Descartes' *Cogito ergo sum*, p. 63; note on "The Son of Man", p. 84; notes on the doctrine of "the two selves", p. 136; translation of passages from the *Kaṭha Upaniṣad*, pp. 260-2; "Mr. Finlayson's Providential Order of Fairplay", pp. 280-3; statement on monarchy, p. 322; "What of India?", pp. 338-41; greeting to Jawaharlal Nehru on his 57th birthday, p. 348; message to commemorate Mahatma Gandhi's 75th birthday, pp. 349-51; "Renaissance of Indian Culture", pp. 356-8; "Indian Opinion on the State Regulation of Vice", pp. 365-8; and "Mind and Myth", pp. 414-17.

An epigraph, excerpted from *The Traditional Theory of Literature*, by Ray Livingston, is printed on page [v].

The blurb on the back flap of the dust-jacket states: "The letters have been compiled by Dorai [*sic*] Raja Singam", and, expressed somewhat differently, on the verso of the title-leaf: "Compiled by Rama Poonambulam [*sic*] Coomaraswamy with assistance from Sabapathi Pillai [*sic*] Durai Raja Singam".

"The IGNCA [i.e. Indira Gandhi National Centre for the Arts, New Delhi] has initiated a programme of publication of works of critical scholarship, reprints and translations. . . . The Collected Works of A.K. Coomaraswamy thematically rearranged with the author's own revisions, is central to the IGNCA's third programme in its division of Textual Research and Publication, Kala Kosa. The present volume . . . commences this series" (p. xviii).

Reviews: V.Y. Kantak, *Indian Literature*, New Delhi, XXXIII. 2 (Mar./Apr. 1990) [133]-150; A. Ranganathan, *Book Review*, New Delhi, XIV. 5 (Sept./Oct. 1990) 11-13.

A90 WHAT IS CIVILISATION? [1989]

First edition:

ANANDA K. COOMARASWAMY | [*rule*] | What is Civilisation? | AND OTHER ESSAYS | FOREWORD BY | SEYYED HOSSEIN NASR | [*short rule*] | GOLGONOOZA | PRESS | [*ornament.* Ipswich]

xii pp., 1 leaf, 193 pp. 24 x 16.3 cm. Claret cloth boards stamped in black down the spine; claret end-papers. Beige dust-jacket printed in claret and black.

Published March 1989 at £21.50; number of copies unknown.

Contents: Foreword—Bibliographical Note [including a list of abbreviations]—1. What Is Civilisation? ["What Is Civilization?"]—2. On the Pertinence of Philosophy—3. On Being in One's Right Mind—4. Beauty, Light and Sound ["Beauté, lumière et son"]—5. Windows of the Soul—6. The Coming to Birth of the Spirit—7. Gradation and Evolution—8. Gradation and Evolution II—9. Fate, Foresight, and Free-will—10. Mahatma [C750 *n.*]—11. On Hares and Dreams—12. The Pilgrim's Way *and* The Pilgrim's Way, A Buddhist Recension—13. Mind and Myth—14. Symbols—15. The Interpretation of Symbols—16. The Symbolism of Archery—17. Khwāja [*sic*] Khaḍir and the Fountain of Life, in the Tradition of Persian and Mughal Art—18. Eckstein—19. *Quod factum est in ipso vita erat*—20. Athena and Hephaistos—Index.

Notes: Three essays are printed here for the first time, "edited from photocopies of the typescripts deposited in the Princeton University Library" (p. ix), as follows: (1) "Windows of the Soul", pp. [50]-57, on the traditional theory of vision, particularly the concept of "the immanent Person in the eye" (with reference to the work of A. A. Bowman), and citing Indian sources, with parallels drawn from the Chinese, Greek, Christian, and Islamic traditions, (2) "*Quod factum est in ipso vita erat*", pp.[178]-182, an exposition of John I. 3-4, and (3) an English version of "Beauté, lumière et son'', pp. [42]-49. The remainder of the essays, with the exception of the first, second, sixth, thirteenth, and twentieth, are printed here for the first time in book-form.

"Many of [AKC's] major studies continue to be unavailable to the general, interested public. Brian Keeble [proprietor of Golgonooza Press and anonymous editor of this book] has, therefore, rendered much service to the cause of traditional studies in making some of these essays available once again in this collection" ("Foreword", p . [vii]).

An Indian issue (hardbound) of this book using the English first-edition sheets was published in New Delhi in 1989 by the Indira Gandhi National Centre for the Arts and Oxford University Press, and an American issue (paperbound) also using the English sheets was published in Great Barrington, Mass., in 1989 by Lindisfarne Press.

Reviews: Arthur Versluis, *Avaloka*, Grand Rapids, V. 1/2 (1990) 92-4; Hilary Williams, *Beshara*, Oxford, 11 (Spring 1990) 42; Usha Hemmadi, *Independent*, Bombay (2 Dec. 1990) 10; Roger Lipsey, *Parabola*, New York, XVI. 1 (Feb. 1991) 126-30.

Translation: Sao Paulo: Editora Siciliano, 1992.

A91 EARLY INDIAN ARCHITECTURE CITIES AND CITY GATES [1991]

First edition:

EARLY INDIAN ARCHITECTURE | Cities and City Gates etc. | Ananda K. Coomaraswamy | [*publisher's device*] | Munshiram Manoharlal | Publishers Pvt Ltd [New Delhi]

3 leaves, 33 pp., 5 text illus., 16 pls. (numbered: CXXII-CXXXIII, also counted as pages, containing 42 illus.). 28.6 x 22.5 cm. Light brown cloth boards stamped in gold down the

spine; end-papers. White dust-jacket printed in brown and black.

Published in 1991 at 100 rupees; number of copies unknown.

Note: A reprint by offset of C563, omitting the addenda and corrigenda.

A92 ... ESSAYS IN EARLY INDIAN ARCHITECTURE 1992

First edition:

ANANDA K. COOMARASWAMY: | ESSAYS IN EARLY INDIAN ARCHITECTURE | Edited and with an Introduction by | Michael W. Meister | INDIRA GANDHI NATIONAL CENTRE FOR THE ARTS, NEW DELHI | OXFORD UNIVERSITY PRESS | DELHI BOMBAY CALCUTTA MADRAS | 1992

xxviii, 151 pp., 30 text illus., 41 pls. (incl. frontis., counted as pages, containing 136 illus.). 31.3 x 23.6 cm. Black-grained red imitation leather boards stamped in gold down the spine; end-papers. White dust-jacket printed in black and grey with, on front, a reproduction of a photograph of a relief at Amarāvatī.

Published in 1992 at 400 rupees; number of copies unknown.

Contents: List of Figures—List of Abbreviations—Foreword [by Kapila Vatsyayan]—Preface—Acknowledgements—Introduction: The Language and Process of Early Indian Architecture—Early Indian Architecture: Parts 1 & 2—Early Indian Architecture: Part 3—Indian Architectural Terms—Early Indian Architecture: Part 4—General Index—Index to Preliminary Pages.

Note: The essays collected in this book are reprinted by offset in facsimile of their original publication in *Eastern Art, Journal of the American Oriental Society,* and *Res*, with new pagination.

A93 JAINA ART [1994]

First edition:

Jaina Art | Ananda K. Coomaraswamy | [*publisher's device*] | Munshiram Manoharlal | Publishers Pvt Ltd [New Delhi]

6 leaves, 57 pp., 1 leaf, 5 text illus., 40 unnumbered pls. (on 20 leaves, containing 66 illus., 5 are coloured). 25 x 18.8 cm. Blue-grey cloth boards stamped in gold on front cover and down the spine; end-papers. White dust-jacket printed in grey and black.

Published in 1994 at 350 rupees; number of copies unknown.

Contents: 1. Introduction—2. Jainism—3. Life of Mahāvīra and Other Jinas—4. Summary of the Story of Kālakācārya—5. Explanation of Various Terms—6. Cosmology—7. Aesthetics and Relationships of Jaina Painting—8. The Illustrated Manuscripts—9. Description of the Figures—Index—Illustrations.

Notes: A reprint (entirely reset) of "Notes on Jaina Art" (1914)—C333.

Page 54 of the index is printed out of order.

Review: Religious Studies Review, Valparaiso, Ind., XXII. (Jan. 1996) 85.

A94 . . . ESSAYS IN ARCHITECTURAL THEORY 1995

First edition:

ANANDA K. COOMARASWAMY: | ESSAYS IN ARCHITECTURAL THEORY | Edited and with an Introduction by | Michael W. Meister | INDIRA GANDHI NATIONAL CENTRE FOR THE ARTS | OXFORD UNIVERSITY PRESS | DELHI BOMBAY CALCUTTA MADRAS | 1995

xxiii, 3-122 pp., 22 text illus., 5 pls. (counted as pages, incl. coloured frontis.), 1 blank leaf. 31.2 x 23.5 cm. Burgundy cloth boards stamped in gold down the spine, with publishers' devices at base; end-papers.

Published late in 1995; number of copies unknown.

Contents: List of Figures—List of Abbreviations—Foreword [by Kapila Vatsyayan]—Preface and Acknowledgements—Introduction: Architecture as Ornament, Essential Form—Pāli *kaṇṇikā*: Circular Roof-plate—The Symbolism of the Dome—*Uṣṇīṣa* and *Chatra*: Turban and Umbrella—Ornament—*Svayamātṛṇṇā*: Janua Coeli—An Indian Temple: The Kandarya Mahadeo—Appendix: Ancient Iron Beams in India—General Index—Index to Preliminary Pages.

Notes: "Princeton University Press has been kind in allowing the Indira Gandhi Centre to make use of the editorial improvements made by Roger Lipsey in their edition of Coomaraswamy's *Selected Papers* [from which five essays are reprinted here, i.e. the first, second, fourth, fifth, and sixth]. . . . I had known for many years that Coomaraswamy's scattered scholarly and philosophic contributions to the understanding of India's architectural traditions were such as to require compilation and reprinting. The previous volume, *Ananda K. Coomaraswamy: Essays in Early Indian Architecture*, collects Coomaraswamy's major contributions to the definition of India's distinctive architectural morphology. This present volume collects those essays that contribute most to architectural theory. These are best read and understood in the order in which they were written. Only by being presented in such a fashion can Coomaraswamy's architectural ideas accumulate a structure comparable to their substance" ("Preface and Acknowledgements", p. xiv).

"Ancient Iron Beams in India" (pp. 111-12), which originally appeared, unsigned, in *The Builder*, London, CIII. 3,634 (27 Sept. 1912) 357-8, is identified by Meister as a work of AKC's. However, as this article contains numerous inapt or uncharacteristic terms and usages as well as wrong or uncouth transliterations of Indian words (some of these silently corrected by Meister), and other infelicities, including the tautologism: "roughly approximate", it can hardly have been written by AKC.

A95 THE DOOR IN THE SKY [1997]

First edition:

The Door in the Sky | Coomaraswamy on Myth and Meaning | Selected and with a preface by | Rama P. Coomaraswamy | PRINCETON UNIVERSITY PRESS | PRINCETON, NEW JERSEY

xxxviii, 3-253 pp., 7 text illus., 8 pls. (counted as pages), 1 leaf, 1 blank leaf. 23.3 x 15.6 cm. Stiff white paper wrappers printed in yellow, black, grey, and blue with, on front, a reproduction of a painting by Hieronymus Bosch.

Published in 1997 at $15.95; number of copies unknown.

Contents: List of Illustrations—Preface—List of Abbreviations and Short Titles—List of Works by A.K. Coomaraswamy Cited in this Volume—1. Mind and Myth—2. *Svayamātṛṇṇā*: Janua Coeli—3. Imitation, Expression, and Participation—4. *Ātmayajña*: Self-Sacrifice—5. A Figure of Speech or a Figure of Thought?—6. The Nature of Buddhist Art—7. An Indian Temple: The Kandarya Mahadeo—8. Literary Symbolism—9. The Symbolism of the Dome—Index.

Notes: This book was issued in the publisher's series "Mythos: The Princeton/Bollingen Series in World Mythology".

"This volume is composed of essays originally published in two volumes of a three-volume work, the eighty-ninth in a series sponsored by Bollingen Foundation: *Coomaraswamy: Metaphysics* . . . and *Coomaraswamy: Traditional Art and Symbolism* . . .1977 by Princeton University Press, both volumes edited by Robert [*sic*] Lipsey; the first essay in the new collection, "Mind and Myth", is reproduced courtesy of Rama P. Coomaraswamy" (p.[iv]).

On page xv of the "Preface", the second sentence in footnote 12 should have been printed as the second sentence of footnote 13.

B. Contributions by Ananda K. Coomaraswamy to Books and Pamphlets

B. Contributions to Books

B1 Mineral Resources [of Ceylon]. *St. Louis World's Fair, 1904. Official Handbook of the Ceylon Court.* Colombo: George J.A. Skeen, Government Printer, Ceylon, 1904, pp. [146]-152, 2 text illus., 1 pl.

A survey of the deposits (particularly graphite and gem stones) with assessments of their economic importance. On page 166 it is noted that "the Government has . . . on view a collection of Mineralogical specimens prepared by Mr. A.K. Coomaraswamy". (The St Louis World's Fair opened on 30 April and closed 1 December.)

B2 The Rocks and Minerals of Ceylon. *Colombo Museum. Guide to the Collections* [3rd edition, edited by Arthur Willey. Colombo: Government Press, 1905], pp. 50-66, 9 text illus., 1 pl.

A general account, incorporating on pages 53-62 "a complete list of the minerals at present known to occur in Ceylon" (seventy-three minerals are briefly described). Addenda to this list is printed in *Spolia Zeylanica*, Colombo, for January 1906—C102. Arthur Willey in his "Preface" (dated 9 February 1905), printed on recto of leaf following the title-leaf, observes that the Museum's "collection of rocks and minerals has been entirely re-arranged and greatly augmented by the Director of the Mineral [*sic*] Survey, Mr. A.K. Coomaraswamy, B.Sc.".

B3 Foreword. *Ālawakadamanaya*, edited by P. Tudāwé Pandita Gunewardene at the request of Dr. Ananda K. Coomaraswamy. Colombo: Printed for the Ceylon Social Reform Society by Sihala Samaya Press, 1907, pp. [1]-7.

Dated December 1906. In the main a synopsis, in English, of the 418 stanzas of this anonymous 17th century poem relating the legend of the conversion to Buddhism of the demon prince Ālavaka (the poem itself is printed in Sinhalese script). "The present edition [is based on a] unique MS. recently purchased by myself in Kandy. It is now published by the Ceylon Social Reform Society, as a small step towards the fulfillment of one of its aims, the revival of interest in Sinhalese literature" (p. [1]).

B4 Geology and Mineralogy [of Ceylon]. *Twentieth Century Impressions of Ceylon: Its History, People, Commerce, Industries, and Resources*, edited by Arnold Wright. London, Durban, Colombo, Perth (W.A.), Singapore, Hong Kong: Lloyd's Greater Britain Publishing Company, Ltd., 1907, pp. 178-9.

A general introduction; graphite and thorianite are singled out for discussion; a descriptive list of gems is provided.

B5 Native Arts and Handicrafts [of Ceylon]. *Twentieth Century Impressions of Ceylon: Its History, People, Commerce, Industries, and Resources*, edited by Arnold Wright. London, Durban, Colombo, Perth (W.A.), Singapore, Hong Kong: Lloyd's Greater Britain Publishing Company, Ltd., 1907, pp. 180-8, 4 text illus., 1 pl. containing 5 illus.

Printed in triple columns, and arranged under two sub-headings: Sinhalese—Tamil. On the traditional character of the old arts and crafts as they survive in the Kandyan provinces, with detailed accounts of the individual crafts; including a note on Sinhalese painting. A "Short Table of Castes of Craftsmen" is provided (p. 187). Concludes with a general survey of the Ceylon Tamils' arts and crafts, of which "no one—certainly not the present writer—has made any detailed study" (p. 187).

B6 [Swadeshi]. *The Swadeshi Movement: A Symposium. Views of Representative Indians and Anglo-Indians . . .* Madras: G.A. Natesan & Co. [1909?], pp. [230]-237.

A reprint, for the first time in book-form, of the article of this title in *Indian Review*, Madras, for January 1907—C143. In the same publisher's "Second Edition Revised and Enlarged" ([1916?]), AKC's article occupies pages 243-51.

B7 The Modern School of Indian Painting in 1910. *Festival of Empire Imperial Exhibition. Indian Section. Guide and Catalogue.* London & Derby: Bemrose & Sons Ltd. [1911], pp. 105-7.

A brief history and description of the work of the small group of painters in Calcutta led by Abanindranath Tagore. AKC also includes a comment on Ravi Varma. The Exhibition was held at the Crystal Palace (London), from May to October 1911.

B8 Foreword. *Introduction to the Study of Indian Music. An Attempt to Reconcile Modern Hindustani Music with Ancient Musical Theory and to Propound an Accurate and Comprehensive Method of Treatment of the Subject of Indian Musical Notation*, by E[rnest]. Clements. London: Longmans, Green, & Co., 1913, pp. [v]-ix.

Dated London, 12 Sept. 1912. In the main, AKC addresses the present-day problems of teaching and preserving the music: he warns against the replacement of the old system of oral transmission by printed scores, and calls attention to the destructive effect upon Indian music of the tempered harmonium. This book was reprinted by Gaurav Publications (New Delhi [1981]).

B9 The Religious Foundation of Life & Art. *Essays in Post Industrialism: A Symposium of Prophecy Concerning the Future of Society*, edited by Ananda K. Coomaraswamy and Arthur J. Penty. London, Edinburgh & Boston: T.N. Foulis, Publisher [1914], pp. 27-42.

Not published; presumably aborted by the publisher at the outbreak of World War I. The information above is based upon a single (bound) dummy in page proof sighted (April 1991) in the collection of Dr Rama P. Coomaraswamy, Greenwich, Conn. AKC's article does not seem to have been printed elsewhere. The "Introduction" to this book (pp. vii-ix), while unsigned, was almost certainly written by AKC, perhaps jointly with Penty. The term employed in the book's title, "Post Industrialism", was coined by AKC; Penty credits AKC with this neologism on page 14 of his *Post-Industrialism* (London, 1922).

B10 [On Rabindranath Tagore]. *The Maharani of Arakan: A Romantic Comedy in One Act Founded on the Story of Sir Rabindranath Tagore*, by George Calderon. London: Francis Griffiths, 1915, pp. 16-20.

The second of four articles, printed under the general heading "A Short Character Sketch of Rabindranath Tagore", compiled by K.N. Das Gupta, pp. 9-30, excerpted from "Poems of Rabindranath Tagore", in *Art and Swadeshi* ([1912])—A25a—pp. [109], 122-3, 124-6. (The last of these articles is by W.B. Yeats.) See also C298.

B11 Intellectual Fraternity. *A Book of Homage to Shakespeare*, edited by Israel Gollancz. London: Humphrey Milford, Oxford University Press, 1916, pp. 317-19.

A publication to commemorate the tercentenary of the death of William Shakespeare. "Alike to those who grieve for Europe in her hour of civil war, and to those who would offer tribute at the shrine of William Shakespeare, it must appear appropriate and significant to publish tokens of the brotherhood of man in art" (p. 317). This article was reprinted in *The Dance of Śiva* (1918)—A38a—pp. [112]-114, and in *Avaloka*, Grand Rapids, Mich., I. 1 (Winter 1986) 18-19.

B11a [Translations of Punjabi and Kashmiri songs]. *Book of Words of Classic East Indian Ragas and Kashmiri Folk Songs Sung by Ratan Devi (Mrs. Ananda K. Coomaraswamy) in Her Costume Recitals.* New York: J.B. Pond Lyceum Bureau [1916], 8 pp.

Texts, with English versions by AKC, of nineteen songs of which sixteen are reprinted, with changes, from *Thirty Songs from the Panjab and Kashmīr* ([1913])—A27a. The translation of the fourteenth song, "Bande Mataram", is not by AKC. This pamphlet was sold at the recitals given by Ratan Devī in New York, Chicago, and elsewhere during her concert tour of North America. Includes tributes to Ratan Devī from Rabindranath Tagore (from his "Foreword" to A27a), Bernard Shaw, W.B. Yeats, Percy Grainger, Kurt Schindler, and Philip Hale; these are printed on the inside of the front and back wrappers.

B12 The Dance of Siva. *Elements of Hindu Iconography*, by T.A. Gopinatha Rao. Madras: The Law Printing House, 1916, *Vol. II*, Pt. 1, pp. 231-52.

A reprint, for the first time in book-form, from *The Light of Truth or the Siddhānta Dipikā and Āgamic Review*, Madras, for July 1912—C293. "Since the work has already been done by [AKC] and if I may respectfully say so, in quite a splendid manner, my task is lightened and I have much pleasure in reproducing . . . the whole of the article" (p. 231). Rao's "Preface", dated Madras, January 1916, includes a further acknowledgement of AKC (pp. ix-x).

B13 Introduction. *Sculpture, Painting and Drawing of Ancient India*. New York: Kevorkian Galleries, 1918, pp. 3-4.

On the proper appreciation of an alien or unfamiliar art. "It is now perhaps for the first time that an exhibition of purely Indian art has been attempted in New York" (p. 3). The exhibition was held in December, and comprised examples selected from Hagop Kevorkian's private collection.

B14 Persian Painting. *Handbook of the Museum of Fine Arts*, Thirteenth Edition. Boston: T.O. Metcalf Company for Museum of Fine Arts, Boston, 1919, pp. 223-9, 4 pls. (i.e. pp. 226-9).

AKC's text is retained in the 14th (1920), 15th (1922), and 16th (1923) editions of the *Handbook*, but beginning with the 17th edition (1925) is replaced by an unsigned introductory note occupying a single page.

B15 Indian Art. *Handbook of the Museum of Fine Arts*, Thirteenth Edition. Boston: T.O. Metcalf Company for Museum of Fine Arts, Boston, 1919, pp. [271]-293, 14 pls. (i.e. pp. 280-93).

"The new edition of the Handbook just issued [replacing the 12th edition (1916)] includes for the first time a section devoted to the art of India" (*Museum of Fine Arts Bulletin*, Boston, for December 1919, p. 63). AKC's text is retained in the 14th (1920), 15th (1922), and 16th (1923) editions of the *Handbook*, but beginning with the 17th edition (1925) is replaced by an unsigned introductory note occupying a single page.

B16 Introduction. *A Catalog of Sculptures by John Mowbray-Clarke Shown at the Kevorkian Galleries at Number Forty West Fifty-seventh St., New York, From May the Seventh to*

June the Seventh, 1919. Notes by H[agop]. Kevorkian, Ananda Coomaraswamy and Amy Murray. [New York: The Sunwise Turn, 1919], pp. [6, 8, 10, 12].

A consideration of the general character of art in our time, and proposing a classification of the modern artist into three types: the Mystic ("the great American example [of which] is [Albert Pinkham] Ryder"), the Olympian, and the Titan.

B17 Introduction. *Dancing and the Drama East and West . . .*, by Stella Bloch. New York: Orientalia, 1922, 3 unnumbered pages (i.e. 2 leaves following title-leaf).

Dated Boston, December 1921. Chiefly on the differences between Oriental and Occidental theory and practice of art.

B18 India, Music in. *A Dictionary of Modern Music and Musicians*, edited by A. Eaglefield-Hull. London: J.M. Dent & Sons, and New York: E.P. Dutton & Co., Inc., 1924, pp. 248-9.

On (1) the music's rôle and status, (2) the typical occasions for its performance, and (3) as compared with European music. The first (alphabetically) of three articles on Indian music that AKC contributed to this *Dictionary*.

B19 Indian Music. *A Dictionary of Modern Music and Musicians*, edited by A. Eaglefield-Hull. London: J.M. Dent & Sons, and New York: E.P. Dutton & Co., Inc., 1924, p. 249.

On (1) the Indian scale, (2) the music's modal character, and (3) the concepts of *rāga* and *tāla*.

B20 Indian Musical Instruments. *A Dictionary of Modern Music and Musicians*, edited by A. Eaglefield-Hull. London: J.M. Dent & Sons, and New York: E.P. Dutton & Co., Inc., 1924, pp. 249-50.

Chiefly on the components and properties of the vīnā, the tambura, and the sārangī.

B21 [Excerpts from "Christian Missions in India"]. *Christian Missions and Oriental Civilizations: A Study in Culture Contact*, by Maurice T. Price. Shanghai: [Privately printed] 1924, pp. 85, 173, 178-80, 186-91, 193, 244, 251, 254-5, 278-9.

Sixteen excerpts, some of considerable length, are reprinted from Chapter XI of *Essays in National Idealism* ([1909])—A18a.

B22 Citra-lakṣana. *Sir Asutosh* [*Mookerjee*] *Memorial Volume*. Patna: J.N. Samaddar, 1926, Part I, pp.[49]-61.

(In English.) An annotated translation by AKC of a 16th century treatise on painting: Śrī Kumāra's *Śilparatna*, Chapter 46. Corrigenda is published with "Viṣṇudharmottara, Chapter XLI" in *Journal of the American Oriental Society*, New Haven, for March 1932—C625—pp. 17-18, and further corrigenda with "The Technique and Theory of Indian Painting" in *Technical Studies in the Field of the Fine Arts*, Cambridge, Mass., for October 1934—C663—pp. 68-85 (i.e. notes 2, 14, 16, 20, and 25). A separately paginated offprint seen (April 1991) in the collection of Dr Rama P. Coomaraswamy, Greenwich, Conn.

B23 Foreword. *Desert Winds*, by Hafsa [*i.e. pseud.* of Russell Meriwether Hughes?]. New York: The Century Co. [1927], pp. vii-viii.

Dated 1 August 1927. AKC commends this account of a journey in Algeria that "gives without sentimentality or patronage a true picture of these people as they are, in themselves . . . such works are all too rare". An English edition, retaining AKC's "Foreword", appeared under the imprint of T. Werner Laurie (London, 1928).

B24 Bronze and Brass Ornamental Work. Indian and Indonesian. *The Encyclopaedia Britannica*. Fourteenth Edition. New York: Encyclopaedia Britannica, Inc. [1929], *Vol. 4*, pp. 249-50, 2 pls. (numbered: XV-XVI) containing 23 illus.

In the main, a description of the *cire perdue* process as it is employed in India for the making of images, utensils, and jewellery; with notes on types of vessels and their decoration, in particular the metal ware known as bidrī. The first (alphabetically) of eight articles on Indian, Ceylonese, and South-East Asian subjects that AKC contributed to this edition of the *Encyclopaedia*.

B25 Dance. India. *The Encyclopaedia Britannica.* Fourteenth Edition. New York: Encyclopaedia Britannica, Inc. [1929], *Vol. 7*, pp. 19-22, 2 pls. (numbered: IV-V) containing 16 illus.

A comprehensive account, that includes notes on the dance of Śiva, as well as the dances associated with other Indian deities, and a description of the traditional education received by a dancer, together with a brief survey of the various folk dances found in India and Ceylon.

B26 Indian and Sinhalese Art and Archaeology. *The Encyclopaedia Britannica.* Fourteenth Edition. New York: Encyclopaedia Britannica, Inc. [1929], *Vol. 12*, pp. 209-19, 9 text illus., XIII numbered pls. (III, X, and XIII are coloured) containing 95 illus.

A detailed and comprehensive survey, beginning with the prehistoric remains. Includes an annotated bibliography.

B27 Indian Architecture. *The Encyclopaedia Britannica.* Fourteenth Edition. New York: Encyclopaedia Britannica, Inc. [1929], *Vol. 12*, pp. 220-8, 2 text illus., VI numbered pls. containing 63 illus.

On the origins, and the successive periods and styles, together with accounts of the special forms peculiar to Indian building. The architecture of Ceylon and South-East Asia is also discussed; bibliographies are included.

B28 Indonesian and Further Indian Art. *The Encyclopaedia Britannica.* Fourteenth Edition. New York: Encyclopaedia Britannica, Inc. [1929], *Vol. 12*, pp. 267-70, 1 pl. (numbered: II) containing 15 illus.

"Our account of the most important artistic developments in each area [of South-East Asia] will be essentially a study of the sculpture" (p. 267); a bibliography is appended.

B29 Iron in Art. Indian and Indonesian. *The Encyclopaedia Britannica.* Fourteenth Edition. New York: Encyclopaedia Britannica, Inc. [1929], *Vol. 12*, pp. 681-2.

A brief account of the history of the manufacture of iron and steel in India, and of the methods of working these metals as traditionally practised.

B30 Textiles and Embroideries. India. *The Encyclopaedia Britannica.* Fourteenth Edition. New York: Encyclopaedia Britannica, Inc.[1929], *Vol. 22*, pp. 3-5, 2 pls. (numbered: VI-VII).

This account includes notes on cotton (and muslin), woolen textiles, silk, brocades, and the traditional techniques of dyeing and printing on fabric.

B31 Yakṣas. *The Encyclopaedia Britannica.* Fourteenth Edition. New York: Encyclopaedia Britannica, Inc. [1929], *Vol. 23*, p. 873, 1 pl. (facing p. 872) containing 10 illus.

A concise account of the nature of these supernatural beings, and of their cult in India.

B32 A Royal Gesture; and Some Other Motifs. *Feestbundel uitgegeven door het Koninklijk Bataviaasch Genootschap van Kunsten en Wetenschappen, 150 Jarig Bestaan 1778-1928.* Weltevreden [Java]: G. Kolff & Co. [1929], pp. [57]-61, 4 text illus., 4 pls. (numbered: II-V).

Dated Boston, 1 Mar. 1928. On "the ancient Indian idea of the king as the source and fountain-head of all prosperity", (p. 61), as expressed in a series of 2nd century BC Āndhra reliefs, at Amarāvatī and Jagayyapeṭa, that represent "a Cakravartin in all his glory". Including notes on the iconographies of (1) the cloud formulae, (2) the "Seven Treasures", and (3) the royal insignia.

B33 Foreword. *Exhibition of Paintings by Rabindranath Tagore. The Fifty-Sixth Street Galleries New York November, 1930.*

[New York: The Fifty-Sixth Street Galleries, 1930], 3 unnumbered pages.

Dated Boston, 20 Oct. 1930. This "Foreword" was pre-printed as "Drawings by Rabindranath Tagore" in *Rupam*, Calcutta, for April/July/October 1930—C575, and reprinted in *Paintings by Rabindranath Tagore: Foreign Comments*, compiled by Joseph Southall (Calcutta: N. Mukerjee, Art Press [1931?]), pp. 18-20, and, in an abridged form, in *Rabindranath Tagore: A Biography*, by Krishna Kripalani (London: Oxford University Press & New York: Grove Press, 1962), pp. 341-2. For a reported comment by AKC on the writing of this foreword, see *Rabindranath Tagore: The Myriad-Minded Man*, by Krishna Dutta and Andrew Robinson (New York: St. Martin's Press [1996]), p. 461.

B34 The Gods of India. *The Golden Book of Tagore. A Homage to Rabindranath Tagore from India and the World in Celebration of His Seventieth Birthday*, edited by Ramananda Chatterjee. Calcutta: The Golden Book Committee, 1931, pp. 283-5.

A brief survey of the Hindu pantheon.

B35 Foreword. *Portrait Sculpture in South India*, by T.G. Aravamuthan. London: The India Society, 1931, pp. ix-xiii.

Dated Boston, 1 June 1930. Chiefly concerning the Indian, and traditional, conception of portraiture as the representation of a type rather than a likeness. Reprinted, as "Votive Sculptures of Ancestors and Donors in Indian Art", in *Fundamentals of Indian Art* (1985)—A88—pp. [31]-34.

B36 Aesthetic of the Śukranītisāra. *Études d'orientalisme publiées par le Musée Guimet à la mémoire de Raymonde Linossier*. Paris: Ernest Leroux, 1932, *Vol. I*, pp. [165]-168.

In the main, a translation by AKC of passages, dealing with the making of images, from the mediaeval treatise of Śukrācārya. Reprinted, with minor revisions, as Chapter IV of *The Transformation of Nature in Art* (1934)—A56a. Excerpts, from the revised version of the translation (only), were printed, with the title "Sukracarya on Making Images", in *Roopa-lekhā*, New Delhi, XXVIII. 1/2 (Mar. 1958) 58.

B37 Dance in India. *The National Encyclopedia*, edited by Henry Suzzallo. New York: P.F. Collier & Son Company [1932], *Vol. Three*, p. 397.

A short, general account. The first (alphabetically) of three articles that AKC contributed to this *Encyclopedia*.

B38 Indian Architecture (Exclusive of Moslem). *The National Encyclopedia*, edited by Henry Suzzallo. New York: P.F. Collier & Son Company [1932], *Vol. Five*, pp. 425-8, 2 text illus., 4 pls. containing 16 illus.

An outline of its history, general character, and influence.

B39 Indian Art. *The National Encyclopedia*, edited by Henry Suzzallo. New York: P.F. Collier & Son Company [1932], *Vol. Five*, p. 428, 3 pls. containing 13 illus.

A very brief account of the history and character of painting and sculpture in India.

B40 Parāvṛtti=Transformation, Regeneration, Anagogy. *Festschrift Moriz Winternitz 1863—23. Dezember-1933*, edited by Otto Stein and Wilhelm Gampert. Leipzig: Otto Harrassowitz, 1933, pp. [232]-236.

On the Buddhist "doctrines of transformation and efficacy of knowledge" (p. [232]), as expressed in the *Mahāyāna Sūtrālaṃkāra*, IX. 41-8, of Maitreya-Asaṅga, with special reference to the renderings of this passage by Sylvain Lévi and Louis de la Vallée Poussin.

B41 Introduction. *Loan Exhibition of Early Indian Sculptures Paintings and Bronzes*, A College Art Association

Exhibition, catalogued by Nasli M. Heeramaneck. New York: Heeramaneck Galleries [1935], pp. 3-6.

Dated Boston, Oct. 1935. AKC provides a guide to what in his view should be the proper reactions to ancient or alien works of art. Including as well a résumé of the history of Indian art. Reprinted as "An Approach to Indian Art", in *Parnassus*, New York, for December 1935—C682.

B42 On the Pertinence of Philosophy. *Contemporary Indian Philosophy*, edited by S. Radhakrishnan and J.H. Muirhead. London: George Allen & Unwin Ltd./New York: The Macmillan Company, 1936, pp. [113]-135.

Comprises two parts, headed: I. Definition and Status of Philosophy, or Wisdom—II. How Divers Wisdoms Have Considered Immortality. Chiefly a meditation upon the purport of Aristotle's First Philosophy (i.e. Metaphysics), and its relation to religion, rationalism, and practical science, and its distinction from the profane meaning of philosophy, with parallels adduced to Christian, Indian, and Islamic doctrine. This article was reprinted in *What Is Civilisation? and Other Essays* ([1989])—A90—pp. [13]-32.

B43 Vēdic "Monotheism". *Dr. S. Krishnaswami Aiyangar Commemoration Volume*, edited by V. Rangacharya, C.S. Srinivasachari, and V.R. Ramachandra Dikshitar. Madras: G.S. Press, 1936, pp. [18]-25.

An earlier version of C687.

B44 An Introduction to Bronze Statuettes of India and Farther India. *Master Bronzes Selected from Museums and Collections in America, February, 1937*. Buffalo, New York: The Buffalo Fine Arts Academy, Albright Art Gallery [1937], 6 unnumbered pages, 14 pls. (numbered: 98-111).

On the proper appreciation of Indian images, with a descriptive list of the plates that illustrate the 14 exhibited bronzes loaned by the Museum of Fine Arts, Boston, and by the Heeramaneck Galleries, New York. Pre-printed as "Indian Bronzes" in *Parnassus*, New York, for January 1937—C698.

B45 The Part of Art in Indian Life. *The Cultural Heritage of India*, edited by the Sri Ramakrishna Centenary Committee. Calcutta: Sri Ramakrishna Centenary Committee [1937], *Vol. III*, "[Section] IV The Arts", pp. [485]-513, 1 pl. (coloured, facing p. [485]).

A comprehensive and documented exposition of the traditional Indian theory of art and beauty; incorporating as well a discussion of the concept of ideal portraiture. In conclusion AKC presents what in his view constitutes the decadence of "the present situation and [cites] some specific instances" (p. 509). In the "Second Edition: Revised and Enlarged" of *The Cultural Heritage of India* (Calcutta: Sri Ramakrishna Mission Institute of Culture [1953-]), AKC's article is to appear in Vol. VII (in preparation at 1992). Reprinted in *Coomaraswamy 1: Selected Papers, Traditional Art and Symbolism* ([1977])—A82—pp. 71-100.

B46 What Use Is Art Anyway? [and] Art for Art's Sake? *What Use Is Art Anyway. Six Broadcasts Sponsored by Boston Museum of Fine Arts January and February 1937*. Newport, R.I.: John Stevens, 1937, pp. 1-5, 6-12.

A reprint, for the first time in book form, of C697.

B47 The Nature of Buddhist Art. *The Wall-Paintings of India Central Asia & Ceylon: A Comparative Study*, by Benjamin Rowland, Jr. . . . with a Foreword by A[lfred]. Townshend Johnson. Boston: The Merrymount Press, 1938, pp. 3-38.

The main theme of AKC's essay, which serves as the introduction to this book, is "the nature and genesis of the anthropomorphic image", and the related questions of "iconoclasm" and "iconolatry". AKC suggests that "the problems of Buddhist art [are not] those of Buddhist art in particular, but rather those of Indian art in a Buddhist application, and in the last analysis the problems of art universally" (p. 4). "For the introductory essay . . . we are indebted to Dr. Ananda K. Coomaraswamy, whose eminence in the field of Indian art bestows on this publication a compliment of which we are more than appreciative" ("Foreword", pp. xii-xiii). Reprinted, in an expanded and slightly revised form, as Chapter XI of *Figures of Speech or Figures of Thought* (1946)—A71, and in *Coomaraswamy 1: Selected Papers, Traditional Art and Symbolism* ([1977])—A82—pp. 147-78. The complete monograph was reprinted by offset, in two volumes, by Alfa Publications (Delhi [1985]), with the pagination of AKC's essay (in Volume I) unaltered.

B48 Mahātmā. *Mahatma Gandhi: Essays and Reflections on His Life and Work, Presented to Him on His Seventieth Birthday, October 2nd, 1939*, edited by S. Radhakrishnan. London: George Allen & Unwin Ltd., 1939, pp. 63-7.

(In English.) A reprint, in an extensively revised and slightly reduced form, of the article of this title in *Calcutta Review*, Calcutta, for April 1939—C750 *n*.

B49 The Coming to Birth of the Spirit. *Ācārya-Puṣpāñjali Volume (In Honour of Dr. D.R. Bhandarkar)*, edited by Bimala Churn Law. Calcutta: Satis Chandra Seal, The Indian Research Institute, 1940, pp. [103]-114.

An analysis of the Indian, neo-Platonic, and other doctrines of "reincarnation", regeneration, transmigration, and metempsychosis. AKC defines each of these terms, differentiating "reincarnation" from transmigration and metempsychosis. "These doctrines, often treated as one, appear to have been more profoundly misunderstood, if that is possible, than any other aspect of Indian metaphysics" (p. [103]). This article was reprinted in *What Is Civilisation? and Other Essays* ([1989])—A90—pp.[58]-69, and, with the omission of the footnotes, in *Tambimuttu: Bridge between Two Worlds*, edited by Jane Williams (London: Peter Owen, 1989), pp. 214-19. A French translation (by Elizabeth Andres) is printed, as "La Mise au monde de l'Esprit", in *Connaissance des Religions*, Avon, France, IV. 3/4 (Dec. 1988/Mar. 1989) 185-94.

B50 The Nature of Medieval Art. *Arts of the Middle Ages* [title on front wrapper adds: *1000-1400*]. *A Loan Exhibition, February 17 to March 24, 1940*. [Boston:] Museum of Fine Arts, Boston, Massachusetts [1940], pp. xi-[xiii].

AKC emphasizes that a proper appreciation of Medieval art "demands an understanding of the spirit of the Middle Ages, the spirit of Christianity itself, and in the last analysis the spirit of . . . the 'Philosophia Perennis' or 'Universal and Unanimous Tradition'" (p. [xiii]). The catalogue is compiled and introduced by Georg Swarzenski, who observes: "The chance location of the Exhibition in galleries adjoining the Museum's famous Oriental collections . . . presents a rare opportunity to see Medieval Art in a wider perspective. This coincidence shows the art of the Middle Ages not as an entr'acte between the two classic periods of European history, but as a phenomenon concurrent to Oriental art and presenting an essential parallel in spirit" (pp. ix-[x]). AKC's essay was printed simultaneously in *Art News*, New York, XXXVIII. 20 (17 Feb. 1940) [6]-7, 23-4, 1 text illus., 1 pl. (i.e. p.[6]), and reprinted as Chapter VI of *Why Exhibit Works of Art?* (1943)—A67, in *Good Work*, Cambridge, Mass., XXVI. 2 (Spring 1963) 54-6, and again in *Studies in Comparative Religion*, Bedfont, Middx., XV. 1/2 (Winter/Spring 1983) 88-91.

B51 Manas. *Woolner Commemoration Volume. (In Memory of the Late Dr. A[lfred]. C[ooper]. Woolner).* Mehar Chand Lachhman Das Sanskrit and Prakrit Series Volume Eight, edited by Mohammad Shafi. Lahore: Mehar Chand Lachhman Das, 1940, pp. [53]-60.

(In English.) On this Sanskrit term, which "in the Saṃhitās and Brāhmaṇas, and sometimes in the Upaniṣads, is the Pure or Possible Intellect, at once a name of God and that in us by which he may be grasped" (p. [53]), including a discussion of "initiation", "dementation", and "intellection", as stages of the soul's journey toward deification. AKC ends by offering some observations on what are in his view the shortcomings of modern scholarship when dealing with the "enigmas" of esoteric doctrine. This article was reprinted in *Coomaraswamy 2: Selected Papers, Metaphysics* ([1977])—A82—pp. 209-19.

B52 Foreword. *The Gesture Language of the Hindu Dance*, by La Meri. New York: Columbia University Press, MCMXLI, pp.[vii]-viii.

Dated Boston, Oct. 1941. On the traditional art of dance as essentially a sacred rite, and contrasting this view of art with that which pertains to the modern secularized and individualistic culture of the West, with parallels adduced to the Platonic doctrine of art. La Meri (i.e. pseud. of Russell Meriwether Hughes) in her "Acknowledgements" (p. [ix]) writes, "I desire to thank . . . Dr. Ananda K. Coomaraswamy for the never-ending inspiration of his writings". This book was reprinted by Benjamin Blom, Inc., New York [1964].

B53 [Letter]. *Temples and Towers: A Survey of the World's Moral Outlook*, compiled by George Vaughan. Boston: Meador Publishing Company, MCMXLI, pp. 156-7.

In reply to a questionnaire circulated by Vaughan between 1933 and 1940. AKC's contribution, of unspecified date, printed in 13 lines, expresses agreement with Vaughan that "we are in a period of rapid drift to lower ideals". AKC further remarks that his "position is analogous to that of René Guénon in *La Crise du Monde Moderne*. I cordially recommend to you all of Guénon's books". A photo-portrait of AKC is reproduced facing page 464.

B54 Wall Paintings of India and Ceylon. *The Iranian Institute Presents an Exhibition of Mural Paintings from the Cave Temples of India in Replicas by Sarkis Katchadourian at the American-British Art Center, 44 West 56th Street, New York, January 8 to February 8, 1942*. [New York: The Iranian Institute, 1942], pp. 8-11, 2 pls. (numbered: II-III).

This exhibition catalogue is also the Institute's *Bulletin*, V. 4 (1942). AKC's essay was originally written for the special exhibition of Katchadourian's work held at the Museum of Fine Arts, Boston, 19 November to 14 December 1941 (the essay was reproduced by mimeograph from typewriting and distributed gratis at that exhibition; a copy seen—June 1991—at the Library of the Museum of Fine Arts). Reprinted, with additionally an appraisal by AKC of Katchadourian as a copyist, in *Indian Murals and Sarkis Katchadourian*, edited by David Olan (New York: The Delphic Press [1942]), pp. 7, 9-11, and again in *Mural Paintings from the Caves of India by Sarkis Katchadourian* (Akron, Ohio: Akron Art Institute [1946]), pp.[3, 5-7].

B55 Foreword. *Related Arts* [by Mary Noreen Gormley and A.J. McDonnell]. Baltimore: College of Notre Dame of Maryland, 1942, p. 3.

Dated 30 Jan. 1942. A formulation of art and human needs; printed in 18 lines. This publication, a pamphlet reproduced from typewriting, was the prospectus for the College's newly-formed atelier, where it was intended that work would be done according to the dictates of the Roman Catholic philosophy of art. Reprinted as the "Foreword" to *On the Traditional Doctrine of Art* ([1977])—A83—p.[3].

B56 India, Education in. *Encyclopedia of Modern Education*, edited by Harry N. Rivlin and Herbert Schueler. [New York: The Philosophical Library, Inc., 1943], pp. 389-90.

Discussing, in the main, the problem of the differences between the ideals of traditional Indian education and those of the modern West. AKC also gives an outline of the history of British educational policy in India. This article was reprinted, as "Education in India", in *Coomaraswamiana* (1960)—A76—pp.[235-40].

B57 Indian Drama. *Dictionary of World Literature. Criticism—Forms—Technique*, edited by Joseph T. Shipley. New York: The Philosophical Library [1943], pp. 317-20.

The first (alphabetically) of four articles that AKC contributed to this *Dictionary*. On *nāṭya* as mimesis and as significant ritual. AKC defines the drama's sacred origins, its purpose, and the various forms it takes (including puppet and shadow plays). The editor comments, in his "Preface", page v: "Many have been helpful, beyond any indication of their initials, in the organization of the material as well as in its final shaping. Suggestions have come most generously from . . . A.K. Coomaraswamy . . .". There is evidence that AKC may have written the entries (unsigned) for "*abhinaya*", "argument", and "dry" (i.e. as opposed to "sentimental"). In the "Revised and Enlarged Third Edition", re-titled *Dictionary of World Literary Terms* (London: George Allen & Unwin, 1970, and reprinted 1979), this entry, considerably altered and reduced, occupies pages 159-60.

B58 Indian Literary Theory. *Dictionary of World Literature. Criticism—Forms—Technique*, edited by Joseph T. Shipley. New York: The Philosophical Library [1943], pp. 320-3.

A survey and exposition beginning with the "prophetic art" of the Vedic period and concluding with a discussion of the later classical period of dramatic and poetic expression. AKC defines *inter alia* "Indian rhetoric", "*rasa*", and "beatitude" (as the ultimate experience of a work of art). In the "Revised and Enlarged Third Edition", re-titled *Dictionary of World Literary Terms* (London: George Allen & Unwin, 1970, and reprinted 1979), this entry, altered and somewhat reduced, occupies pages 160-1.

B59 Ornament. *Dictionary of World Literature. Criticism—Forms—Technique*, edited by Joseph T. Shipley. New York: The Philosophical Library [1943], p. 416.

An entry printed in 12 lines. AKC explains how the word "originally referred to the proper ordering of [the] parts [of a work of art] with a view to efficient operation". In the "Revised and Enlarged Third Edition", re-titled *Dictionary of World Literary Terms* (London: George Allen & Unwin, 1970, and reprinted 1979), this entry, unaltered but for a minor addition, appears on page 228.

B60 Symbolism. *Dictionary of World Literature. Criticism—Forms—Technique*, edited by Joseph T. Shipley. New York: The Philosophical Library [1943], pp. 564-7.

On the general nature of symbols, the doctrine of analogy (or adequacy), and on symbolism as forming a traditional and universal lingua franca. As a demonstration of *le symbolisme qui sait* (in contradistinction to *le symbolisme qui cherche*), and to show the consistency of the metaphysical content of symbols regardless of time or place, AKC discusses the symbolism of (1) the "thread" or "cord", (2) the "chariot", and (3) the notion of "hesitation". In the "Revised and Enlarged Third Edition", re-titled *Dictionary of World Literary Terms* (London: George Allen & Unwin, 1970, and reprinted 1979), this entry appears, with a few minor omissions and alterations, on pages 322-5. Reprinted, with the addition of notes, and with the title "Literary Symbolism", as Chapter VII of *Figures of Speech or Figures of Thought* (1946)—A71, and again, incorporating further addenda, in *Coomaraswamy 1: Selected Papers, Traditional Art and Symbolism* ([1977])—A82—pp. 323-30.

B61 Introduction. *It All Goes Together; Selected Essays,* by Eric Gill. New York: The Devin-Adair Company, MCMXLIV, pp. v-xiv.

"I knew Eric Gill in England as a lovable person and as an artist, and after 1917 never saw him again. We were both of us beginning to grow up then; and since then we have corresponded regularly and were in very close agreement about fundamentals . . ." (p. v). AKC summarizes Gill's views on the problems of human work, vocation, and responsibility in a modern industrialized society. "Of [Gill's] powers as an artist I shall not say anything here except to remark that the precision of his writing corresponds to that of the lettering of which he was an acknowledged master. I shall only allude to one of his outstanding qualities: an ability to recognise the truth, not only in Christian contexts, but wherever he found it" (p. xi).

B62 Some Sources of Buddhist Iconography. *B*[*imala*]. *C*[*hurn*]. *Law Volume*, Part I, edited by D.R. Bhandarkar, K.A. Nilakanta Sastri, B.M. Barua, B.K. Ghosh, and P.K. Gode. Calcutta: The Indian Research Institute, 1945, pp.[469]-476.

"The five notes [that form this paper, i.e. 1. The Buddha as a Pillar of Fire—2. The Kindling of the Dry Wood—3. The Flame on a Buddha's Head—4. The Māra Dharṣaṇa—5. Māra's Headless Troops] are intended to collate a number of texts which can be regarded as the original prescriptions or sanctions that underlie and serve to elucidate the corresponding narratives and representations in Buddhist literature and art" (p.[469]). Reprinted in *Sources of Wisdom* ([1981])—A85—pp. 159-71.

B63 Tanūkṛt. *Bhārata-Kaumudī (Studies in Indology in Honour of Dr. Radha Kumud Mookerji)*, Part I, edited by N.K. Sidhanta, B.C. Law, C.D. Chatterjee, and V.S. Agrawala. Allahabad: The Indian Press Ltd., 1945, pp. 221-5.

On the meaning of this Sanskrit word as it occurs in *Ṛgveda*, VIII. 79, 3 (together with a specimen translation by AKC of that passage).

B64 Understanding and Reunion: An Oriental Perspective. *The Asian Legacy and American Life*, edited by Arthur E. Christy. New York: The John Day Company, An Asia Press Book, Published in Co-operation with The East and West Association [1945], pp. 215-30, 269-70.

A summary of the differences, similarities, and influences between the cultures of Asia and America, with special reference to theatre, music, and dance. A list compiled by AKC of recommended books on the performing arts of Asia is incorporated on pages 222-4.

B65 Brahmanism. *The Encyclopedia Americana*, edited by A.H. McDannald. New York & Chicago: Americana Corporation [1945], *Vol. 4*, pp. 394-394b.

A comprehensive general account. The first (alphabetically) of two articles that AKC contributed to this *Encyclopedia*. AKC's article was retained in all editions to 1952; editions subsequent to that have not been sighted by the compiler.

B66 Persian Mythology. *The Encyclopedia Americana*, edited by

A.H. McDannald. New York & Chicago: Americana Corporation [1945], *Vol. 21*, pp. 629d-630.

A general introduction, but singling out for discussion the rôle of the Sīmurgh (Falcon, or Eagle) in art and myth. AKC's article was retained in all editions of the *Encyclopedia* to 1952; editions subsequent to that have not been sighted by the compiler.

B67 [Comment on the dancing of La Meri]. *La Meri*. [Camden, Maine: Herald Publishing Co., 1945?], p.[11].

A souvenir programme. AKC's is the third of eight comments printed on this page in appreciation of La Meri, i.e. pseud. of the American ethnological danseuse, Russell Meriwether Hughes, 1898?-1988.

B68 What Is Civilization? *The Albert Schweitzer Jubilee Book*, edited by A.A. Roback, J.S. Bixler, and George Sarton. Cambridge, Mass.: Sci-Art Publishers [1946], pp. 261-74 (*i.e.* Pt. IV, Chap. XII).

An historical analysis of the concept of civilization, based on Eastern and Western sources. AKC also considers the etymological significance, or intrinsic meaning, of the words "civilization", "city", "politics", and the Sanskrit word "*puruṣa*". This article was reprinted, with words in Greek script romanized, in *Sources of Wisdom* ([1981]) —A85—pp. 57-75, and again, but with the word "Civilization" in the title spelled "Civilisation", in *What Is Civilisation? and Other Essays* ([1989])—A90—pp.[1]-12.

B69 Inspiration. *Encyclopedia of the Arts*, edited by Dagobert D. Runes and Harry G. Schrickel. New York: Philosophical Library [1946], pp. 468-9.

AKC points out that the term has always implied "the inward breathing of an informing spirit", but is "nowadays frequently misused by art critics . . . when they mean 'stimulate'". As evidence for how "inspiration" has traditionally been understood, AKC cites passages from Hesiod, Homer, Plato, Plotinus, St John, Dante, Meister Eckhart, and the *Aitareya*

Brāhmaṇa. The first (alphabetically) of two articles that AKC contributed to this *Encyclopedia*. Reprinted by Peter Owen (London, 1965).

B70 Participation. *Encyclopedia of the Arts*, edited by Dagobert D. Runes and Harry G. Schrickel. New York: Philosophical Library [1946], p. 724.

That "the material work . . . *participates* in the reality of its thesis . . .", also "that the formal cause (or meaning) is really *present* in the actual shape of the work of art", and furthermore, "that all existences are what they are 'by participation' in their principle". Reprinted by Peter Owen (London, 1965).

B71 [Supplementary footnotes]. *Myths and Symbols in Indian Art and Civilization*, by Heinrich Zimmer, edited by Joseph Campbell. New York: Pantheon Books Inc., Bollingen Series VI, 1946, pp. 14, 24, 27, 39, 60, 76, 90, 98, 103, 116, 123, 125, 128, 134, 136, 137, 138, 142, 143, 144, 157, 160, 162, 163, 169, 172, 175, 177, 183, 184, 189-90, 219.

"Dr. Ananda K. Coomaraswamy very kindly supplied a number of supplementary notes to complete the work [left unfinished by Heinrich Zimmer, who died in New York on 20 March 1943]. His additions have been introduced in square brackets and initialed AKC; undoubtedly they would have met with the approval of Dr. Zimmer. I am indebted to Dr. Coomaraswamy, also . . . for many indispensable emendations throughout the length of the text" ("Editor's Foreword", dated 28 Oct. 1945, p.[vi]). Among AKC's notes is a discussion of the metaphysical significance of grammatical gender (p. 123), and the "difficult Christian doctrine" of *extra Ecclesiam nulla salus*, together with a brief comment on *The Perennial Philosophy*, by Aldous Huxley (p. 219).

B72 Symplegades. *Studies and Essays in the History of Science and Learning Offered in Homage to George Sarton on the Occasion of His Sixtieth Birthday 31 August 1944*, edited by M.F. Ashley Montagu. New York: Henry Schuman [1946], pp.[463]-488.

AKC considers the many forms of the Active Door (e.g. the "Clashing Rocks" of Greek myth and the "strait gate" of Christianity), and the universal distribution and significance of this motif of a passage to the Otherworld; with reference to the appendix on "Floating Islands" in A.B. Cook's *Zeus*. "The materials collected even in the present short article [i.e. from Indian, American Indian, and Celtic, as well as from Greek sources] should suffice to convince the reader that, as the late Sir Arthur Evans once wrote, 'The coincidences of tradition are beyond the scope of accident'" (p. 480). On page 477 (and again on page 481), AKC refers to a work-in-progress, "The Early Iconography of Sagittarius-Kṛṣānu". This essay remained unfinished at the time of his death, and has not been published. Reprinted, with minor omissions and other changes, in *Studies in Comparative Religion*, Bedfont, Middx., VII. 1 (Winter 1973) 35-56, and, without those changes, but incorporating some minor addenda, in *Coomaraswamy 1: Selected Papers, Traditional Art and Symbolism* ([1977])—A82—pp. 521-44. Also reprinted, in a reduced form, as "The Crack Between Two Worlds", in *Parabola*, New York, XV. 1 (Feb./Spring 1990) 40-3, 1 text illus. AKC's original submission to the Sarton Festschrift, an article entitled "On the Indian and Traditional Psychology, or Rather Pneumatology", was rejected (see Roger Lipsey, *Coomaraswamy 3: His Life and Work* ([1977])—E116—pp. 188-9).

B73 For What Heritage and to Whom Are the English-Speaking Peoples Responsible? *The Heritage of the English-Speaking Peoples and Their Responsibility. Addresses at the Conference, October 1946, Kenyon College.* [Gambier, Ohio: Kenyon College, 1947], pp.[48]-65.

A critical analysis of the implications of the West's educational and missionary activities in India, and on the problems in general of intercultural relations. AKC's address to the Conference was given on 4 October. Reprinted, as "Responsibility of the English-Speaking Peoples", in *Mint*, London, II. (1948) 17-33, and, with this title, but substituting: People, for "Peoples", in *Cross Currents*, New York, VI. 1 (Winter 1956) [33]-43, and again, in *Sources of Wisdom* ([1981])—A85—pp. 20-40. A report of the Conference, by Walter W. Ruch, in *The New York Times*, New York, for 5 October 1946, p. 2, entitled "Appeals for India at Kenyon Meeting", incorporates in 41 lines excerpts from AKC's address. Another excerpt is printed as "The 'Curse' of Foreign Rule", in *United Nations World*, New York, for February 1947—C878.

B74 The Sea. *India Antiqua: A Volume of Oriental Studies Presented by His Friends and Pupils to Jean Philippe Vogel, on the Occasion of the Fiftieth Anniversary of His Doctorate*, edited by the Kern Institute – Leyden. Leyden: E.J. Brill, 1947, pp.[89]-94.

On the sea as a symbol of man's entelechy. AKC adduces, by means of a montage of passages excerpted from Hindu, Greek, Jewish, Buddhist, Christian, and Islamic scriptural texts, that this symbolism is the common property of all traditions. AKC also considers the related symbols of the "river" and the "fountain". Reprinted in *Coomaraswamy 1: Selected Papers, Traditional Art and Symbolism* ([1977])—A82—pp. 405-11.

B75 [Letter to K. Bharatha Iyer]. *Art and Thought; Issued in Honour of Dr. Ananda K. Coomaraswamy on the Occasion of His 70th Birthday*, edited by K. Bharatha Iyer. London: Luzac & Company Ltd., 1947, p. xiii.

An excerpt from a letter written in 1944, quoted by the editor in his "Introduction" to this Festschrift. AKC explains to Iyer why he is not interested in writing an autobiography.

B76 Art, Man and Manufacture. *Our Emergent Civilization*, edited by Ruth Nanda Anshen. Science of Culture Series Volume IV. New York & London: Harper & Brothers, Publishers, 1947, pp. 152-74 (*i.e.* Chap. VIII).

A reprint of *The Christian and Oriental or True Philosophy of Art* (1939)—A65, slightly revised, with a reduction of the footnotes, and augmented with the addition of a newly-written concluding section. Reprinted, with these changes, in *Sources of Wisdom* ([1981])—A85—pp. 193-224.

B76a Songs of the Love of Radha and Krishna . . . A Punjabi Love Song . . . Kashmiri Love Song . . . Lachhi . . . New England Woods. *This Strange Adventure: An Anthology of Poems in English by Indians: 1828-1946*, chosen and edited with an introduction and notes by Fredoon Kabraji. [London: New India Publishing Co., Ltd., 1947], pp. 29-36, 130-1.

Reprinted from *Thirty Songs from the Panjab and Kashmīr* ([1913])—A27a, *Vidyāpati: Bangīya Padābali* (1915)—A32, and *Three Poems* (1920)—A41.

B77 [Supplementary footnotes]. *The King and the Corpse. Tales of the Soul's Conquest of Evil*, by Heinrich Zimmer, edited by Joseph Campbell. [New York] The Bollingen Series XI,

Pantheon Books [1948], pp. 39, 40, 48, 77, 79, 83, 166, 257, 270.

"The late Dr. Ananda K. Coomaraswamy generously read the galleys, offered valuable suggestions, and supplied a few supplementary notes to complete the references [left by Heinrich Zimmer, who died in New York on 20 March 1943]. The latter appear in bracketed footnotes, with his initials" ("Editor's Foreword", dated 9 September 1947, p.[v]).

B78 [A comment on the symbolism of the "hook" in William Law]. *Selected Mystical Writings of William Law*, edited by Stephen Hobhouse. Second Edition Revised. London: Rockliff, 1948, "Appendix Three: Additional Notes for Second Edition", pp. 393-4.

A lengthy passage excerpted from a letter, of unspecified date, from AKC to Hobhouse.

B79 [Excerpt from a letter to S. Durai Raja Singam, etc.]. *Homage to Ananda K. Coomaraswamy. A Garland of Tributes*, edited by S. Durai Raja Singam. [Kuala Lumpur: Printed for the editor by The Malayan Printers, 1948], pp. 24, 144-5, 176.

The following material by AKC is printed here for the first time or for the first time in book-form: an excerpt (on Gandhi) from a letter to S. Durai Raja Singam [15 Aug. 1947], in facsimile of AKC's handwritten original, p. 24; the text of his seventieth birthday speech, i.e. "Dr. Coomaraswamy's Talk at His Boston Dinner" (1947)—C875, printed as part of James Marshall Plumer's "The Farewell Dinner", pp. 140-6; and a line, concerning his retirement plans, excerpted from a letter of [Aug.] 1947 to Jayanta Padmanabha, p. 176.

B80 [Excerpt from a letter to Eric Gill]. *Letters of Eric Gill*, edited by Walter Shewring. London: Jonathan Cape [1947, *i.e.* 1948], p. 404.

An excerpt, printed in 15 lines, from a letter dated 29 June 1938. Comprises criticism of a passage in Gill's lecture "Work and Culture", together with comments on Lucien Lévy-Bruhl and "primitive" societies. Gill's reply is printed on the same page. (This volume includes eight letters in all from Gill to AKC.) Evan R. Gill, in his *Bibliography of Eric Gill* (1953), says that the date of publication was January 1948, not "1947" as stated on the copyright page.

B81 Buddhism. *Religion in the Twentieth Century*, edited by Vergilius Ferm. New York: The Philosophical Library, Inc. [1948], pp. 61-79.

A general introduction to this tradition's history, doctrine and method, Buddhology, and cosmogony, together with a bibliography comprising 33 items. A brief biographical note on AKC by the editor is printed on page [60]. Reprinted as *Living Schools of Religion* (Ames, Iowa: Littlefield, Adams & Co., 1958), with the text of AKC's article unaltered and the original pagination preserved. The article was also reprinted in *Sources of Wisdom* ([1981])—A85—pp. 111-36.

B82 Gradation, Evolution and Reincarnation. *Vishveshvaranand Indological Series—2: Siddha-Bhāratī . . . or The Rosary of Indology. Presenting 108 Original Papers on Indological Subjects in Honour of the 60th Birthday of Dr. Siddeshwar Varma . . . Part Two*, edited by Vishva Bandhu. Hoshiarpur, India: Vishveshvaranand Vedic Research Institute, Printing and Publishing Organization [1950], pp.[25]-28.

An exact reprint, for the first time in book-form, of the article with this title in *Main Currents in Modern Thought*, Port Chester, N.Y., for July 1946—C866. A list of "Errata" is printed on page 345. The publication of this Festschrift was to have coincided with Siddeshwar Varma's birthday, 3 November 1947.

B83 Correspondence from Dr. Ananda K. Coomaraswamy. *The Methods of Construction of Celtic Art*, by George Bain. Glasgow: MacLellan [1951], p. 20.

Two letters to George Bain, dated 26 February and 13 June 1947, are printed under this heading. In the first, on fibulae, AKC acknowledges Bain's "excellent booklets on Celtic Art", and says he is sending him "The Iconography of Dürer's 'Knots' and Leonardo's 'Concatenation'" (1944)—C838; the second letter discusses the meaning of the motif of the "two birds". (I am indebted to Mr Ken White for drawing my attention to this item.) Reprinted by Dover Publications, Inc. (New York, 1972).

B84 Some Survivals in Sinhalese Art. *Souvenir and Guide to the Colombo Exhibition. February 16th to March 16th 1952.*

Colombo: Government Information Department [1952], pp. 23-32, 22 text illus.

A reprint, for the first time in book-form, with the omission of the footnotes and other (minor) omissions, from *Journal of the Royal Asiatic Society (Ceylon Branch)*, Colombo, for 1906—C93.

B85 [Contra Cartesium, etc.]. *Homage to Ananda Coomaraswamy: (A Memorial Volume) A Garland of Tributes*, edited by S. Durai Raja Singam. [Kuantan & Singapore: Printed for the editor by Liang Bros., & Co.] 1952, pp. ix, 137-48, unnumbered plate facing p. 292, 324.

The following material by AKC is printed here for the first time or in book-form for the first time: "Contra Cartesium" (1944)—C846, p. ix; "I Meet Ananda K. Coomaraswamy" (1947)—C882, pp. 137-48; letter (complete) to B.S. Sitholey, 6 Oct. 1935, in facsimile of AKC's holograph, unnumbered plate facing p. 292; excerpts from letters of unspecified date (on Theosophy) to Wesley N. Needham, p. 324. Brief excerpts from other letters and articles by AKC are printed *passim*. The letters to Wesley N. Needham are printed in full in *Selected Letters of Ananda K. Coomaraswamy* (1988)—A89—pp. 39, 127-8.

B86 [Letters to S. Durai Raja Singam]. *Letters of the Great; Received by S. Durai Raja Singam, Kuantan, Malaya*, edited by S. Durai Raja Singam. [Singapore: Reproduced from typewriting for the editor by Kwok Yoke Weng & Co., 1954], pp. 33-55.

Nineteen letters from AKC to S. Durai Raja Singam, and to his son, Gandhikijai Singam, written between 13 December 1945 and 2 September 1947, occupy these pages. Title on front wrapper has the word "*to*" in place of the words "*Received by*". Sixty copies were printed (for private circulation). The letter of May 1946 (p. 35) was reprinted in *Span*, New Delhi, for March 1973—C897, and this letter together with those of 26 October 1946, 26 April and 21 July 1947, were reprinted in *Selected Letters of Ananda K. Coomaraswamy* (1988)—A89—pp. 351-2, 365, 380. All nineteen letters were also printed separately as *Letters of Ananda Coomaraswamy* (1972)—A78.

B87 Art and Craftsmanship. *Reflections on Art: A Source Book of Writings by Artists, Critics and Philosophers*, edited by

Susanne K. Langer. Baltimore: The Johns Hopkins Press, 1958, pp. 240-2.

A reprint, for the first time in book-form, from *Rupam*, Calcutta, for April 1920—C426.

B88 What Might Have Been: The Village Community and Modern Progress. *Organising for Development: Progress and Reaction in Ceylon, 1947-1963*, edited by C.R. Hensman. Colombo: *Community* Series No. 7, 1964, pp. 36-48.

A reprint, for the first time in book-form, of "The Village Community and Modern Progress" in *Ceylon National Review*, Colombo, for August 1908—C181. Information from H. A. I. Goonetileke, *A Bibliography of Ceylon* (Zug, Switzerland, 1970), *Vol. II*, no. 4822.

B89 [The Meaning of Death]. *What Happens When You Die? Twentieth Century Thought on Survival After Death*, edited by August H. Wagner. New York: Abelard-Schuman [Limited, 1968], pp. 46-9.

A letter, written *circa* 1943-44, in reply to a questionnaire circulated by Wagner. (I am indebted to Mr George Pollard for calling my attention to this item.) Reprinted, with this title, with minor changes and the addition of a new concluding sentence, in *Coomaraswamy 2: Selected Papers, Metaphysics* ([1977])—A82—pp. 426-9 (the letter is mistakenly referred to there, in an editorial note on page 426, as a hitherto "unpublished work").

B90 [Excerpts from letters to William Rothenstein]. *Imperfect Encounter; Letters of William Rothenstein and Rabindranath Tagore 1911-1941*, edited by Mary M. Lago. Cambridge, Mass.: Harvard University Press, 1972, pp. 5, 31, 33.

Mary Lago quotes from three letters to Rothenstein dated 22 December 1909 (mustering support for E.B. Havell), 10 October 1910 (on the Indian element in Mughal art), and 17 February [1911] (urging Rothenstein to visit Tagore at Santiniketan, Bengal). The second of these letters is printed complete in "Sir William Rothenstein and His Indian Correspondence", by Kenneth Romney Towndrow, in *Art and Letters*, London (1951)—C893, and in *Selected Letters of Ananda K. Coomaraswamy* (1988)—A89—pp. 372-3.

B91 [Lecture notes, articles, letters, etc.]. *Ananda Coomaraswamy: Remembering and Remembering Again and Again*, edited by S. Durai Raja Singam. [Kuala Lumpur: Printed for the editor by Khee Meng Press] 1974, pp. xix, xxix-xxxii, 67, [170], 188, 221, 223, 247, [251], 261, 273-6, 312-14, 327, 331, 373.

The following material by AKC is printed here for the first time or in book-form for the first time: excerpts from a letter to S. Durai Raja Singam, 15 Aug. 1947, in facsimile of AKC's holograph, pp. xix, [170]; "A Yale University Address (Fragmentary) Unpublished of Dr. Ananda Coomaraswamy [,] Yale, April 13, 1942" (on the traditional doctrine of art), with an editorial note on p. xxxii: "These lecture notes, never before published, appear in this Volume by arrangement with Princeton University Press and Rama P. Coomaraswamy, M.D.", pp. xxix-xxxii; annotations to *The Thirteen Principal Upanishads*, translated by Robert Ernest Hume, a spread from AKC's interleaved copy reproduced in facsimile, p. 67; the text, including the title-page and tail-piece, of *Three Poems* (1920)—A41, reproduced in facsimile of the printed pamphlet, p. 188; slips containing drafts of entries for words of Indian origin, submitted to the General Editor of *Webster's New International Dictionary of the English Language*, Second Edition (1934)—D2, reproduced in facsimile of AKC's handwritten and typewritten originals, p. 221; excerpt from a letter (mainly on René Guénon) to Kurt F. Leidecker, 16 Nov. 1941, p. 223; a quatrain (on a teapot) sent to his landlady, *circa* 1897, p. 247; "Doverow Once More" (1895)—Cl, reproduced in facsimile of the printed article, p.[251]; a typewritten genealogical chart of the Coomaraswamy family, reproduced in facsimile, p. 261; "The Farewell Dinner" (1948)—C875 *n.*, pp. 273-6; excerpts from four letters to Arthur Sibly, 8 Dec. 1930, 14 Nov. 1931, 12 and 18 Jan. 1932, pp. 312-14; "War—in India and Outside. [Letter]" (1932)—C624, p. 314; an undated note to K.N. Iengar(?), reproduced in facsimile of AKC's holograph, p. 327; "Foreword", *Related Arts* (1942)—B55, p. 331; and "A Message" (1944)—C843, p.373. There are other (brief) excerpts from letters and articles by AKC printed *passim*. "A Yale University Address . . . 1942" was reprinted, in part, in *Ananda Coomaraswamy Day 1975. 09. 09* [*Souvenir Programme*] (Peradeniya, Sri Lanka: The Arts Council, University of Sri Lanka, 1975), p. 4. The letter to Kurt F. Leidecker is printed complete in *Selected Letters of Ananda K. Coomaraswamy* (1988)—A89—pp. 49-50.

B92 Who Is "Satan" and Where Is "Hell"? *Disguises of the Demonic; Contemporary Perspectives on the Power of Evil*, edited by Alan M. Olson. New York: Association Press, 1975, pp. 57-68.

A reprint, for the first time in book-form, from *Review of Religion*, New York, for November 1947—C887.

B93 [Articles, letters, etc.]. *Ananda Coomaraswamy: A Study*, by Moni Bagchee. Varanasi: ["Bharata Manisha Research Series 9"] Bharata Manisha [1977], pp. 135-84.

"Appendix I. Some Writings of Coomaraswamy", occupies these pages and prints the following: "Mahatma" (1939)—B48, pp. 135-9; an excerpt, entitled "At Seventy", from "Dr. Coomaraswamy's Talk at His Boston Dinner" (1947)—C875, pp. 139-41; excerpts, the first of which is entitled "The Problem of Untouchability", from *The Religious Basis of the Forms of Indian Society* (1946)—A70, pp. 141-4; excerpts from "What India Has Contributed to Human Welfare?" [*sic*] (1915)—C354, pp. 145-8; "The Goods [*sic*] of India" (1931)—B34, pp. 148-51; an excerpt, entitled "The Mahabharata", from *Myths of the Hindus & Buddhists* (1913)—A29, pp. 152-3; an excerpt, entitled "Aesthetics and Relationships of Jaina Paintings", from "Notes on Jaina Art" (1914)—C333, printed here in book-form for the first time, pp. 153-7; excerpts, entitled "Philosophy of Art", from *Why Exhibit Works of Art?* (1943)—A67, pp. 157-60; "Paintings of Tagore", i.e. "Drawings by Rabindranath Tagore" (1930)—C575, pp. 160-3; "Four Days in Orissa", (1911)—C271, printed here in book-form for the first time, pp. 163-7; "Indian Images with Many Arms" (1913)—C305, pp. 167-71; "Three Letters", comprising "War—in India and Outside" (1932)—C624, pp. 172-3, and two letters to Jaideva Singh, 14 Feb. and 19 May 1947, printed here for the first time, pp. 173-5; "Two [Rabindranath] Tagore Poems", comprising AKC's translations of "Janmakatha" (with Ajit Chakravarti) and "Bidaya" [*sic*] (1911)—C270, 272, pp. 176-9; and excerpts from *Spiritual Authority and Temporal Power in the Indian Theory of Government* (1942)—A66, pp. 179-84. The material on pp. 40-1, described as written by AKC is in fact a report by Ardelia Ripley Hall of AKC's conversation, excerpted from Hall's article "The Keeper of the Indian Collection: An Appreciation of Ananda Kentish Coomaraswamy"—E80—p. 108.

B94 [Articles, letters, etc.]. *Ananda Coomaraswamy—the Bridge Builder; a Study of a Scholar-Colossus*, by S. Durai Raja Singam. [Kuala Lumpur: Printed for the author by Khee Meng Press] 1977, pp. [6, 34, 59, 63-4, 65-79, 123-4, 127, 131, 132, 157-8, 159, 164-5, 197, 201-4, 228, 247, 259, 278-80, 282-6, 297-304, 320, 332, 343, 350, 379, 403-4, 443-5, 446, 451, 453, 454, 459, 461, 472, 494, 495, 496, 497, 498, 500, 502-3, 512, 523, 596].

The following material by AKC is printed here for the first time or in book-form for the first time: an excerpt (?) from a letter to Columba Cary-Elwes, 18 Aug. 1947, p.[6]; excerpts from letters to James Marshall Plumer, René Guénon, 2 Apr. 1946, Stanley Nott, 15 Feb. 1945, and a translation from Apollonius of Tyana, *Ep.* LVIII, p.[34]; letter to S. Durai Raja Singam, May 1946, in facsimile of AKC's typewritten original, p.[59]; "Public Reception to Dr. A. K. Coomaraswamy . . ." (1906)—C114, pp.[63-4]; excerpts from letters to William Rothenstein, 23 June 1910, James Marshall Plumer, 16 Nov. 1942, Sidney Lewis Gulick, 21 July 1943, Hermann Goetz, 17 and 22 Jan. 1947, Vasudeva S. Agrawala, 23 Mar. and 31 May 1939, Howard C. Hollis, 3 and 9 Aug. 1934, 15 July 1942, K. Bharatha Iyer, 6 June 1944 and 19 Mar. 1945, Albert Gleizes, Walter Shewring, 26 June 1945 and 6 Aug. 1947, Joseph Campbell, 23 Aug. 1947, Jaideva Singh, 6 Aug. 1947, Marco Pallis, 20 Aug. 1944, Ethel Mairet, 1 June 1945, K. M. Talgeri, 29 Aug. 1946 (the complete letter is printed on p.[494]), unnamed correspondent, 5 Apr. 1947, Fernando Nobre, 31 Oct. 1946, Robert Allerton Parker, 19 Nov. 1944, 27 Jan. 1945, and 20 Oct. 1946, F.S.C. Northrop, 4 July 1944 and 5 June 1946, M.(?), Margaret F. Marcus, 23 Nov. 1931, Porter Sargent, 19 Mar. 1945, Artemas Packard, 26 Mar. 1941, George Sarton, 2 Nov. 1942, Ade Bethune, 16 June 1939 (further excerpts from this letter are printed on pp.[459, 495]), Jean David, 15 July 1944, H.C.P. Bell, 29 Oct. 1900, pp.[65-79, 123-4]; "Testimonial", dated 11 Oct. 1905, contained in a printed advertisement for Kandyan furniture, reproduced in facsimile, p.[127]; "The Word Cingalese" (1904), "A Mineral from Dimbula" (1905), "Opium, 'Logic' and Hongkong" (1905), "'Thorianite' and Its Evidences" (1905), "Kandyan Art: Some Enquiries" (1905), "Mispronunciation of Ceylon Names" (1906), "An Evening Shadow of Adam's Peak" (1906), reproduced in facsimile of the printed letters—C34, 57, 73, 80, 85, 105, 109, p. [131]; *Borrowed Plumes* ([1905])—A3, reproduced in facsimile of the printed pamphlet, p.[132]; letter (complete) to Secretary, Ceylon University Association, 1 Jan. 1906—C111, pp.[157-8]; excerpt from letter to Patrick Geddes, 15 Jan. 1912, p.[159] (two further excerpts from this letter are printed on pp.[259, 280]); "Ceylon Social Reform Society. The Jaffna Branch" (1906)—C116, pp.[164-5]; letter (complete?) to Janet Ashbee, 16 Mar. 1909, p. [197]; translations (hitherto unpublished) of poems by Rabindranath Tagore, reproduced in facsimile of AKC's holograph, pp.[201-4]; excerpt from "Lecture at Trincomalee" (1905)—C59, p.[228]; excerpt from letter to Helena Mowbray-Clarke, 1 Oct. 1920, and excerpts from interview with AKC, *Japan Advertiser*, Tokyo, 26 July 1920(?), p.[247]; excerpts from letters to Paul Hanley Furfey, 29 Aug. 1935, and *Boston Traveller*, Boston, Dec. 1945, p.[259]; a reading list, sent to S. Durai Raja Singam, 1946, pp.[278-9]; excerpts from letters to Patrick Geddes, 30 Mar. 1912, Walter Shewring, 27 Feb. 1938 (further excerpts from this letter are printed on pp.[284-6]), 2 Jan. 1946, pp. [279-80]; excerpts from letters to Joseph T. Shipley, 6 Apr. 1942, Margaret F. Marcus, 18 Dec. 1939, Murray Fowler, 4 Mar.1944, George Sarton, 6 Feb. 1945, Bernard Kelly, 9 Apr. 1947, pp.[282-3, 285]; 29 letters and postcards to Duggirala Gopalakrishnayya, 1914-16, pp. [297-304]; excerpts from letters to George Sarton, Margaret F. Marcus, William Rothenstein, and M.N. Rao, 6 Jan. 1945, pp. [320, 332, 343, 350]; letter (complete) to G. & C. Merriam Co., 15 Apr. 1929, p. [379]; letter (complete) to Romain Rolland, 22 Aug.1920, pp.[403-4]; excerpts from 5 letters to Arthur Sibly, written between 18 Dec. 1930 and 6 Dec. 1943, pp. [443-5]; excerpts from letters to unnamed recipients, 23 June 1910, 6 Feb. 1916, p. [446]; letter (complete) to *Boston Traveller*, Boston, ? Dec. 1943, p.[451]; note (complete) to Joseph T. Shipley, 23 Oct. 1944, in facsimile of AKC's holograph, p.[453]; notes to A. Graham Carey, 24. Feb. 1936, in facsimile of AKC's holograph, p.[454]; excerpt from a letter to Richard Ettinghausen, 26 Aug. 1942, p.[459]; a page from AKC's notebooks, in facsimile of his typewritten and handwritten original, p.[461]; letter (complete) to Alfred Stieglitz, 4 Mar. 1923, in facsimile of AKC's holograph, p.[472]; postcard to Eric Gill and Walter Shewring,

13 Jan. 1936, in facsimile of AKC's holograph, p. [495]; letter (complete) to Robert Allerton Parker, containing "Contra Cartesium" (1944)—C846, 10 Nov. 1944, in facsimile of AKC's typewritten original, p.[496]; letter (complete) to Duggirala Gopalakrishnayya, 1 June 1911, in facsimile of AKC's holograph, p.[497]; letter (complete) to Kodando Rao, 10 Apr. 1947, p. [498]; postcard to James Marshall Plumer, 26 Jan. 1942, and letters (complete) to F.L. Woodward, 18(?) Aug. 1931, G.A. Natesan, 30 Dec. 1910, Howard C. Hollis, 10 Mar. 1942, Joseph T. Shipley, 20 Feb. and 21 Apr. 1942, Walter Shewring, 21 Aug. 1946, Schuyler Cammann, 8 Feb. 1947, in facsimile of AKC's handwritten and typewritten originals, pp.[500, 502-3]; excerpt from letter to Margaret F. Marcus, 29 Sept. 1946, p.[512]; excerpts from letters to Helen B. Chapin, 21 Oct. 1945, and George Sarton, 4 Nov. 1934, pp.[523, 596]. Numerous (brief) excerpts from other letters and articles are printed *passim*.

B94a [Excerpts from articles, letters, etc.]. *Coomaraswamy 3: His Life and Work*, by Roger Lipsey. Bollingen Series LXXXIX. Princeton: Princeton University Press [1977], pp. 10, 18, 22-5, [27], 28-9, 30, 51, 65, 105, 127-8, 141, 149, 155, 156-7, 158, 166-7, 169-70, 174, 178, 179, 180-1, 184, 187, 190-1, 202, 206, [208], 211-12, 218, 219, 220, 221, 225-6, 228-9, 230, 233, 243, 246, 248-9, 250, 252-4, 256, 273, 277-8, 279.

Contains on these pages, quotations from articles, letters, and other material by AKC, printed here for the first time, or in book-form for the first time, as follows: "Public Reception to Dr. A.K. Coomaraswamy . . .", pp. 10, 18; "The Ceylon Social Reform Society. Manifesto", anonymous, but almost certainly in part by AKC, pp. 22-5; a synopsis of "Some Kandyan Crafts" (lecture), contained in a printed advertisement, reproduced in facsimile as Figure 6, p.[27]; "Kandyan Art: What It Meant and How It Ended", pp. 28-9; "Anglicisation of the East", pp. 29, 30; letter to Meyer Schapiro, 30 Apr. 1932, pp. 51, 279; epigram from a Christmas (1918) greeting card, p. 65; "Love and Art", p. 105; "The Cave Paintings of Ajanta . . .", pp. 127-8; two letters to Mary Mowbray-Clarke, 29 Oct. 1920(?), p. 141, 1 Oct. 1920, p. 155; introduction to *A Catalog of Sculptures by John Mowbray-Clarke* . . ., p. 149; four letters to Alfred Stieglitz, 4 March 1923, 25 Apr. 1923, 7 Feb. 1924, 7 Mar. 1924, pp. 156-7; "A Gift from Mr. Alfred Stieglitz", p. 158; "Maha-Pralaya and Last Judgement", pp. 166-7; introductory note to a translation of "Sacred and Profane Science", by René Guénon, pp. 169-70; four letters to S.E., 26 Feb. 1942, p. 174, 27 May 1941, p. 202, 1941, pp. 206, 230, 20 Feb. 1941, p. 233, and two letters to Walter Shewring, 27 Feb. 1938, p. 178, 4 Mar. 1936, pp. 219, 249; "On Translation: Māyā, Deva, Tapas", p. 179; "Two Vedântic Hymns from the *Siddhântamuktâvalī*", pp. 180-1; letter to Marco Pallis, 20 Aug. 1944, pp. 184, 249; letter addressed to but not used by *Apollo*, London, 23 Feb. 1938, p. 187; letter to Stella Bloch, 15 Nov. 1939, pp. 190-1; a page of manuscript notes, reproduced in facsimile as Figure 30, p.[208]; letters to Hermann Goetz, 17 Jan. 1947, pp. 211-12, Paul Dinkins, 1 Aug. 1944, p. 218, S. L. G., 21 July 1943, p. 219, John Layard, 11 Aug. 1947, p. 220, Aldous Huxley, 28 Sept. 1944, p. 220, unnamed correspondents, Summer 1947, pp. 221, 250, 7 July 1947, p. 246, and Hilla Rebay, 29

Aug. 1947, pp. 225-6; "The Relation of Art to Life in India" (radio broadcast), pp. 228-9; two letters to *The New English Weekly*, London, 1 Apr. 1943, 4 Oct. 1945, p. 230; "The Symbolism of Archery", p. 243; letters to K. Bharatha Iyer, 19 Mar. 1945, p. 248, and Ethel Mairet, 1 June 1945, pp. 248-9; "Dr. Coomaraswamy's Talk at His Boston Dinner" (complete), pp. 252-4; translation of an excerpt (on death) from Apollonius of Tyana, *Ep.* LVIII, p. 256 (the second paragraph of which, although captioned "Note by AKC", is by Apollonius); note, p. 273; "A Lecture on Comparative Religion", p. 275; and "Gradation and Evolution—II", pp. 277-8. There are brief quotations *passim* from other articles and letters by AKC. See also A82 and E116.

B95 Archaic Indian Terracottas. *From River Banks and Sacred Places: Ancient Indian Terracottas. An Exhibition to Commemorate the One-Hundredth Anniversary of the Birth of Ananda K. Coomaraswamy . . . August 23–December 31, 1977*, introductory remarks by Pramod Chandra and reprinted essay by Ananda K. Coomaraswamy. Catalogue by Joyce Paulson. [Boston] Museum of Fine Arts, Boston [1977], pp. 6-24, 51 text illus.

A reprint, for the first time in book-form, from *Ipek*, Leipzig (1928)—C514. AKC's dating and classifications have in some cases been revised in the light of new archaeological evidence. These emendations, cross-referenced to the article, are incorporated by Joyce Paulson in her catalogue, which occupies pages 24-47. Pramod Chandra's remarks, on pages 4-5, are headed "A Tribute to Ananda Coomaraswamy (1877-1947)"—E22. There is also a "Preface" (on AKC), by Jan Fontein, page 3.

B96 [Conversations with, and letters to, Dorothy Norman]. *Encounters: A Memoir*, by Dorothy Norman. San Diego, New York, London: "A Helen and Kurt Wolff Book", Harcourt Brace Jovanovich, Publishers [1987], pp. 77, 78-83, 141-3.

In the course of this memoir AKC's reported conversation is given in quotation marks as his direct words; excerpts are printed from two letters: the date of the first is not specified, the second is of November 1938. See also "The Last Time I Saw Coomaraswamy"—E138, where Norman reproduces a conversation she had with AKC in 1947.

C. Contributions by Ananda K. Coomaraswamy to Periodicals, including Newspapers, Annuals, Reports, Proceedings and Transactions of Societies, Etc.

C. Contributions to Periodicals

1895

C1 Doverow Once More. *Wycliffe Star*, Stonehouse, Glos., XXXIV. (Apr. 1895) 2-5.

On the geology of Doverow Hill in Gloucestershire. This article was written by AKC when he was seventeen, while a pupil at Wycliffe College, and published in the magazine of that school. Reprinted, in facsimile of the printed article, in *Ananda Coomaraswamy: Remembering and Remembering Again and Again*, edited by S. Durai Raja Singam (1974)—B91—p. [251].

1899

C2 Excursion to Guildford and Godalming. Saturday, July 15th, 1899. *Proceedings of the Geologists' Association*, London, XVI. 5 (Nov. 1899) 254-5.

AKC's report as excursion director. "The objects of the excursion were to trace the succession from London Clay to Weald Clay, and to see the Peasemarsh anticline" (p. 254). AKC was elected a member of the Geologists' Association on 15 June 1896.

1900

C3 On Ceylon Rocks and Graphite. *Quarterly Journal of the Geological Society*, London, LVI. 223 (Aug. 1900) 590-614, 4 text illus., 1 pl. (numbered: XXXIII, facing p. 614).

A paper read to the Society on 6 June 1900. On the physical geography of Ceylon: the recent deposits, including detailed notes on the crystalline rocks examined *in situ*, and on the origin and mode of occurrence of graphite, with a bibliography comprising thirty items on Ceylon geography and geology, pp. 612-13. A summary of the discussion which followed the reading of this paper is subjoined on p. 615. AKC was made a Fellow of the Geological Society on 7 December 1898.

C4 Excursion to Guildford. Saturday, June 23rd, 1900. *Proceedings of the Geologists' Association*, London, XVI. 10 (Nov. 1900) 512-13.

AKC's report as excursion director.

1901

C5 [A review of] E. Weinschenck [*sic*, for Weinschenk]. *Zur kenntniss der graphitlagerstätten.* III. "Die graphitlagerstätten der Insel Ceylon". *Geological Magazine*, London, N.S. Decade IV, VIII. 4 (Apr. 1901) 175-7.

(In English.) "I have attempted in this review merely to give an abstract of Professor Weinschenck's [*sic*] views as expressed in his important paper" (p. 177). A separately paginated offprint seen (April 1973) at the National Museum Library, Colombo.

C6 Note on the Occurrence of Corundum as a Contact-Mineral at Pont Paul near Morlaix (Finistère). *Quarterly Journal of the Geological Society*, London, LVII. 226 (May 1901) 185-8, 3 text illus.

A paper read at a meeting of the Society on 9 January 1901. On p. 209 of the same issue some reported comments from AKC are printed in six lines under the heading: "Discussion of J. Parkinson's Notes on the Geology of South Central Ceylon" (pp. 206-10).

C7 The Circulation of Salt. [Letter]. *Geological Magazine*, London, N.S. Decade IV, VIII. 12 (Dec. 1901) 575-6.

Calling attention to "The Sea Mills of Cephalonia", by F.W. and W.O. Crosby, in *Technology Quarterly*, Boston, for March 1896.

1902

C8 [A review of] *Mémoire sur l'Histoire Géologique du Graphite*, by E. Weinschenck [*sic*, for Weinschenk].

Geological Magazine, London, N.S. Decade IV, IX. 4 (Apr. 1902) 180-1.

(In English.)

C9 Excursion to Guildford and Godalming. Saturday, May 10th, 1902. *Proceedings of the Geologists' Association*, London, XVII. 7/8 (May/July 1902) 371-2, 1 text illus.

AKC's report as director and excursion secretary.

C10 Occurrence of Radiolaria in Gondwána Beds Near Madras. *Geological Magazine*, London, N.S. Decade IV, IX. 7 (July 1902) 305-6, 1 pl.(numbered: XVII, facing p. 306).

On some fossilized animalcules obtained by AKC at Sripermatur in 1901.

C11 Origin of the Crystalline Limestones of Ceylon. *Geological Magazine*, London, N.S. Decade IV, IX. 8 (Aug. 1902) 375-8.

AKC outlines his theory that whatever their origin the limestones have existed in a state akin to fusion and, as seen by the intrusion of the granulites, behaved much as igneous rocks.

C12 The Crystalline Limestones of Ceylon. *Quarterly Journal of the Geological Society*, London, LVIII. 231 (Aug. 1902) 399-422, 7 text illus., 2 fold. maps (numbered: XIII, XIV, inserted at p. 422).

A paper read to the Society on 12 March 1902. "A somewhat more complete account than has yet been attempted of the crystalline limestones and their relation to the (igneous) granulites (Charnockite Series) among which they are found. It is based on observations made in Ceylon in 1901, and refers especially to the Kandy and Hakgala districts" (p. 401). The maps are geological sketch-maps drawn by AKC and dated 1902; they show the country between Kandy and Talatuoya, and south-east of Hakgala. A summary of the discussion that followed the reading of this paper is subjoined on pp. 422-4.

C13 Note on the Scenery of Ceylon. *Geological Magazine*, London, N.S. Decade IV, IX. 10 (Oct. 1902) 476-7.

Summary of a paper, mainly on the south central region, that was read at a meeting of the British Association at Belfast on 16 September 1902. This summary was also printed in

Report of the Seventy-Second Meeting of the British Association for the Advancement of Science Held at Belfast in September 1902 (London: John Murray, 1903), pp. 613-14.

C14 The Point-de-Galle Group (Ceylon): Wollastonite-Scapolite Gneisses. *Quarterly Journal of the Geological Society*, London, LVIII. 232 (Nov. 1902) 680-9, 7 text illus., 1 pl. (numbered: XXXIV, facing p. 689).

A paper read to the Society on 18 June 1902. The plate is a geological sketch map by AKC, dated 1901, of Galle Fort and environs.

1903

C15 Serendibite, a New Borosilicate from Ceylon. *Mineralogical Magazine*, London, XIII. 61 (Feb. 1903) 224-7, 1 text illus.

A paper written with G[eorge]. T[hurland]. Prior, and read to the Mineralogical Society on 4 February 1902. On the mode of occurrence, physical characters and chemical composition of a deep indigo-blue coloured mineral discovered by AKC at Gangapitiya (12 miles east of Kandy). "The name 'serendibite', given [by AKC and Prior] to the mineral, is derived from 'Serendib', an old Arab name for Ceylon" (p. 227). This paper was summarized in *Nature*, London, LXV. 1,686 (20 Feb. 1902) 383. AKC gives further details as to serendibite's mode of occurrence in "The Crystalline Limestones of Ceylon"—C12—pp. 420-2.

C16 Observations on the Tiree Marble, with Notes on Others from Iona. *Quarterly Journal of the Geological Society*, London, LIX. 233 (Feb. 1903) 91-103, 5 text illus., 2 pls. (numbered: VI-VII).

A paper read to the Society on 17 December 1902. "Embodies observations made by me in the summer of the present year (1902) . . . Although so well known, and represented in many mineralogical collections, the Tiree Marble has never been described in detail" (p. 91). A summary of the discussion that followed the reading of this paper is subjoined on pp. 103-4.

C17 The *Geologisches Centralblatt*. [Letter]. *Geological Magazine*, London, N.S. Decade IV, X. 5 (May 1903) 239-40.

Dated Peradeniya, Ceylon, 23 March 1903. Commenting on the poor standard of geological abstracting.

C18 List of Fish Teeth from the Bagshot Sands (London Basin). *Proceedings of the Geologists' Association*, London, XVIII. 2 ([June] 1903) 83-4.

A paper read to the Association on 5 December 1902.

C19 Are Factories Necessary. [Letter]. *New Age*, London, XV. 455 (18 June 1903) 398-9.

Dated Kandy, 17 May 1903. On the degradation of labour in industrialized society, with reference to a letter by W.E. Larkin in the issue for 23 April 1903. (For AKC's association with this Socialist weekly, see *Coomaraswamy 3: His Life and Work*, by Roger Lipsey (1977)—E116—pp. 110-11.)

C20 Contributions to Ceylon Geology [I]: Occurrence of Corundum *in sitû* Near Kandy, Ceylon. *Geological Magazine*, London, N.S. Decade IV, X. 8 (Aug. 1903) 348-50.

The first of four instalments. "The present notes are based on field observations made in 1900" (p. 348). This article was reprinted in *Tropical Agriculturist (Literary Register Supplement)*, Peradeniya, XXIII. (Dec. 1903) 127-8.

C21 Corundum in Ceylon. [Letter]. *Tropical Agriculturist (Literary Register Supplement)*, Peradeniya, Ceylon, XXIII. (Nov. 1903) 123.

Dated 29 Sept. [1903]. Seeking information of further localities where corundum may be observed in the matrix; with a list of other Ceylon gems not yet discovered *in situ*. This letter was to have accompanied a reprint in *Tropical Agriculturist* of "Contributions to Ceylon Geology [I]: Occurrence of Corundum *in sitû* Near Kandy, Ceylon"—C20, the appearance of which was held over until the issue for December 1903.

C22 Comparisons. [Letter]. *New Age*, London, XV. 480 (10 Dec. 1903) 799.

Dated Ceylon, 16 Nov. 1903. On the high incidence of venereal disease in the British Army.

1904

C23 Mineralogical Survey. Report of the Director of the Mineralogical Survey for 1903. *Ceylon Administration*

Reports for the Year 1903. Colombo: George J.A. Skeen, Government Printer, Ceylon, 1904, Pt. IV, pp. Ll-Ll2, 11 text illus., 2 fold. maps, 2 pls.

The first of AKC's four reports. "Arrangements were made in the latter part of 1902 for the establishment of a mineralogical survey in Ceylon to last for a period of three years. . . . The staff consists of a Director, A.K. Coomaraswamy, B.Sc., F.L.S., F.G.S., and an Assistant Director, James Parsons, B.Sc., F.G.S., who arrived in Ceylon on 7th March [1903]" (p. Ll). The report is dated January 1904, and comprises observations on the general geology of Ceylon and on the mode of occurrence and the distribution of minerals of economic importance, i.e. mica, graphite, iron ore, corundum, moonstone, garnet, and uraninite, with notes on production and methods of working the deposits. Includes a note on the new mineral gallery (renovated by AKC) at the Colombo Museum.

C24 Contributions to the Geology of Ceylon: II. Silicification of Crystalline Limestones. *Geological Magazine*, London, N.S. Decade V, I. 1 (Jan. 1904) 16-19, 1 text illus.

A detailed account of chert occurring as a replacement in limestone, based on observations made in 1903.

C25 The Crystalline Rocks of Ceylon. *Spolia Zeylanica*, Colombo, I. 4 (Feb. 1904) 105-11, 1 text illus., 1 pl.

"[This] paper is intended to give a brief account of the crystalline rocks of Ceylon, so far as at present known and studied" (p. 105).

C26 Uraninite. *Spolia Zeylanica*, Colombo, I. 4 (Feb. 1904) 112-13, 1 text illus.

On a specimen from Gampola, in the Balangoda district of Ceylon, that was forwarded to the Mineralogical Survey by W.D. Holland in 1903. (Most probably this specimen was not pitchblende, as AKC then supposed, but the new mineral, thorianite; see "Mineralogical Notes" (1904)—C32, p. 59.)

C27 Some Reviews. [Letter]. *New Age*, London, XVI. 494 (17 Mar. 1904) 175.

Dated Ceylon, 13 Feb. 1904. On fairy tales, and heroes of legendary story; taking exception to a reviewer's commendation, in the issue for 21 January 1904, of a modern fairy tale by Mark Lemon. AKC also comments on *Phantastes*, by George Macdonald, and the stories of W.W. Jacobs.

C28 A New Mineral from Ceylon. [Letter]. *Ceylon Observer*, Colombo (30 Apr. 1904) 5.

Dated 27 Apr. [1904]. AKC reports on the recent discovery of thorianite, specimens of which had been forwarded to London for analysis. Thorianite is a rare, heavy black mineral occurring in cubic crystals and consisting chiefly of oxides of thorium and uranium. The name was suggested by Wyndham R. Dunstan, the Director of the Imperial Institute, who was the first to publish the discovery, in *Nature*, London, LXIX. 1,796 (31 Mar. 1904) 510-11. A brief (unsigned) announcement appeared simultaneously in the *Bulletin of the Imperial Institute*, London, II. 1 (31 Mar. 1904) 13. AKC's letter was reprinted, as "Thorianite in Ceylon", in *Tropical Agriculturist*, Peradeniya, XXIII. 12 (1 June 1904) 853.

C29 Wesleyans and Gothic Architecture. [Letter]. *New Age*, London, XVI. 511 (14 July 1904) 445-6.

Dated Ceylon, 6 Apr. 1904. That by adopting the defunct Gothic Revival style the Wesleyans will only produce deplorable buildings, with reference to an unsigned article of this title in the issue for 12 May.

C30 The "Peridot" of Ceylon. [Letter]. *Ceylon Observer*, Colombo (20 July 1904) 5.

Dated Kandy, 19 July [1904]. On the mistaken application of the name peridot to a variety of yellow tourmaline. This letter was reprinted in *Tropical Agriculturist*, Peradeniya, XXIV. 3 (1 Sept. 1904) 174.

C31 Contributions to the Geology of Ceylon: III. The Balangoda Group. *Geological Magazine*, London, N.S. Decade V, I. 8 (Aug. 1904) 418-22, 2 text illus.

A detailed account of the types of rock that form this Group—a name proposed by AKC "for a series of granitic and pegmatite rocks . . . first met with in the Balangoda district, but evidently distributed over a large area between Balangoda and Hatton" (p. 418). Erratum to this article is printed in the issue for December 1904, p. 622.

C32 Mineralogical Notes. *Spolia Zeylanica*, Colombo, II. 6 (Aug. 1904) 57-64.

The first of these notes, headed "The New Mineral", pp. 57-60, is a detailed report of the discovery in Ceylon of thorianite. This note (only) was reprinted as "The New Ceylon Mineral"—C36. The other notes concern corundum, sillimanite, phlogopite, kyanite, chert, opal, steatite (talc), stilbite, serendibite, moonstone, kaolin, sphene, and mispickel.

C33 The "Peridot" in Ceylon: In Conclusion. [Letter]. *Ceylon Observer*, Colombo (3 Aug. 1904) 5.

Dated Colombo, 3 Aug.[1904]. This letter was reprinted in *Tropical Agriculturist*, Peradeniya, XXIV. 3 (1 Sept. 1904) 174.

C34 The Word Cingalese. [Letter]. *Nature*, London, LXX. 1,814 (4 Aug. 1904) 319.

Dated Ceylon, 6 July [1904]. AKC points out that "the word should be spelt Sinhalese, the form above quoted being a quite incorrect transliteration".

C35 British Governors-Elect and German Steamers. [Letter]. *Times of Ceylon*, Colombo (30 Aug. 1904).

Signed "Liberty of the Subject", and dated Ratnapura, Ceylon, 28 Aug. 1904. AKC registers his disgust at the indignation expressed by "ardent Imperialists in Ceylon" over the preference, shown by certain high officials, for travel by German instead of British vessels. (This item is known to the compiler only from a clipping.) This letter was reprinted, in a slightly different version, signed A.K.C., and under the heading "Imperial Exclusiveness", in *New Age*, London, XVI. 524 (13 Oct. 1904) 655.

C36 The New Ceylon Mineral. *Tropical Agriculturist*, Peradeniya, XXIV. 4 (1 Oct. 1904) 242-3.

On thorianite. Excerpted from "'Mineralogical Notes" in *Spolia Zeylanica*, Colombo, for August 1904—C32.

C37 The Eton College Beagles: A Protest Against Uncalled-For "Cruelty to Animals". [Letter]. *Ceylon Observer*, Colombo (22 Oct. 1904) 5.

Dated 20 Oct. [1904]. On Dr Edmond Warre (the then headmaster of Eton) and the school's hare hunt.

C38 Celtism—A Reply. [Letter]. *New Age*, London, XVI. 526 (27 Oct. 1904) 687.

Dated Ceylon, 28 Sept. 1904. Chiefly on jingoistic opposition to the Celtic revival, with reference to an article "Celtism", by "Macrobius", in the issue for 8 September.

C39 [A review of] *On Some Important Occurrences of Granular Carbonate Rocks, with Special Reference to their Origin and Structure*. By Bernhard Lindemann. *Geological Magazine*, London, N.S. Decade V, I. 12 (Dec. 1904) 613-15.

In this review AKC summarizes the history of the theory of the origin of crystalline limestones. Two brief references are made by AKC where the theory is applicable to the rocks of Ceylon.

C40 Tamil Plays in Colombo. [Letter]. *Ceylon Observer*, Colombo (5 Dec. 1904) 5.

Dated Kandy, 3 Dec. [1904]. On the Europeanization of these productions.

C41 Socialism and Standing Armies. [Letter]. *Times of Ceylon*, Colombo (6 Dec. 1904).

Dated 26 Nov. [1904]. A reply to a statement in the issue for 30 September that AKC claims is a misrepresentation of the principles of Socialism. (This item is known to the compiler only from a clipping.)

1905

C42 Mineralogical Survey. Report of the Director of the Mineralogical Survey for 1904. *Ceylon Administration Reports for the Year 1904*. Colombo: George J.A. Skeen, Government Printer, Ceylon, 1905, Vol. II, Pt. 4, pp. E1-E21, 10 text illus., 1 fold. map, 3 pls.

The second of AKC's four reports is dated 31 December 1904; some portions are written by the Assistant Director, James Parsons. Comprises accounts detailing the mode of occurrence and commercial value of the deposits of corundum, thorianite, thorite, allanite, the samarskite group, fergusonite, baddeleyite, geikielite, cassiterite, rutile, beryl, chrysoberyl, topaz, tourmaline, spinel, the crystalline limestones, mica, and graphite. Also contains "Manufacture of Iron and Steel" (a description by AKC of the barely surviving traditional processes of iron-smelting and steel-making in Ceylon), pp. E4-E6; "General Account of Gemming in Ceylon", with James Parsons, pp. E11-E15; "Glossary of [Sinhala] Terms Used in Gemming", compiled with James Parsons, pp. E15-E17; and "Museum Work", p. E21. The plates are reproductions of photographs taken by Ethel M. (Mrs A.K.) Coomaraswamy of workings in Ceylon.

C43 Notes on Paddy Cultivation Ceremonies in the Ratnapura District (Nawadun and Kuruwiti Korales). *Journal of the Royal Asiatic Society (Ceylon Branch)*, Colombo, XVIII. 56 (1905) 413-28, 3 text illus.

A paper read (by C.M. Fernando in AKC's absence) to the Society on 17 July 1905. "The *kamat-hẹlla* or threshing-floor song [the words of which are given in Sinhalese script with AKC's English translation facing] forms the main feature of this paper . . . full details [are given] of the proper preparation of the *arak* or talisman that is deposited in the *arakwaḷa* or 'arak-hole' in the threshing-floor" (p. 413). Charms and a fire-walking ceremony are also described. AKC concludes with an entreaty to fellow scholars to collect agrarian and other traditional songs before it is too late. A summary of the discussion that followed the reading of this paper is subjoined on pp. 429-31. AKC had been elected a member of the Ceylon Branch of the Society on 22 June 1903. A separately paginated offprint seen (April 1991) in the collection of Dr Rama P. Coomaraswamy, Greenwich, Conn.

C44 Occurrence of Thorianite in Ceylon. *Proceedings of the Royal Society*, London, Series A, LXXVI. (1905) 254-6.

Forms part of a paper, "Thorianite, a New Mineral from Ceylon", by Wyndham R. Dunstan and G.S. Blake, pp. 253-65, that was read to the Royal Society on 18 May 1905. Apparently excerpted from AKC's otherwise unpublished official reports to the Imperial Institute, London. Dunstan and Blake's paper was also printed, in two parts, in *Chemical News*, London, XCII. 2,380 (7 July 1905) 13-15, and 2,382 (21 July 1905) 26-8; AKC's report occupies pp. 13-14.

C45 The Rope Trick: in Ceylon and Southern India. [Letter]. *Ceylon Observer*, Colombo (3 Feb. 1905) 5-6.

Dated 3 Feb. 1905. Citing a parallel from Irish folklore, and calling for accounts of the trick's performance in Ceylon.

C46 An Open Letter to the Kandyan Chiefs: An Expert on Kandyan Architecture and Painting in the Days of Old. [Letter]. *Ceylon Observer*, Colombo (17 Feb. 1905) 5-6.

An appeal for the better preservation of Buddhist buildings in Ceylon, with particular reference to those of the 17th and 18th centuries; incorporating a description of the wall-paintings in the Degaldoruva temple. This letter was reprinted as a separate ([1905])—A4.

C47 [Unexplored Kandyan Literature]. *Kandyan*, Colombo, II. 5 [*i.e.* 1] (Mar. 1905) 112-15.

Dated Kandy, 29 Dec. 1904. A letter addressed to the editor requesting that more space be given in the periodical to unpublished Sinhalese literature, with reference to an article on William Wordsworth in a previous issue. Reprinted with this title in *Ceylon Observer*, Colombo (23 June 1905) 7.

C48 Irregularly Developed Crystals of Zircon (Sp. Gr. 4·0) from Ceylon. *Spolia Zeylanica*. Colombo, II. 8 (Mar. 1905) 189-90, 1 text illus.

An abstract by AKC of a paper of this title, by L.J. Spencer, that was published in the *Mineralogical Magazine*, London, for October 1904. Concerning "some small isolated crystals from gem-washings in Ceylon [that were forwarded by AKC] to the British Museum for determination and study . . . at first thought to be rutile, but on detailed examination proved to be zircon of a rather unusual type" (Spencer).

C49 The Rocks and Minerals of Ceylon. *Spolia Zeylanica*, Colombo, III. 9 (Mar. 1905) 50-66.

AKC's article forms part of a complete reprinting of the *Colombo Museum. Guide to the Collections* ([3rd edition, 1905])—B2—in this issue of *Spolia Zeylanica*, pp. 1-66. The original pagination and illustrations of the Guide have been preserved.

C50 Tin in Ceylon. *Ceylon Observer*, Colombo (24 Mar. 1905).

Dated Ratnapura, 13 Mar. [1905]. AKC's announcement of the discovery of alluvial tin occurring in small deposits at Niriella in the Ratnapura district. (This item is known to the compiler only from a clipping.) Reprinted in *Tropical Agriculturist*, Peradeniya, XXIV. 10 (15 Apr. 1905) 636, and in *Report on the Occurrence of Cassiterite* . . . ([1905])—A5—p.[1].

C51 Socialism Not a Stomach Question. [Letter]. *New Age*, London, XVII. 548 (30 Mar. 1905) 207.

Dated Kandy, 28 Feb. 1905. On the danger to the Socialist movement of a lapse into materialism, with reference to writers in recent issues who have expressed merely "stomachic considerations".

C52 Western Civilisation and the Sinhalese. [Letter]. *Ceylon Observer*, Colombo (13 Apr. 1905) 5.

Dated Ratnapura, 12 Apr. [1905]. On the debilitating influence of Western encroachment, and, to remedy this, the need to strengthen public opinion amongst the Sinhalese; expressing sympathy with the views of the Anagarika Dharmapala.

C53 Reformation of Sinhalese Dress. [Letter]. *Ceylon Independent*, Colombo (17 Apr. 1905).

Dated 14 Apr. 1905. Written with Ethel M. (Mrs A.K.) Coomaraswamy. On the need to halt the wholesale adoption of English dress among the Sinhalese. (This item is known to the compiler only from a clipping.)

C54 Churches in Ceylon and Their Sites. [Letter]. *Ceylon Observer*, Colombo (22 Apr. 1905) Supplement (i.e. a single unnumbered leaf laid in this issue with AKC's letter printed on the recto).

Dated Kandy, 21 Apr. [1905]. A protest against badly sited Christian churches; AKC singles out St. Paul's in Kandy as a particularly insensitive example.

C55 Social Reform. [Letter]. *Ceylon Independent*, Colombo (25 Apr. 1905).

Dated 21 Apr. [1905]. A reply to a letter (signed: Tom-foolery) in the issue for 18 April, the writer of which reports sighting AKC wearing a Tamil costume. (This item is known to the compiler only from a clipping.)

C56 The Wearing of the Fez. [Letter]. *Times of Ceylon*, Colombo (15? May 1905).

Dated Mawanella, Ceylon, 13 May 1905. Defining the fez, in connection with a recent incident in Colombo where the Chief Justice ordered a Muslim advocate to uncover his head in court. (This item is known to the compiler only from a clipping.)

C57 A Mineral from Dimbula. [Letter]. *Ceylon Observer*, Colombo (8 June 1905) 5.

Dated Kandy, 7 June [1905]. Printed in seven lines, identifying a reader's specimen of tourmaline.

C58 Note [on mica] by the Director of the Mineralogical Survey. *Ceylon Government Gazette*, Colombo, 6,057 (9 June 1905), Pt. I, pp. 459-60.

Dated 19 May 1905. On the commercial feasibility of mining mica in Ceylon. AKC's note is appended to "Report on a Consignment of Mica Forwarded by the Government of Ceylon", by Wyndham R. Dunstan.

C59 Lecture at Trincomalee. *Hindu Organ*, Jaffna (19 July 1905).

A reply to an address by the Tamil community, at the Hindu School (Jaffna) on 12 July. AKC exhorts the Tamils to preserve their language and literature, and to retain their traditional dress. Printed simultaneously in *Ceylon Independent*, Colombo (19 July 1905) 3, and reprinted in *Ceylon Observer*, Colombo (20 July 1905). Information from S. Durai Raja Singam, *Ananda Kentish Coomaraswamy: A Bibliographical Record . . . Part I: 1895-1927* (1981)—E194—pp. 52-4.

C60 Chinese Deficiences. [Letter]. *New Age*, London, XVII. 565 (27 July 1905) 479.

Dated Kandy, 27 June 1905. Highlighting a passage in an issue of the *Proceedings of the*

Royal Artillery Institute that exhibits a contemptuous attitude of the British towards Korean anti-militarism.

C61 Contributions to the Geology of Ceylon: 4. Intrusive Pyroxenites, Mica-Pyroxenites, and Mica-Rocks in the Charnockite Series or Granulites in Ceylon. *Geological Magazine*, London, N.S. Decade V, II. 8 (Aug. 1905) 363-9, 1 pl. (numbered: XX).

Dated Kandy, 19 June 1905. Summarized (by AKC) in *Spolia Zeylanica,* Colombo, III. 11 (Jan. 1906) 201.

C62 The Ceylon Social Reform Society. *Sandaresa*, Colombo, English Supplement, I . 11 (4 Aug. 1905) 3-4.

AKC's address upon being elected the first President of the Society on 29 July, at the Masonic Hall, Galle Face, Colombo. AKC implores the Ceylonese to resist the pernicious effects of the West's cultural hegemony. Reprinted in *Theosophist*, Madras, XXVII. 2 (Nov. 1905) 136-40, with additionally an editorial note, p.136. The Ceylon Social Reform Society was inaugurated on 22 April 1905, at Musaeus College, Colombo. An unsigned statement (almost certainly partly, if not wholly, written by AKC) that appeared in the Society's "Annual Report, 1905-6", a supplement to the *Ceylon National Review*, Colombo, for July 1906, outlines the Society's programme: "[to] foster the growth of an enlightened public opinion amongst Ceylonese, re-awaken in them a sense of the value of their own traditions and national culture—language, literature, art, music, dress—and to promote amongst them that unity and mutual respect which alone can enable them to act together and exert influence of a political character, and assist each other in preserving these invaluable elements of national individuality which are now neglected and in danger of final loss" (p.[5]).

C63 Forced Labour: and Batticaloa P[lanters']. A[ssociation]. [Letter]. *Ceylon Observer*, Colombo (11 Aug. 1905) 5-6.

Dated Nuwara Eliya, Ceylon, 10 Aug. 1905. On a resolution by coconut planters that the traditional Sinhalese mode of cultivation (*chena*) be stopped to provide labour for the estates. Reprinted, under the heading "Forced Labour", in *Sandaresa*, Colombo, English Supplement, I. 13 (18 Aug. 1905) 2-3, and again in *New Age*, London, XVII. 571 (7 Sept. 1905) 572-3.

C64 Education in Ceylon. [Letter]. *Hindu Organ*, Jaffna (16 Aug. 1905).

Dated Kandy, 12 Aug. 1905. That a Westernized curriculum for the Ceylonese is at the cost of an estrangement from their spiritual and traditional inheritance. (This item is known to the compiler only from a clipping.)

C65 The Social Reform Society. [Letter]. *Ceylon Independent*, Colombo (28 Aug. 1905).

Dated Kandy, 25 Aug.[1905]. That the Society did not begin as "a Sinhalese Dress Reform Society"; concluding with a note on the tortoise-shell comb as a "comparatively modern", and effeminate, addition to Sinhalese fashion. (This item is known to the compiler only from a clipping.)

C66 The Social Reform Society. [Letter]. *Sandaresa*, Colombo, English Supplement, I. 16 (8 Sept. 1905) 2.

Dated Ruanwella, 6 Sept. 1905. On Lord Avebury's acceptance of honorary membership.

C67 Molybdenite. [Letter]. *Times of Ceylon*, Colombo (8 Sept. 1905).

Dated Ruanwella, 6 Sept.[1905]. Confirming the occurrence of this sulphide in Ceylon, and describing its physical properties. (This item is known to the compiler only from a clipping.)

C68 Civilization—at Home and Abroad. *Sandaresa*, Colombo, English Supplement, I. 17 (15 Sept. 1905) [1].

On Western influence in Ceylon, South Africa, and Turkey.

C69 Manufacture of Iron and Steel in Ceylon. *Ceylon Observer*, Colombo (18 Sept. 1905), Morning edition, p. [3].

An account of the barely surviving traditional processes of iron-smelting and steel-making, excerpted from "Mineralogical Survey. Report of the Director of the Mineralogical Survey for 1904" (1905)—C42—pp. E4-E6. Reprinted again, as "The Early Iron and Steel Industry of Ceylon", in *Ceylon Geographer*, Colombo, XV. 1/4 (Jan./Dec. 1961) 31-7, 3 text illus., with an editorial note: "The early indigenous iron and steel industry of Ceylon was in its last dying stage when Ananda K. Coomaraswamy wrote his accounts in 1903 and 1904. The location of the industry at this time, and a description of the methods of manufacture employed by the workers are of great interest to the historical geographer. Coomaraswamy's account has been unavailable in print for a considerable time, and in response to many requests, is now being reprinted" (p. 31).

C70 Esperanto—and Local Tongues. [Letter]. *Ceylon Observer*, Colombo (18 Sept. 1905).

Dated Ruanwella, 16 Sept. [1905]. AKC argues that a knowledge of commercial English, when acquired at the expense of Sinhala and Tamil, has no more value to a Ceylonese than that of an artificial language like Esperanto. (This item is known to the compiler only from a clipping.)

C71 A Chinese View of Western Civilization. I. *Sandaresa*, Colombo, English Supplement, I. 18 (22 Sept. 1905) 3.

The first of three instalments. A review of *Letters from a Chinese Official* (by Goldsworthy Lowes Dickinson, anonymously).

C72 Soul. [Letter]. *Sandaresa*, Colombo, English Supplement, I. 18 (22 Sept. 1905) 3.

On Buddhism and the soul.

C73 Opium, "Logic" and Hongkong [*sic*]. [Letter]. *Ceylon Observer*, Colombo (23 Sept. 1905) 7.

Dated Ruanwella, 22 Sept. [1905]. AKC argues that since Australia has prohibited the importation of opium, Britain should either declare war as she did when China was unwilling to allow opium to be imported, or apologize to China and give her back Hong Kong. AKC's point was taken up and expanded to form an editorial comment in the issue for 25 September.

C74 A Chinese View of Western Civilization. II. *Sandaresa*, Colombo, English Supplement, I. 19 (29 Sept. 1905) [1].

C75 Social Reform. *Ceylon*, Colombo, I. 1 (Oct. 1905) [50]-54.

AKC, as President of the Ceylon Social Reform Society (Colombo), replies to accusations that the Society is "opposed to the progress of civilization".

C76 Kandyan Horn Combs. *Spolia Zeylanica*, Colombo, III. 10 (Oct. 1905) 151-4, 2 text illus., 3 pls. (lettered: A-C, following p. 154).

Written in collaboration with Ethel Mary (Mrs A.K.) Coomaraswamy. "A short account of the making of the ordinary 10-cent [buffalo] horn comb . . . more purely native in form and decoration [than the ivory, and the comparatively modern tortoise-shell comb]" (p. 151), with a note on the motifs employed in the carved ornamentation. This article was reprinted, with the omission of the illustrations, in *Ceylon Observer*, Colombo, for 27 October 1905, p. 7, and, in part, with changes, in *Mediaeval Sinhalese Art* ([1908])—A14a—pp. 187-8.

C77 A Chinese View of Western Civilization. III. *Sandaresa*, Colombo, English Supplement, I. 20 (6 Oct. 1905) 4.

C78 The Teaching of Sinhalese. [Letter]. *Sandaresa*, Colombo, English Supplement, I. 21 (13 Oct. 1905) 3.

Dated Avissawella, 7 Oct. [1905]. Pointing out that the vernacular is not taught in Buddhist schools.

C79 Recent Kandyan Architecture. *Sandaresa*, Colombo, English Supplement, I. 21 (13 Oct. 1905) 4.

On two "examples of modern buildings in a would-be Kandyan style": the Ruanwella *ambalama* (resthouse), and the Kandy Bandstand. A separately paginated offprint seen (July 1992) at the Adyar Library and Research Centre, Madras.

C80 "Thorianite" and Its Evidences. [Letter]. *Ceylon Observer*, Colombo (17 Oct. 1905) 5.

Dated Avissawella, 16 Oct. [1905]. On the suppositious occurrence of this mineral in India.

C81 Mr. Henry Holiday on English Dress. *Sandaresa*, Colombo, English Supplement, I. 22 (20 Oct. 1905) [1].

Comprised of two parts, headed: "Monotony" and "Fashion", respectively. Holiday's strictures on modern clothing are applied by AKC in his criticism of the Ceylonese imitation of European fashions (and décor). This article was reprinted, as "Monotony and Fashion", in *Dress Review*, London, II. 1 (1906) 3-6.

C82 The Teaching of Sinhalese. [Letter]. *Sandaresa*, Colombo, English Supplement, I. 22 (20 Oct. 1905) 3.

Dated Avissawella, 16 Oct. 1905. AKC exhorts the Sinhalese to preserve their language.

C83 Recent Marine Clays at Kuchavelli, Ceylon. *Geological Magazine*, London, N.S. Decade V, II. 11 (Nov. 1905) 508-9.

On deposits containing crab and marine shell fossils. Subjoined is a "Note on Some Post-Tertiary Mollusca from Ceylon" (i.e. on fossils collected by AKC at Kuchavelli), by R. Bullen Newton, pp. 509-10. Both articles were summarized by AKC, and augmented with the addition of addenda and corrigenda, in *Spolia Zeylanica*, Colombo, III. 11 (Jan. 1906) 199-200.

C84 A Treatise on the "Dipavamsa" and "Mahavamsa": Correction. [Letter]. *Ceylon Observer*, Colombo (30 Nov. 1905) 5.

Dated Kandy, 29 Nov.[1905]. On Ethel Mary (Mrs A.K.) Coomaraswamy's proposal to translate into English Wilhelm Geiger's prolegomena to his translation of the Pāli chronicles of the early kings of Ceylon, if the Government of Ceylon will print it; correcting an editorial misstatement in the issue for 28 November. (Mrs AKC's translation was published by the Government in 1908.)

C85 Kandyan Art: Some Enquiries. [Letter]. *Ceylon Observer*, Colombo (4 Dec. 1905) 5.

Dated 1 Dec.[1905]. Seeking technical information.

C86 Wearing the Fez in Ceylon. [Letter]. *New Age*, London, XVII. 584 (7 Dec. 1905) 782.

Dated Kandy, 7 Nov. 1905. On a recent ruling by Justices of the Supreme Court that a Muslim advocate might not appear in Court wearing the fez; and quoting a resolution sent by the Ceylon Social Reform Society to the Colonial Secretary in Colombo, appealing for the right to wear national head-dress.

C87 Kandyan Art: Some Further Points. [Letter]. *Ceylon Observer*, Colombo (8 Dec. 1905) 5.

C88 "The Blue Room". [Letter]. *Daily News*, London (8 Dec. 1905).

Dated Ceylon, 15 Nov. 1905. On a photograph published in the 27 October issue of *The Sketch*, London, showing Mr Passmore, an actor in a play of this title, "hiding" in a statue of the Buddha. (This item is known to the compiler only from a clipping.) Reprinted in other newspapers, and, under the heading "Blasphemy", in *New Age*, London, XVII. 585 (14 Dec. 1905) 798, and again, with additional comment (dated Kandy, 2 Jan. [1906]), under the heading "A Blasphemous Play", in *Ceylon Observer*, Colombo (3 Jan. 1906) 5.

C89 Swadeshism in Ireland. *Sandaresa*, Colombo, English Supplement, I. 29 (8 Dec. 1905) 3.

On the Sinn Fein as an example to the Ceylonese.

C90 The Social Reform Society Meeting at Kandy. *Sandaresa*, Colombo, English Supplement, I. 29 (8 Dec. 1905) 4.

The text of AKC's speech of 25 November 1905 at Trinity College Hall: on the Society's decision to form a Kandy branch.

C91 A Rare Bird Shot. [Letter]. *New Age*, London, XVII. 586 (21 Dec. 1905) 815.

Dated Kandy, 12 Nov. 1905. AKC protests against the shooting of a species of quail on Lopham Fen, Norfolk.

1906

C92 Mineralogical Survey. Report of the Director of the Mineralogical Survey for 1905. *Ceylon Administration Reports for the Year 1905*. Colombo: H.C. Cottle, Government Printer, Ceylon, 1906, Vol. II, Pt. 4, pp. E1-E19, 1 text illus., 1 fold. map, 5 pls.

The third of AKC's four reports is undated; portions of this report were written by the Assistant Director, James Parsons. On the mode of occurrence and commercial value of graphite, gold, platinum, thorianite, thorite, monazite, niobates, cassiterite, rutile, galena, molybdenite, and the crystalline limestones, with notes on gemming districts, the Sinhalese method of hand dredging, recent deposits and sub-aerial denudation, the Balangoda Group, intrusive pyroxenites, mica-pyroxenites, and mica-rocks in the granulites, land subsidence at Manippai, museum work, and minerals exported from Ceylon in 1905. Also includes errata and addenda to the glossary of gemming terms that was printed in the Report for 1904—C42. "In October [1905] it was decided that the Mineralogical Survey, originally appointed for three years ending March 7, 1906, should be continued to the end of 1906" (p.E1). The second of the plates (facing page E16) is a reproduction of a photograph of an exposure of crystalline limestone, with AKC, wearing a sola topee and puttees, sitting on the exposure.

C93 Some Survivals in Sinhalese Art. *Journal of the Royal Asiatic Society (Ceylon Branch)*, Colombo, XIX. 57 (1906) 72-89, 20 text illus., 2 pls.

AKC spoke on this paper to the Society on 6 August 1906. An attempt to demonstrate that the origin of several characteristic patterns in Sinhalese (Kandyan) art of the 18th century can be traced to the early art of northern India. "My object in bringing the matter forward now is to provoke discussion and invite criticism, and also to demonstrate the historical value of the study of Sinhalese art and the importance of carefully preserving its remains, as much from the intellectual as from the artistic point of view" (p. 87). This article was reprinted, with omissions, in *Souvenir and Guide to the Colombo Exhibition* ([1952])—B84. See also C125.

C94 Kandyan Art: What It Meant and How It Ended. *Ceylon National Review*, Colombo, I. 1 (Jan. 1906) [1]-12.

An account of traditional Sinhalese art: its national character and the conditions under which it was produced, together with an indictment of the effects of Western encroachment on this old order. *The Ceylon National Review*, a periodical in ten numbers, the organ of the Ceylon Social Reform Society, was founded by AKC and edited by him (he also designed and executed the cover), with the assistance of Wilmot Arthur de Silva and Frank Lee Woodward. To each number, excepting the eighth and ninth, AKC contributed articles and book reviews. The last number appeared in January 1911. In a letter of 21 October 1905 to the Archaeological Commissioner in Ceylon, H.C.P. Bell (in the Bell Collection, National Museum Library, Colombo), AKC described the forthcoming *Review* as: "a magazine, on the one hand to foster national sentiment by historical method, a sort of continuation of the *Orientalist* and *Taprobanian*, and on the other to contain articles on the present situation".

C95 Two Kandyan Brass Boxes. *Ceylon National Review*, Colombo, I. 1 (Jan. 1906) 84-6, 1 pl. (facing p. 86).

A description of 18th or 19th century containers for tobacco or betel leaves: one with an illustration of the *Canda Kinnara Jātaka* chased on the lid, the other decorated with six conventional Kandyan motifs. The plate (only) was reprinted, as three separate text illustrations, in *Mediaeval Sinhalese Art* ([1908])—A14a—pp. 82, 91, 110.

C96 [A review of] *Indian Art at Delhi 1903*, by Sir George Watt. *Ceylon National Review*, Colombo, I. 1 (Jan. 1906) 103-5.

"[The Delhi Exhibition is] in the main a lamentable illustration of the decay of Indian taste and decline of craftsmanship". AKC questions the criteria for the selection of exhibits, being "at a loss to understand how such rubbish [e.g. an epergne made by Indian craftsmen for a "distinguished official"] was admitted to the exhibition at all" (p. 103). "However the book [which is the official catalogue] . . . contains much valuable information and will for a long time remain an indispensible [*sic*] handbook of Indian art, second in importance only to that of Sir George Birdwood" (p. 105).

C97 [A review of] *The Meat Fetish; Two Essays on Vegetarianism* by Ernest Crosby and Elisee Reclus. *Ceylon National Review*, Colombo, I. 1 (Jan. 1906) 106-7.

AKC concludes this review with: "Perhaps some of the Ceylonese who have adopted the eating of dead flesh along with other aspects of Western civilization, will bethink themselves that they are a little behind the times and if they would be really up to date, should return to their former simple diet" (p. 107).

C98 [A review of] *Ivories*. By Alfred Maskell. *Ceylon National Review*, Colombo, I. 1 (Jan. 1906) 111.

AKC upbraids Maskell for his superficial treatment of Indian and Sinhalese art.

C99 [A review of] *Buddhist Art in India* . . . [by] Albert Grünwedel revised and enlarged by James Burgess. *Ceylon National Review*, Colombo, I. 1 (Jan. 1906) 112-13.

AKC commends Grünwedel as "indispensible [*sic*] to the student of Indian art in its historical aspect", but regrets that little reference is made to decorative designs or to late Buddhist art in Ceylon. AKC contributes an epitome of the history of Buddhist art, and derives a chronological table from Grünwedel.

C100 [A review of] *Corporal Punishment in India*. By Sir Henry Cotton. *Ceylon National Review*, Colombo, I. 1 (Jan. 1906) 114-15.

AKC endorses "the need for reform in respect of Prison administration in India"; he concludes with: "We are glad that Indian questions are now so much more widely discussed in England, and that amongst Englishmen who are able to speak with authority, India has such friends as Sir Henry Cotton" (p. 115).

C101 [A review of] *Asia and Europe*; [by] Meredith Townsend. *Ceylon National Review*, Colombo, I. 1 (Jan. 1906) 117-18.

"We believe that Mr. Townsend's book conduces to a better understanding of the complexity of Eastern problems [especially those problems associated with "the present attempt . . . to anglicise India"]; and it emphasises the uselessness of mere imitation of Western civilization by Indians".

C102 Minerals New or Rare in Ceylon. *Spolia Zeylanica*, Colombo, III.11 (Jan. 1906) 198-9.

Mainly addenda to the list printed with "The Rocks and Minerals of Ceylon" (1905)—B2, with notes on six minerals discovered in Ceylon since that list was compiled.

C103 "How We British Do It". [Letter]. *New Age*, London, XVIII. 588 (4 Jan. 1906) 13.

Dated Ceylon, 12 Nov. 1905. AKC reproduces a letter (signed: W.) from the *Ceylon Observer*, Colombo, for 10 Oct. 1905, that condemns the "punitive expedition to the New Hebrides, of September 14 [1905, led by] Captain Doyley of H.M.S. 'Pegasus'", because, as AKC puts it in an introductory note, the letter "deserves a wider distribution".

C104 The Loan Exhibition of Kandyan Art, Kandy Kachcheri, January 5th and 6th [1906]. *Sandaresa*, Colombo, English Supplement, I. 33 (12 Jan. 1906) 3.

A review with special reference to the exhibits of textiles, illuminated books, and jewelled objects. This article was reprinted, as "Loan Exhibition of Kandyan Art, January 5 and 6, 1906", in *Ceylon National Review*, Colombo, I. 2 (July 1906) 233-5.

C105 Mispronunciation of Ceylon Names. [Letter]. *Ceylon Observer*, Colombo (1 Mar. 1906) 2.

Dated 28 Feb.[1906]. Concerning as well the question of transliteration.

C106 The Theosophical Society. [Letter]. *Ceylon Observer*, Colombo (2 Mar. 1906) 6.

Dated Dehiowita, 1 Mar.[1906]. On the Society's example of religious tolerance. "I may add that I am not a member of the Theosophical Society". (Nevertheless, shortly after this disclaimer, AKC joined the Society, on 20 January 1907; his sponsors were Annie Besant and W.A. English; see *Theosophist*, Madras, XXVIII. (Mar. 1907) Supplement, p. xxx.)

C107 Tolerance. [Letter]. *Sandaresa*, Colombo, English Supplement, I. 40 (2 Mar. 1906) 3.

Dated, 27 Feb. 1906.

C108 Ceylon Spelling—Kandyan Art—Theosophy. [Letter]. *Ceylon Observer*, Colombo (10 Mar. 1906) 2.

Dated Kandy, 9 Mar.[1906]. Continuing the subjects of earlier letters (C85, 105, 106).

C109 An Evening Shadow of Adam's Peak. [Letter]. *Ceylon Observer*, Colombo (22 Mar. 1906) 5.

Dated Maskeliya, 21 Mar. [1906]. On how this phenomenon differs from the well-known morning shadow.

C110 The [Ceylon] Social Reform Society. [Letter]. *Sandaresa*, Colombo, English Supplement, I. 44 (30 Mar. 1906) 2.

Quoting Thomas William Rhys Davids' letter accepting the Society's offer of honorary membership.

C111 [Letter to the Secretary of the Ceylon University Association]. *Journal of the Ceylon University Association*, Colombo, I. 1 (Apr. 1906) 28.

Dated Kandy, 1 Jan. 1906. On the proposal to establish a university in Ceylon, with suggestions as to what should be the educational ideals of such an institution. (May have title, "The Question of a University for Ceylon".) Information from S. Durai Raja Singam, *Ananda Kentish Coomaraswamy: A Bibliographical Record... Part I: 1895-1927* (1981)—E194—p. 68. This letter was reprinted in *Ananda Coomaraswamy—the Bridge Builder; a Study of a Scholar-Colossus*, by S. Durai Raja Singam (1977)—B94—pp. [157-8].

C112 Scorpion Stings. *Spolia Zeylanica*, Colombo, III. 12 (Apr. 1906) 215-16.

Excerpts from AKC's correspondence with E. Ernest Green (the Ceylon Government entomologist) are printed under this heading, together with a prefatory note from Green printed in four lines. AKC describes some traditional Sinhalese cures for scorpion or centipede stings, and quotes a *mantra* for snake bite.

C113 Education and Agricultural Progress in Denmark and Ceylon. *Tropical Agriculturist*, Peradeniya, XXVI. 3 (16 Apr. 1906) 233-5.

A comparison. This article was printed simultaneously in *Journal of the Ceylon University Association*, Colombo, I. 1 (Apr. 1906) 83-6. Reprinted in *Sandaresa*, Colombo, English Supplement, I. 48 (4 May 1906) 3-4, and again in *Vaidyeshivaran*, Jaffna, X. (Dec. 1958) 1-4.

C114 Public Reception to Dr. A.K. Coomaraswamy, D.Sc. (London) F.L.S., F.G.S. *Ceylon Observer*, Colombo (7 June 1906) 5-6.

A report of the reception given by the Tamils of Jaffna at the Hindu College Hall (Jaffna), 4 June 1906 (here erroneously dated 14 June), incorporates AKC's reply in which he rebukes the Tamils for the readiness with which they have absorbed Western influences, and calls for a united body of Tamil and Sinhalese public opinion to resist the encroachment of an alien government. This report was reprinted, as "Dr. Coomaraswamy's Reply", in *Sandaresa*, Colombo, English Supplement, II. 6 (22 June 1906) 3-4, and, in two parts, with the title "East and West", in *Indian Education*, Bombay, V. 2 (Sept. 1906) 61-5, and 3 (Oct. 1906) 107-10; also reprinted, with slight alterations, in *Two Addresses* (1906)—A8—pp. [3]-12. A lengthy excerpt from AKC's reply is printed in *Ceylon National Review*, Colombo, I. 2 (July 1906) 226-8.

C115 Mr. Coomaraswamy Explains. [Letter]. *Ceylon Observer*, Colombo (12 June 1906) 5.

Dated Jaffna, 10 June [1906]. Clarifying points in his talk of 4 June at Jaffna—see C114.

C116 Ceylon Social Reform Society. The Jaffna Branch. *Ceylon Observer*, Colombo (15 June 1906) 2-3.

A report of a meeting held under the auspices of the Jaffna Young Men's Hindu Association, at the Hindu College (Jaffna), on 9 June, to decide the formation of a Society branch there. Incorporates AKC's address in which he describes the origin, aims, and future activities of the Society. This report was reprinted, as "The Jaffna Branch", in *Ceylon National Review*, Colombo, I. 2 (July 1906) Supplement, pp. 12-15. S. Durai Raja Singam, in *Ananda Kentish Coomaraswamy: A Bibliographical Record . . . Part I: 1895-1927* (1981)—E194—p. 85, records the first appearance of this report in *The Hindu Organ*, Jaffna (10 June 1906).

C117 Dr. Coomaraswamy . . . Another Explanation. [Letter]. *Ceylon Observer*, Colombo (18 June 1906) 6.

Dated Kandy, 17 June [1906]. Further on his remarks of 4 June made at Jaffna.

C118 Anglicisation of the East. *Ceylon National Review*, Colombo, I. 2 (July 1906) [181]-195.

The text of AKC's first Presidential Address to the Ceylon Social Reform Society, 17 April 1906. On (1) the neglect of the vernacular in Ceylonese and Indian schools, (2) the destruction of the native arts and crafts, and the concomitant loss of the craft-songs, and (3) the abandonment of native dress. "We have to deal, not with the due influence of one civilization upon another, but with the obliteration of one and its replacement by another" (p. 182).

C119 Legends of a Celtic Type. *Ceylon National Review*, Colombo, I. 2 (July 1906) 239-41.

A note on some Indian and Sinhalese legends that present parallels to Irish folklore.

C120 [A review of] *Apitanakocham* (Tamil Classical Dictionary), by A. Muttuttambippillai, and *The Philosophy of Hinduism*, by a Member of the Jaffna Vivekananda Sabhai. *Ceylon National Review*, Colombo, 1. 2 (July 1906) 246.

"The dictionary is . . . invaluable . . . and we take this opportunity of suggesting the desirability of the production of a similar work in Sinhalese''.

C121 [A review of] *Missionary Study of Hinduism*, by J. N. Farquhar. *Ceylon National Review*, Colombo, I. 2 (July 1906) 246-7.

"[An] interesting pamphlet which we recommend to all enquirers who are prepared to take an intelligent interest in India and its people".

C122 [A review of] *Ribeiro's History of Ceilao, with Notes from de Barros, de Couto and Antonio Bocarro*. [Part I]. Translated from the Portuguese by P.E. Pieris. *Ceylon National Review*, Colombo, I. 2 (July 1906) 248-50.

"This valuable work has been carried out by Mr. Pieris with . . . care and exactness . . . [Joao Ribeiro] provides an interesting account of the state of the low-country, contemporaneous with [Robert] Knox's description of the Kandyan districts (published 1681 A.D.)" (pp. 248-9).

C123 Sinhalese Earthenware. *Spolia Zeylanica*, Colombo, IV. 13 (July 1906) [1]-18, 9 text illus., 3 pls.(following p. 18).

The first of two instalments. On the domestic, ecclesiastical, and architectural pottery, with observations on the potter and his appliances. The plates are reproductions of photographs taken in Ceylon by Ethel M. (Mrs A.K.) Coomaraswamy. This instalment was reprinted, with minor alterations and additions, in *Mediaeval Sinhalese Art* ([1908])—Al4a—as "Chapter XIII. Earthenware", pp. 218-28.

C124 Mr. Coomaraswamy on the "Ceylon Churchman". [Letter]. *Times of Ceylon*, Colombo (10 July 1906).

Dated Madugoda, 7 July [1906]. A reply to a suggestion from the editor of the *Ceylon Churchman* that the Ceylon Social Reform Society is purveying anti-Christian propaganda. (This item is known to the compiler only from a clipping.)

C125 Royal Asiatic Society [Ceylon Branch]. *Sandaresa*, Colombo, English Supplement, II. 11 (10 Aug. 1906) 2-3.

Under this heading, a report of the Society's meeting on 6 August incorporates, in twenty-five lines, AKC's prefatory words to presenting his paper "Some Survivals in Sinhalese Art". These words are not included with the paper as published—C93.

C126 A Plea for the Teaching of Indian Music in Ceylon. *Journal of the Ceylon University Association*, Colombo, I. 2 (Oct. 1906) [142]-150.

"All of the Indian instruments were once used amongst the Sinhalese . . . [they] have a right to the heritage of Indian music no less than to every other aspect of Indian culture, for historically speaking, they are perhaps more Indian than the Indians themselves" (p. 143). AKC outlines his belief in the educational value of music, and discusses briefly the character of Indian music itself, taking into account the European objection to the "seemingly arbitrary" Hindu scale, the profusion of modes, and the absence of harmony.

C127 The Game Protection Society. [Letter]. *Times of Ceylon*, Colombo (4 Oct. 1906).

AKC's is the second of two letters printed under this heading. Dated 2 Oct. [1906]. Opposing "the unnecessary slaughter of animals" in Ceylon, with reference to views expressed by a local huntsman, Colonel E. Gordon Reeves. (This item is known to the compiler only from a clipping.)

C128 Sportsmen and the Preservation of Game. [Letter]. *Times of Ceylon*, Colombo (6? Oct. 1906).

Dated Kandy, 5 Oct.[1906]. That the solution is to create more sanctuaries. (This item is known to the compiler only from a clipping.)

C129 The Ceylon Game Preservation Society. Dr. Coomaraswamy and Colonel Gordon Reeves. [Letter]. *Times of Ceylon*, Colombo (13 Oct. 1906).

Dated Kandy, 12 Oct. [1906]. A reply to Reeves's defence of hunting as a sport. (This item is known to the compiler only from a clipping.)

C130 Sinhalese Earthenware. (Second Paper). *Spolia Zeylanica*, Colombo, IV. 14/15 (Dec. 1906) 135-41.

The text of a traditional song describing the potter's art and craft, printed in Sinhalese script followed by AKC's translation into English. Addenda and corrigenda to "Sinhalese Earthenware"—C123—is subjoined. This translation, with minor alterations, was reprinted in *Mediaeval Sinhalese Art* ([1908])—A14a—as "Appendix to Chapter XIII. Potter's Song", pp. 229-31.

C131 Indigenous Arts and Crafts. *Ceylon Observer*, Colombo (4 Dec. 1906) 7.

A paper read by AKC at the 26th annual meeting of the Board of Agriculture in Colombo on 3 December. AKC recommends Government assistance for traditional Ceylonese architects and artisans. Incorporates criticism of a modern *ambalama* (resthouse) built at Ruanwella. This paper was reprinted, as "Suggestions for the Encouragement of Indigenous Arts and Crafts in Ceylon", in *Sandaresa*, Colombo, English Supplement, II.

26 (7 Dec. 1906) 3, and again, with this title, in *Tropical Agriculturist*, Peradeniya, XXVII. 6 (15 Dec. 1906) 497-500.

C132 Farewell Interview with Dr. Coomaraswamy. *Times of Ceylon*, Colombo, Morning Edition (28 Dec. 1906) 4.

AKC's answers are given in quotation marks as his direct words. This interview was conducted on the occasion of AKC's retirement as Director of the Mineralogical Survey, and on the eve of his departure from Ceylon. AKC discusses (1) the revival of Ceylonese national ideals, (2) the need for education in Ceylon to include the vernacular languages and national culture, (3) the need to establish a local university, and (4) the European-style furnishing of Ceylonese homes. AKC concludes by remarking how "the Ceylonese will neither respect themselves nor be respected by others so long as their own attitude towards the West remains one of abject imitation".

1907

C133 Mineralogical Survey. Report of the Director of the Mineralogical Survey for 1906. *Ceylon Administration Reports for the Year 1906*. Colombo: H.C. Cottle, Government Printer, Ceylon, 1907, Vol. II, Pt. 4, pp. E1-E14, 2 text illus., 3 fold. maps.

The last of AKC's four reports is dated 31 December 1906. Comprising accounts of thorianite, copper, asbestos, graphite, nitre, corundum, andalusite, moonstone, khondalite, serpentine, and alluvial deposits, with notes on mapping the Kandy District, earth movements in Ceylon, and a "Bibliography of Ceylon Geology" (listing 116 items), pp. E10-E14. The first of the folding maps bears the caption: "Geological Sketch Map of a Part of the Kandy District Surveyed by A.K. Coomaraswamy D.Sc., 1898-1906". The following announcement is printed on page E1: "It [was] decided that the Mineralogical Survey should be continued for a further period of three years, and that Mr. [James] Parsons should be Director, the present Director not desiring to carry on the work".

C134 Notes on Painting, Dyeing, Lacwork, Dumbara Mats, and Paper in Ceylon. *Journal of the Royal Asiatic Society (Ceylon Branch)*, Colombo, XIX. 58 (1907) [103]-121, 1 text illus.

On the traditional methods of manufacture. A reprint, in a revised and expanded form, of excerpts from *Handbook to the Exhibition of Arts & Crafts* . . . (1906)—A9.

C135 Teaching of Drawing in Ceylon. *Ceylon National Review*, Colombo, I. 3 (Jan. 1907) [302]-312, 5 text illus.

A description of the traditional and highly systematic course of instruction given to apprentices when draughtsmanship was still an essential prerequisite for the superior craftsman. Also includes suggestions as to how the present-day methods of teaching drawing in Ceylon schools might be improved. A separately paginated offprint seen (April 1973) at the National Museum Library, Colombo. This article was reprinted, with revisions, as "Appendix to Chapter III. 1. Teaching of Drawing", in *Mediaeval Sinhalese Art* ([1908])—A14a—pp. 64-9.

C136 [A review of] *The Web of Indian Life*, by [Sister] Nivedita. *Ceylon National Review*, Colombo, I. 3 (Jan. 1907) [376]-380.

"The book [an interpretation of the traditional ideals of Hindu society] must be read by all who care for India's past or India's future" (p. 380). In the course of this review AKC comments briefly upon (1) the relation of Ceylon and India, (2) Indian assimilation of Western science, (3) Indian womanhood, (4) the *Mahābhārata* and *Rāmāyaṇa* as national epics, and (5) caste.

C137 [A review of] *Swami Vivekananda, a Collection of His Speeches and Writings. Ceylon National Review*, Colombo, I. 3 (Jan. 1907) 380-1.

AKC quotes at length from Vivekananda's exhortations to his countrymen to preserve their ethos *vis-à-vis* modern social reformers' efforts to "engraft" upon India "Western means and methods". Unsigned, but almost certainly by AKC.

C138 [A review of] *Dadabhai Navroji* [*sic*], *a Sketch of His Life and Work*. Anonymous. *Ceylon National Review*, Colombo, I. 3 (Jan. 1907) 381-2.

"Very touching is [Naoroji's] persistent faith in English justice and loyalty to British rule which is a characteristic feature of even the most active agitators for the abolition of the present system of Government; it deserve a better return than the repeated disappointment which it has hitherto experienced" (p. 382). (Naoroji, 1825-1917, a wealthy Parsi, emigrated to England in 1886 and became the first Indian to be elected a member of the House of Commons. He was President of the Indian National Congress in 1906.)

C139 [A review of] *Malabar and Its Folk*, by T.K. Gopal Pannikar. *Ceylon National Review*, Colombo, I. 3 (Jan. 1907) 382-3.

AKC notes Pannikar's deference to Western influences in S.W. India, but concedes that "the main value of this work is ethnological . . . [an] interesting and useful volume, which we commend to every student of Indian folklore and social economy".

C140 [A review of] *Ribeiro's History of Ceilao, with Notes from de Barros, de Cowto* [*sic*], *and Antonio Bocarro*. [Part II]. Translated from the Portuguese by P.E. Pieris. *Ceylon National Review*, Colombo, I. 3 (Jan. 1907) 383-4.

AKC commends Pieris's "painstaking and admirable work".

C141 [A review of] *The Thirty-Seven Nats*, by R.C. Temple. *Ceylon National Review*, Colombo, I. 3 (Jan. 1907) 384.

"[This] is an example of the sort of work that ought to be undertaken in Ceylon, where equally interesting material exists". AKC thinks Temple's treatment of Burmese animistic worship "not especially sympathetic".

C142 The Decline of Vegetarianism in Ceylon. *Humane Review*, London, VII. 28 (Jan. 1907) 1-8.

This article was reprinted, with this title, in *Siddhānta Dīpika*, Madras, VII. 12 (Mar. 1907) [359]-365, and, with revisions, as "Vegetarianism in Ceylon", in *Ceylon National Review*, Colombo, for February 1908—C160.

C143 Swadeshi. *Indian Review*, Madras, VIII. 1 (Jan. 1907) 4-7.

AKC points to weaknesses in the movement, in particular the casting aside of traditional Indian industries (in favour of establishing new industries to produce poor imitations of mostly worthless European manufactures). This article was reprinted in *The Swadeshi Movement* ([1909?])—B6, and, in a revised and expanded form, as Chapter XII of *Essays in National Idealism* ([1909?])—A18a.

C144 Degaldoruwa Vihare. *Kandyan*, Colombo, II. 3 (Feb. 1907) 163-8.

(In English.) Chiefly concerning the tempera wall-paintings, that depict Jātaka stories, in this 18th century Buddhist cave-temple near Kandy, Ceylon. Shortly before March 1905, AKC copied the *Vessantara Jātaka* section of the murals. This replica was published, in colour, as the frontispiece to *Mediaeval Sinhalese Art* ([1908])—A14a; it was moved to the back and printed in black-and-white in the second edition (1956)—A14b.

C145 Aspects of Swadeshi. *Dawn*, Calcutta, X. 8 (Apr. 1907) [33]-36.

Printed under the general heading: Topics for Discussion. A reprint, with changes, of "Swadeshi" in *Indian Review*, Madras, for January 1907—C143.

C146 Mata Bharata. *Modern Review*, Calcutta, I. 4 (Apr. 1907) 369-71.

(In English.) The history of India's relations with England presented in the form of an allegory. Reprinted in *The Deeper Meaning of the Struggle* ([1907])—A10, and as Chapter III of *Essays in National Idealism* ([1909?])—A18a, and again in *Ananda Coomaraswamy—the Bridge Builder; a Study of a Scholar-Colossus*, by S. Durai Raja Singam (1977)—B94—pp.[462-3].

C147 India and Ceylon. *Ceylon National Review*, Colombo, II. 4 (July 1907) [15]-22.

AKC's Presidential address to the Ceylon Social Reform Society in April 1907. On their cultural and other ties, and the necessary realization of a national self-consciousness in Ceylon, and of the concomitant ideal of an internationalism. Excerpts from this address were reprinted, under the heading "The Doctrine of Nationality: The Individuality of a Nation", in *Dawn*, Calcutta, XIII. 7 (July 1910) [25]-28.

C148 Wanted: National Education in India. *Hindustan Review*, Allahabad, XVI. 95 (July 1907) [19]-22.

The text of a lecture given by AKC in Madras sometime in May 1907. AKC says that an anglicized education is sterilizing the intelligence of India, and that the remedy for this is a system, controlled by Indians, that aims for the development of the people's intelligence through the medium of their own national culture. Reprinted in the *Ceylon National Review*, Colombo, II. 4 (July 1907) [39]-55 (where a footnote on p.[39] says reproduced from *Indian Patriot*—this periodical has not been sighted by the compiler), and, in a reduced form, in *Dawn*, Calcutta, XI. 12 (Oct. 1908) [7]-8.

C149 The Present State of Indian Art I.—Painting and Sculpture. *Modern Review*, Calcutta, II. 2 (Aug. 1907) [105]-110, 1 pl. (facing p.[105]).

The first of two instalments. Considering as well the future prospects; prefaced with an epitome of the history of the fine arts in India; and including a discussion of the paintings of Ravi Varma (p. 107) and Abanindranath Tagore (p. 108). A separately paginated offprint seen (April 1991) in the collection of Dr Rama P. Coomaraswamy, Greenwich, Conn.

C150 The Present State of Indian Art II.—Architecture and Decorative Art. *Modern Review*, Calcutta, II. 5 (Nov. 1907) 405-13.

On the causes, both internal and external, of the degeneration of the Indian (and Ceylonese) crafts, and the prospect of their revival, citing at length the "opinions of Western artists and students of art and industry [George Birdwood, James Fergusson, George Watt, and others]" (p. 405). AKC criticizes the Swadeshi movement as "too purely commercial . . . too unimaginative, too solely based on the ideal of dull prosperity to greatly help the cause of Indian art" (p. 411). This article is probably the text of AKC's lecture, "The Influence of Western Civilisation on Indian Arts and Industries", given at Madras, under the auspices of the Madras Mahajana Sabbha, on 23 January 1907. This instalment, together with C149, was reprinted, with revisions, as Chapter VI, "The Influence of Modern Europe on Indian Art", of *Essays in National Idealism* ([1909?])—A18a.

1908

C151 The Relations of Art and Religion in India. *Transactions of the Third International Congress for the History of Religions*. Oxford: Clarendon Press, 1908, Vol. II, pp. 70-4.

An abstract of a paper read by AKC at the Congress on 17 September. An "elementary study of the religious psychology of Indian art" (p. 73).

C152 Beauty and Efficiency in Dress. *Dress Review*, London, III. (1908) 181-9.

That clothing's adaption to function and hygiene should go hand in hand with a sensuous beauty that reflects pride or respect in one's physical health. AKC points to the relevance this formula has to the aims of modern dress reformers. AKC includes as well some observations on the wearing of jewellery.

C153 The Aim of Indian Art. *Modern Review*, Calcutta, III. 1 (Jan. 1908) 15-21, 1 text illus., 3 pls. lettered: A-C (pl. C is frontis. to this issue, i.e. facing p.[1]).

This article (which differs almost entirely from *The Aims of Indian Art* ([1908])—A12) was intended by AKC as a postscript to "The Present State of Indian Art I[-II]", in the issues for August and November 1907—C149, 150. AKC gives expression to his conviction that "the artistic achievement of India at various times, has been as great as any that the world has seen" (p. 16). His thesis centres on the doctrine of Idealism: to express the Ideal has been the consistent aim and special characteristic of Indian art, and "should still be before the Indian artist" (p. 15). AKC includes as well an explanation and a vindication of the role of tradition and convention in art. A separately paginated offprint seen (April 1991) in the collection of Dr Rama P. Coomaraswamy, Greenwich, Conn. An excerpt was printed, as "Convention in Traditional Society", in *Good Work*, Cambridge, Mass., XXXI. 2 (Spring 1968) 34-8, 3 text illus., and further excerpts were printed in *Bhavan's Journal*, Bombay, XVIII. 24 (25 June 1972) [39]-41.

C154 [A review of] *Memoirs of Mistral*. Translated by C.E. Maud. *Modern Review*, Calcutta, III. I (Jan. 1908) 86.

AKC likens the present conditions in India to those of Provence, before Frédéric Mistral's revivification of Provençal culture. "Do we not need Mistrals in India? Have we not a false and unnatural education in our schools? Do not the schools wage war against the native and historic languages of the Indians?" This review was reprinted, with slight changes, in *Ceylon National Review*, Colombo, II. 5 (Feb. 1908) [153].

C155 [A review of] *Daily Practice of the Hindus*, by Sris [*sic*] Chandra Vasu. *Modern Review*, Calcutta, III. 1 (Jan. 1908) 88-9.

AKC gives an epitome of the practices described by Vasu, and "strongly recommend[s] this little volume to all interested in mental culture, or who wish to know more of Hinduism as it really is" (p. 89). This review was reprinted in *Ceylon National Review*, Colombo, II. 5 (Feb. 1908) 155-7.

C156 [A review of] *Two New Worlds*, by E.E. Fournier d'Albe. *Siddhānta Dīpikā*, Madras, VIII. 10 (Jan. 1908) [308]-313.

AKC considers the author's thesis of "an infinity of material universes", and compares this with the traditional Indian cosmological doctrines. In the course of his review AKC makes the following prescient remark, "I do not doubt that within a hundred years the culture of India will be valued in the West as that of Greece is today; her achievements in philosophy, literature, science and art cannot ultimately be ignored, but must take their right place in the scheme of human culture and civilization" (p. 312). This review was reprinted, with revisions, in *Ceylon National Review*, Colombo, II. 5 (Feb. 1908) 157-60.

C157 The Royal Asiatic Society; the Government Printing Office; and Diacritical Type. *Ceylon Observer*, Colombo (9 Jan. 1908).

An editorial with this title quotes three comments from AKC relevant to these topics. (This item is known to the compiler only from a clipping.)

C158 Sinhalese Labour for Estates . . . Dr. Coomaraswamy's Views—II. [Letter]. *Ceylon Observer*, Colombo, Weekly Edition (28 Jan. 1908) 128.

Dated Campden [Gloucestershire], 5 Jan. 1908. A protest against a scheme, proposed by James Westland in the issue for 3 December 1907, to induce labour by the imposition of a hut-tax on "unemployed" villagers who refuse to work on tea estates and rubber plantations. A letter from Westland, explaining his proposal, is printed above AKC's, under the heading: Sinhalese Labour for Estates—I.

C159 The Hon. Mr. J. P. Lewis on Indian Music—Criticised by Dr. Coomaraswamy. [Letter]. *Ceylon Observer*, Colombo (30 Jan. 1908).

Dated Campden [Gloucestershire], 7 Jan.[1908]. A reply to the reported words of John Penry Lewis (Government Agent of the Central Province of Ceylon) that express a "contemptuous disparagement . . . [of] all Eastern music". (This item is known to the compiler only from a clipping.) Reprinted, as "Mr. Lewis on Indian Music", in *Ceylon National Review*, Colombo, II. 5 (Feb. 1908) 151-2.

C160 Vegetarianism in Ceylon. *Ceylon National Review*, Colombo, II. 5 (Feb. 1908) [125]-131.

A revised and expanded version of an article that first appeared, with the title "The Decline of Vegetarianism in Ceylon", in *Humane Review*, London, for January 1907—C142. Reprinted in *Ceylon Daily News*, Colombo, Vesak Number (May 1937) 21-2, and in *Vegetarian News*, London, XXIX. 269 (Autumn 1950) 74-7.

C161 [A review of] *The Other Side of the Lantern*, by Sir Frederick Treves. *Ceylon National Review*, Colombo, II. 5 (Feb. 1908) 160.

"A fair specimen of the balderdash written by passing tourists in Ceylon and India, who feel called upon to proclaim their ignorance in print."

C162 Indian Music. *Hindustan Review*, Allahabad, XVII. 103 (Mar. 1908) [248]-260.

On the neglect and precarious survival of Indian (and Ceylonese) music: its loss of status in education, the decline in its general appreciation, and its vulgarization through the introduction of the harmonium and gramophone. AKC recounts some personal experiences of listening to music in India. This article was reprinted, to form in part Chapters XIII and XIV of *Essays in National Idealism* ([1909?])—A18a.

C163 Art of the East and of the West. *New Age*, London, N.S. II. 21 (21 Mar. 1908) 408-9.

Excerpted from a lecture delivered by AKC to the Art-workers' Guild at Clifford's Inn Hall, London, 10 January 1908. On (1) the essential distinctions of (Phidian) Greek art from Indian art, (2) the difficulty in appreciating alien artefacts, and (3) the present and future status of art in England and India. Reprinted, in *Ceylon National Review*, Colombo, II. 6 (May 1908) [229]-233, simultaneously in *Modern Review*, Calcutta, III. 5 (May 1908) 397-9, and as Chapter VII of *Essays in National Idealism* ([1909?])—A18a, where, in a footnote on page 82, AKC explains that this article is "primarily phrased as if for European readers".

C164 Memory in Education. *Journal of the Ceylon University Association*, Colombo, II. 5 (Apr. 1908) 1-12.

A critique of the prevailing system of colonial English education in India and Ceylon. AKC points to the dangers inherent in education and culture being made matters of book-learning only. He describes some characteristic operations of memory and the related faculty, concentration, and notes how "memory, in the Indian view, is itself a most important part of personal character". AKC adduces evidence for the existence of a living national literature in earlier times "not dependent altogether on a knowledge of reading and writing"; furthermore, that the memorising of epics, legends, and heroic literature, was the vehicle for the transmission of a common culture (which English education ignores and destroys) where "all [were] united . . . however varying the extent of their knowledge". This article was reprinted as Chapter X of *Essays in National Idealism* ([1909?])—A18a.

C165 [*Entry deleted.*]

C166 Sir Henry Craik on Education in India. *Modern Review*, Calcutta, III. 4 (Apr. 1908) 330-3.

AKC expresses agreement with Craik's censure of the present system (in articles contributed by Craik to *The Scotsman*), and puts the case for a radical reform based on the principle "that if modern education is to add anything to the greatness and nobility of the Oriental ideal, it can only be by the fulfilment and not by the rejection of the existing culture" (p. 332). A separately paginated offprint seen (April 1991) in the collection of Dr Rama P. Coomaraswamy, Greenwich, Conn.

C167 A Note on the Number of Craftsmen in the Kandyan Population. *Ceylon National Review*, Colombo, II. 6 (May 1908) 239-40.

AKC estimates that craftsmen in the 18th century formed about one tenth of the population.

C168 [A review of] *Ceylon, the Paradise of Adam*, by Caroline Corner. *Ceylon National Review*, Colombo, II. 6 (May 1908) 242-3.

"We are surprised that anyone should have thought it worth while [*sic*] to publish a book of this degree of ineptitude . . . the gossipy impressions of an Anglo-Indian lady resident for some years in Colombo."

C169 [A review of] *The Inward Light*, by H. Fielding Hall. *Ceylon National Review*, Colombo, II . 6 (May 1908) 244-6.

"We are continually in sympathy with [Hall's] point of view; but his style is . . . vague and wordy . . . What he wishes to say is mainly this, and it might have been said in a much smaller book: that religion is not in the East, as it is in the West, a formula or a doctrine, but a way of looking at life, and includes all life, so that there is no division into sacred and profane: that it cannot be understood in any effective way by an unsympathetic study, or even by sympathetic study if of a purely intellectual or scholarly character" (p. 244). This review was printed simultaneously in *Modern Review*, Calcutta, III. 5 (May 1908) 463-4.

C170 The Assumption of Maou Ying. *Modern Review*, Calcutta, III. 5 (May 1908) 460, 1 pl.(facing p. 460).

A brief note to accompany the reproduction of a painting from an 18th century Chinese MS, *Yun t'ai hsien jui*, in the British Museum. (Maou Ying was a Taoist saint of the late Chou Dynasty.)

C171 The Indian Craftsman. *Modern Review*, Calcutta, III. 6 (June 1908) 507-10.

A lecture given by AKC at the Campden School of Arts and Crafts, in Gloucestershire, on 6 March 1908. On the status of the village craftsman, and the function of the craft guilds of the cities. This article was reprinted, in an expanded form, as Chapters I and II of *The Indian Craftsman* (1909)—A16a. This expanded version was reprinted, in two parts, as "The Village Craftsman" and "The Craft Guilds of the Great Cities", in *Silpi*, Madras, I. 1 (Aug. 1946) 40-1, and 2 (Sept. 1946) 2-8, 4 text illus. See also C177 and 189.

C172 Dr. Rodolphe Broda on Indian Art. *Modern Review*, Calcutta, III. 6 (June 1908) 556-7.

On "The Future of Art in East and West", in the January 1908 issue of *The International*, London, "that betrays in every sentence gross ignorance of Oriental art" (p. 556).

C173 [A review of] *New Ideas in India*. By the Rev. John Morison. *Modern Review*, Calcutta, III. 6 (June 1908) 560-2.

AKC highlights the "moral obliquity" involved in a typical Christian missionary's accommodation of Indian religion and culture. An excerpt from this review was printed, under the heading "The Christian Missionary's Moral Attitude Towards Caste", in *Dawn*, Calcutta, XI. 11 (Sept. 1908) [41]-42.

C174 The Florence Press Books. [Letter]. *New Age*, London, N.S. III. 8 (20 June 1908) 159.

AKC, as the proprietor of a private press (i.e. the Essex House Press), disputes the opinions of Jacob Tonson, expressed in an earlier issue, concerning the market for hand-printed books.

C175 Ideal of Indian Nationalism. *Dawn*, Calcutta, XI. 9 (July 1908) 34-5.

An excerpt reprinted from *The Deeper Meaning of the Struggle* ([1907])—A10.

C176 The Future of Dress in India. *Hindustan Review*, Allahabad, XVIII. 107 (July 1908) [99]-101.

Printed under the general heading: Criticisms and Discussions. AKC's reply to an article of this title, by Rama Sastri, in the issue for April: on the question of the adoption of English dress.

C177 The Feudal Craftsman in India and Ceylon. *Modern Review*, Calcutta, IV. 1 (July 1908) 30-4.

In the main on the organization, work, and status of the royal craftsman in Ceylon. A continuation of the subject treated in C171. This article was reprinted, considerably expanded, as Chapter III of *The Indian Craftsman* (1909)—A16a. This expanded version was reprinted in *Silpi*, Madras, I. 5 (Dec. 1946/Jan. 1947) 16-26, and again in *Festival of the Arts. Souvenir Published by The Ceylon Society of Arts in Connection with the Second Anniversary* (Colombo: Printed for The Ceylon Society of Arts by The Times of Ceylon Ltd., 1950), pp. [46]- 47, 49-50, 57, 59, 65.

C178 Professor Wallace on the Failure of Lord Morley. *Modern Review*, Calcutta, IV. 1 (July 1908) 77-8.

A note by AKC, printed in seven lines, introduces Alfred Russel Wallace's criticism of the Secretary for India's policy.

C179 [A review of] *Oriental School Drawing Books,* by E.B. Havell. *Modern Review*, Calcutta, IV. 1 (July 1908) 86.

AKC remarks that these "admirable drawing books [are] for teaching freehand drawing in schools. They differ from the old patterns in being the decorative forms of Indian art, instead of containing the, to an Indian student, less interesting and valuable forms of Classic and Gothic ornament". AKC expresses the hope that model drawing might be similarly reformed. This review was reprinted in *Ceylon National Review*, Colombo, II. 7 (Aug. 1908) 314.

C180 The Injustice of Votes for Women. [Letter]. *New Age*, London, N.S. III. 13 (25 July 1908) 258.

Opposing the views expressed in an article of this title, by C.H. Norman, in the issue for 18 July.

C181 The Village Community and Modern Progress. *Ceylon National Review*, Colombo, II. 7 (Aug. 1908) [249]-260.

"[AKC's] Presidential Address to the Ceylon Social Reform Society, May, 1908" (p.[249]). On traditional Sinhalese social organization, and its disintegration under British rule; with some observations on the personal character of the unspoilt Sinhalese villager. A separately paginated offprint is in the possession of the compiler. This article was reprinted, as "What Might Have Been: The Village Community and Modern Progress", in *Organising for Development*, edited by C.R. Hensman (1964)—B88.

C182 The Future of the [Ceylon Social Reform] Society. *Ceylon National Review*, Colombo, II. 7 (Aug. 1908) 302-3.

AKC's prefatory remarks that accompanied his Presidential address in May, "The Village Community and Modern Progress", that were not printed with the published version of that address—C181.

C183 [A review of] *The Book of Ceylon*, by H.W. Cave. *Ceylon National Review*, Colombo, II. 7 (Aug. 1908) 313-14.

AKC remarks of this guidebook that although it "gives to the visitor a good general idea of the country . . . we notice many errors . . . we have most fault to find with the journalese . . . and the superficiality of the treatment". AKC singles out as "an excellent feature of the work . . . Mr. [John Penry] Lewis' admirable and adequately illustrated account of Kandyan architecture". This book was also reviewed by AKC, at greater length, in *Hindustan Review*, Allahabad, for September 1908—C188.

C184 National Self-Consciousness and Its Relation to Racial Self-Consciousness. *Dawn*, Calcutta, XI. 10 (Aug. 1908) 40.

A paragraph, with changes, excerpted from *The Deeper Meaning of the Struggle* ([1907])—A10—pp.15-16.

C185 The "New Birth" in India: "A Living Movement". *Hindustan Review*, Allahabad, XVIII. 108 (Aug. 1908) [109]-120.

A reprint, with changes (including the omission of "Mata Bharata"), of *The Deeper Meaning of the Struggle* ([1907])—A10. The quoted portions of the title are the words of Bishop Lefroy of Lahore and Viscount Morley, respectively.

C186 The Aims of Indian Art. *International*, London, III. 9 (Aug. 1908) 59-72, 1 pl. (frontis. to this issue).

A reprint of A12. This article was reprinted again in *Studies in Comparative Religion*,

Bedfont, Middx., IX. 1 (Winter 1975) 2-19, 1 text illus. A revised and expanded version was reprinted as Chapter IV of *Essays in National Idealism* ([1909?])—A18a.

C187 The Bhadda Sala Jataka. *Modern Review*, Calcutta, IV. 2 (Aug. 1908) 148-9.

This translation was reprinted in *Mediaeval Sinhalese Art* ([1908])—A14a—pp. 121-2, with additionally the following note: "I have endeavoured to put the unsympathetic prose and doggerel verse of the original translation [by Edward Byles Cowell] into passable English."

C188 Ceylon of To-day. *Hindustan Review*, Allahabad, XVIII. 109 (Sept. 1908) [309]-318.

Printed under the general heading: Views and Reviews. A review of *The Book of Ceylon: Being a Guide to Its Railway System and an Account of Its Varied Attractions for the Visitor and Tourist*, by H.W. Cave, and *Ceylon: A Hand-Book for the Resident and the Traveller*, by J.C. Willis. AKC calls attention to a "really valuable and original" feature of Cave's book: the descriptions and photographs of paddy cultivation ceremonies. Of the second book under review, AKC comments that it is "a very useful and comprehensive . . . guide, particularly for the European traveller of more intelligence than the 'mere tourist'" (p. 317).

C189 The Indian Craftsman. *Modern Review*, Calcutta, IV. 3 (Sept. 1908) 191-6.

On (1) the maintenance by the state, by guilds, and by the institution of caste, of standard in the crafts, and the latter-day degradation of this order; (2) the craftsman's conception of his craft as intrinsically religious; (3) the apprentice craftsman and his education; and (4) the craftsman's economic and spiritual status in society. A continuation of the subject treated in C171 and 177. This article was reprinted, considerably expanded, to form Chapters IV, V, and VI of *The Indian Craftsman* (1909)—A16a. Chapter V of *The Indian Craftsman* was in turn reprinted, as "Religious Ideas in Craftsmanship", in *Silpi*, Madras, I. 4 (Nov. 1946) [10]-14.

C190 Education in India. *Modern Review*, Calcutta, IV. 4 (Oct. 1908) 338-43.

An indictment of 19th and 20th century colonial English education for its part in the destruction of the indigenous culture. In suggesting some reforms of this system, AKC enumerates (on pp. 341-2) seven "points of view which are intrinsic in Indian culture, and must be recognized in any sound educational ideal for India". A separately paginated offprint seen (May 1991) among The Coomaraswamy Papers in the Firestone Library at

Princeton University. This article was reprinted as Chapter IX of *Essays in National Idealism* ([1909?])—A18a, and in *National Education. (A Symposium by the Friends & Leaders of India.)*, edited by H.V. Dugvekar (Benares: Balabodha Office, 1917), pp. 41-61.

C191 An Educationist's Indian Impressions. *Hindustan Review*, Allahabad, XVIII. 112 (Dec. 1908) [566]-568.

Printed under the general heading: Views and Reviews. A review of *Impressions of India*, by Henry Craik. AKC thinks the head of the Scottish Education Board's observations on India superficial, when they are not either prejudiced or ignorant, but concludes his review by quoting lengthy excerpts from "the really solid chapter in the book . . . that concerned with education".

1909

C192 The Book of the Month: Mr. Binyon's Painting in the Far East. *Hindustan Review*, Allahabad, XIX. 113 (Jan. 1909) [70]-79.

A review of *Painting in the Far East: An Introduction to the History of Pictorial Art in Asia, Especially in China and Japan*, by Laurence Binyon. AKC considers this work even more valuable "as a contribution to a true understanding of the aims of art, than as a history of Chinese and Japanese painting", but cautions that "the references to religion and religious art are perhaps the least satisfying parts", and furthermore that Binyon "is handicapped by a limited knowledge of Indian art" (pp. [70], 76, 75).

C193 The New Spirit in India. *Hindustan Review*, Allahabad, XIX. 113 (Jan. 1909) [80]-85.

Printed under the general heading: Views and Reviews. A review of *The New Spirit in India*, by H.W. Nevinson. "This is certainly the best book written by an Englishman, that has yet appeared, dealing with the political aspects of the National movement in India" (p.[80]).

C194 Christian Missions in India. *Indian Review*, Madras, X. 2 (Feb. 1909) 110-16.

On the conversion of Hindus and Muslims "to some form of dogmatic Christianity". AKC questions the legitimacy of missionary aims and methods, and examines (1) the fate of girls sent to mission schools, and (2) proselytizing camouflaged as general education.

Excerpts from this article were reprinted in *Central Hindu College Magazine*, Benares, N.S. IX. 6. (1 June 1909) 136. The entire article was reprinted, combined with "Missionary Misrepresentation", from the issue for March 1909—C197, to form Chapter XI of *Essays in National Idealism* ([1909?])—A18a; also reprinted, considerably reduced, in *Indian Review*, Madras, LXXVII. 11 (Feb. 1982) 33-6.

C195 Note on the Silpa Sastras in Ceylon. *Modern Review*, Calcutta, V. 2 (Feb. 1909) 121-4.

"Read at the Oriental Congress, Copenhagen [19 August 1908]" (footnote, p. 121). On the artistic canons of measurement and proportion known as the *Rūpāvaliya*, the *Vaijayantaya*, and the *Sāriputra* (the last a purely Buddhist canon). In part identical with the (more detailed) discussion and translation of this material in *Mediaeval Sinhalese Art* ([1908])—A14a—"Appendix to Chapter VIII. Sāriputra", pp. 150-63.

C196 The Book of the Month. Mr. E.B. Havell's Indian Sculpture and Painting. *Hindustan Review*, Allahabad, XIX.115 (Mar. 1909) [271]-280.

A review of *Indian Sculpture and Painting*, by E.B. Havell. AKC calls this work "the first serious attempt to understand and appreciate Indian art" (p. 271), and elsewhere, "this is the only important work on the subject of Indian art, considered as art, and not merely as material for the archaeologist" (*Mediaeval Sinhalese Art* ([1908])—A14a—p. 258).

C197 Missionary Misrepresentation. *Indian Review*, Madras, X. 3 (Mar. 1909) 187-92.

AKC reviews, and cites at length, some common misstatements of missionaries concerning India. Includes as well a plea for the establishment of a national education controlled by Indians. This article was reprinted, combined with "Christian Missions in India"—C194, to form Chapter XI of *Essays in National Idealism* ([1909?])—A18a.

C198 Art and Archaeology. [Letter]. *Modern Review*, Calcutta, V. 3 (Mar.1909) 272.

With reference to an article, "The Flight of Laksman [*sic*] Sen", by Akshay Kumar Maitra, in the issue for January, that concerns a painting of this subject by Surendra Nath Ganguly.

C199 The Book of the Month: The British in Egypt. *Hindustan Review*, Allahabad, XIX. 116 (Apr. 1909) [386]-389.

A review of *La mort de Philae*, by Pierre Loti. AKC endorses Loti's abhorrence of British Imperialism, and draws attention to the relevance for India of Loti's appeal to the Egyptians to defend their heritage against the disintegrating influence of "the Occidental incubus".

C200 Mahayana Buddhist Images from Ceylon and Java. *Journal of the Royal Asiatic Society*, London (Apr. 1909) [283]-297, 3 pls.

On bronze statuettes, chiefly of AD 7th to 9th century, in the British Museum, and from AKC's own collection. (AKC was elected a member of the Royal Asiatic Society of Great Britain and Ireland on 10 April 1906.)

C201 The Message of the East [I]. *Modern Review*, Calcutta, V. 5 (May 1909) 427-9.

The first of three instalments. The series as a whole concerns itself with the mutual influence exerted by the cultures and civilizations of India and Europe, remarking in particular on the "subtle Indianisation of the West", and moreover, that "the East has . . . revealed a new world to the West, which will be the inspiration of a 'Renaissance', more profound and far-reaching than that which resulted from the re-discovery of the classic world of the West" (p. 427). In this first instalment, AKC contrasts the realism, or naturalism, of modern European art with the ideal art of the East. Separately paginated offprints of each of the three instalments seen (April 1991) in the collection of Dr. Rama P. Coomaraswamy, Greenwich, Conn. The three instalments, together with "Art and Svadeshi"—C203, were reprinted as *The Message of the East* ([1909])—A17.

C202 Gramophones—and Why Not. *Modern Review*, Calcutta, V. 5 (May 1909) 436-8.

On the problem of the relation of mechanism to art, condemning the use of the gramophone (i.e. as a substitute for music as an art) and the harmonium. "These two instruments, if care be not taken, will in a few years more complete the vulgarisation of Indian music" (p. 438). This article was reprinted, with the title question-marked, as Chapter XV of *Essays in National Idealism* ([1909?])—A18a.

C203 Art and Svadeshi. *Central Hindu College Magazine*, Benares, N.S. IX. 5 (1 May 1909) 111-14.

That Swadeshi "must be something more than a political weapon. It must be a religious-artistic ideal" (p. 113): AKC considers (1) the plight of an "Anglicised India", (2) "the degradation of Indian craftsmanship", (3) the shoddy Indian "imitations of the productions of European commerce", and (4) that, in his view, "the regeneration of India [will be] through art, and not by politics and economics alone" (p.112). This article was reprinted in *The Message of the East* ([1909])—A17—pp. 39-50, and as Chapter I of *Art and Swadeshi* ([1912])—A25a.

C204 Dr. Coomaraswamy on His Lecture, Etc. [Letter]. *Ceylon Observer*, Colombo (17 May 1909) 5.

Disclaiming responsibility for the words of his lecture (on Indian art, at a meeting of the Royal Asiatic Society in Colombo on 14 May) as they were reported in the issue for 15 May. This letter was reprinted in *Journal of the Royal Asiatic Society (Ceylon Branch)*, Colombo, XXI. 62 (1909) 294.

C205 Indian Art: Further Views. [Letter]. *Ceylon Observer*, Colombo (18 May 1909) 5.

Replying to editorial criticism, in the issue for 15 May, concerning his lecture at a meeting of the Royal Asiatic Society in Colombo on 14 May. This letter was reprinted in *Journal of the Royal Asiatic Society (Ceylon Branch)*, Colombo, XXI. 62 (1909) 295-6.

C206 The Nationalisation of Education. *New Age*, London, N.S. V. 4 (20 May 1909) 70-1.

Dated Colombo, Apr. 1909. AKC opines that since becoming an Imperialist power, England has lost her true self; he suggests educational and other reforms that might serve to "leaven and spiritualise the English character". The by-line has erroneously: Professor [for, Doctor] Ananda K. Coomaraswamy.

C207 [Letter]. *Times Literary Supplement*, London, 385 (27 May 1909) 198.

AKC's is the sixth of nine items printed under the general heading: Notes. On a review of *Mediaeval Sinhalese Art* ([1908])—A14a—in the issue for 25 March; pointing out that neither William Morris nor Indian art preach the gospel of art for art's sake.

C208 The Message of the East [II]. *Modern Review*, Calcutta, V. 6 (June 1909) 506-11.

On the "fatal confusion" in the West of science with art: "The message of the East is . . . that there exists a greater beauty and truth than that of this phenomenal world; and that the artist . . . must imitate the beauty which is in Heaven, rather than its imperfect reflection in individual physical forms" (p. 508).

C209 Art and Yoga in India. *Orpheus: The Art-Movement of the Theosophical Society*, London, 7 (June 1909) 62-6, 1 pl.

On certain aspects of the aims and methods of Indian art that possess a yogic character, and in this connection quoting from Patañjali and a 12th century AD Tantric text. AKC also compares the Indian conception of the artistic imagination with that which prevails in modern Europe. This article was reprinted as Chapter V of *Essays in National Idealism* ([1909?])—A18a.

C210 The Dhyani Buddha from Borobodur. *Central Hindu College*

Magazine, Benares, N.S. IX. 6 (1 June 1909) 139-40, 1 pl. (i.e. frontis. to this issue).

A brief exposition of the seated Buddha type, citing *Bhagavadgītā*, VI. 12-15. The first of an intended monthly series of twelve articles by AKC on Indian art. The series appeared concurrently in *Theosophist*, Madras. In all only nine instalments were published, and the monthly schedule was not maintained. "These notes may serve to suggest to readers . . . that the history of Indian religious thought is written as clearly in Indian art as in Indian literature" (p. 140). This article was printed simultaneously, as "A Ḍhyani Buḍḍha from Boro Budur", in *Theosophist*, Madras, XXX. 9 (June 1909) [374]-375, 1 pl. (facing p. 290).

C211 A Prize for Craft Similies. *Central Hindu College Magazine*, Benares, N.S. IX. 6 (1 June 1909) 140.

Calling for the best collection assembled of such similies, from the Sanskrit literature, and giving as an example: "Causing all things to revolve as though mounted on a potter's wheel" (*Bhagavadgītā*, XVIII. 61). Unsigned, but almost certainly by AKC; see C231.

C212 The Function of Schools of Art in India [I]. *Hindu*, Madras (23 June 1909) 4-5.

Dated Tanjore, India, 20 June [1909]. The first of two instalments. On a lecture of this title by Cecil L. Burns (Principal of the Sir Jamsetjee Jeejeebhoy School of Art, Bombay), given at the Royal Society of Arts, London, 27 May 1909 (Burns' lecture was subsequently published in the 18 June 1909 issue of the Society's *Journal*). AKC, in the course of his critique of Burns' "un-Indian" regime, says that "the true function of Schools of Art in India, is not to introduce European methods and ideals but to *gather up and revitalise the broken threads of Indian tradition* [AKC's emphasis], to build up the idea of Indian art as an integral part of the national culture, and to relate the work of Indian craftsmen to the life and thought of the Indian people" ([II], p. 6). Reprinted, with changes, in *Modern Review*, Calcutta,VII. 2 (Feb. 1910) 125-9, and as Chapter V of *Art and Swadeshi* ([1912])—A25a. Reprinted, in part, in *Indian Review*, Madras, XI. 3 (Mar. 1910) 212.

C213 The Function of Schools of Art in India [II]. *Hindu*, Madras (24 June 1909) 5-6.

C214 The Message of the East [III]. *Modern Review*, Calcutta, VI. 1 (July 1909) 9-10.

The last of the three instalments with this title comprises some reflections on the consequences of the Indian attempt to assimilate Western industrial culture: "Indians are destroying their civilization as a compliment to England" (p.10).

C215 "Extinction". *Central Hindu College Magazine,* Benares, N.S. IX. 7 (1 July 1909) 165-6.

Correcting an unnamed "English lady artist['s]" misapprehensions about Hinduism.

C216 Shiva as Nataraja. *Central Hindu College Magazine*, Benares, N.S. IX. 7 (1 July 1909) 174, 1 pl. (i.e. frontis. to this issue).

(The plate only, a reproduction of a Naṭarāja image from the Colombo Museum, was reprinted in *Theosophist*, Madras, for December 1909, facing p. 361, with a substitute text, by Ernest Wood and S.V. Subrahmanyam, as AKC's copy had failed to arrive.)

C217 The Philosophy of Indian Art. *Hindustan Review*, Allahabad, XX. 120 (Aug. 1909) [138]-149.

A reprint, in a reduced form, and with changes, of *The Aims of Indian Art* ([1908])—A12.

C218 Dr. Coomaraswamy on European Commercial Production: Superiority of the Eastern Craftsman Over the Western Workman. *Dawn*, Calcutta, XII. 9 (Sept. 1909) 35-6.

Excerpted from *Mediaeval Sinhalese Art* ([1908])—A14a—"Foreword", p. vii.

C219 The International Congress of Applied Chemistry: and Aniline Dyes. *Modern Review*, Calcutta, VI. 3 (Sept. 1909) 275-8.

AKC points to the detrimental effect of the new chemical dyes upon the traditional dyer's craft in India, with reference to "The International Congress of Applied Chemistry—a Lesson for India", by Praphulla Chandra Ray, in the issue for August 1909. This article was reprinted as Chapter IV of *Art and Swadeshi* ([1912])—A25a.

C220 The Paintings of Nanda Lal Bose. *Modern Review*, Calcutta, VI. 3 (Sept. 1909) 300-2.

AKC singles out for discussion two works by this artist of the modern Calcutta School: "Sati" (reproduced in the April 1908 issue) and "Siva Tandava"; and adds some comments on the educational role the Calcutta School might perform within the Indian nationalist movement.

C221 Gold Embedding. *Spolia Zeylanica*, Colombo, VI. 22 (Sept. 1909) 76-7, 1 text illus.

Notes on the process of incrusting gold with gems (Sinhala, *tahadu kola bemma*, Tamil, *idu tarigam*) taken from observation made of a Tamil jeweller working in Colombo. This article was reprinted, as an item in the list of "Errata and Additional Addenda", in *Mediaeval Sinhalese Art*, Second Edition ([1956])—A14b—pp. 319-20.

C222 Bhairava, or Dharmapala. *Central Hindu College Magazine*, Benares, N.S. IX. 9 (1 Sept. 1909) 224, 1 pl. (i.e. frontis. to this issue).

On a Javanese bronze of *circa* AD 9th century. This article was reprinted, as "Ḍharmapāla or Bhairava", in *Theosophist*, Madras, XXXI. 1 (Oct. 1909) [140], 1 pl. (facing).

C223 Eugenics. [Letter]. *New Age*, London, N.S. V. 20 (9 Sept. 1909) 371.

Quoting two paragraphs that express "the true principles of Eugenics" from an unnamed Persian book.

C224 Sundara Murti Swami. *Central Hindu College Magazine*, Benares, N.S. IX.10 (1 Oct. 1909) 255, 1 pl. (i.e. frontis. to this issue).

(In English.) On the bronze image of a Tamil Shaiva saint, "recently discovered at Polonnaruwa in Ceylon, and now in the Colombo Museum". This article was reprinted, as "Sunḍara Mūrṭi Svāmi", in *Theosophist*, Madras, XXXI. 2 (Nov. 1909) [273], 1 pl. (facing), and, with revisions, in *Selected Examples of Indian Art* ([1910])—A21—pp. 15-16.

C225 The Evolution of Music in East and West. *Journal of the Ceylon University Association*, Colombo, II. 7 (Nov. 1909) [178]-191.

A review of *Analysis of the Evolution of Musical Form*, by Margaret Glyn, with copious excerpts. This review was reprinted, in two parts, in *Hindustan Review*, Allahabad, XXV. 152 (Apr. 1912) [384]-389, and 153/154 (May/June 1912) [472]-480.

C226 A Plea for National Education. *Dawn*, Calcutta, XII. 12 (Dec. 1909) [197]-204.

The reported words of a lecture, entitled "National Education", given by AKC at the Bengal National College, Calcutta, on 18 August 1909. "A very faithful report [by Rabindranarayan Ghosh], which is here presented to the public as an article. Owing to Dr. Coomaraswamy's rather sudden departure for England almost immediately after the delivery of the address, we had no opportunity of getting it revised by him" (*editorial note*, p. [197]).

C227 Figure of Kapila at Isurumuniya Vihara, Anuradhapura. *Spolia Zeylanica*, Colombo, VI. 23 (Dec. 1909) 132-3.

Dated 18 Sept. 1909. AKC suggests "that the sculpture represents the sage Kapila, with the horse, in Patála (the nether regions of the earth)" (p.133).

1910

C228 National Self-Consciousness in India. *Hindustan Review*, Allahabad, XXI. 125 (Jan.1910) [16]-20.

Excerpts, with changes, from *The Deeper Meaning of the Struggle* ([1907])—A10—pp. 15-21, 23.

C229 Shipping in Ancient India. *Modern Review*, Calcutta, VII. 1 (Jan. 1910) 108-9.

Printed under the general heading: Notes. AKC quotes from *Ancient Ceylon*, by Henry Parker, and from a circa AD 1st century Tamil poem, the *Pattinappalai*, i.e. sources additional to those cited in a series of articles on the ancient sea-borne trade, by Radha Kumud Mookerji, in the issues for October, November, and December 1909.

C230 Kansallinen liike indiassa. *Valvoja*, Helsinki, XXX. 1 (Jan. 1910) [7]-18.

("Indian national movement".) With reference to *The New Spirit in India*, by H.W. Nevinson.

C231 The Prize for Craft Similies. *Central Hindu College Magazine*, Benares, N.S. X. 1 (1 Jan. 1910) 12-13.

As none of the entries received—see C211—was considered worthy of a prize, AKC announces a new competition: the best essay received on Viśvakarma.

C232 Recent Studies of Buddhism and Hinduism. *Hindustan Review*, Allahabad, XXI. 126 (Feb.1910) [217]-229.

Printed under the general heading: Views and Reviews. Unsigned, but credited to AKC on the front cover of this issue. An omnibus review of *Early Buddhism*, by T.W. Rhys Davids; *Buddhist Essays*, by Paul Dahlke; *Buddhism, Primitive and Present, in Magadha and in Ceylon*, by R.S. Copleston; *The Essence of Buddhism*, by P. Lakshmi Narasu; *The Way of the Buddha*, by Herbert Baynes; *Brahma Knowledge*, *The Heart of India*, and *Hinduism*, by L.D. Barnett. "Nothing can be more interesting and significant than the interest now taken by Western nations in the religious thought of the East . . . Every student of Buddhism should possess Prof. Rhys Davids' history . . . Dahlke's essays . . . present a clear and logical exposition of Buddhism . . . Bishop Copleston's book is of another order . . . it is written throughout in the manner of a criticism of the Buddha and his teachings, by 'one who knows' . . . Of the three booklets by Dr. Barnett, the first seems to us the best . . . Prof. Lakshmi Narasu's volume . . . is in many ways an excellent account of Buddhism but is named [*sic*, for marred?] by a controversial and patronising attitude towards Hinduism, which the author hardly seems to understand . . . 'The Way of the Buddha', by Herbert Baynes . . . is to be regarded as a useful introduction."

C233 Indo-Persian Miniatures. *Modern Review*, Calcutta, VII. 2 (Feb. 1910) 205.

Printed under the general heading: Notes. A translation by AKC of some passages from *Manuel d'art musulman, II. Les Arts plastiques et industriels*, by Gaston Migeon.

C234 The Influence of Musalman Art on the Arts of Western Europe. *Modern Review*, Calcutta, VII. 3 (Mar. 1910) 239-42.

A translation by AKC of the "Conclusion" to *Manuel d'art musulman, II. Les Arts plastiques et industriels*, by Gaston Migeon.

C235 Khwaja Kidar. *Modern Review*, Calcutta, VII. 3 (Mar. 1910) 294-5, 1 pl. (facing p. 212).

(In English.) Printed under the general heading: Notes. On the cult in India of the "genius of inland waters, as rivers and wells", and his typical representation in paintings of the Mughal period.

C236 On the Study of Indian Art [I]. *Hindu*, Madras (26 Mar. 1910) 7-8.

The first of three instalments. A paper read by AKC at a meeting of the Royal Asiatic Society in London, on 8 March 1910. AKC contends that Western understanding of Indian art is "fettered by . . . academic conventions", by cultural prejudice, by "the extremely materialistic character of most European religious thought since the Reformation", and by the current notion of naturalism as the aim of art. He proposes an improved methodology which takes as its prerequisite that an "understanding of Indian art can only be attained through a realisation of the mental atmosphere in which it grew". AKC calls attention to certain inadequacies in the works of Albert Grünwedel, Vincent Smith, and Alfred Foucher, and notes how by "some extraordinary oversight" no European writer has yet studied the *śilpa-śāstras*. The three instalments were reprinted together to form Chapter VI of *Art and Swadeshi* ([1912])—A25a.

C237 On the Study of Indian Art [II]. *Hindu*, Madras (28 Mar. 1910) 5-6.

C238 On the Study of Indian Art [III]. *Hindu*, Madras (31 Mar. 1910) 3-4.

C239 The Book of the Month. The Mind of the Artist. *Hindustan Review*, Allahabad, XXI. 127/128 (Mar./Apr. 1910) 323-6.

A review of *The Mind of the Artist: Thoughts and Sayings of Painters and Sculptors on Their Art*, edited by Mrs Laurence Binyon. AKC thinks the book "of great value to the student of the psychology of art", and excerpts from Binyon's anthology "some of the sayings of those artists whose aims and work are most nearly allied to those of classic Indian art" (p. 324).

C240 Mediaeval Indian Painting. *Modern Review*, Calcutta, VII. 4 (Apr. 1910) 314-22, 7 text illus.

An inquiry into the special character of Mughal painting, and the contemporaneous "Mediaeval Hindu school" (i.e. Rājput painting). Prefaced with some remarks on the Buddhist work at Ajaṇṭā. AKC expects "a better knowledge and understanding of Mediaeval Indian painting than is now general" (p. 322).

C241 Aniline Dyes. [Letter]. *Manchester Guardian*, Manchester, 19,866 (11 Apr. 1910) 12.

Dated Campden [Glos.], 9 Apr. [1910]. AKC points out that while English manufacturers may express regret over their loss of pre-eminence in the aniline dye trade, these dyes have destroyed throughout the world the traditional art of dyeing; with reference to correspondence on this topic in previous issues.

C242 "The Madras House". [Letter]. *New Age*, London, N.S. VI. 24 (14 Apr. 1910) 574.

The second of two letters printed under this heading: on a play of this title by Granville Barker.

C243 Indian Bronzes. *Burlington Magazine*, London, XVII. 86 (May 1910) 86-94, II numbered pls.

A brief guide to the proper appreciation of some Hindu and Buddhist statuettes from India, Nepal, Tibet, Ceylon, and Java.

C244 Chank and Other Objects from the Maha Devale, Kandy. *Spolia Zeylanica*, Colombo, VI. 24 (May 1910) 185-6, 1 pl. (facing p. 185).

Dated Campden, Glos., 13 Dec. 1909. On a gold-mounted conch shell trumpet, and other royal treasures of Ceylon.

C245 The Oriental View of Woman. *Votes for Women*, London, N.S. III. 114 (13 May 1910) 531.

Correcting the European assumption that woman is looked down upon in the East. This article was reprinted, in part, in *Indian Review*, Madras, XI. 6 (June 1910) 451. The complete article was reprinted in *Vivekananda Kendra Patrika,* Madras, VI. 2 (Aug. 1975) 125-7, and, in a slightly expanded form, by Essex House Press ([1910])—A19.

C246 Domestic Handicraft and Culture. *Education*, London, II. (17 June 1910) 369-71.

Printed under the general heading: Association of Teachers of Domestic Science—(2). Annual Conference in London. A lecture read by AKC before the Association, at the University of London, on 28 May. On the modern "substitution of mechanical production under factory conditions, for hand production under domestic . . . conditions", and how this innovation "is directly destructive of culture" (p.371), incorporating quotations from Plato, William Blake, and William Morris. This lecture was reprinted by Essex House Press ([1910])—A20, and as Chapter III in *Art and Swadeshi* ([1912])—A25a, and again in *Good Work*, Cambridge, Mass., XXVII. 2 (Spring 1964) 44-51. Also reprinted, in an abridged form, in *Dawn*, Calcutta, XV. 7 (July 1912) [129]-132.

C247 Originality in Mughal Painting. *Journal of the Royal Asiatic Society*, London (July 1910) 874-81.

Dated Campden [Glos.], Mar. 1910. A vindication of this branch of Islamic art, and drawing attention to the characteristics that distinguish Mughal work from both Persian and Rājput.

C248 Night Effects in Indian Pictures. Golden Rain by Muhammad Afzal. *Modern Review*, Calcutta, VIII.1 (July 1910) 103-4, 2 text illus.

On two 17th century miniatures that depict groups of Hindu girls with fireworks. The second of these paintings is also discussed in an article by AKC, that is in part identical with this, "Night Effects in Indian Pictures", in *Studio*, London, for September 1910—C253.

C249 The Birth of Ganga. *Modern Review*, Calcutta, VIII. 2 (Aug. 1910) 220-1, 1 text illus.

A note to accompany the reproduction of a painting of this title by Abanindranath Tagore and Nanda Lal Bose: in the main a retelling by AKC of the myth of the Descent of the Ganges as found in the *Rāmāyaṇa*; with a brief critical comment on the picture itself.

C250 Rāgiṇī Torī. *Theosophist*, Madras, XXXI. 11 (Aug. 1910) [1473]-1474, 1 pl. (facing p. [1473]).

On a Rāgmālā miniature, tentatively assigned to the 17th century and thought to be from Jaipur; including a general discussion of the connection of musical modes with painting. (The plate reproduces the same painting as that in *Rajput Painting* (1916)—A34a—Pl. XIIB.) This article was reprinted in *Central Hindu College Magazine*, Benares, N.S. X. 9 (1 Sept. 1910) 229-30, 1 pl. (facing p. 229), and, in a slightly revised form, in *Selected Examples of Indian Art* ([1910])—A21—pp. 2-3.

C251 The Book of the Month. Ancient Ceylon. *Hindustan Review*, Allahabad, XXII. 133 (Sept. 1910) 323-8.

A review of *Ancient Ceylon: An Account of the Aborigines and of Part of the Early Civilisation*, by Henry Parker. AKC calls attention to and discusses Parker's accounts of (1) the religion of the Veddas, in particular the "Hill god . . . whose identity is merged and survives in that of the later Śiva" (p. 325), (2) the ancient cities and structural works, including irrigation works, and (3) the ancient and modern games. AKC commends the book as having "great merit . . . and quite indispensible [*sic*] to the student of Ancient India and Ceylon, especially to those concerned with Buddhist antiquities, and with folk-lore and anthropology" (p. 328).

C252 Notes on Kandyan Art. *Spolia Zeylanica*, Colombo, VII. 25 (Sept. 1910) 39-42, 2 pls. (one following p. 42).

On (1) a chank (shell) trumpet, (2) a carved powder horn, (3) a stock-drill weight, (4) a *kendiya* (spouted water vessel), (5) gold beads (including a list of Sinhala names for gold necklaces, additional to those given in *Mediaeval Sinhalese Art* ([1908])—A14a—p. 211), and (6) the bo-leaf as a decorative motif.

C253 Night Effects in Indian Pictures. *Studio*, London, L. 210 (Sept. 1910) 305-7, 4 text illus.

On this motif as a "very characteristic feature of Indian painting", and discussing its occurrence in four miniatures (all reproduced, and ascribed by AKC to the late 17th century) that "belong, broadly speaking, to the Rajput School". AKC concludes with a paragraph on the proper application of the term "Indo-Persian" in classifying Indian pictures—"hitherto it has been usual to class all Indian paintings as Indo-Persian, or even frankly as

Persian". This article was reprinted, revised and with the omission of the final paragraph, as Chapter IX of *Art and Swadeshi* ([1912])—A25a.

C254 Shiva's Dance. *Theosophist*, Madras, XXXI. 12 (Sept. 1910) [1620]-1621, 1 pl. (facing p. [1620]).

On the iconography of a Kāngrā Valley School miniature, depicting Shiva, surrounded by his orchestra, dancing on Mount Kailāsa. This article was reprinted in *Central Hindu College Magazine*, Benares, N.S. X. 10 (1 Oct. 1910) 262-3, 1 pl. (frontis. to this issue), and, in a slightly revised and expanded form, in *Selected Examples of Indian Art* ([1910])—A21—pp. 1-2.

C255 Shiva Rāṭri. *Theosophist*, Madras, XXXII. 1 (Oct. 1910) [140], 1 pl. (facing).

(In English.) A note in 14 lines on an Indian miniature of *circa* 17th or 18th century that depicts a night scene where three *sannyāsinīs* are performing Shiva *pūjā*. This article was reprinted in *Central Hindu College Magazine*, Benares, N.S. X. 11 (1 Nov. 1910) 281, 1 pl. (facing).

C256 An International Symposium on the Art of the Theatre. *New Age*, London, N.S. VII. 23 (6 Oct. 1910) 533.

AKC's is the fourth of ten contributions printed under this heading. The symposium was conducted by Huntly Carter. AKC's contribution is captioned: India. On the present state of the Indian dramatic arts; with a paragraph on the nautch dancing of southern India.

C257 About Pictures [I]. *Modern Review*, Calcutta, VIII. 5 (Nov. 1910) 523-4.

The first of two instalments. In the main, on the "fallacy of illusion", i.e. that the greatest painting is that which achieves a photographic resemblance to some object chosen as the model. An essay written expressly to exemplify the "conception of art-criticism as a high calling" (p. 523).

C258 Calligraphy. *Modern Review*, Calcutta, VIII. 5 (Nov. 1910) 552-3.

Printed under the general heading: Reviews and Notices of Books . . . Persian. On the special status accorded calligraphy in the East, and the threat to calligraphy's survival in the age of machines; calling attention to *The Tadhkira-i-Khushnavisan of Mawlana Ghulam Muhammad Dihlavi*, edited by M. Hidāyat Husain.

C259 Lailā and Majnūn. *Theosophist*, Madras, XXXII. 2 (Nov. 1910) [297]-298, 1 pl. (facing p. [297]).

On an "Indo-Persian" miniature, tentatively dated early 17th century, that typically depicts the tragic lovers at their "Last Meeting". This article was reprinted in *Central Hindu College Magazine*, Benares, N.S. X. 12 (1 Dec. 1910) 307-8, 1 pl. (facing p. 307). Also printed, in a revised and expanded form, in *Selected Examples of Indian Art* ([1910])—A21—pp. 6-8.

C260 A Prince of Swadeshists. *Young Behar*, Bhagalpur, India, II. 5 (Nov. 1910) 89.

A note in praise of Lord Curzon (Viceroy and Governor-General of India, 1898-1905) for his advocacy of India's traditional arts and crafts.

C261 About Pictures [II]. *Modern Review*, Calcutta, VIII. 6 (Dec. 1910) 592-4.

A brief guide to the appreciation of painting in general, and on discerning the truth or greatness of a work of art.

C262 Baz Bahāḍur and Rūpmaṭī. *Theosophist*, Madras, XXXII. 3 (Dec. 1910) [450], 1 pl. (facing).

A note, printed in 17 lines, accompanying the reproduction of a "characteristically Rājput" picture of the celebrated lovers riding together by night. This note was reprinted in *Central Hindu College Magazine*, Benares, N.S. XI. 2 (Feb. 1911) 54, 1 pl. (facing).

C263 Indian maalaustaide. *Valvoja*, Helsinki, XXX.12 (Dec. 1910) [661]-681, 10 text illus.

("Indian painting".)

1911

C264 The New School of Indian Painting. *Ceylon National Review*, Colombo, IV. 10 (Jan. 1911) [201]-206, 1 pl. (facing p. [201]).

"A very brief account of the origins and work of the New School [in Calcutta, led by Abanindranath Tagore]" (p. 206). Preceded by a discussion of how the "conditions established by the occupation of India by Europeans . . . [brought about] the destruction of great artistic traditions, in the interests of commercial exploitation" (pp. [201], 202).

C265 Indian Art at the United Provinces Exhibition. *Hindustan Review*, Allahabad, XXII. 137 (Jan. 1911) [15]-21.

Briefly describing some of the exhibits: paintings of the modern Calcutta School; Christiana Herringham's copies of Ajaṇṭā frescoes; Mughal and Rājput miniatures; textiles; embroidery; etc. At the invitation of the Indian Society of Oriental Art (Calcutta), AKC was Officer in Charge of the Courts of Fine Arts, Wood, Stone, and Metal, at the Exhibition, held at Allahabad, from 1 December 1910 to 28 February 1911.

C266 On Mughal and Rajput Painting. *Modern Review*, Calcutta, IX. 1 (Jan. 1911) 71-5, 7 pls. (facing pp. 4, 36, 48, 70, 72, 74, 80).

An abstract of a lecture given by AKC at a meeting of the Indian Society of Oriental Art, held at the Calcutta home of Sir John Woodroffe (Arthur Avalon), sometime in the latter part of 1910. A detailed account of the characteristic and distinguishing features of the two schools. This article was reprinted, in a revised and enlarged form, as Chapter VIII of *Art and Swadeshi* ([1912])—A25a.

C267 Indian Opinion on the State Regulation of Vice. *Shield: The Official Organ of the British Committee of the International Federation for the Abolition of State Regulation of Vice*, London, N.S. XIII. 123 (Jan. 1911) 7-8.

Dated India, October 1910. On the current status of the prostitute in India. This article was reprinted, with the omission of two sentences from the penultimate paragraph, in *Selected Letters of Ananda K. Coomaraswamy* (1988)—A89—pp. 365-8.

C268 Indian Sculpture at Allahabad. *Modern Review*, Calcutta, IX. 3 (Mar. 1911) [221]-226, 10 text illus.

A review of old and modern exhibits at the United Provinces Exhibition (1910-11). AKC singles out for praise the work of "one of the most real artists I have ever met", the sculptor Mali Ram of Jaipur. Includes a plea for "sympathetic and *critical* patronage" (AKC's emphasis) of those traditional craftsmen that still survive.

C269 Prize Essays on Trade Guilds in India. *Modern Review*, Calcutta, IX. 3 (Mar. 1911) 253-9.

AKC introduces Mukandi Lal's winning essay on the Benares Silk-weavers' Guild (which essay is reproduced on pp. 254-7); with brief summaries of two of the other prize essays received. The announcement of AKC's offer to award a prize of 250 rupees for the best essay on the Guilds in India (in connection with the United Provinces Exhibition at Allahabad, 1910-11) had appeared in the issue for November 1910, on p. 576.

C270 Janmakatha (Birth-Story). *Modern Review*, Calcutta, IX. 3 (Mar. 1911) 296.

A translation from the Bengali into English by AKC of a poem by Rabindranath Tagore, with assistance from Ajit Chakravarty. This translation was reprinted in *Art and Swadeshi* ([1912])—A25a—pp. 118-20.

C271 Four Days in Orissa. *Modern Review*, Calcutta, IX. 4 (Apr. 1911) 345-50, 10 text illus.

"A very brief account of a short architectural pilgrimage" (p. 350). Comprises descriptions of (1) the sacred city of Purī, (2) the Koṇārak Sun temple, (3) the Hindu temples at Bhuvaneśvara, and (4) the Buddhist monuments at Udayagiri and Khandagiri. The illustrations, with the exception of the first two, are reproductions of photographs, taken in Orissa, by AKC. Erratum is printed in this same issue of the *Modern Review*, p. 449. This article was reprinted, with the omission of the illustrations, in *Ananda Coomaraswamy; a Study*, by Moni Bagchee ([1977])—B93—pp. 163-7.

C272 Biday (Farewell). *Modern Review*, Calcutta, IX. 4 (Apr. 1911) 371, 1 pl. (facing).

A translation from the Bengali by AKC of a poem by Rabindranath Tagore, in collaboration with the poet. This translation was reprinted, with minor revisions, and repeating the first stanza at the end, in *Art and Swadeshi* ([1912])—A25a—pp. 120-2. The plate is a reproduction of a photograph of Tagore and AKC taken by Hiralal Sen.

C273 The Woman's Suffrage Movement and Indian Unrest. [Letter]. *New Age*, London, N.S. VIII. 24 (13 Apr. 1911) 571-2.

AKC argues that women are not claiming "political rights because they are different from men and wish to turn the world upside down", but because "they want a share in the inestimable privilege of maintaining the status quo . . . It is . . . profound self-distrust which is the most essential weakness in the English woman's movement, as well as in the Indian Nationalist movement. Neither women nor Indians really wish to be themselves" (p. 572). This letter was reprinted, in the form of an article, with a few minor changes, as "The Woman's Suffrage Movement: Criticism and Parallel to Indian Unrest", in *Modern Review*, Calcutta, IX. 5 (May 1911) 462-3.

C274 Indian Drawings. [Letter]. *Athenaeum*, London, 4,356 (22 Apr. 1911) 452-3.

Dated Bombay, 29 Mar. 1911. On a review in the issue for 18 February of his *Indian Drawings* ([1910])—A22.

C275 Selected Examples of Indian Art. [Letter]. *Burlington Magazine*, London, XIX. 98 (May 1911) 106.

Dated India, 21 Feb. 1911. On the review by W.H. J[ames]. W[eale]. of *Selected Examples of Indian Art* ([1910])—A21, in the issue for February. AKC defends his advocacy of the modern Calcutta school, and explains as well some of the distinctions between Mughal and Rājput painting.

C276 Avalokitesvara. *Modern Review*, Calcutta, IX. 5 (May 1911) 542-3, 1 text illus.

(In English.) Printed under the general heading: Notes. A brief comment, excerpted from Chapter V of *Essays in National Idealism* ([1909?])—A18a, to accompany the reproduction of an 8th century bronze from Ceylon.

C277 Prajna-Paramita. *Modern Review*, Calcutta, IX. 5 (May 1911) 543, 1 text illus.

(In English.) Printed under the general heading: Notes. A brief comment, excerpted from Chapter IV of *Essays in National Idealism* ([1909?])—A18a, to accompany the reproduction of a Mahāyāna Buddhist image from Java.

C278 Indian Music, and Harmoniums. *Dawn*, Calcutta, XIV. 7 (July 1911) 74-7.

At the request of the periodical's editor, AKC replies to an article of this title, by A.H. Fox Strangways, which is printed on pp. 65-73. AKC objects to the harmonium (which he considers to be no more a musical instrument than "the steam-organ of the circus and merry-go-round"), especially when used to accompany the voice, and comments on the harmonium's deleterious effect generally on Indian music and musicianship.

C279 Song-Words of a Panjabi Singer. *Modern Review*, Calcutta, X. 4 (Oct. 1911) 329-33.

Dated Kashmir, Aug. 1911. Comprises (1) a discussion of how in Indian music "there is no marked distinction between art and folk songs", (2) a biographical cameo of Abdul Rahīm, a modern *ustād* of Kapurthala, and (3) a brief annotated anthology of twenty-one Panjabi, Urdu, Hindi, Sindhi, Persian, and Arabic songs taken from this singer's repertory. The translations of these songs are by AKC, with the assistance of Paira Mall. This article was reprinted, with minor revisions, together with the song "Panjabi Ghazal" that was omitted, erroneously, from the article as originally printed, and with the addition of four new sentences, as Chapter X of *Art and Swadeshi* ([1912])—A25a, and, with further revisions and expansions, as *Thirty Songs from the Panjab and Kashmīr* ([1913])—A27a. See also C308.

1912

C280 Rajput Painting. *Dawn*, Calcutta, XV. 1 (Jan. 1912) 12-16.

A note on the Hindu character of Rājput work, and the relation this school bears to Persian and Mughal painting. Some explanatory comments by the editor of *Dawn* are subjoined, pp. 16-23. A considerably expanded version of this article was printed in *Burlington Magazine*, London, for March 1912—C285.

C281 [Letter]. *Indian Education*, Bombay, X. 6 (Jan. 1912) 274.

Printed under the general heading: Correspondence. Replying to an editorial, in the issue for August 1911, that misunderstood his position concerning pictures suitable for exhibition in Indian art schools. AKC concludes with a paragraph on the paintings of Ravi Varma. A rejoinder from the editor of *Indian Education* is appended.

C282 Art and Ethics [I]. *Modern Review*, Calcutta, XI. 1 (Jan. 1912) 88-9.

The first of two instalments. A brief meditation on the relation of art to morality.

C283 The Book of the Month: Mr. Havell's Ideals of Indian Art. *Hindustan Review*, Allahabad, XXV. 150 (Feb. 1912) [185]-188.

A review of *The Ideals of Indian Art*, by E.B. Havell. AKC finds Havell best in his arguments with the Western philistine, though Havell is "perhaps . . . a little over-combative for a battle already won" (p. [185]). AKC is critical of Havell's method: "his directly aesthetic, rather than literary enquiry . . . goes too far in ignoring scholarship" (p. 188); nevertheless, AKC acknowledges that "Havell's . . . very great service . . . is the way in which he has laboured to make [Indian] art better known" (pp. [185]-186).

C284 Art and Ethics [II]. *Modern Review*, Calcutta, XI. 2 (Feb. 1912) 150-2.

In the main, on the question of censorship.

C285 Rajput Paintings. *Burlington Magazine*, London, XX. 108 (Mar. 1912) 315-24, 4 pls. (facing pp. 315, 318, 323, and 324).

This article, which AKC says is the "first published account of the Rajput Schools, the Hindu painting of Rajputana and the Punjab Himalayas" (in his *Bibliographies of Indian Art* (1925)—A48—p. 23), is concerned with the essentially indigenous character of Rājput work, arguing its distinction from the Mughal. AKC demonstrates how Rājput painting derives from, and continues, the older Indian classical tradition, in particular the fresco painting at Ajaṇṭā. He proposes a classification of Rājput painting into two groups: Rājasthānī and Pahāṛī, and describes in some detail their respective characters.

C286 Parasitic Art. *Hindu*, Madras (21 Mar. 1912) 7-8.

AKC reproves the modern Indian artist who feels only contempt for India's past achievements, and who adopts European pictorial conventions that are alien to his own mode of vision. Including some comments on the European appreciation of Oriental art, illustrated by quotations from Laurence Binyon, Roger Fry, and W.R. Lethaby.

C287 Drawing-room Charades. *Hindu*, Madras (27 Mar. 1912) 6-7.

A review of two recently-staged "Indian" plays in London: *Buddha, the Light of Asia, His Life and Great Renunciation* (an adaptation of Sir Edwin Arnold's *Light of Asia*), and *Kumārasambhavạ* (based on the poem of Kālidāsa), objecting to "the rhetorical design and false sentiment": the "scenery and costumes were more suggestive of Bombay Parsi drawing-rooms".

C288 Rajput Cartoons; a Criticism after Nietzche [*sic*]. *Rajput Herald*, London, II. 6 (June 1912) 21-5, 1 text illus., 2 pls. (one is coloured, facing p. 21).

AKC employs Nietzschean terms and ideas in his estimation of 18th century cartoons (depicting Rādhā and Krishna dancing) for wall-paintings in the Jaipur palace.

C289 The Suggested Change of Capital for Ceylon: A Home Protest. [Letter]. *Ceylon Observer*, Colombo, Weekly Edition (16? June 1912) 1027.

Dated London, 30 May 1912. AKC opposes suggested improvements to Kandy, and observes that "whatever civic beauty Kandy possesses, and that is much, is due to Buddhist town-planning and the survival of Buddhist buildings". (This item is known to the compiler only from a clipping.)

C290 The Book of the Month. Sir Marc Stein's "Ruins of Desert Cathay". *Hindustan Review*, Allahabad, XXVI. 155 (July 1912) [56]-61.

A review of *Ruins of Desert Cathay*, by Marc Aurel Stein. AKC discusses the significance to social and political history, and to the history of art, of Stein's archaeological discoveries in Chinese Central Asia.

C291 Siva and Parvati. *Modern Review*, Calcutta, XII. 1 (July 1912) 107.

Printed under the general heading: Notes. A brief comment on the subject of a painting attributed to Mola Rām of Gaṛhwāl (d. 1833), which is reproduced, in colour, as the frontispiece to this issue.

C292 Rājput Painting. *Ostasiatische Zeitschrift*, Berlin, I. 2 (July 1912) 125-39, 7 text illus.

Differs from "Rajput Paintings" (Mar. 1912)—C285. An offprint is held by the Victoria & Albert Museum, National Art Library, with others by AKC in a bound volume lettered on the spine: Indian Art.

C293 The Dance of Siva. *The Light of Truth or the Siddhānta Dipikā and Āgamic Review*, Madras, XIII. 1 (July 1912) [1]-13, 1 pl. (facing p. [1]).

On the Naṭarāja image; an explication of "the general significance of the dance [and] the details of its concrete symbolism", by extensive reference to the contemporary literature. Some quotations are printed in Tamil script. This article was reprinted in *Elements of Hindu Iconography*, by T.P. Gopinatha Rao (1916)—B12, and, with the omission of Tamil script, in *The Dance of Śiva* (1918)—A38a—pp. [56]-66.

C294 On Indian Art in China. *Dawn*, Calcutta, XV. 8 (Aug. 1912) [133]-137.

Drawing upon the researches of Victor Goloubew, Marc Aurel Stein, Stephen Wootton Bushell, *et al.*, AKC traces the direct influence of Indian (Buddhist) art on Chinese and Japanese sculpture, painting, and architecture, from AD 5th to 15th century. Explanatory notes by Rabindranarayan Ghosh and Haran C. Chakladar are subjoined, pp. 137-48.

C295 The Book of the Month. Bengalee [*sic*] Language and Literature. *Hindustan Review*, Allahabad, XXVI. 156 (Aug. 1912) [157]-163.

A review of *History of Bengali Language and Literature*, by Dinesh Chandra Sen. AKC praises this "first living history of any Indian vernacular literature", and in the course of his review discusses Bengali versions of the *Mahābhārata* and *Rāmāyaṇa*, the Vaiṣṇava poets Caṇḍīdāsa and Vidyāpati, and *yātrās* or "popular theatrical shows".

C296 Art for Life's Sake. *Hindu*, Madras (2 Sept. 1912) 4-5.

A review of *On the Truth of Decorative Art: A Dialogue between an Oriental and an Occidental*, by Lionel de Fonseka, with copious excerpts. "Hitherto no Oriental writer has . . . attempted to measure modern Western by ancient Eastern art. It is to me a matter for congratulation that a countryman of mine should have published a little work in which this task is undertaken with conspicuous success . . . it is surely the best general criticism of modern Western civilisation, and diagnosis of our modern Indian incoherence, which any one of us has yet written".

C297 The Historical Sense in India. *Hindu*, Madras (11 Sept. 1912) 4.

AKC's reply to the oft-made accusation by European scholars that Indians lack this faculty.

C298 Introduction to Indian Music. *Indian Music Journal*, Mysore, II. 4 (Sept./Oct. 1912) 81-3.

The revised version of a lecture by AKC, which, together with a recital of Indian songs by Ratan Devī (i.e. Mrs AKC), preceded the performance of the play, *The Maharani of Arakan*, by George Calderon, at the Royal Albert Hall, London, on 12 October 1912. See also B10.

C299 The Modern School of Indian Painting. *Journal of Indian Art and Industry*, London, XV. 120 (Oct. 1912) 67-9, 1 pl. (numbered: 15).

A revised and expanded version of the article with the same title printed in *Festival of Empire Imperial Exhibition. Indian Section. Guide and Catalogue* ([1911])—B7. This article was reprinted as Chapter XII of *Art and Swadeshi* ([1912])—A25a.

C300 Mughal Portraiture. *Orientalisches Archiv*, Leipzig, III. 1 (Oct. 1912) 12-15, 3 pls. (numbered: I-III) containing 14 illus.

A brief survey of the development of this type of Mughal painting, illustrated by reproductions of examples from the British Museum and AKC's own collection. Reference is also made to the reproductions published in *Indian Drawings* ([1910])—A22, *Indian Drawings: Second Series, Chiefly Rājput* ([1912])—A26, and in *Selected Examples of Indian Art* ([1910])—A21. Corrigendum to *Indian Drawings* ([1910]) is incorporated with this article.

C301 The New Delhi. [Letter]. *Manchester Guardian*, Manchester, 20,645 (7 Oct. 1912) 4.

That the suppression of national character in modern Indian building is in all likelihood an aim of British Imperialist policy, with reference to a leader headed "Imperialism and Architecture" in *The Builder*, London, for 27 September 1912. AKC expresses as well some apprehension over the style of the proposed buildings for the new seat of Indian government. (AKC was a signatory to a petition "urging the desirability of the employment of Indian master-builders and craftsmen in the construction of the new City of Delhi", presented to Lord Crewe, the Secretary of State for India, on 6 February 1913. This petition, together with a list of the signatories, was published the following day on page 5 of *The Times*, London, under the heading, "The New Delhi. Indian Craftsman or Western Architect".)

C302 The Understanding of Indian Art. *Modern Review*, Calcutta, XII. 5 (Nov. 1912) 482-4.

A translation by AKC from the German of William Cohn in *Ostasiatische Zeitschrift*, Berlin, for June 1912.

C303 Fine Art in India and the East—I. *Hindustan Review*, Allahabad, XXVI. 160 (Dec. 1912) 494-501.

The first of two instalments, printed under the general heading: Views and Reviews. In the main, a review of *A History of Fine Art in India and Ceylon from the Earliest Times to the Present Day*, by Vincent A. Smith, followed by brief discussions (illustrated by copious excerpts) of *L'Art*, by Auguste Rodin, *Two Drawings by Hokusai*, by William Rothenstein, *Nietzsche and Art*, by Anthony M. Ludovici, *The Flight of the Dragon*, by Laurence Binyon, and *Aesthetic as Science of Expression and General Linguistic*, by Benedetto Croce. AKC says of Smith's book, that "its fundamental coldness is evidence of an unsurmountable barrier between the author and his material" (p. 495), but concedes that "this work will be indispensable to every student of Indian art . . . and it is not likely as a text book of archaeology to be superseded for many years" ([II], p. 82). AKC also discusses (1) notions of "universality" and "progress" in art, (2) the judging of aesthetic merit, (3) the problem of appreciating alien works of art, and (4) the assumption (by Smith) that art is good insofar as it succeeds in "photographing" nature.

1913

C304 The Preservation of the Kandyan Village Crafts. *Ceylon Morning Leader Vesak Supplement*, Colombo (1913) 25-6.

Information from H.A.I. Goonetileke, *A Bibliography of Ceylon* (Zug, Switzerland, 1970), Vol. II, no. 9712.

C305 Indian Images with Many Arms. *Burlington Magazine*, London, XXII. 118 (Jan. 1913) 189-96, 2 pls.

The iconography of "the multiplication of members" is discussed in detail, with special reference to the figures of Durgā, Śiva (Naṭarāja), Tārā, and Gaṇeśa. AKC argues "that the excellence or defect of a work of art can no more be attributed to its human or super- or semi-human form, than it can be judged by any other special convention" (p. 196). This article was reprinted, in a revised and reduced form, in *The Dance of Śiva* (1918)—A38a—pp.[67]-71.

C306 Fine Art in India and the East—II. *Hindustan Review*, Allahabad, XXVIII [*i.e.* XXVII]. 161 (Jan. 1913) [79]-86.

C307 The Sacred Drama of Cambodia. *Mask*, Florence, V. 3 (Jan. 1913) 206-8.

A translation by AKC of a passage from [Chapter] XII of *Un Pèlerin d'Angkor*, by Pierre Loti.

C308 Five Indian Folk-songs. *Rajput Herald*, London, III. 1 (Jan. 1913) 12.

A reprint, incorporating further revisions, of the fourth, eighth, tenth, eleventh, and twentieth of the translations by AKC and Paira Mall that were printed in Chapter X of *Art and Swadeshi* ([1912])—A25a—pp. 103-4, 105-6, 109.

C309 Universal Compulsory Education. *Rajput Herald*, London, III. 2 (Feb. 1913) 66-7.

AKC questions the value of literacy by itself, and outlines a reform of English educational policy for India. Corrigenda to this article is printed in the issue for March, p. 144.

C310 The Purpose of Art. *Path*, London, III. 9 (Mar. 1913) 325-30.

The text of a lecture by AKC given at the Newcastle-under-Lyme School of Art, on 14 January 1913. On the arts and crafts as a means to a revolution and re-education in sensibility: "the greatest art means the greatest life", with reference to the Platonic doctrine of art, and to the writings of W.R. Lethaby. This article was reprinted in *Modern Review*, Calcutta, XIII. 6 (June 1913) 605-8.

C311 Dr. F.R. Martin and Oriental Painting . . . The Indian Paintings. *Burlington Magazine*, London, XXIII. 121 (Apr. 1913) 50-1.

AKC challenges Fredrik Robert Martin's supercilious dismissal of the question of Rājput painting, with reference to that writer's *The Miniature Painting and Painters of Persia, India and Turkey from the 8th to the 18th Century*. This book is also reviewed by AKC, somewhat differently, and at greater length, in *Hindustan Review*, Allahabad, for April and May 1913—C312, 314.

C312 The Book of the Month. Eastern Miniature Painting—I. *Hindustan Review*, Allahabad, XXVII. 164 (Apr. 1913) [232]-237.

The first of two instalments. A review of *The Miniature Painting and Painters of Persia, India and Turkey from the 8th to 18th Century*, by Fredrik Robert Martin. Discussing and summarizing Martin's treatment of the history of Persian painting, with copious excerpts.

C313 Sati: A Vindication of the Hindu Woman. *Sociological Review*, Manchester & London, VI. 2 (Apr. 1913) 117-35.

A paper read by AKC at a meeting of the Sociological Society on 12 November 1912. "What I have tried to explain is that notwithstanding that the formula of woman's status in Oriental society may have ere now crystallised—as the formulae of classic art have become academic—nevertheless this formula represented once and still essentially represents, although 'unfelt' in realisation, a veritable expression of woman's own nature" (from the version of this article in *The Dance of Śiva* (1918)—A38a—p. 101). Includes (1) a consideration of the ideals of the modern West's "assertive feminism", (2) a comparison of the Hindu arranged marriage with the Western "self-chosen marriage", (3) a review of the history and significance of the institution of satī/suttee, and (4) a note on purdah (seclusion of women). The discussion is illustrated by passages chosen from the *Mahābhārata*, the *Purāṇas*, the *Laws of Manu*, Tantric texts, the *Sūz-u-gudāz* of Muhammad Riza Nau'i, as well as from Celtic and Teutonic mythology, and English folk-song. An "Appendix", comprising quotations (compiled by the editor of *Sociological Review*?), is subjoined on p. 135, and a response to AKC's paper, by H[elena]. M[aria]. Swanwick, entitled "Eastern Ideals of Women . . .", follows on pp. 136-8. A separately paginated offprint seen (April 1991) in the collection of Dr. Rama P. Coomaraswamy, Greenwich, Connecticut. This article was reprinted, with revisions, as "Status of Indian Women", in *The Dance of Śiva* (1918)—A38a—pp. [82]-102, and in *Religion for a New Generation*, edited by Jacob Needleman, A.K. Bierman, and James A. Gould (New York: The Macmillan Company [1973]), pp. 197-211. Excerpts were printed, as "Hindu Ideals of Marriage", in *Oriental Magazine*, New York, for June/July 1928—C521.

C314 The Book of the Month. Eastern Miniature Painting [—II]. *Hindustan Review*, Allahabad, XXVII. 165 (May 1913) [312]-314.

A critical discussion of the chapter devoted to Indian painting in *The Miniature Painting and Painters of Persia, India and Turkey . . .* , by Fredrik Robert Martin. This second instalment (only) of AKC's review appeared almost simultaneously, in a somewhat different form, in *Burlington Magazine*, London, for April 1913—C311.

C315 [A Kashmiri song]. *Modern Review*, Calcutta, XIII. 5 (May 1913) 552.

An article, "The Musalmans of Kashmir", by Mukandi Lal, pp. 547-52, incorporates a translation by AKC of a "pseudo-philosophic religious song . . . from the original of a Kashmiri minstrel . . . specially sent by the Doctor [i.e. AKC] for my use".

C316 The Royal Palaces of Rajputana. *Rajput Herald*, London, III. 5 (May 1913) [230]-240, VI numbered pls. (also counted as pages).

An account (supported by lengthy excerpts from the work of James Fergusson) of the characteristic features of six palaces: the palace fortress of Mān Siṅgh at Gwāliar, the fort and palace at Jodhpur, the Gopal Bhavan palace at Dīg, the Halwad palace at Kathiawar, the palace fortress at Urcha, and the palace and hostel of the Rajas of Nagpur (also known as the Ghosla Ghat) at Varanasi. AKC laments the decline in the progress of Indian architecture, and says (1) it is now in the hands of the Rajput princes to save or destroy Indian building traditions, and (2) that the palaces of Rajputana, because they are exemplary expressions of national character, are ideal Indian models for the planners of the new Delhi.

C317 ["The Good, the Beautiful and the True" a Monopoly of the White Skin]. *Rajput Herald*, London, III. 7 (July 1913) [383].

Printed under the general heading: Reviews. AKC translates, from the German, a racialist pronouncement of Karl Jentsch in *Die Grenzboten*, Berlin, LXXII. 1 ([Jan.?] 1913) 292-3, with a brief comment. Reprinted, with this title, in *Modern Review*, Calcutta, XIV. 2 (Aug. 1913) 214.

C318 Notes on Indian Dramatic Technique. *Mask*, Florence, VI. 2 (Oct. 1913) 109-28, 2 text illus., 3 pls.

On puppets and human actors, quoting passages of some length from Indian and Ceylonese literature that contain references to puppet theatre. A modern example of a puppet show in Thailand is also described. Incorporating a reply to some misgivings, expressed by Edward Gordon Craig (the editor of *Mask*), concerning "the bodies of men and women as the material of dramatic art".

C319 Some Aspects of Modern India. *Hindustan Review*, Allahabad, XXVIII. 70/71 [*i.e.* 170/171] (Oct./Nov. 1913) 838-9.

Printed under the general heading: Views and Reviews. A review of *India To-day*, by Oliver Bainbridge. AKC offers a sampler of Bainbridge's "perversions and misapprehensions". A supplementary footnote from the editor of the *Hindustan Review* is printed on p. 839.

C320 Limitations of Nietzsche. *Indian Review*, Madras, XIV. 11 (Nov. 1913) 867-70.

An estimation of Friedrich Nietzsche's philosophy, in the light of Hindu and Buddhist metaphysics. This article was reprinted, with amendments, in *Path*, London, IV. 7 (Jan. 1914) 246-51. Errata is printed in the March 1914 issue of *Path*, p. 249. This article forms a part of a much longer, projected work, to have been titled "Nietzsche, Blake and Hinduism", referred to by AKC in his review of *Reflections on the Problems of India*, by A.S. Wadia, in *Hindustan Review*, Allahabad, for September 1914—C335. A sequel, "Nietzsche and His Teachings: A Rejoinder", is printed in the *Hindustan Review* for July 1918—C394.

C321 Music of East and West. *Hindustan Review*, Allahabad, XXVIII. 172 (Dec. 1913) [927]-929.

A translation by AKC and Kali Mohan Ghose from the Bengali of Rabindranath Tagore (from his *Jivan Smriti*). The concluding paragraphs of this translation, in a revised form, were reprinted in *The Dance of Śiva* (1918)—A38a—pp. 78-9.

C322 Modern Indian Architecture. *Hindustan Review*, Allahabad, XXVIII. 172 (Dec. 1913) 943-5.

A review of *Report on Modern Indian Architecture: Types of Modern Indian Buildings at Delhi, Agra, Etc.*, by Gordon Sanderson and John Begg. Unsigned, but credited to AKC on the front cover of this issue. AKC says this book "demonstrates, what some have doubted, that there do exist in Hindustan a living architectural tradition, and master craftsmen of real ability [and furthermore, that their existence is] of vital interest, in connection with the immediate problem of the architecture of the new Delhi" (p. 944).

1914

C323 [A review of] *Indian Music*. By [A.H.] Fox-Strangways [*sic*]. *Oxford Indian Magazine*, Oxford, I. (1914) [88]-91.

AKC calls this "a work that is not merely one of scholarship, but . . . one of the few books really indispensible [*sic*] to the student who seeks to have some knowledge of the inner life of the Indians" (p. 91). AKC adds a note on the general character of Indian music (and on the appreciation of Indian music by Westerners). This review was reprinted in *Hindustan Review*, Allahabad, XXXI, 189/190 (May/June 1915) 550-3.

C324 Hands and Feet in Indian Art. *Burlington Magazine*, London, XXIV. 130 (Jan. 1914) 204-11, 14 text illus., 1 pl.

A brief introduction to the Indian language of gesture, emphasizing its importance iconographically in both painting and sculpture. The illustrations are reproductions of sketches, tracings, and photographs, of *mudrās*, selected mainly from the Ajaṇṭā frescoes, and from Buddha and Śiva images.

C325 The Book of the Month: Havell's Indian Architecture. *Hindustan Review*, Allahabad, XIX [*i.e.* XXIX]. 173 (Jan. 1914) [67]-71.

A review of *Indian Architecture: Its Psychology, Structure, and History from the First*

Muhammadan Invasion to the Present Day, by E.B. Havell. "This volume . . . is the first serious and extensive contribution to the history of Indian architecture since [James] Fergusson" (p. [67]). AKC adds his own reflections on what he considers the likely outcome of plans for the new Delhi, see pp. [67]-68, 70-1. AKC has a much shorter review of Havell's book in *Burlington Magazine*, London, for March 1914—C328.

C326 What Is Essential in Art? *Path,* London, IV. 8 (Feb. 1914) 314-22.

Printed under the general heading: The International School. A report which summarizes and quotes from AKC's lecture (and from his contribution to the ensuing discussion), given at Peebles, Scotland, on 23 July 1913.

C327 Some Ancient Elements in Indian Decorative Art. *Ostasiatische Zeitschrift*, Berlin, II. 4 (Jan./Mar.? 1914) [383]-392, 21 text illus.

"It is the purpose of these notes to illustrate, in particular, the parallels [early Indian decorative art presents to] old Aegean art of the sixth century BC and earlier . . . I do not always mean to predicate Aegean origins; for both may derive from older common sources in Western Asia. I wish rather to show that a certain stratum in Indian decorative art represents a common inheritance shared alike by all countries from the Aegean to Ceylon" (pp. 384, 385). This article was reprinted in *Modern Review*, Calcutta, XVI. 6 (Dec. 1914) 172-7, 21 text illus.

C328 [A review of] *Indian Architecture*. By E.B. Havell. *Burlington Magazine*, London, XXIV. 132 (Mar. 1914) 351.

Also reviewed by AKC, at greater length, in *Hindustan Review*, Allahabad, for January 1914—C325.

C329 The Art of India. [Letter]. *New Age*, London, N.S. XIV. 22 (2 Apr. 1914) 702-3.

A reply to Anthony M. Ludovici's review of *The Arts & Crafts of India & Ceylon* (1913)—A28, in the issue for 26 March.

C330 Modern Art Criticism. *New Age*, London, N.S. XIV. 24 (16 Apr. 1914) 761-3.

A review of *Art*, by Clive Bell, adding Oriental parallels. "Undoubtedly the most important contribution to aesthetics since [Benedetto] Croce . . . though [written] with rather more of mere smartness than quite accords with its own principles" (p. 761). This review was reprinted in *Hindustan Review*, Allahabad, XXXI. 188 (Apr. 1915) 437-45.

C331 The Songs of Rabindranath Tagore. [Letter]. *Manchester Guardian*, Manchester, 21,128 (25 Apr. 1914) 12.

Under the general heading: Western Orientalism in Music. On a leader in the issue for 21 April concerning John Alden Carpenter's settings of selections from *Gitanjali*. AKC asks: "is it not rather futile to set Mr. Tagore's poems to Western or pseudo-Oriental music when they were originally composed by the author himself as songs with music?".

C332 The Book of the Month: The Truth About Woman: by Mrs. W.M. Gallichan. *Hindustan Review*, Allahabad, XXIX. 177/178 (May/June 1914) [560]-565.

A review of *The Truth About Woman*, by C. Gasquoine Hartley (Mrs. Walter M. Gallichan). AKC adds his own thoughts on (1) the English movement for the emancipation of women (and the parallel this presents to Indian political nationalism), and (2) the significance of the "physical and mental sexual differentiations" of man and woman. This review was reprinted, as "The Truth About Woman", in *Living Age*, Boston, CCLXXXII. 3,661 (5 Sept. 1914) 613-16.

C333 Notes on Jaina Art. *Journal of Indian Art and Industry*, London, XVI. 127 (July 1914) [81]-97, 5 text illus., 15 numbered pls., containing 66 illus. (pl.1 is coloured).

Comprises (1) a general introduction to Jainism and the life of Mahāvīra, (2) a summary of the story of Kālakācārya, (3) explanations of various Jaina terms, (4) notes on the Jaina cosmology, (5) a discussion of the aesthetics and relationships of Jaina painting, (6) notes on illustrated manuscripts, and (7) a descriptive list of the plates. "This paper forms a contribution to our knowledge of Jain painting and minor arts, concerning which nothing has yet been published except the valuable *Miniaturen zum Jinacarita* . . . by Dr. [W.] Hüttemann in the 'Baessler Archiv' for [1913]" (p.[81]). Corrigenda is printed in the issue for October 1914, p. 113. This article was reprinted separately as *Jaina Art* ([1994])—A93.

C334 Woman Under Polygamy. [Letter]. *Athenaeum*, London, 4,532 (5 Sept. 1914) 251.

Dated Britford [Wilts.], 30 Aug. 1914. On a review of *Women Under Polygamy*, by Walter M. Gallichan, in the issue for 29 August.

C335 Reflections on the Problems of India. *Hindustan Review*, Allahabad, XXX. 181 (Sept. 1914) 229-33.

Printed under the general heading: Views and Reviews. A review of a book of this title, by A.S. Wadia. "Another encouraging sign of incipient Indian dissatisfaction with the aims of Western democracies" (p. 229). AKC adds his own criticisms (supported by quotations from Friedrich Nietzsche) of the wholesale adoption by Indians of what are in reality outmoded Western conventions.

C336 On Drawing and Painting. *Hindustan Review*, Allahabad, XXX. 181 (Sept. 1914) 233-6.

Printed under the general heading: Views and Reviews. A review of a book of this title, by Denman Waldo Ross. AKC addresses himself to that portion of Ross's book that makes a plea for (1) the restoration of the traditional values of craftsmanship, and (2) the restoration of vocation as a principle of social order, and points to the relevance Ross's programme has to the solution of present-day sociological problems in India.

C337 [A review of] *Antiquities of India: An Account of the History and Culture of Ancient Hindustan*, by L.D. Barnett. *Burlington Magazine*, London, XXVI. 139 (Oct. 1914) 38.

"A trustworthy handbook of Indian archaeology is so much needed, that we think it a pity that the present volume, in a series actually devoted to the archaeology of various countries, should as an exception be concerned rather with the 'Antiquities', in the sense of history and culture. The historical and theological portions are certainly very good".

C338 The Eight Nāyikās. *Journal of Indian Art and Industry*, London, XVI. 128 (Oct. 1914) [99]-112, 8 numbered pls.

Quoting extensively from the *Rasikapriyā* of Keśava Dās (Chap. VII), AKC describes the classes and types of heroines (*Nāyikās*) as employed by Indian writers and painters, discussing in detail the classification, into eight, of *Svakīyā* ("One's own") heroines, "according to the immediate circumstances of their relations with their Lovers . . . especially in relation to the representation of these types in Pahārī paintings, such as we reproduce in the accompanying Plates" (p. 100). A note on the geographical grouping of Pahārī paintings is included on p. 111. Corrigendum is subjoined on p. 113. A considerably reduced and revised version of this article is incorporated with *Rajput Painting* (1916)—A34a—pp. 43-6.

C339 Painted Ceiling at Kẹlaṇiya Vihāra, Ceylon. *Journal of Indian Art and Industry*, London, XVI. 128 (Oct. 1914) 113, 1 pl. (numbered: Plate 9).

A brief description of the interior of a Buddhist temple near Colombo.

C340 Indian War. *Manchester Guardian*, Manchester, 21,275 (14 Oct. 1914) 10.

On the traditional Indian conception of warfare.

C341 Indian Aid [I]. [Letter]. *New Age*, London, N.S. XV. 24 (15 Oct. 1914) 580.

On the question of India's co-operation with Britain in World War I. This letter was reprinted, with minor omissions and revisions, in *Selected Letters of Ananda K. Coomaraswamy* (1988)—A89—pp. 334-7.

C342 Indian Aid [II]. [Letter]. *New Age*, London, N.S. XV. 25 (22 Oct. 1914) 603.

A postscript to his letter, printed under the same heading, in the issue for 15 October.

C343 A World Policy for India. *New Age*, London, N.S. XVI. 8 (24 Dec. 1914) 192-3.

AKC argues that as World War I "does not cause but marks a crisis in the history of Western culture", and although it is inconceivable that Indians should fight on behalf of their oppressor, "it is the duty of India to throw in her lot with the world". A separately paginated offprint, with additionally a dedication to Romain Rolland, printed under the title on page [1], seen at the State Library of Victoria, Melbourne. This article was reprinted, in a French translation, as "La crise Européene, opinions Hindoues", in *La Semaine Littéraire*, Geneva, for 27 February 1915, pp. 107-8.

1915

C344 The Idealistic Reaction Against Science. *New Age*, London, N.S. XVI. 10 (7 Jan. 1915) 225-6.

A review of a book of this title, by Antonio Aliotta. Reprinted, with minor revisions, in *Hindustan Review*, Allahabad, XXXI. 186 (Feb. 1915) 208-11.

C345 Books of the Month. Mr. G. Lowes Dickinson on "Appearances" and "Civilization". *Hindustan Review*, Allahabad, XXXI. 187 (Mar. 1915) 343-5.

A review of *Appearances; Being Notes of Travel* and *An Essay on the Civilizations of India, China and Japan*, by G. Lowes Dickinson.

C345a [A review of] *The Ancient and Mediaeval Architecture of India. A Study of Indo-Aryan Civilisation.* By E.B. Havell. *Manchester Guardian*, Manchester, 21,393 (2 Mar. 1915) 4.

This book was also reviewed (differently) by AKC in *Burlington Magazine*, London, for May 1915—C348, and in *Hindustan Review*, Allahabad, for September 1915—C352. An unsigned review of Havell's book in *Athenaeum*, London, for February 1915, pp. 171-2, is almost certainly by AKC.

C345b Problems of India. *Manchester Guardian*, Manchester, 21,405 (16 Mar. 1915) 5.

A review of *Sva*, by George Birdwood. "No European—not even Sister Nivedita—has better understood or more whole-heartedly admired the constitution of Hindu society". Also reviewed by AKC (at greater length) in *Hindustan Review*, Allahabad, for January 1916—C361.

C346 That Beauty Is a State. *Burlington Magazine*, London, XXVII. 145 (Apr. 1915) 7-14, 2 pls.

A discussion (employing the terms of Indian aesthetics) of the concept of an absolute beauty, i.e. beauty identified with God. AKC also considers (1) the question of the relativity of taste, (2) the role of the critic, and (3) the problem of ethnocentrism in art appreciation. "The reproductions on the accompanying plates are . . . selected to illustrate only one point; that Beauty is not determined by subject" (p.14). This article was reprinted in *The Dance of Śiva* (1918)—A38a—pp. [38]-45, and in *Revision*, Cambridge, Mass., VI.1 (Spring 1983) 53-4. A considerably reduced version was printed in *Changing India*, edited by Raja Rao and Iqbal Singh (London: George Allen & Unwin Ltd. [1939]), pp. [183]-189. Excerpts were printed with "An Obvious Statement (for the Millionth Time)", by Margaret Anderson, in *Little Review*, New York, VII. 3 (Sept./Dec. 1920) [8]-16, as an appendix occupying pp. 12-16.

C347 The Hindu View of Art. *Quest*, London, VI. 3 (Apr. 1915) 480-98.

An elucidation of orthodox Hindu (and Buddhist) aesthetics, drawing on ancient and medieval Indian texts, and demonstrating "close agreement with conclusions that have been advanced at other times and elsewhere" (p. 497), including some modern parallels. AKC discusses in particular "the important part once played in Indian thought by the concept of Art as a means of Yoga" (p. 484). A separately paginated offprint seen (May 1991) among The Ananda Coomaraswamy Papers in the Firestone Library at Princeton University. This article was reprinted, in two parts, in *The Dance of Śiva* (1918)—A38a—pp. [18]-29, [30]-37, and, in a Sinhala translation, in *Sanskruti*, Colombo, III. 3 (July/Sept. 1955) [1]-8.

C348 [A review of] *Ancient and Mediaeval Architecture of India: A Study of Indo-Aryan Civilization*, by E.B. Havell. *Burlington Magazine*, London, XXVII. 146 (May 1915) 79.

AKC remarks that "the strength of Mr. Havell's position lies in his constant effort to trace back the forms of Indian art to still-operating conditions of life and thought, of which it is the expression . . . and above all, in his insistence upon the political and social significance of craftsmanship". But AKC objects to Havell's methodology: his "reading of . . . symbols [is] based on the appearance of the actual works, rather than upon the technical literature . . . amongst [his] many poetical suggestions, we find but little rigorous proof".

C349 Love and Art. *Modern Review*, Calcutta, XVII. 5 (May 1915) 574-84.

AKC argues that if the activities of empirical science are to benefit man the results of inventions will have to made use of under the guidance and censorship of artists, saints, and philosophers.

C350 [A review of] *Footfalls of Indian History*. By Sister Nivedita. *Hindustan Review*, Allahabad, XXXI. 189/190 (May/June 1915) 553-4.

Printed under the general heading: Views and Reviews. "Taken collectively, the essays clearly expound some of the pressing problems of Indian research. Perhaps the best considered chapters are those on 'The Ancient Abbey of Ajanta', and 'The Rise of Vaishnavism under the Guptas'" (p. 554). AKC also remarks, in passing, of another work by Sister Nivedita, *The Web of Indian Life*, that this gives "the truest picture of Hindu society ever presented by a Western writer" (p. 553).

C351 The Gods of Mahāyāna Buddhism. *Burlington Magazine*, London, XXVII. 148 (July 1915) 139-41, 1 pl. (facing p. 139).

A review of *The Gods of Northern Buddhism*, by Alice Getty. AKC prefaces this review with an outline of the distinction between Hīnayāna and Mahāyāna Buddhism. He objects to inaccuracy and prejudice in J. Deniker's introductory essay. However, Getty's "clearly systematized and well illustrated guide to [the Mahāyāna pantheon] . . . has been compiled with the utmost care, and is of quite remarkable accuracy" (p. 140). "Mr. H[enry H.]. Getty's collection, which is alone drawn upon for illustration, contains important examples; as well as many of inferior value, regarded as works of art. . . . In order to supply an avoidable deficiency I have reproduced here a few examples of Mahāyāna divinities chosen from the areas least fully represented in Mr. H. Getty's collection, and I have taken the opportunity of correcting in the Description of the Plate certain statements in my text to my selection of reproductions, 'Visvakarmā' [(1914)]" (p. 141).

C352 The Book of the Month. Mr. Havell on Indo-Aryan Civilization. *Hindustan Review*, Allahabad, XXXII. 193 (Sept. 1915) 144-8.

A review of *The Ancient and Mediaeval Architecture of India: A Study of Indo-Aryan Civilisation*, by E.B. Havell. "In this volume and in his other works Mr. Havell has clearly shown that the accepted history of Indian architecture needs drastic revision. But I do not think Mr. Havell can claim to have accomplished this revision himself" (p. 146). AKC discusses in detail some of Havell's "solutions" of "highly controversial points" (p. 148). A comment on AKC's review from E.B. Havell, "Dr. Coomaraswamy on Indian Art: A Rejoinder", is printed in the issue for April 1916, pp. [306]-307.

C353 Vidyapati. [Letter]. *New Age*, London, N.S. XVII. 18 (2 Sept. 1915) 439.

Replying to an anonymous review of *Vidyāpati: Bangīya Padābali Songs of the Love of Rādhā and Krishna* (1915)—A32—in the issue for 19 August 1915.

C354 What Has India Contributed to Human Welfare? *Athenaeum*, London, 4,588 (2 Oct. 1915) Supplement, pp. 1-8.

In the main, on the application of Indian religious philosophy to present-day problems of sociology. This article was reprinted in *The Dance of Śiva* (1918)—A38a—pp. [1]-17, and, separately, in a Dutch translation, by A. van de Linde, with a foreword by W.H. Denier van der Gou, as *Wat heeft het Oosten bijgedragen tot het welzijn der Menschheid* (Amersfoort: Valkhoff & Co., 1916), and again, in a revised and considerably reduced form, as "India's Share in World Civilization", in *Fair Play*, New York, X. 8 (19 Aug. 1916) 120-2.

C355 Mechanism and Art. *Author*, London, XXVI. 3 (Dec. 1915) 75-6.

AKC questions the value of the cinema and the gramophone as educative instruments.

C356 [A review of] *Elements of Hindu Iconography* [by] T.A. Gopinatha Rao . . . Vol. I, pts. I and II, in 2 vols. *Burlington Magazine*, London, XXVIII. 153 (Dec. 1915) 106.

AKC congratulates Rao on "a good beginning" in a subject of which "the scientific and systematic study has only very recently been initiated", but at the same time detects some modernist tendencies in Rao's exposition: "it is particularly futile to pass judgement on ancient Indian art in terms of modern and generally Europeanized taste". An unsigned review of Rao's book in *Athenaeum*, London, 4,583 (28 Aug. 1915)148-9, is almost certainly by AKC.

C357 The Book of the Month. A Historical Survey of South Indian Sculpture. *Hindustan Review*, Allahabad, XXXII. 196 (Dec. 1915) [428]-431.

A review of *South Indian Bronzes: A Historical Survey of South Indian Sculpture, with Iconographical Notes Based on Original Sources*, by O.C. Gangoly. "Mr. Gangoly has made an important contribution to the growing literature of Indian iconography" (p. 431). AKC is critical of the "uncouth transliterations", and also notes that Gangoly's naming of *mudrās* does "not [always] agree with authoritative books . . . some are certainly incorrect" (p. 430). Also reviewed differently by AKC in *Burlington Magazine*, London, for February 1916—C362.

C358 [A review of] *Indian Thought, Past and Present*. By R.W. Frazer. *Athenaeum*, London, 4,597 (4 Dec. 1915) 413-14.

AKC finds Frazer's systematic exposition of Indian thought "admirable and careful", but regrets that Frazer "scarcely raises" the question of the part Hinduism might play in *modern* life. AKC offers some immediate applications of Hindu thought to "the problems of the West". Unsigned, but almost certainly by AKC.

1916

C359 Indisk Skulptur. *Ord och Bild*, Stockholm, XXV. 1 (1916) [19]-32, 16 text illus.

Translated by Andrea Butenschön. A general account, that includes as well a discussion of the sculpture of Ceylon.

C360 Buddhist Primitives. *Burlington Magazine*, London, XXVIII. 154 (Jan. 1916) 151-5, 1 pl.

The first of two instalments; these were reprinted together to form a single essay in *The Dance of Śiva* (1918)—A38a—pp. [46]-55. On the Indian formulae and ideas that characterize early Buddhist art, and on the problem of the Western formulae in the art of Gandhāra, with reference to the work of Alfred Foucher.

C361 The Book of the Month.—A Lover of India. *Hindustan Review*, Allahabad, XXXIII. 197 (Jan. 1916) 86-90.

A review of *Sva*, by George Birdwood. AKC considers this "one of [the] few works by Anglo-Indians combining knowledge with sympathy, and that sympathy far removed from patronage and arising from genuine community of sentiment. It . . . deserves the careful attention of Indian readers, and in especial of those who would identify advantageous 'progress' with increasing 'civilization'" (p. 90).

C362 [A review of] *South Indian Bronzes: A Historical Survey of*

South Indian Sculptures, with Iconographical Notes Based on Original Sources [by] O.C. Gangoly. *Burlington Magazine*, London, XXVIII. 155 (Feb. 1916) 199-200.

Also reviewed by AKC, at greater length, in *Hindustan Review*, Allahabad, for December 1915—C357.

C363 Buddhist Primitives (Conclusion). *Burlington Magazine*, London, XXVIII. 156 (Mar. 1916) 224-30, 2 pls. (numbered: II and III).

Reprinted, together with C360 to form a single essay, in *The Dance of Śiva* (1918)—A38a—pp. [46]-55.

C364 The Book of the Month. The Rajputs. *Hindustan Review*, Allahabad, XXXIII. 199 (Mar. 1916) 279-81.

A review of *The Rajputs: A Fighting Race*, by Thakur Shri Jessraj Singhji Sessodia. AKC remarks "this volume . . . admirably fulfils its . . . purpose of introducing the Rajput princes . . . to the reading public of England", and adds his own views on the significance of the interference by the British Raj with the princely order.

C365 To India the Great War Is a Civil Conflict. *New York Tribune*, New York, LXXV. 25,312 (5 Mar. 1916) Part V, "Special Features Section", page 2, 2 text illus.

An interview, with AKC's replies given in quotation marks as his direct words.

C366 The Destructive Sword. An Analysis of Blake's Attitude to War. *Poetry Review*, London, VII. 2 (Mar./Apr. 1916) 125-32.

Although signed only with the initials A.K.C., textual evidence suggests that this article was almost certainly written by Ananda K. Coomaraswamy. (The first three words of the title are taken from the 27th of William Blake's "Proverbs of Hell".)

C367 [A review of] *Catalogue of the Museum of Archaeology at Sārnāth* [by] Daya Rama Sahni. *Burlington Magazine*, London, XXIX. 157 (Apr. 1916) 29-30.

AKC enumerates some of the earlier and more important of the Museum's Buddhist sculptures reproduced in this "detailed and systematic, and indispensable" catalogue.

C368 Oriental Poetry More Realistic Than Ours. *New York Times*, New York, (2 Apr. 1916) Section Six, "Magazine Section", page 12, 1 text illus.

The reported words of an interview with AKC and Ratan Devī (i.e. Mrs. AKC), on the occasion of their concert tour of North America. The interview was conducted by the American poet [Alfred] Joyce Kilmer. On Indian poetry, English mystical verse, and Rabindranath Tagore. The illustration is a photomontage of portraits of the interviewees.

C369 Buddhist Art in India. *Scribner's Magazine*, New York, LX. 1 (July 1916) 127-30, 7 text illus.

A general introduction.

C370 Rajput Painting and Its Artistic Sisterhood to "Modernist" Art. *Vanity Fair*, New York, VI. 5 (July 1916) 39, 1 text illus.

A general introduction, with some parallels to modern European and American painting.

C371 The Cave Paintings of Ajanta an Almost Unique Type of Classic Indian Art Which Appeals Strongly to Modernists. *Vanity Fair*, New York, VII. 1 (Sept. 1916) 67, 98, 3 text illus.

A general introduction, with a consideration of the question of how modern painters might respond to the Ajaṇṭā frescoes.

C372 The Book of the Month. A.M. Ludovici's Defence of Aristocracy: A Text-book for Tories. *Hindustan Review*, Allahabad, XXXIV. 208 (Dec. 1916) 453-64.

A review of *A Defence of Aristocracy. A Text Book for Tories*, by Anthony Ludovici. AKC weighs the principles of aristocracy and democracy, mainly with reference to the traditional Hindu social system, and to "certain passages of Mr. Ludovici's book [that] are of special significance in modern India" (p. 458).

1917

C373 Section of Indian Art [I]. *Forty-second Annual Report for the Year 1917*. Boston: Museum of Fine Arts, Boston, 1917, pp. [102]-105.

AKC's first report to the Director of the Museum of Fine Arts, Boston, following his appointment in April to the position of Keeper of the Section of Indian Art. After 1919, AKC's reports were summarized in the Director's report (after 1936 the activities of the Department of Indian Art, as it then came to be named, were communicated by Kojiro Tomita in his report for the Department of Asiatic Art). So, although AKC's term of office at the Museum continued to 1947, he only had occasion to publish three reports. "The Museum of Fine Arts has been the first in America to organize a Department of Indian Art, and possesses a collection of Indian paintings and bronzes unequalled outside India" (p. [102]).

C374 The Book of the Month: The Frescoes in Ajanta Caves. *Hindustan Review*, Allahabad, XXXV. 209 (Jan. 1917) 59-63.

A review of *Ajanta Frescoes*, by Christiana Herringham. AKC expresses his admiration for Herringham's copies done at Ajaṇṭā; and quotes in the course of this review extensively from Herringham, and from the other contributors to *Ajanta Frescoes*, Dorothy Larcher, Laurence Binyon, and William Rothenstein.

C375 References to the Theory and Practise [*sic*] of Art in the Silpa Sastras and Other Indian Literature. *Modern Review*, Calcutta, XXI. 1 (Jan. 1917) 40-5.

Chiefly concerning (1) the artist's preliminary practice of mental visualization, (2) the requisite integrity of the craftsman, and (3) the co-existence of religious and secular art in ancient and medieval India.

C376 Aesthetic. *Hindustan Review*, Allahabad, XXXV. 210 (Feb. 1917) [77]-81.

On the general tendency nowadays to depreciate the idea of art as a spiritual activity. This article was reprinted, in a reduced form, under the general heading "Indian Periodicals", in *Modern Review*, Calcutta, XXI. 4 (Apr. 1917) 470-1.

C377 The Book of the Month. Mr. Clutton-Brook [*sic*] on the "Ultimate Belief". *Hindustan Review*, Allahabad, XXXV. 211 (Mar. 1917) 215-18.

A review of *The Ultimate Belief*, by Arthur Clutton Brock. "This is a valuable contribution to the problem of what may be taught in schools as unsectarian religion" (p. 215).

C378 Spiritual Freedom Expressed in India's Dances. A Philosophy of Life the Basic and Abiding Idea in Oriental Movement, with Occidental Imitations but Mere Mimicry.

Modern Dance Magazine, New York, II. 4 (Mar. 1917) 15-16.

AKC discusses (1) what characterizes the Indian art of dance, (2) the type of the dancing girl, and (3) what is required of the would-be Western exponent; incorporating as well his first-hand impressions of dance performances in Lahore, Lucknow, and Madura.

C379 Love in Hindu Literature: A Rejoinder. *Hindustan Review*, Allahabad, XXXV. 212 (Apr. 1917) [286]-287.

On the assertion, in *Love in Hindu Literature*, by Benoy Kumar Sarkar, that AKC's purpose in *Vidyāpati: Bangīya Padābali Songs of the Love of Rādhā and Krishna* (1915)—A32—was "to offer an apology for Vidyāpati's sensuousness and extollation of human desires". See also Sarkar's "Love in Hindu Literature: Examination of a Rejoinder", in the issue for December 1917, pp. [415]-417.

C380 Indian Music. *Musical Quarterly*, New York, III. 2 (Apr. 1917) 163-72.

A general introduction, written expressly for the Western concert-goer. Includes (1) an outline of the chief characteristics of Indian vocal and instrumental music, compared with the European, (2) a definition of the term *raga*, and (3) notes on the metaphysical implications of Indian music. A separately paginated offprint seen at the State Library of Victoria, Melbourne. This article was reprinted, incorporating addenda (as footnotes), in *The Dance of Śiva* (1918)—A38a—pp. [72]-81, and in *Traditional India*, edited by O.L. Chavarria-Aguilar (Englewood Cliffs, N.J.: Prentice-Hall, Inc. [1964]), pp. 114-23. An excerpt (from pp. 168-9) was printed, with the title "Song and Tune", in *Indian Music Journal*, New Delhi, V. 1 (Apr./May 1968) 21-2.

C381 Oriental Dances in America and a Word or Two in Explanation of the Nautch. *Vanity Fair*, New York, VIII. 3 (May 1917) 61, 1 text illus., 1 pl. (facing p. 61).

On the theory and character of the nautch—compared with modern Western dance and drama—incorporating brief comments on performances by Ruth St. Denis, Roshanara, and Ratan Devī. This article was reprinted, in a French translation, reduced and revised, as "A propos des Danses Orientales en Amérique: Qu'est-ce que le Nautch?", in *Bulletin de l'Association Française des Amis de l'Orient*, Paris, 2 (Dec. 1921)[21]-25; this version was reprinted, in English, as "Oriental Dances in America", in *Dial*, New York, LXXII. 1 (Jan. 1922) 17-19.

C382 Illustrated Jaina Manuscripts. *Museum of Fine Arts Bulletin*, Boston, XV. 90 (Aug. 1917) 40-1, 4 text illus.

Some general remarks on Jainism, and on the stories related in the manuscripts, are followed by technical, historical, and aesthetic notes on 15th century examples recently acquired by the Museum. This article is the first of sixty-two contributions by AKC to the Museum's *Bulletin*; his last contribution is printed in the issue for June 1943. AKC's association with the Museum of Fine Arts, Boston, began on 5 April 1917, when Denman Waldo Ross gave to the Museum a collection of Indian art which incorporated AKC's Indian Collection that had recently been purchased by Ross. This became the founding collection (thereafter known as the Ross-Coomaraswamy Collection) of the Museum's Section of Indian Art, to which AKC was appointed Keeper on 26 April 1917. He assumed his curatorial duties on 1 October of that year. "In 1931 when Mr. [Kojiro] Tomita was appointed curator of the Asiatic department, Dr. Coomaraswamy's title was changed to Fellow for Research in Indian, Persian and Mohammedan Art, which was better related to the manner in which he then exercised his mind. So it remained until his . . . death on 9 September 1947" (Walter Muir Whitehill, *Museum of Fine Arts Boston: A Centennial History* (Cambridge, Mass.: The Belknap Press of Harvard University Press, 1970), *Vol. One*, p. 370).

C383 The Music of India Its Constantly Increasing Popularity in America. *Vanity Fair*, New York, IX. 2 (Oct. 1917) 67, 96, 2 text illus.

A brief guide to its appreciation, written expressly for the American concert-goer.

1918

C384 Section of Indian Art [II]. *Forty-third Annual Report for the Year 1918*. Boston: Museum of Fine Arts, Boston, 1918, pp. [95]-96.

C385 [Letter]. *Game*, Ditchling, Sussex, II. 1 (Jan. 1918) 24.

Dated New York, 25 Dec. 1916. On defining beauty. A reply from Eric Gill, dated 23 January 1918, is printed as a footnote on the same page.

C386 Young India [I]. *Modern School*, Ferrer Colony, Stelton, N.J., V. 2 (Feb. 1918) 34-41.

The first of two instalments. Comprises some reflections on the implications of India's "arrival" in the modern world. This article, combined with the second instalment—C389, was reprinted in *The Dance of Śiva* (1918)—A38a—pp. [122]-136.

C387 Mughal Painting. (Akbar and Jahangir). *Museum of Fine Arts Bulletin*, Boston, XVI. 93 (Feb. 1918) 2-8, 8 text illus.

On this "dramatic episode in the history of Indian art" (p. 2), and noting some examples in the Museum collections that were executed under the patronage of these emperors.

C388 Note on the Study of Indian Art. *Young India*, New York, I. 2 (Feb. 1918) 6-8.

On the indifference of Indians nowadays (especially on the part of those concerned with education) to their own past achievements, and present abilities, in the arts.

C389 Young India [II]. *Modern School*, Ferrer Colony, Stelton, N.J., V. 3 (Mar. 1918) 66-74.

C390 In Defense of Mr. Penty. [Letter]. *New Republic*, New York, XIV. 176 (16 Mar. 1918) 208.

On Randolph Bourne's review of *Old Worlds for New*, by Arthur Joseph Penty, in the issue for 2 March.

C391 [On Indian sculpture in the Pennsylvania Museum]. *Bulletin of the Pennsylvania Museum*, Philadelphia, XVI. 61 (Apr. 1918) 24.

An article "Indian Sculpture", signed H[amilton]. B[ell]., pp. 20-4, incorporates excerpts from a letter from AKC identifying some items in the Museum collection, e.g. a Sūrya image from Bengal of *circa* AD 12th century.

C392 Indian Bronzes. *Museum of Fine Arts Bulletin*, Boston, XVI. 95 (June 1918) [31]-41, 20 text illus.

On three Buddhist images from Ceylon, seven Buddhist and two Hindu examples from Nepal (also a reliquary and a stand), and four Hindu examples from North and South India, from the 8th to 16th centuries, in the Museum collections.

C393 What Is Beautiful? *Young India*, New York, I. 6 (June 1918) 12-13.

"Without adhering strictly to Indian modes of expression, I shall try to state a Theory of Beauty from an Indian point of view, meaning by this a theory consistent with totalistic monism" (p.12). This article was reprinted in *Hindustan Review*, Allahabad, XXXIX. 233 (Jan. 1919) [10]-12.

C394 Nietzsche and His Teachings: A Rejoinder. *Hindustan Review*, Allahabad, XXXVIII. 227 (July 1918) [23]-29.

A sequel to "Limitations of Nietzsche"—C320, prompted by B.K. Mukerji's review of *The Complete Works of Friedrich Nietzsche* in the issue for May/June 1917. AKC explains, "I do not write as a 'Nietzschan', or from any other sectarian standpoint, but rather with a view to proving that he represents a positive and spiritual force, which we should be strong enough to use constructively, and not merely fear" (p. [23]). AKC concludes with eight quotations from Nietzsche chosen to illustrate his "brilliant powers of sarcasm . . . [and because] so much of what he says has direct and very poignant application to the situation in India" (p. 28).

C395 Indian Art in the Boston Museum of Fine Arts. *Hindustan Review*, Allahabad, XXXVIII. 228 (Aug. 1918) [99]-104.

An outline of the history and chief characteristics of Indian art precedes a brief survey of the collections at Boston. This article was reprinted, in a reduced form, under the general heading "Indian Periodicals", in *Modern Review*, Calcutta, XXIV. 5 (Nov. 1918) 499-500.

C396 Rajput Painting [I]. *Museum of Fine Arts Bulletin*, Boston, XVI. 96 (Aug. 1918) 49-62, 16 text illus.

The first of two instalments. A general introduction, including (1) a discussion of Rāgmālā painting and (2) the school of Jammu. This article is illustrated by examples taken from the Museum collections.

C397 Portraits of Akbar, Raja Man Singh, and Others. *Journal of the Royal Asiatic Society*, London (Oct. 1918) 536-40.

AKC considers some published Mughal paintings in the interests of dating and identification of subjects, correcting faulty data in *Akbar the Great Mogul 1542-1605*, by Vincent Smith; *The Music of Hindostan*, by A.H. Fox Strangways; *Exposition des Arts Musulmans*, by G. Migeon; *Miniature Painting and Painters of Persia, India and Turkey*, by F.R. Martin; *Miniatures Persanes*, by Georges Marteau and Henri Vever; *History of Bengali Language and Literature*, by D.C. Sen; and in other publications.

C398 Asiatic Art—1. India. *Art World and Arts & Decoration*, New York, [X.1] (Nov. 1918) 5-8, 7 text illus. (one facing p. 5).

The first of three instalments. A general survey.

C399 The Indian Epics—I. Notes on the Ramayana. *Young India*, New York, II. 11 (Nov. 1918) 11-12.

In the main, on the error of interpreting the *Rāmāyaṇa* from the standpoint of present-day Western morals.

C400 Asiatic Art. Part II.—The Far East. *Art World and Arts & Decoration*, New York, [X.2] (Dec. 1918) 71-4, 7 text illus.

C401 Burmese Glazed Tiles. *Museum of Fine Arts Bulletin*, Boston, XVI. 98 (Dec. 1918) 85, 2 text illus.

On examples in the Museum collection, from pagodas at Pāgan, that depict episodes from the *Jātakas*.

C402 Severe Consolation. *Youth: Poetry of Today*, Cambridge Mass., I. 2 (Dec. 1918) 36.

An original aphorism by AKC printed in two lines. (AKC is listed as the periodical's "Corresponding Editor for India", in an editorial note on p. 53.)

1919

C403 Section of Indian Art [III]. *Forty-fourth Annual Report for the Year 1919*. Boston: Museum of Fine Arts, Boston, 1919, pp. [110]-112.

C404 Asiatic Art. Part III.—Persia. *Art World and Arts & Decoration*, New York, [X.3] (Jan. 1919) 134-7, 180, 6 text illus.

C405 [A review of] *The Beginnings of Buddhist Art*, by A. Foucher. *Burlington Magazine*, London, XXXIV. 190 (Jan. 1919) 40-1.

AKC considers (1) Alfred Foucher's treatment of the aniconic character of early Buddhist art, and (2) his "controversial" theory of the "Greek origin of the Buddha type". "After the actual pioneers, no one has done more . . . to add to our knowledge of early Buddhist art" (p. 40). This review was reprinted in *Hindustan Review*, Allahabad, XL. 238 (July 1919) 76-8. For another (brief) review by AKC of this book of Alfred Foucher's, see "Twelfth Critical Bibliography of the Philosophy of Science and of the History of Civilization" (1922)—C448—pp. 615-16.

C406 Religion and Art. [Letter]. *Burlington Magazine*, London, XXXIV. 190 (Jan. 1919) 41-2.

Dated Boston, 10 November [1918]. On a review by Eric Gill of *The Dance of Śiva* (1918)—A38a—in the issue for October 1918.

C407 Notes on the Epics II. Mahabharata: Bhagavat Gita. *Young India*, New York, II. 1 (Jan. 1919) 12-14.

A discussion of the "problem in ethics . . . raised at the commencement of the Bhagavat Gita" (p. 12).

C408 The New Temple. *Youth: Poetry of Today*, Cambridge, Mass., I. 3 (Feb. 1919) 66-7.

A poem on the modern problems of Indian political and religious unity, translated by AKC (with assistance of Lala Lajpat Rai) from the Urdu of Muhammad Iqbal. This translation was reprinted in *Young India*, New York, II. 4 (Apr. 1919) 74.

C409 Buddhist Art in Asia. Its Origin and Development in India. *Asia*, New York, XIX. 4 (Apr. 1919) 353-60.

AKC provides "a summary of the history of Buddhist art, in the fewest possible words" (p. 355).

C410 Portrait of Gosain Jadrup. *Journal of the Royal Asiatic Society*, London (Apr. 1919) [389]-391, 1 pl. (facing p. [389]).

On a Mughal painting of *circa* AD 1617 ("shown to me by the owner, a resident of Ajmere, but of whose name, unfortunately, I made no note, at Allahabad in 1911") that depicts a famous Sādhu who was a friend and teacher of the Emperor Jahāngīr.

C411 Whitman as Prophet. *Modern School*, Ferrer Colony, Stelton, N.J., VI. 4/5 (Apr./May 1919) 98-102.

AKC discusses Walt Whitman's spiritual, non-puritanical view of human love, and his mysticism; also how through the example of Whitman "it is possible for an Oriental to believe that Western civilization may ultimately from the resources of its own vitality correct its own one-sidedness" (p. 100). The initial letter of this article is designed by Rockwell Kent, as is the front wrapper of this special issue devoted to Whitman on the centenary of his birth. This article was reprinted in *Hindustan Review*, Allahabad, XLI. 247 (Apr. 1920) [266]-269.

C412 Whether Art or Skill? *Young India*, New York, II. 6 (June 1919) 137-8.

On the tendency of the public when confronted with works of art to pay more honour to skill than to imagination.

C413 New England Woods. *Modern School*, Ferrer Colony, Stelton, N.J., VI. 8 (Aug. 1919) 209, 1 text illus.

A 16-line poem by AKC. The illustration, which serves as a headpiece, reproduces an engraving, "The Bride", by Edward Calvert. This poem was reprinted in *Three Poems* (1920)—A41.

C414 Rajput Painting [II]. *Museum of Fine Arts Bulletin*, Boston, XVII. 102 (Aug. 1919) [33]-43, 10 text illus.

On the Kāngrā Valley school, and on the Vaiṣṇava and Śaiva themes that form the common subjects of the paintings; illustrated by examples drawn from the Museum collections.

C415 A Note on Urdu Poetry. *Youth: Poetry of Today*, Cambridge, Mass., I. 6 (Aug. 1919) 115.

AKC's note is based upon materials supplied by Dr Paira Mall.

C416 The Mystic Vision. [Letter]. *Athenaeum*, London, XCIII. 4,661 (29 Aug. 1919) 823.

Dated Boston, 13 Aug. 1919. Correcting some notions of mysticism expressed by Arthur Clutton Brock, Bertrand Russell, and others, in the issues for 20 June, 4 and 11 July.

C417 The Significance of Oriental Art. *Art Bulletin*, New York, II. 1 (Sept. 1919) 17-22.

The text of a paper read by AKC at the Eighth Annual Meeting of the College Art Association of America in New York on 12 May 1919. On the traditional relation of art to life in the East, contrasted with the conditions under which art is produced in the modern West. This article was reprinted in *Hindustan Review*, Allahabad, XLI. 244 (Jan. 1920) [35]-38.

C418 Indian Stone Sculptures. *Museum of Fine Arts Bulletin*, Boston, XVII. 104 (Dec. 1919) [57]-63, 6 text illus.

Of the Gandhāra and Gupta periods. This article was reprinted, as "Indian Art in America: Indian Stone Sculptures in the Museum of Fine Arts, Boston", in *Modern Review*, Calcutta, XXVII. 4 (Apr. 1920) 407-13, 7 text illus.

1920

C419 Indian Art in America I. Paintings of Musical Modes in Boston and New York. *Art in America*, New York, VIII. 2 (Feb. 1920) 58-67, 2 pls.

The first of three instalments. A discussion of a typical group of 16th century Rājasthānī works (from the Museum of Fine Arts, Boston, the Metropolitan Museum of Art, New York, and from AKC's private collection) that originally formed a set of illustrations to "a *Rāgmālā*, or 'Garland of *Rāgas*', a class of poetry describing the thirty-six modes . . . in Indian music" (p. 58).

C420 Psychical Research. *Hindustan Review*, Allahabad, XLI. 245 (Feb. 1920) [79]-81.

"We do not propose to question here the 'results' of psychical research, nor to discuss the veridity of spiritualistic phenomena: but rather to ask what ultimate significance for us might lie in empirical proof of the survival of personality and the existence of an 'other world, beyond', or 'next life'" (p. [79]).

C421 To a Migrant Bird. *Modern Review*, Calcutta, XXVII. 3 (Mar. 1920) 267-8.

A 52-line poem, comprising 13 stanzas, on the subject of pilgrimage, "by Kolapi [*sic*, for Kalāpi, i.e. 'the Peacock'], Darbar Sura Singh-ji, Prince of Lathi in Kathiawad, India. Translated from Gujarati by Ananda Coomaraswamy and Premanand V. Vaishya" (p. 267). AKC regarded this as among the best of his translations of Indian poetry; see his letter, dated 13 August 1946, to S. Durai Raja Singam, in *Letters of the Great* ([1954])—B86—pp. 37-8.

C422 Todi Ragini. *Young India*, New York, III. 3 (Mar. 1920) 50, 1 pl. (facing p. 50).

Printed under the general heading: Our Art Section. On the nature of Rāgmālā painting, with reference to a 16th century Rājput miniature in the collections of the Museum of Fine Arts, Boston. This article is the first of a series of monthly contributions on Indian art by AKC to be printed in this periodical; the last appeared in the issue for December 1920. The contribution to the November issue takes the form solely of a reproduction (facing p. 242) of a photograph by AKC captioned: Bathing Ghat at Benares.

C423 A Nepalese Buddhist Painting. *Museum of Fine Arts Bulletin*, Boston, XVIII. 106 (Apr. 1920) 14-17, 6 text illus.

On a recent gift to the Museum, dated equivalent to AD 1716. The painting illustrates the *Pindapatra* and *Kapisa Avadanas*: two stories on the merit of almsgiving. This article was reprinted in *Modern Review*, Calcutta, XXVIII. 6 (June 1920) 622-4, 1 text illus.

C424 Siamese Bronzes. *Museum of Fine Arts Bulletin*, Boston, XVIII. 106 (Apr. 1920) 17-19, 4 text illus.

A description of four Buddhist examples in the Museum's possession: a standing figure of a Bodhisattva of the Sukothai-Savankolok period; the head of a Bodhisattva from the early Ayuthia period; the upper part of a standing figure of a Buddha and an entire standing figure of Dipankara Buddha, both of the late Ayuthia period.

C425 Khmer Sculpture. *Museum of Fine Arts Bulletin*, Boston, XVIII. 106 (Apr. 1920) 20-1, 4 text illus.

On two Śaiva and two Buddhist sandstone heads of the 9th to 14th century, in the Museum collections.

C426 Art and Craftsmanship. *Rupam*, Calcutta, 2 (Apr. 1920) 4-5.

A definition of these terms from the standpoint of the traditional doctrine of art. Reprinted, with minor revisions, and with the addition of a new concluding sentence, in *Dial*, New York, LXVIII. 6 (June 1920) [744]-746, and, without these changes, in *Reflections on Art* . . ., edited by Susanne K. Langer (1958)—B87.

C427 Krishna's Flute. *Young India*, New York, III. 4 (Apr. 1920) 74, 1 pl. (facing p. 74).

Printed under the general heading: Our Art Section. An elucidation of this Vaiṣṇava motif as represented in a 17th century Rājput miniature in the collections of the Museum of Fine Arts, Boston. "Krishna may be the prototype of the Pied Piper of Hamelin".

C428 Head of Apsaras. *Young India*, New York, III. 5 (May 1920) 98, 1 pl. (facing p. 98).

Printed under the general heading: Our Art Section. A brief note on an AD 10th or 11th century Hindu sandstone sculpture in the collections of the Museum of Fine Arts, Boston.

C429 Indian Art in America, Part Two, the Krishna Cycle in Rajput Painting. *Art in America*, New York, VIII. 4 (June 1920) 160-[165], 1 text illus.

A discussion of Kāngrā Valley painting: the characteristic delineation ("tinted drawings rather than . . . paintings"), the dominant themes, and leading symbols.

C430 Avalokitesvara Bodhisattva. *Young India*, New York, III. 6 (June 1920) 122, 1 pl. (facing p. 122).

Printed under the general heading: Art Section. A note on an AD 8th century Ceylonese bronze in the collections of the Museum of Fine Arts, Boston.

C431 Rama, Sita and Lakshmana. *Young India*, New York, III. 7 (July 1920) 146, 1 pl. (facing p. 146).

Printed under the general heading: Art Section. A note on a 17th century Rājput miniature, in the collection of Arthur B. Davies (New York), that illustrates the "forest asylum" section of the *Rāmāyaṇa.*

C432 Indian Art in America, Part Three, Indian Painting, Eleventh to Sixteenth Century. *Art in America*, New York, VIII. 5 (Aug. 1920) 223-32, 2 pls.

Illustrations from early Indian manuscripts are compared with Rājput art to demonstrate the continuity of Indian painting. A *circa* AD 1136 Nepalese manuscript of *Aṣṭasāhasrikā Prajñāpāramitā* that contains representations of scenes from the life of the Buddha, and Jain paintings from manuscripts of the 15th century, including an illustration that depicts the Tonsure of Mahāvīra, are discussed in detail. All of the manuscripts are from the collections of the Museum of Fine Arts, Boston. See also C447.

C433 The Dying Men [*sic*, for Man]. *Young India*, New York, III. 8 (Aug. 1920) 170, 1 pl. (facing p. 170).

A comment on a Mughal painting of *circa* AD 1620-30 in the Bodleian Library at Oxford; with a note on what distinguishes Mughal work from that of the Rājput schools. See also C465.

C434 First Impressions of Japan. *Asian Review*, Tokyo, I. 6 (Aug./ Sept. 1920) 596-7.

Dated Tokyo, 10 Aug. 1920. (AKC was granted a year's leave of absence by the Museum of Fine Arts, Boston, beginning June 1920. He embarked upon a world tour, that was, in part, a study and buying trip; see the Museum's *Bulletin* for June 1920, p. 30.)

C435 Infant Krishna with Yasoda. *Young India*, New York, III. 9 (Sept. 1920) 194, 1 pl. (facing p. 194).

Printed under the general heading: Art Section. In the main, a critical assessment of the modern Calcutta school, with a brief note on a painting of this title by Asit Kumar Haldar.

C436 The Rasikapriya of Kesava Das. *Museum of Fine Arts Bulletin*, Boston, XVIII. 109 (Oct. 1920) 50-2, 3 text illus.

On three leaves and eighteen detached illustrations from a manuscript (*circa* AD 1600) of this Hindi treatise on rhetoric and literary analysis in the Museum collections.

C437 Leaf of a Koran. *Museum of Fine Arts Bulletin*, Boston, XVIII. 109 (Oct. 1920) 52-3, 2 text illus.

An 11-line note accompanying reproductions of Kufic script of the 13th century.

C438 A Peacock's Feather. *Rupam*, Calcutta, 4 (Oct. 1920) 27, 1 pl. (tipped in on p. 27).

On a Rājput painting in the Museum of Fine Arts, Boston, that treats a feather realistically in colours and gold. (See also AKC's note on this same painting in *Catalogue of the Indian Collections in the Museum of Fine Arts, Boston Part V Rājput Painting* (1926)—A49—p. 194.)

C439 The Dance of Siva. *Young India*, New York, III. 10 (Oct. 1920) 218, 1 pl. (facing p. 218).

A brief explication of the Naṭarāja motif, with reference to a copper image of *circa* 12th century in the Madras Museum.

C440 Sujata's Offering to Buddha. *Young India*, New York, III. 12 (Dec. 1920) 268, 1 pl. (facing p. 268).

A note on this subject as represented in a relief at Borobudur, Java.

1921

C441 Notice sur l'entité et les noms de Çiva. *Ars Asiatica*, Brussels & Paris, III. (1921) 15-17, XII numbered pls.

This issue also carries the title: *Sculptures Civaites* [*de l'Inde*]. A résumé of the philosophical concept of Shaivism, and the place of Shiva in his various aspects in Indian religious thought. An English translation of this article by D.M. Moore is printed in *Ananda*

Coomaraswamy—the Bridge Builder, by S. Durai Raja Singam ([Kuala Lumpur] 1977)—E192—pp. [275-6].

C442 A Nepalese Tara. *Rupam*, Calcutta, 6 (Apr. 1921) [1]-2, 1 pl. (facing p. [1]).

A note on a copper figure of a goddess, which AKC tentatively dates AD late 12th or 13th century.

C443 Svadhinapatika. [Letter]. *Rupam*, Calcutta, 6 (Apr. 1921) 43.

(In English.) Under this heading, editorial comment on "Some Notes on Hindu Erotics", by Kannoomal, in the issue for October 1920, incorporates a letter from AKC correcting the caption to a picture of a *Nāyikā* (heroine) that was reproduced with Kannoomal's article.

C444 America and India. *Indian Review*, Madras, XXII. 5 (May 1921) [281]-283.

AKC contrasts India's traditional, and theocratic, social order with the West's democratic ideal, and concludes with some reflections on Asia's precarious position in the modern world. This article was reprinted in *Orient*, New York, I. 1 (Feb. 1923) 15-17.

C445 Notes on the Javanese Theatre. *Rupam*, Calcutta, 7 (July 1921) 5-11, 6 pls. (2 tipped in, pp. 5, 7).

A description of "the leading forms of the drama as it exists in Java and Bali at the present day" (p. 6); including as well some observations on Asiatic dramatic technique in general. AKC visited Indonesia in January(?) 1921, while on a world tour (see C434 *n.*). His travelling companion, Stella Bloch, contributes two drawings, i.e. the tipped in plates; the other illustrations are reproductions of photographs taken in Indonesia by AKC. In a note concerning this article, in *Isis*, Cambridge, Mass., IV. 3 (1922)—C448—p. 607, AKC says he is "not responsible for the incorrect descriptions of [i.e. the captions to] the illustrations".

C446 The Book of the Month. Mythology of All Races. *Hindustan Review*, Allahabad, XLIV. 263 (Aug. 1921) [89]-91.

A review of *Mythology of All Races*, edited by L.H. Gray, Vol. VI: *Indian, Iran*, by Arthur Berriedale Keith and A.J. Carnoy, and Vol. IX: *Oceania*, by R.B. Dixon. AKC gives a summary of the contents of these two volumes "of an admirable series".

C447 An Illustrated Nepalese Manuscript. *Museum of Fine Arts Bulletin*, Boston, XIX. 114 (Aug. 1921) 47-9, 4 text illus.

On the recent acquisition by the Museum of a *circa* AD 12th century manuscript of the Buddhist sūtra *Aṣṭasāhasrikā Prajñāpāramitā*, "of primary interest as a document of Indian painting [because it] links the early schools of Buddhist painting with the later productions of Nepalese art" (p. 48).

1922

C448 Twelfth Critical Bibliography of the Philosophy of Science and of the History of Civilization. *Isis*, Cambridge, Mass., IV. 3 (1922) 573, 574, 578, 586, 597, 607-8, 615-17.

Under this heading, brief critical notes, signed with the initials A.K.C., are appended to 22 entries, s.v. P.K. Acharya; W. Cohn; Ananda K. Coomaraswamy; K. Döhring; Alfred Foucher; G.A. Grierson and L.D. Barnett; G. Groslier; A.K. Haldar; J.E. Jasper and Mas Pirngadie; K.P. Jayaswal; Sten Konow; Stella Kramrisch; Mukandi Lal; P.G. Nahar and K. Ghosh; L.D.S. Pillai; H.A. Popley; Bhavanrao Pratinidhi; T.A. Gopinatha Rao; Auguste Rodin, Ananda K. Coomaraswamy, E.B. Havell, and Victor Goloubew; Dinesh Chandra Sen. AKC also contributed notes to the Thirteenth (1922), Fourteenth (1923), and Sixteenth (1925) instalments of this bibliography—C449, 457, 479—compiled under the direction of George Sarton.

C449 Thirteenth Critical Bibliography of the Philosophy of Science and of the History of Civilization. *Isis*, Cambridge, Mass., V. 1 (1922) 207, 212, 271.

Under this heading, brief critical notes, signed with the initials A.K.C., are appended to three entries, s.v. H.T.D., and G. Jouveau-Dubreuil.

C450 Saiva Sculptures. Recent Acquisitions. *Museum of Fine Arts Bulletin*, Boston, XX. 118 (Apr. 1922) [15]-24, 10 text illus.

The eleven examples discussed comprise Umā-Maheśvara groups and South Indian bronzes, AD 800-1800. The discussion is preceded by an essay on the use of images and the Śaiva cults, pp. [15]-17. "All the objects described in the present article, with the exception of one . . . were purchased through Dr. Ananda Coomaraswamy in India" (p.[15]).

C451 Bibliography of Indian Painting. (Not Including Moghul). *Rupam*, Calcutta, 10 (Apr. 1922) 57-8.

A select list of materials in Western languages, arranged in alphabetical order by author, and comprising thirty-eight monographs and thirty-nine contributions to periodicals.

C452 Buddhist Sculpture. Recent Acquisitions. *Museum of Fine Arts Bulletin*, Boston, XX. 120 (Aug. 1922) [45]-53, 13 text illus.

The objects discussed (the majority of which were purchased by AKC in India in 1921) comprise sculptures from Amarāvatī, Māyā Devī or Lakshmī coins from Ceylon, sculptures from Mathurā (Kuṣāna and Gupta), a Southern Gupta Buddha figure, Mediaeval stone and metal figures, a Khmer head of the Buddha from Cambodia, and a Bodhisattva from Ceylon (the last mentioned stolen in transit to the Museum). The discussion is preceded by a summary of the history of Buddhism and Buddhist art.

C453 Jaina Sculpture. Recent Acquisition. *Museum of Fine Arts Bulletin*, Boston, XX. 120 (Aug. 1922) 53, 1 text illus.

On an AD 9th century sandstone figure of Mahāvīra, the historical founder of Jainism.

C454 Ajanta Fresco Fragment in the Boston Museum. *Rupam*, Calcutta, 12 (Oct. 1922) 121-3, 1 pl.

From Cave XVI, and "perhaps the only part of the original frescoes now surviving apart from the remains *in situ*" (p. 122). This article was reprinted as part of "Recent Acquisitions of the Department of Indian Art" in *Museum of Fine Arts Bulletin*, Boston, for December 1922—C456, under the subheading "A Fragment of Fresco from Ajanta", pp. 70-2.

C455 [A review of] *Serindia: A Detailed Report of Explorations in Central Asia and Westernmost China*, by Aurel Stein; with Appendices by L. Binyon, E. Chavannes, R. Petrucci and others . . . [and] *The Thousand Buddhas: Ancient Buddhist Paintings from the Cave Temples of Tun-huang on the Western Frontier of China* . . . by Aurel Stein, with an Introductory Essay by Laurence Binyon. *Asia*, New York, XXII. 11 (Nov. 1922) 904.

"These results are equally important to the geographer and to the student of the history of Asiatic civilization and art . . . A profound interest attaches to the [Tun-huang] paintings . . . mainly Buddhist and therefore based on Indian formulae; but . . . everything . . . is translated into Chinese terms, terms that belong to the indigenous Chinese tradition of secular art, otherwise hardly known . . . All are invaluable to the student of Buddhist iconography."

C456 Recent Acquisitions of the Department of Indian Art. *Museum of Fine Arts Bulletin*, Boston, XX. 122 (Dec. 1922) 69-73, 5 text illus.

On two Rājput paintings, a fragment of fresco from Ajaṇṭā, and a *circa* 1st century stone image of Sūrya (the Indian sun god).

1923

C457 Fourteenth Critical Bibliography of the Philosophy of Science and of the History of Civilization. *Isis*, Cambridge, Mass., V. 2 (1923) 528, 529.

Under this heading, brief critical notes, signed with the initials A.K.C., are appended to two entries, s.v. Berthold Laufer and H. Parmentier.

C458 Indian Art in Boston. *Arts*, New York, III. 1 (Jan. 1923) 36-[46], 2 text illus., 6 pls.

A description of the most important of the recent acquisitions by the Museum of Fine Arts, Boston, including a fresco fragment from Ajaṇṭā, a Umā-Maheśvara group, a Naṭarāja image, a Buddha head and casing slab from Amarāvatī, and Rājput paintings. "The Museum is now easily first in America in respect of the quality and range of its Indian exhibits, and is not surpassed in these respects by any museum outside India" (p. 36).

C459 Early Persian Paintings in America. *Arts*, New York, III. 3 (Mar. 1923) 175-84, 15 text illus., 1 pl.

On examples from the Museum of Fine Arts, Boston, the Hagop Kevorkian collection (New York), and AKC's personal collection, that comprise manuscripts of the *Kitāb fī ma'arifat al-ḥiyal al-handasiya* of al-Jazari (on automata), an Arabic translation of the *Materia medica* of Dioscorides by Abdulla ibn Fadl, the chronicle of Muhammad ibn Jarīr ut-Tabarī, the *Manāfi al-Hayawān*, and the *Shāh Nāma*. See also C464.

C460 Medieval and Modern Hinduism. *Asia*, New York, XXIII. 3 (Mar. 1923) 203-6, 230, 4 text illus.

A general account, written in collaboration with Stella Bloch (i.e. Mrs AKC). The illustrations (and one other printed in the same issue on p. [160], captioned: "Returning from the Temple") are reproductions of photographs taken by AKC in India.

C461 The Nine Planets. Indian Sculpture. *Worcester Art Museum Bulletin*, Worcester, Mass., XIV. 1 (Apr. 1923) 6-10, 2 text illus.

A description of a sandstone relief in the Museum that represents planetary and stellar deities (the Navagraha), here tentatively assigned by AKC to the Gupta period. This article was reprinted, as part of "Some Indian Sculptures in American Museums", in *Rupam*, Calcutta, for April 1924—C473, and again, as "Some Indian Images in the Worcester Art Museum: Navagraha", in *Marg*, Bombay, VI. 3 (June 1953) 18, 1 text illus.

C462 Hindu Culture. *Freeman*, New York, VII. 168 (30 May 1923) 285-6.

A review of *The Futurism of Young Asia, and Other Essays on the Relation Between the East and the West*, by Benoy Kumar Sarkar. AKC is critical of Sarkar's attempt "to prove the material rather than the spiritual character of Hindu culture".

C463 Notes on Rajput Painting. *Rupam*, Calcutta, 15/16 (July/Dec. 1923) 72-3.

On costume as material for use in dating and localization of paintings, with reference to "Studien zur Rājputen-Malerei [Part I]", by Hermann Goetz (1923). AKC revises the dates given to the Rāgamālā paintings published in his *Rajput Painting* (1916)—A34—and in *Portfolio of Indian Art* (1923)—A43. This article was reprinted, in an expanded version, and with the addition of seven illustrations, in *Ostasiatische Zeitschrift*, Berlin, N.S. I. (1924) [17]-21, 2 pls. (numbered: 3-4).

C464 Early Arabic and Persian Paintings. Mainly Recent Acquisitions. *Museum of Fine Arts Bulletin*, Boston, XXI. 126 (Aug. 1923) 49-53, 8 text illus.

On a leaf from al-Jazari's *Kitāb fī ma'arifat al-ḥiyal al-handasiya* (a treatise on automata), two leaves from a *Manāfi al-Hayawān*, and five leaves from two manuscripts of the *Shāh Nāma*, all of the 13th century AD.

C465 The Dying Man ('Inayat Khan). *Museum of Fine Arts Bulletin*, Boston, XXI. 126 (Aug. 1923) 54.

On the identification, by S.C. Clarke, of the subject of a Mughal drawing in the Museum collections (that exactly corresponds to a finished picture in the Bodleian Library at Oxford) as one of the Emperor Jahāngīr's courtiers who died in AD 1618.

C466 [A review of] *Modern Indian Artists, Vol. I, Khsitindranath Mazumdar*, [by] O.C. Gangoly. *Orient*, New York, I. 4 (Oct./Nov. 1923) 49-50.

AKC discusses the principal strengths and weaknesses of the modern Calcutta School of painters—"the pre-Raphaelites of India"—led by Abanindranath Tagore, of whom

Mazumdar was a pupil and follower. AKC remarks that "like Rabindranath Tagore, the modern Indian artists know what they ought to feel and to experience, but there is no evidence in their work that they have actually felt". AKC singles out Gaganendranath Tagore and Nandalal Bose as having produced the best works of the School.

C467 The Appreciation of Art. *Art Bulletin*, New York, VI. 2 (Dec. 1923) [61]-64.

Written in collaboration with Stella Bloch (i.e. Mrs AKC). A critique of the modern conception of art and the teaching of art appreciation. This article was reprinted in *Ceylon Daily News*, Colombo (11 Sept. 1975) 6.

C468 Hindī Rāgmālā Texts. *Journal of the American Oriental Society*, New Haven, XLIII. 4 (Dec. 1923) 396-409.

A discussion and translation by AKC of three Rāgmālā poems (two versions each of the Rāgiṇīs *Madhu-mādhavī*, *Vibhāsa*, and *Gandhāra*) inscribed on Rājput paintings from the 16th and 17th centuries in the Museum of Fine Arts (Boston), the Metropolitan Museum of Art (New York), the Freer Gallery of Art (Washington, D.C.), and other collections. The poems describe situations in human experience appropriate to the moods illustrated in Rāgmālā pictures, i.e. paintings whose themes have been evoked by the different musical modes of the thirty-six Rāgas and Rāgiṇīs. Two of these translations were reprinted with the expanded version of "Notes on Rajput Painting"—C463 *n*.

C469 Photographs in the Print Department. *Museum of Fine Arts Bulletin*, Boston, XXI. 128 (Dec. 1923) 79.

On photography as a valid "medium for artistic expression", and the Museum's decision to form a collection of artistic photographs; including an announcement of "a promise of twelve prints from Mr. Alfred Stieglitz". See also C472.

1924

C470 The Invention of the Buddha Figure. *Ostasiatische Zeitschrift*, Berlin, N.S. I. (1924) [51]-55.

Printed under the general heading: Miszellen. A review of *L'art gréco-bouddhique du Gandhāra*, Vol. II, by Alfred Foucher.

C471 Cambodian Dancers and Other Khmer Sculptures Recently Acquired. *Museum of Fine Arts Bulletin*, Boston, XXII. 130 (Apr. 1924) [9]-13, 9 text illus.

On a bronze figure of an *apsaras*; architectural stone fragments bearing relief figures of dancers and heads of horses; a frieze of *apsarases* from Angkor Wat; a 14th or 15th century stone head of the Buddha, and another of a *deva* "from about the ninth century". This article was printed simultaneously, as part of "Some Indian Sculptures in American Museums", in *Rupam*, Calcutta, for April 1924—C473.

C472 A Gift from Mr. Alfred Stieglitz. *Museum of Fine Arts Bulletin*, Boston, XXII. 130 (Apr. 1924) 14, 1 text illus.

On the Museum's recent acquisition of photographs by Stieglitz, together with remarks on the nature of photography itself. AKC was personally acquainted with Stieglitz, and in 1923 asked him for some of his photographs for the Museum. When Stieglitz made his eventual choice of twenty-seven prints, Boston became the first American museum to acquire a group of photographs by one artist. This article was reprinted, with the omission of the first two sentences, as part of Perry T. Rathbone's "Foreword" to *Alfred Stieglitz: Photographer*, by Doris Bry (Boston: Museum of Fine Arts [1965]), p. [5]. For further on AKC and Alfred Stieglitz, see *Coomaraswamy 3: His Life and Work*, by Roger Lipsey ([1977])—E116—pp. 155-60.

C473 Some Indian Sculptures in American Museums. *Rupam*, Calcutta, 18 (Apr. 1924) 65-8, 1 text illus., 2 pls. (one facing p. 65).

On the identification, and iconography, of seven recent acquisitions: two figures of Vishnu, a Brahmā, and a Mahesha-mūrti in the Pennsylvania University Museum; a Mañjuśrī in the Metropolitan Museum of Art (New York); a Navagraha in the Worcester Art Museum; and a Cambodian *apsaras* in the Museum of Fine Arts, Boston. Corrigendum to this article is printed with "A Statuette of Vishnu from Kashmir" in the *Pennsylvania University Museum Journal* for March 1926—C486, p. 93, fn. 1.

C474 A Reply to Mr. Wadia. *Eolian Review*, New York, III. 3 (May 1924) 8-12.

Analysing an Indian listener's dissatisfaction with modern Western music, i.e. "his complaint of a lack of intelligible *meaning* and *purpose* [AKC's emphases]", with reference to "A Question from the Orient", by B.P. Wadia, in the issue for June 1923.

C475 Todi Ragini. *Orient*, New York, II. 1 (May/June 1924) 36, 1 pl. (facing p. 41).

An anonymous Rāgmālā poem, translated by AKC into English from the Hindi of British Museum MS. Or 2821, and printed here in 17 lines. This translation was reprinted in *Coomaraswamiana*, edited by S. Durai Raja Singam (1960)—A76—pp. [221-4].

C476 Ragmala Poems. *Orient*, New York, II. 1 (May/June 1924) 76-8.

An annotated sampler from this particular branch of Hindi literature where poetry, painting, and music, supply a mutual commentary. These translations were reprinted in *Coomaraswamiana*, edited by S. Durai Raja Singam (1960)—A76—pp.[213-18], and in *Ananda Coomaraswamy—the Bridge Builder; a Study of a Scholar-Colossus*, by S. Durai Raja Singam (1977)—B94—pp. [370-2].

C477 A Buddhist Sculpture. Recent Acquisition. *Museum of Fine Arts Bulletin*, Boston, XXII. 132 (Aug. 1924) 30, 1 text illus.

On the iconography of a Pāla stone sculpture of the 10th or 13th century AD, "probably from Bengal", and representing "the Eight Great Miracles or significant events in the Buddha's life".

1925

C478 Catalogue des pièces khmères conservées dans les musées de l'Amérique du nord. *Arts et Archéologie Khmèrs*, Paris, II. 2 (1925) 235-40, 3 pls. (numbered: 25-7) containing 17 illus.

"Ce catalogue est dressé sur l'invitation de M. [George] Groslier" (p. 235). Altogether forty pieces are briefly described from the collections of seven museums: the Museum of Fine Arts, Boston, the Fogg Art Museum, the Worcester Art Museum, the Cleveland Museum of Art, the Philadelphia Museum, the Metropolitan Museum, and the Art Institute, Chicago.

C479 Sixteenth Critical Bibliography of the Philosophy of Science and of the History of Civilization. *Isis*, Cambridge, Mass., VII. 2 (1925) 183, 221, 254.

Under this heading, brief critical notes, signed with the initials A.K.C., are appended to three entries: s.v. J. Kats; E. Kühnel and Hermann Goetz; and Stella Kramrisch.

C480 Dīpaka Rāga. *The Year Book of Oriental Art and Culture 1924-1925*, edited by Arthur Waley. London: Ernest Benn Limited, 1925, *Volume One: Text:* pp. 29-30; *Volume Two: Plates:* 1 pl. (numbered: 20).

(In English.) A discussion and translation of a Rāgmālā poem text inscribed on a 17th century picture in the Museum of Fine Arts, Boston.

C481 Two Mughal Paintings, with Portraits of ʻAlī Mardān Khān. *The Year Book of Oriental Art and Culture 1924-1925*, edited by Arthur Waley. London: Ernest Benn Limited, 1925, *Volume One: Text:* pp. 66-9; *Volume Two: Plates:* 2 pls. (numbered: 48, 49).

Identification, dating, and description of the subject: "a Persian who occupied a very important position at the Mughal court in the latter part of Shāh Jahān's reign" (p. 66). The paintings are from the collections of Babu Sītārām Lāl of Benares and Messrs. Parish-Watson of New York.

C482 The Chinese Theatre in Boston. *Theatre Arts Monthly*, New York, IX. 2 (Feb. 1925) 113-22, 4 text illus., 2 pls.

Written in collaboration with, and illustrated with drawings by, Stella Bloch (i.e. Mrs AKC). On the stage arrangements, music, technique, and audience, of a recently opened repertory theatre.

C483 Indian Sculptures. Ross Collection. *Museum of Fine Arts Bulletin*, Boston, XXIII. 139 (Oct. 1925) 57-62, 7 text illus.

On five pieces recently acquired from India, Siam, Cambodia, and Java, and so not included in the *Catalogue of the Indian Collections in the Museum of Fine Arts, Boston . . . Part II, Sculpture* (1923)—A44: a Medieval Indian stone image of a devotee or donor; a basalt head of the Buddha, probably from Borobudur; a 17th or 18th century Siamese standing figure of the Buddha; a 10th to 12th century Siamese head of the Buddha; and "a second gigantic head of a *deva*, probably from one of the causeways at Angkor Thom" of about the late 9th century (p. 59). AKC concludes with a note on the evolution of Siamese sculpture, based upon the "admirable discussion" in *Sculpture in Siam*, by Alfred Salmony.

C484 [A review of] *Sculpture in Siam*. By A. Salmony. *Arts*, New York, VIII. 5 (Nov. 1925) 289-91, 1 text illus.

"Until lately the history of Siamese art has been very imperfectly known . . . Dr. Salmony's book exhibits in an admirable way the main lines of development" (p. 289).

C485 Three Fragments of Gandhara Sculpture. *Museum of Fine Arts Bulletin*, Boston, XXIII. 140 (Dec. 1925) 73-5, 4 text illus.

On some recent acquisitions by the Museum. One of these fragments, that depicts an episode from the *Vessantara Jātaka*, is discussed at length. AKC concludes with a brief survey of the representation of this *Jātaka* in the art of India and Ceylon.

1926

C486 A Statuette of Vishnu from Kashmir. *Pennsylvania University Museum Journal*, Philadelphia, XVII. 1 (Mar. 1926) 91-3, 1 pl.

On this piece from the Museum collections, dated to AD 9th century, that is uniquely armed with a dagger. Another description by AKC of this same Vishnu is printed as part of "Some Indian Sculptures in American Museums", in *Rupam*, Calcutta, for April 1924—C473.

C487 Rājput Paintings. *Bulletin of the Museum of Fine Arts*, Boston, XXIV. 142 (Apr. 1926) 23-6, 5 text illus.

Notes on recent acquisitions by the Museum: (1) a miniature that depicts Rādhā and Krishna, "tentatively described as Gujarātī, early or mid-sixteenth century", (2) a "portrait of a seated Jodhpur rājā", probably of the 17th century, (3) "two smaller paintings of uncertain provenance and representing Paurānic subjects", and (4) a *circa* late 17th century picture from an illustrated manuscript of "a Hindī poetical version of the story of Madhu and Mālati".

C488 The New Edition of Vincent Smith's *Early History of India*: A Correction. *Journal of the Royal Asiatic Society*, London (Apr. 1926) 305-6.

On the identification of objects connected with the first Jina that are mentioned in the Hāthī-gumphā inscription of Emperor Khāravela.

C489 Frescoes at Elūrā. *Ostasiatische Zeitschrift*, Berlin, N.S. III. 1/2 (Jan./June 1926) [1]-8, 3 pls. (one facing p. 8).

A note describing remnants of late AD 8th century and later Hindu painting in the porch of the Kailāsa temple and in some of the caves. The footnotes on pp. [1]-2 list thirty-one references in the scholarly literature to the early history of painting in India and Ceylon.

C490 The Indian Origin of the Buddha Image. *Journal of the American Oriental Society*, New Haven, XLVI. 2 (June 1926) 165-70.

"I have thought that it would be interesting to gather together a number of quotations . . . from well known scholars already committed to the theory of Greek origin. These extracts are admittedly selected *ad hoc*, and do not always fairly represent the author's real views; they are rather, at least in some cases, to be regarded as incidental admissions. My object in gathering them . . . is to show that there actually exists a great deal of evidence in favour of an Indian origin" (p. 165).

C491 [A review of] *The Indian Buddhist Iconography, Mainly Based on the Sadhanamala and Other* (sic) *Cognate Tantric Texts of Rituals.* [By] B. Bhattacharyya. *Journal of the American Oriental Society*, New Haven, XLVI. 2 (June 1926) 187-9.

"This is a well documented volume and will be indispensable to all scholars interested in Mahāyāna theology and in the identification of Mahāyāna, especially Vajrayāna deities" (p. 187). Concerning the text of the *Sādhanamālā*, AKC disagrees with Bhattacharyya's assertion that the artist's "imaginative self-identification with the form evoked" is a practice exclusive to Buddhists. He also disagrees with the significance ascribed by Bhattacharyya to the *Brahma-kapāla*. The "(sic)" is AKC's interpolation.

C492 The Bee-Song of Sur Das. *New Orient*, New York, III. 2 (July 1926) 51-4.

A literal translation by AKC of the *Bhramar-Gīt* (on the Krishna Līlā theme), from the collection *Sūr Sāgar* of the 16th century Hindī poet Sūr Dās.

C493 Early Indian Sculptures. Six Reliefs from Mathura. *Bulletin of the Museum of Fine Arts*, Boston, XXIV. 144 (Aug. 1926) 54-60, 12 text illus. (one is printed on the front cover of this issue, i.e. p. [53]).

On decorated Buddhist cross-bars and railing pillars, mainly from the 3rd century BC to AD 3rd century, in the Museum collections. Some of the reliefs that depict Bodhi tree temples are discussed at length because these contribute to the knowledge of early Indian architecture.

C494 [A review of] *Ancient India: From the Earliest Times to the Guptas, with Notes on the Architecture and Sculpture of the Mediaeval Period.* By C[*sic*, for K]. de B. Codrington. With a Prefatory Essay on Indian Sculpture by William Rothenstein. *Journal of the American Oriental Society*, New Haven, XLVI. 3 (Sept. 1926) 253-6.

"Mr. Codrington's book, so far as it goes . . . may well be described as the best account of Indian art that has yet been published . . . an original and important work . . . The supposed foreign elements in Mauryan, Śuṅga and Kuṣāna art are judiciously discussed". AKC notes some "caprices of transcription [and] the extreme carelessness of the proof-reading".

C495 A Connection Between Indian Aesthetics and Philosophy. *Rupam*, Calcutta, 27/28 (July/Oct. 1926) 91-4.

A translation by AKC of "Une connexion dans l'Esthétique et la Philosophie de l'Inde. La Notion de Pramāna", by P. Masson-Oursel, from *Revue des Arts Asiatiques*, Paris, II. 1 (1925) 34-6.

C496 Military Origin of the Minuet. *Dial*, New York, LXXXI. 4 (Oct. 1926) [340]-344.

A review of *The Dance Over Fire and Water*, by Elie Faure. AKC discusses Faure's thesis that art "appears in the world as the result of conflict, and typically as the result of wars" (p.[340]).

1927

C497 Notes on Indian Paintings 1. A Contribution to Mughal Iconography. *Artibus Asiae*, Ascona, II. 1 (1927) [4]-11, 5 pls. (tipped in).

The first of four instalments. Comprises detailed descriptions of five Mughal portraits: four from the Museum of Fine Arts, Boston, and one from a private collection.

C498 Notes on Indian Paintings 1. A Contribution to Mughal Iconography (Part II). *Artibus Asiae*, Ascona, II. 2 (1927) 132-7, 5 pls. (tipped in).

Comprises detailed descriptions of six Mughal portraits (two of which depict Kabīr) from the Worcester Art Museum, the Freer Gallery of Art, the British Museum, the Museum of Fine Arts, Boston, and from AKC's personal collection.

C499 Notes on Mughal Painting, 2. *Artibus Asiae*, Ascona, II. 3 (1927) 202-12, 10 pls. (tipped in).

On a 15th century illustrated Fables of Bīdpaī, the *Kalīla va Dimnah*, in the British Museum (MS. Add. 18579). AKC comments on the signatures of Āqā Riẓā, Mirza Ghulām, Nānhā, and other painters' names preserved on some of the miniatures.

C500 Notes on Indian Painting, 4. Bishndās and Others. *Artibus Asiae*, Ascona, II. 4 (1927) 283-94, 5 pls. (tipped in).

A list, with brief comments, of ten known (and two attributed) works by the 17th century Mughal painter Bishndās; also included are notes on the painters Ḥūn Karmānī and Muḥammad Afṣal, and miscellaneous corrigenda concerning portraits of 'Alī Mardān Khān, Jahāngīr, and Shāh Jahān.

C501 An Early Indian Buddha Head. *Bulletin of the Detroit Institute of Arts*, Detroit, VIII. 6 (Mar. 1927) 65-6, 1 text illus.

A description of a Gupta piece (Mathurā school), recently acquired by the Institute.

C502 A Pallava Relief: Durgā. *Bulletin of the Museum of Fine Arts*, Boston, XXV. 148 (Apr. 1927) 22-5, 3 text illus.

On the Museum's recent acquisition of an AD 7th century sculpture from South India representing the goddess Durgā (or Mahākālī): AKC describes her appearance, explains her role in the Hindu theological scheme, and adds some general comments on the art of the Pallava dynasty. This article was reprinted in *Modern Review*, Calcutta, XLII. 1 (July 1927) 62-4, 2 text illus.

C503 Sthānam. *Journal of the Royal Asiatic Society*, London (Apr. 1927) 323.

A seven-line note correcting a mistranslation of this Sanskrit term in "A Note on the Sanskrit Monologue-Play (Bhana), with Special Reference to the Caturbhani", by S.K. De, in the issue for January 1926.

C504 The Task Before Us. *Oriental Magazine*, New York, I. 2 (May/June 1927) 34.

A reprint of the concluding paragraphs from the essay "What Has India Contributed to Human Welfare?" in *The Dance of Śiva* (1918)—A38a.

C505 The Origin of the Buddha Image. *Art Bulletin*, New York, IX. 4 (June 1927) 287-328, 12 pls. (pl.[1] faces p. 287, pl. [12] faces p. 328) containing 73 illus.

AKC offers a refutation of the theory propounded by Alfred Foucher that the Indian Buddha type is of Hellenistic origin. Drawing upon verbal and plastic evidences AKC argues "that practically every element essential to the iconography of Buddha and Bodhisattva figures appears in early Indian art before the Buddha figure of Gandhāra or Mathurā is known" (p. 313). As AKC remarks elsewhere, "The Gandhāran sculptor . . . did not so much make an Apollo into a Buddha, as a Buddha into an Apollo" (*History of Indian and Indonesian Art* (1927)—A50—p. 52). The thesis is expounded under six headings: 1. What Is the Buddha Image?—2. The Early Representation of Deities by Means of

Symbols—3. The Necessity for a Buddha Image—4. Elements of the Later Anthropomorphic Iconography Already Present in Early Indian Art—5. Style and Content: Differentiation of Indian and Hellenistic Types—6. Dating of Gandhāra and Mathurā Buddhas. There is a descriptive list of the plates, and an "Appendix" which comprises quotations selected to illustrate "the psychology of those whose devotional feelings led to the use of Buddha images" (p. 327). Footnote 45, on p. 309, discusses the significance of the "lotus" in Indian art. AKC assumes that the reader of this article is familiar with his earlier "The Indian Origin of the Buddha Image" (1926)—C490. A separately paginated offprint, that has additionally a corrigenda slip containing eight items printed in fifteen lines, seen at the National Library of Australia, Canberra. This article was reprinted, in two parts, in *Journal of Ancient Indian History*, Calcutta, II. 1/2 (1968/69) [424]-433, and III. 1/2 (1969/70) 395-450, with annotations by D.C. Sircar printed as footnotes enclosed within square brackets and initialled: D.C.S. A separately paginated offprint from the *Journal of Ancient Indian History*, that has additionally an index, is in the compiler's possession. Also reprinted, in an abridged form and with the omission of the footnotes and plates, in six instalments, in *Ceylon Daily News*, Colombo, from 8 to 19 May 1971. This condensed version was reprinted in *Buddhist*, Colombo, XLII. 6/8 (Oct./Dec. 1972) 3-15. Reprinted separately by Munshiram Manoharlal, New Delhi ([1972])—A77.

C506 A Hamsa-Laksana Sari. *Bulletin of the Museum of Fine Arts*, Boston, XXV. 149 (June 1927) 36-7, 3 text illus.

On a 17th or 18th century Indian muslin brocade, in the Museum collections, patterned with rows of *haṁsas* (geese). AKC cites some other examples of this motif's occurrence in India.

C507 Relation of Moghul and Rajput Paintings. *Rupam*, Calcutta, 31 (July 1927) 88-91, 2 pls.

On evidence for the existence of a mixed Rājput-Mughal school, apropos of "Relation Between Rajput and Moghul Painting: A New Document", by Laurence Binyon, in the issue for January 1927.

C508 Sculptures from Mathurā. *Bulletin of the Museum of Fine Arts*, Boston, XXV. 150 (Aug. 1927) 50-4, 5 text illus.

Chiefly on the Museum's recent acquisition of an early Kuṣāna half-pediment slab from a temple doorway, containing reliefs that depict scenes from the life of the Buddha.

C509 [A review of] *Studies in Indian Painting*. By N.C. Mehta. *Journal of the American Oriental Society*, New Haven, XLVII. 3 (Sept. 1927) 275-8.

"This is a solid contribution to our knowledge" (p. 275).

C510 [A review of] *Ajanta. Les peintures de la première grotte.* Par V. Goloubew. *Journal of the American Oriental Society*, New Haven, XLVII. 3 (Sept. 1927) 278-9.

(In English.) "Too many volumes of *Ars Asiatica* [of which series this work by Victor Goloubew forms volume X] have hitherto been dedicated to desultory descriptions of selected examples of Asiatic art in scattered collections. The present work is a solid and permanent contribution to our knowledge of Indian archaeology and art" (p. 278). Also reviewed (differently) by AKC in *American Journal of Archaeology* for January/March 1929—C535.

C511 Sahaja—A Phase of Hindu Love. *Oriental Magazine*, New York, I. 3 (Sept./Oct. 1927) 89-90.

On the doctrine and practical discipline (or "rule") of the cult of Sahaja, in which "the adoration of young and beautiful girls was made the path of spiritual evolution and ultimate emancipation" (p. 90); incorporating a discussion of the work of the 14th century Bengali poet Caṇḍīdāsa. A reprint of the essay "Sahaja" from *The Dance of Śiva* (1918)—A38a—pp. [103]-111.

C512 Two Suṅga Railing Pillars. *Journal of the Royal Asiatic Society*, London (Oct. 1927) 847.

AKC rectifies a factual inaccuracy in *Ancient India*, by Kenneth de Burgh Codrington.

C513 Early Indian Terra Cottas. *Bulletin of the Museum of Fine Arts*, Boston, XXV. 152 (Dec. 1927) 90-6, 1 text illus., 3 pls. (containing 19 illus.).

A description of examples from the Museum collections, with notes on their stylistic evolution, and on the cult of the Mother Goddess. A considerably expanded version of this article is printed, with the title "Archaic Indian Terracottas", in *Ipek* for 1928—C514.

1928

C514 Archaic Indian Terracottas. *Ipek. Jahrbuch für prähistorische und ethnographische Kunst*, Leipzig, III. (1928) 64-76, 7 pls. (containing 51 illus.).

A detailed description of examples that comprise divine and human, or semi-human, images, assigned by AKC to dates before 100 BC, from the Indus Valley and from Mathurā, now in the Museum of Fine Arts, Boston. AKC suggests some identifications for these oldest known Indian sculptures, shows analogies with later types of Indian sacred art, and discusses the occurrence of the Mother, or Nude, Goddess as a popular deity in ancient India. This article is an expansion of a preliminary account of the Boston terracottas published as "Early Indian Terra Cottas" in *Bulletin of the Museum of Fine Arts*, Boston, for December 1927—C513. Reprinted in *Marg*, Bombay, VI. 2 (1953) 22-35, 50 text illus., and in *From River Banks and Sacred Places: Ancient Indian Terracottas* ([1977])—B95.

C515 Notes on Indian Coins and Symbols. *Ostasiatische Zeitschrift*, Berlin, N.S. IV. 4 (1927/28) [175]-188, 7 text illus., 3 pls. (numbered: 27-9).

The first of these notes concerns the motif of three or more superimposed arches that commonly appears on Indian coins and that is in AKC's view erroneously interpreted by the older numismatists as representing a *caitya* (i.e. a *stūpa*): AKC gathers examples of the motif's occurrence from world-wide sources in attempt to demonstrate by comparative study that the device always represents a mountain. The second note deals with a symbol "which may be described as a circle surmounted by a trident", occurring in Hindu, Buddhist, and Jain contexts. The third note discusses in detail the Sanskrit term *Vardhamāna(ka)*; for addendum and corrigendum to this see "*Vaḍḍhamāna*" in *Journal of the Royal Asiatic Society*, London, for October 1931—C616.

C516 Notes sur la sculpture bouddhique. *Revue des Arts Asiatiques*, Paris, V. 4 (1928) 244-52, 3 pls. (numbered: LVII-LIX) containing 8 illus.

A discussion arranged under three headings: I. Un fragment de la haute époque d'Amarāvatī—II. Autres sculptures d'Amarāvatī—III. Trois bas-reliefs du Gandhāra. A separately paginated offprint seen (April 1991) in the collection of Dr. Rama P. Coomaraswamy, Greenwich, Connecticut.

C517 An Early Khmer Head of Vishnu. *Bulletin of the Museum of Fine Arts*, Boston, XXVI. 153 (Feb. 1928) 16-17, 1 text illus.

A note on an example coifed with a "mitre" head-dress; a recent gift to the Museum by Denman W. Ross.

C518 An Elder Art. A Few Examples from One of the Finest Collections in the World. *Independent*, Boston, CXX. 4,054 (11 Feb. 1928) 131-4, 11 text illus.

Comments on reproductions of paintings and sculptures from the collections of Indian art at the Museum of Fine Arts, Boston. Unsigned, but the text and the captions to the illustrations are almost certainly written wholly, or at least in part, by AKC.

C519 Ganesha. *Bulletin of the Museum of Fine Arts*, Boston, XXVI. 154 (Apr. 1928) 30-1, 2 text illus.

(In English.) On this elephant-headed Indian deity's general character and iconographic evolution; with reference to his representation in a Rājput painting, and as a late Gupta sculpture. Both examples discussed are from the Museum collections.

C520 Some Early Buddhist Reliefs Identified. *Journal of the Royal Asiatic Society*, London (Apr. 1928) 390-8.

Dated Boston, 28 Oct. 1927. In the main, concerning sculptures at Bharhut, Mathurā, Pāṭaliputra, and Amarāvatī, that depict episodes from the *Jātakas*.

C521 Hindu Ideals of Marriage. *Oriental Magazine*, New York, II. 1 (June/July 1928) 19-24.

Reprinted from *The Dance of Śiva* (1918)—A38a—pp. 85-91, i.e. excerpts from the essay "Status of Indian Women".

C522 Early Indian Iconography I. Indra, with Special Reference to "Indra's Visit". *Eastern Art*, Philadelphia, I. 1 (July 1928) 32-41, 8 text illus., 3 pls. (numbered: XV-XVII).

An account of the principal, mainly pre-Gupta, representations on coins and early sculptures of this "Vedic and Hindu deity, who plays an important part also in Buddhist legends" (p. 33). (The text illustrations on p. 35 are printed upside-down.) The first of a proposed "series of articles . . . to study one by one the iconography of the Indian deities" (p. 33). Only two instalments of the series appeared: "Early Indian Iconography III. Śiva", announced by AKC as "in preparation" (see *Eastern Art*, II. (1930), p. 242), was never published. Corrigenda and addenda are printed in the issues for October 1928, p. 122; 1930, p. 240; and 1931, p. 217.

C523 Erakapatra Nāgarāja. *Journal of the Royal Asiatic Society*, London (July 1928) 629-30.

(In English.) The story of this Nāga king, with a detailed explanation of the relief at Bhārhut.

C524 Indian Architectural Terms. *Journal of the American Oriental Society*, New Haven, XLVIII. 3 (Sept. 1928) 250-75, 2 pls.

A review of *Indian Architecture According to the Mānasāra-śilpaśāstra* and *A Dictionary of Hindu Architecture*, by P.K. Acharya. AKC contributes a list of additional notes on 129 technical terms (of which sixteen are "not in the *Dictionary*"), as well as the names of fourteen historical architects, and one architectural treatise, not noticed by Acharya. This review was reprinted in *Essays in Early Indian Architecture*, edited by Michael W. Meister (1992)—A92.

C525 Mudrā, Muddā. *Journal of the American Oriental Society*, New Haven, XLVIII. 3 (Sept. 1928) 279-81.

(In English.) A critical note on Otto Francke's rendering of this Sanskrit word in his article "Mudrā=Schrift (oder Lesekunst)?" in *Zeitschrift der Deutschen Morgenländischen Gesellschaft*, Leipzig, XLVI. (1892). AKC appends a list of fourteen bibliographical references to the language of gesture.

C526 *Daṇḍarāsa*, *Vaṁśanartin*, and *Caturaśratva*. *Journal of the American Oriental Society*, New Haven, XLVIII. 3 (Sept. 1928) 281-3.

(In English.) A discussion of three terms associated with Indian dance, respectively "staff-dance", "pole-dancer", and "the position where the arms are at right angles to the body", with reference to the various translations of these terms by Sten Konow, Charles Rockwell Lanman, M. Monier-Williams, Franklin Edgerton, *et al.*

C527 Miniatures from Turkish and Persian Books of Fables. *Bulletin of the Museum of Fine Arts*, Boston, XXVI. 157 (Oct. 1928) 89-91, 5 text illus.

AKC attempts the identification of fables as represented in illuminations contained in two 16th century manuscripts from the Museum's Goloubew and Ross collections: 'Alī Celebī bin Sālih's *Humāyūn Nāma* and Sanāī's *Hadīqatu'l-Haqīqa*.

C528 The Buddha's *Cūḍā*, Hair, *Uṣṇīṣa*, and Crown. *Journal of the Royal Asiatic Society*, London (Oct. 1928) [815]-841, 1 text illus., 2 pls. (numbered: IV-V).

A detailed inquiry into some iconographic problems presented by these four characteristic *lakṣaṇas* (lineaments) associated with the Buddha image.

C529 Early Reference to Fly Fishing [I]. [Letter]. *Fishing Gazette*, London, XCVII. 2,688 (27 Oct. 1928) 427.

Dated Boston, 5 Oct. 1928. AKC cites two literary sources: Wolfram von Eschenbach's *Parzival* and the *Śatapatha Brāhmaṇa*. A reply from William Radcliffe, commenting on AKC's evidence, is printed on the same page.

C530 Early Reference to Fly Fishing [II]. [Letter]. *Fishing Gazette*, London, XCVII. 2,693 (1 Dec. 1928) 531.

AKC's rejoinder to the letter of William Radcliffe that was printed with C529.

C. CONTRIBUTIONS TO PERIODICALS

1929

C531 A Chinese Buddhist Water Vessel and Its Indian Prototype. *Artibus Asiae*, Ascona, III. 2/3 (1928/29) 122-41, 31 text illus.

Written with Francis Stewart Kershaw. AKC would appear to be wholly responsible for pp. 131-9. On a type of bottle-cum-drinking vessel with two openings (Chinese *p'ing* or *bin*, Indian *kuṇḍikā*): its actual use, before the end of the medieval period, and its representation iconographically, where it forms one of "the insignia of an ascetic vocation" (p.139). Concluding with an explanation of the *kuṇḍikā's* distinction from another Indian vessel, the *amṛta kalaśa* (with a note on the latter's employment as an architectural element). Kershaw (1869-1930) was a sometime Keeper of the Department of Chinese and Japanese Art at the Museum of Fine Arts, Boston.

C532 Early Indian Iconography II. Śrī-Lakṣmī. *Eastern Art*, Philadelphia, I. 3 (Jan. 1929) [174]-189, 8 text illus., 5 pls. (numbered: XXIV-XXVIII).

An inquiry into the early Hindu literary references to, and actual iconography of, this Indian goddess of abundance: the etymology of her name; her special associations with the Waters and the lotus; the meaning of the *abhiṣeka* (lustration) type; her relation to the Yakṣas; with reference to her representation at Bhārhut, Mathurā, and elsewhere. Corrigenda and addenda to this article are printed in the issue for 1930—C564.

C533 Nâgara Painting. *Rupam*, Calcutta, 37 (Jan. 1929) 24-9.

On the characteristics and special functions of an Indian genre where amateurs executed "urban" or "secular" portraits and erotic subjects on panels. AKC translates some relevant passages in the *Viṣṇudharmottara*, III. 41, and collects and comments upon other references to *nāgara* painting from various sources within the classical literature. Addendum to this article is printed in the issue for October 1929—C557.

C534 Sāhîb Rām, etc. [Letter]. *Rupam*, Calcutta, 37 (Jan. 1929) 61.

Dated Boston, 22 Nov. 1928. On this 18th century Jaipur painter; and incidentally providing addendum to *Indian Drawings: Second Series, Chiefly Rājput* ([1912])—A26.

C535 [A review of] *Ajanta. Les Peintures de la Première Grotte*, by V. Goloubew [and] *Les Collections archéologiques du Musée National de Bangkok*, by G. Coedès. *American Journal of Archaeology*, New York, Second Series, XXXIII. 1 (Jan./ Mar. 1929) 163-4.

Victor Goloubew's *Ajanta* was also reviewed (differently) by AKC in *Journal of the American Oriental Society*, New Haven, for September 1927—C510. AKC commends George Coedès' work: the first "clear and accurate summary of the history of Siamese art . . . modifications have to be made accordingly in . . . my *History of Indian and Indonesian Art*".

C536 A Passage in the *Uttara-Rāma-Carita* of Bhavabhūti. *Journal of the American Oriental Society*, New Haven, XLIX. 1 (Mar. 1929) 61.

On I. 15, 5 (Sītā describing Rāma's hair) as translated in the Harvard Oriental Series: suggesting a different reading.

C537 [A review of] *Samarāṅganasūtradhāra*. By King Bhojadeva. Edited by Mahāmahopādhyāya T. Gaṇapati Śāstrī. Volume II. *Journal of the American Oriental Society*, New Haven, XLIX. 1 (Mar. 1929) 69.

"It is high time that the numerous Śilpa-śāstras now available as edited texts should be translated and compared."

C538 [A review of] *Principles of Indian Śilpaśāstra; with the text of Mayaśāstra*. By P.N. Bose. *Journal of the American Oriental Society*, New Haven, XLIX. 1 (Mar. 1929) 69-70.

"Unfortunately this volume does not fulfil the functions suggested by the title"(p. 69).

C539 [A review of] *Pallava Architecture*. By A.H. Longhurst. Parts I and II [and] *Two Statues of Pallava Kings and Five Pallava Inscriptions in a Rock Temple at Mamallapuram*. By H.K. Sastri. *Journal of the American Oriental Society*, New Haven, XLIX. 1 (Mar. 1929) 70-1.

"These monographs are exceedingly welcome, and all scholars will look forward to Mr. Longhurst's subsequent volumes" (p. 70).

C540 [A review of] *Manimekhalai in its Historical Setting*. By S. Krishnaswami Aiyangar. *Journal of the American Oriental Society*, New Haven, XLIX. 1 (Mar. 1929) 71-2.

In the course of this review AKC discusses some parallels the Indian story presents to European forms of the Grail legend.

C541 [A review of] *Masterpieces of Rajput Painting*, by O.C. Gangoly. *Journal of the American Oriental Society*, New Haven, XLIX. 1 (Mar. 1929) 72-3.

"The author and publishers are to be congratulated on the production of a work which is at once scholarly and elegant. I acknowledge gratefully the dedication" (p. 73).

C542 [A review of] *Costumes et parures khmèrs d'après les Devatā d'Angkor Vat*. Par Sappho Marchal. *Journal of the American Oriental Society*, New Haven, XLIX. 1 (Mar. 1929) 73.

(In English.) "An admirable work". AKC approves of the designation "Devatā".

C543 [A review of] *Dances cambodgiennes*. [By] Sappho Marchal. *Journal of the American Oriental Society*, New Haven, XLIX. 1 (Mar. 1929) 73.

"An excellent account of the modern dramatic dances in traditional manner which may be seen at Angkor."

C544 Āndhra Sculptures. *Bulletin of the Museum of Fine Arts*, Boston, XXVII. 160 (Apr. 1929) 20-3, 4 text illus. (one is printed on the front cover of this issue, i.e. p. [19]).

On the iconography of five Buddhist reliefs (the largest bears a representation of a complete stūpa), that were recently acquired by the Museum from a stūpa located in the Godāvari-Kistna delta (Veṅgī).

C545 A Very Ancient Indian Seal. *Bulletin of the Museum of Fine Arts*, Boston, XXVII. 160 (Apr. 1929) 28-9, 2 text illus.

On an Indus Valley intaglio seal (*circa* 3000 BC), recently acquired by the Museum, that bears the device "of a bull and 'crib', accompanied by a pictographic script" (p. 28). An abstract of this article, with the title "The Pre-Aryan Culture of India", is printed in *Art and Archaeology*, Washington, D.C., XXIX. 5 (May 1930) 234.

C546 Indian Sculpture. *Art News*, New York, XXVII. 30 (27 Apr. 1929), Section One, pp. 35-45, 8 pls. (i.e. pp. 37-44) containing 22 illus.

A general introduction.

C547 Buddhist Reliefs from Nāgārjunikoṇḍa and Amarāvatī. *Rupam*, Calcutta, 38/39 (Apr./July 1929) 70-6, 4 pls.

Identification of sculpture from AD 2nd and 3rd centuries in the Musée Guimet, Paris; the Government Museum, Madras; the Metropolitan Museum of Art, New York; and the British Museum, London; with a detailed discussion of the iconography. AKC weighs accounts by James Burgess and Alfred Foucher, and concludes with comments, in agreement with O.C. Gangoly, on the significance of certain resemblances between Āndhra art and that of Cambodia and Indonesia. Corrigenda is incorporated with "Indian Sculpture: A Review", in the issue for Apr./July/Oct. 1930—C574.

C548 The Origin and Use of Images in India. *International Studio*, New York, XCIII. 384 (May 1929) 21-6, 94, 8 text illus.

An exposition of the traditional concept and practice of iconolatry. This article was reprinted, in a revised and expanded form, but with the omission of the illustrations, as Chapter VII of *The Transformation of Nature in Art* (1934)—A56a, in *The Spirit of Modern India: Writings in Philosophy, Religion & Culture*, edited by V.S. Naravane and Robert Allen McDermott (New York: Thomas Y. Crowell Co., 1974), pp. 136-49, and in *Art, Creativity and the Sacred: An Anthology in Religion and Art*, edited by Diane Apostolos-Cappadona (New York: Crossroad/Continuum, 1984), pp. [127]-137.

C549 The Tree of Jesse and Indian Parallels or Sources. *Art Bulletin*, New York, XI. 2 (June 1929) [216]-220, 4 text illus., 1 pl.

Pointing out that "the whole group of ideas involved [in the Jesse motif] appears much earlier in India than anywhere else" (p. 217), and that "for students of Christian mediaeval art the Indian forms provide analogies and parallels which cannot be neglected if all the problems are to be seen in proper perspective" (p. 220). This article is based on a paper read by AKC, on 29 December 1928, at the 18th Annual Joint Meeting of the Archaeological Institute and the College Art Association held at the Metropolitan Museum of Art, New York. Summaries were printed, as "The Tree of Jesse and Indian Parallels or Origins", in *Parnassus*, New York, I. 3 (15 Mar. 1929) 23, and as "Tree of Jesse and Indian Parallels Have Influenced Christian Era", in *Art and Archaeology*, Washington, D.C., XXVII. 2 (Feb. 1929) 91. Addenda to this article is incorporated with "The Tree of Jesse and Oriental Parallels" (1935)—C667.

C550 An Early Cambodian Statue of Harihara. *Bulletin of the Museum of Fine Arts*, Boston, XXVII. 161 (June 1929) 40-1, 3 text illus.

On an AD 6th or 7th century stone figure, acquired by the Museum, representing a deity "who combines in one the persons of Viṣṇu (Hari) and Śiva (Hara)" (p. 40); including brief notes on the chronology and stylistic sequence of Cambodian art.

C551 Picture Showmen. *Indian Historical Quarterly*, Calcutta, V. 2 (June 1929) [182]-187.

On the practice in India of picture showmen who publicly exhibit and explain their own pictures of deities, legends, etc., citing as earliest extant evidence the *Mahābhāṣya* of Patañjali (*circa* 140 BC). Other references in Indian literature are discussed, as well as evidence for this custom in Indonesia and Persia.

C552 [A review of] *Indian Serpent Lore, or the Nāgas in Hindu Legend and Art.* By J.Ph. Vogel. *Journal of the American Oriental Society*, New Haven, XLIX. 2 (June 1929) 186-90, 1 pl.

AKC gives additional literary references for Nāgas, and notes other Indian (and Sinhalese) sculptures and paintings of serpents and snakes either not mentioned or not illustrated by Vogel.

C553 [A review of] *India: the Landscape, the Monuments, and the People.* By Martin Hürliman [*sic*]. *Journal of the American Oriental Society*, New Haven, XLIX. 2 (June 1929) 190-1.

"The author's admirable and well-chosen photographs present an adequate picture of a living culture in vital relation to its actual environment" (p. 190).

C554 [A review of] *Basreliefs of Bādāmī.* By R.D. Banerji. *Journal of the American Oriental Society*, New Haven, XLIX. 2 (June 1929) 191-3, 4 text illus.

In the course of this review AKC contributes some illustrated notes on the motif of two animals sharing a common head.

C555 The Javanese Theater. *Asia*, New York, XXIX. 7 (July 1929) 536-9, 8 text illus.

A general account written in collaboration with Stella Bloch (i.e. Mrs AKC), who "has provided drawings of characters in the gala theatrical performances at Surakarta, in 1921, as two of the illustrations" (editorial note in this issue, p. [521]); the other illustrations are reproductions from photographs taken in Indonesia by AKC. This article was reprinted, reduced and with the omission of the illustrations, in *Baker's Drama-Gram*, Boston, VII. 1 ([Fall] 1929) 15-17.

C556 Arabic and Turkish Calligraphy. *Bulletin of the Museum of Fine Arts*, Boston, XXVII. 162 (Aug. 1929) 50-7, 13 text illus.

A general survey of its development based on examples from AD 800 to 1927 as represented in the Museum collections. On p. 50 AKC announces: "Later Persian and Indian Mughal calligraphy will be dealt with in another article"; but this intention was not fulfilled.

C557 Nāgara Painting: Addendum. *Rupam*, Calcutta, 40 (Oct. 1929) 127-9.

Some references to this genre, excerpted from the Indian classical literature, additional to those given in "Nâgara Painting" in the issue for January 1929—C533.

C558 A Yaksi Torso from Sanchi. *Bulletin of the Museum of Fine Arts*, Boston, XXVII. 164 (Dec. 1929) 90-4, 5 text illus.

On a female figure, tentatively dated by AKC to about 100-75 BC, recently acquired by the Museum, that once served as a bracket to the lower architrave of one of the gateways of the Great Stūpa; including brief notes on the Yakṣīs as tree spirits, and the application to Buddhist purposes of this older indigenous cult. Addendum to this article is printed in the issue for February 1930, p. 18.

C559 [A review of] *The Poems of Nizami*, by Laurence Binyon. *Journal of the American Oriental Society*, New Haven, XLIX. 4 (Dec. 1929) 329.

"This is a book that all students of Persian painting will want to possess."

C560 [A review of] *Le Bayon d'Angkor et l'evolution de l'art khmer*, by Philippe Stern. *Journal of the American Oriental Society*, New Haven, XLIX. 4 (Dec. 1929) 330-1.

"This very careful and valuable study revolutionises the accepted chronology of Cambodian monuments" (p. 330). AKC gives an epitome of the new dating.

C561 [A review of] *Chalukyan Architecture*. By H. Cousens. *Journal of the American Oriental Society*, New Haven, XLIX. 4 (Dec. 1929) 331.

Cousens' work is "little more than a convenient compilation of matter already published in the Annual Reports and other volumes of the [Archaeological] Survey [of India]".

1930

C562 Early Indian Architecture [I. Cities and City-gates, Etc.; II. Bodhi-gharas]. *Eastern Art*, Philadelphia, II. (1930) [208]-

235, 3 text illus., 12 pls. (numbered: CXXII-CXXXIII; also counted as pages) containing 42 illus.

The first of two parts of a projected series of articles on Indian architecture "mainly as referred to in the Pali literature and as represented in the reliefs of Bharhut, Sāñcī, and Amarāvatī" (p. 209); only three parts were published, as *Eastern Art* succumbed during the Depression. A fourth part, "Early Indian Architecture: IV. Huts and Related Temple Types", is printed in *Res*, Cambridge, Mass., for Spring 1988—C909. Also intended for inclusion in the series were articles on "towers . . . arches, and doorways; and pillars" (p. 222). Incorporates *passim* addenda and corrigenda to "Indian Architectural Terms" (1928)—C524. Addenda and corrigenda to both parts of this article are printed in the issue for 1931, p. 217. This article was reprinted separately, but omitting the list of addenda and corrigenda, in 1991 by Munshiram Manoharlal Pvt., Ltd., New Delhi—A91, and, including the addenda and corrigenda, in *Essays in Early Indian Architecture*, edited by Michael W. Meister (1992)—A92.

C563 An Illustrated Śvetambāra Jāina Manuscript of A.D. 1260. *Eastern Art*, Philadelphia, II. (1930) [236]-240, 2 pls.

Also discussed in "An Early Illustrated Jaina Manuscript" (1930)—C568. The present article is a fuller account, with additional illustrations and a transcription and translation into English (by L.D. Barnett) of the manuscript's colophon. Corrigenda to this article is printed in the issue for 1931, p. 217.

C564 Early Indian Iconography . . . Corrigenda and Addenda. *Eastern Art*, Philadelphia, II. (1930) 240-2.

To "Early Indian Iconography I. Indra, with Special Reference to 'Indra's Visit'" in the issue for July 1928—C522, and "Early Indian Iconography II. Śrī-Lakṣmī" in the issue for January 1929—C532.

C565 The Art of Bookmaking in Islam. *International Studio*, New York, XCV. 392 (Jan. 1930) 71-2, 1 text illus.

A review of *The Islamic Book. A Contribution to Its Art and History from the VII-XVIII Century*, by Thomas W. Arnold and Adolf Grohmann. ". . . as a whole it belies its title . . . there is still room and need for a systematic work on the art of bookmaking" (p. 71).

C566 A New South Indian Bronze. *Rupam*, Calcutta, 41 (Jan. 1930) [1]-2, 1 pl. (facing p. [1]).

On some iconographic problems presented by a female figure of *circa* AD 1100, tentatively identified here as a "deified queen", recently acquired by the Freer Gallery of Art, Washington, D.C. This article was reprinted, in a German translation, as "Eine neue südindische Bronze", in *Pantheon*, Munich, VI. 7 (July 1930) 338-40, 1 pl.; excerpts from this translation, are printed under the heading "Eine südindische Bronze", in *Atlantis*, Berlin, V. 5 (May 1933) 316-17, 3 text illus.

C567 [A review of] *Mussulman Painting*. By E. Blochet. *Rupam*, Calcutta, 41 (Jan. 1930) 21.

A brief notice, printed in 17 lines; "of value for the numerous reproductions of Persian paintings in the Bibliothèque Nationale ... The very discursive text is mainly devoted to the thesis 'Only one art has ever existed, and that is Classic Art' ... Comment is needless". This review was reprinted in *International Studio*, New York, XCVI. 397 (June 1930) 68.

C568 An Early Illustrated Jaina Manuscript. *Bulletin of the Museum of Fine Arts*, Boston, XXVIII. 165 (Feb. 1930) 7-8, 2 text illus.

A note on the Museum's recent acquisition of an AD 1260 manuscript of the *Sāvaga-paḍikkamaṇa-sutta-cunnī*. AKC continues this discussion in *Eastern Art*, Philadelphia, for 1930—C563.

C569 The Sanchi Yaksi Torso. *Bulletin of the Museum of Fine Arts*, Boston, XXVIII. 165 (Feb. 1930) 18, 1 text illus.

Addendum to "A Yaksi Torso from Sanchi" in the issue for December 1929—C558. AKC points out that the torso was first published in 1854 in *The Bhilsa Topes*, by Alexander Cunningham.

C570 Early Indian Art Traced Through Six Centuries of Stylistic Change. *International Studio*, New York, XCV. 393 (Feb. 1930) 68-9, 1 text illus.

A review of *Early Indian Sculpture*, by Ludwig Bachhofer. Also reviewed by AKC (at greater length) in *Rupam*, Calcutta, for April/July/October 1930—C574.

C571 [A review of] *La miniature persane*. By Armenag Bey Sakisian. *Journal of the American Oriental Society*, New Haven, L. 1 (Mar. 1930) 81.

"Probably the best, most sober, best documented, and altogether most reliable of all the books on Persian painting that have appeared in recent years". Also reviewed by AKC (at greater length) in *American Journal of Archaeology*, New York, for October/December 1930—C592.

C572 [A review of] *Iconography of Buddhist and Brahmanical Sculptures in the Dacca Museum*. By N.K. Bhaṭṭaśāli. *Journal of the American Oriental Society*, New Haven, L. 1 (Mar. 1930) 82.

"The Dacca Museum, and its learned curator, Mr. Bhaṭṭaśāli, are to be heartily congratulated on the production of this richly documented volume, which will be indispensable to the student of mediaeval Indian art and iconography". AKC highlights the "valuable features" of this work.

C573 Miniatures from an Early Persian Shāh Nāmah. *Bulletin of the Museum of Fine Arts*, Boston, XXVIII. 166 (Apr. 1930) 27-9, 2 text illus.

AKC contributes notes on three leaves from a 14th century *Shāh Nāmah* in the Museum collections.

C574 Indian Sculpture: A Review. *Rupam*, Calcutta, 42/43/44 (Apr./July/Oct. 1930) 2-11.

A review of *Early Indian Sculpture*, by Ludwig Bachhofer. AKC questions Bachhofer's dating, and the conclusions reached, concerning the origin of the Buddha image, and contributes corrections and supplementary notes to the iconographical descriptions of the plates. Shorter reviews by AKC of this book are printed in *International Studio*, New York, for February 1930—C570, and in *Journal of the American Oriental Society*, New Haven, for March 1931—C604.

C575 Drawings by Rabindranath Tagore. *Rupam*, Calcutta, 42/43/44 (Apr./July/Oct. 1930) 31-2.

An advance printing of the "Foreword" written by AKC for the catalogue of the exhibition of Tagore's work at the Fifty-Sixth Street Galleries, New York, in November 1930—B33. "This . . . is not 'Art' with a capital A, on the one hand—nor, on the other, a merely pathological self-expression; nor art intended to improve our minds, nor to provide for the artist himself an 'escape'; but without ulterior motives, truly innocent, like the creation of a universe" (p. 32). This article was reprinted, as "Exhibition of Paintings by Rabindra Nath Tagore Introduction", in *Roopa-lekhā*, Delhi, II. 7/8 (Autumn/Winter 1930) 22-5, and, as "Paintings by Rabindranath Tagore", in *Indian Review*, Madras, LXXI. 12 (Mar. 1976) 28-9, and again, as "Paintings of Tagore", in *Bhavan's Journal*, Bombay, XXIV. 1 (14 Aug. 1977) [161]-169, 4 text illus.

C576 Sense About Art. *International Studio*, New York, XCVI. 396 (May 1930) 76, 1 text illus.

A review of *Art-Nonsense and Other Essays*, by Eric Gill.

C577 Two Pallava Marble Pillars. *Bulletin of the Museum of Fine*

Arts, Boston, XXVIII. 167 (June 1930) 55-8, 5 text illus.

Identification, dating, and description of an AD 7th century pair probably from the Guṇṭūr District (India) and now in the Museum collections.

C578 Origin of the Lotus- (So-Called Bell-) Capital. *Indian Historical Quarterly*, Calcutta, VI. 2 (June 1930) [373]-375, 1 pl. (facing p. [373]).

Printed under the general heading: Miscellany. A reply to "A Bell-Capital from Bhuvaneśvara", by Achyuta Kumar Mitra, in the issue for September 1929. AKC discusses (1) the capital's morphology: "the bell, torus and abacus are respectively the [lotus] petals, stamens, and pericarp" (p. [373]), and (2) provides an explanation of the significance of the lotus motif with reference to the Vedic sources.

C579 [A review of] *The Lights of Canopus: Anvār i Suhailī.* Described by J.V.S. Wilkinson, with a preface by Laurence Binyon. *Journal of the American Oriental Society*, New Haven, L. 2 (June 1930) 170-1.

"A description, at once scholarly and readable, of . . . one of the finest examples of Mughal bookmaking known" (p. 170).

C580 [A review of] *A Javanese Period in Sumatran History.* By W.P. Stutterheim. *Journal of the American Oriental Society*, New Haven, L. 2 (June 1930) 171.

AKC thinks Stutterheim's argument "accounts better than the older view for the magnificence of the Central Javanese monuments (Borobudur, etc.) at this time".

C581 The Shadow-Play in Ceylon. *Journal of the Royal Asiatic Society*, London (July 1930) 627.

A note, printed in 12 lines, calling attention to a reference in the *Mahāvaṁsa* to "leather puppets".

C582 A Pastoral Paradise. *Bulletin of the Museum of Fine Arts*, Boston, XXVIII. 168 (Aug. 1930) 64-5, 1 text illus. (printed on the front cover of this issue, i.e. p. [63]).

On a 17th century Rājasthānī painting on cloth, recently acquired by the Museum, depicting a herd of cows in connection with the Divine Cowherd (Kṛṣṇa); including notes on the idea of paradise in Vaiṣṇava theology. This article is also printed in *Rupam*, Calcutta, 42/43/44 (Apr./July/Oct. 1930) 14-16, 2 pls. (one is coloured).

C583 New Data on Indian Painting. *International Studio*, New York, XCVII. 400 (Sept. 1930) 72, 74.

A review of *La Peinture Indienne à l'Époque des Grands Moghols* and *Les Miniatures Indiennes de l'Époque des Grands Moghols au Musée du Louvre*, by Ivan Stchoukine. "One of the most original and valuable features of [*La Peinture Indienne*] is the recognition of the fact that the style and formulae of Jaina . . . painting . . . underlie and survive in Rajput and Mughal painting" (p. 72). But AKC expresses disagreement over other aspects of Stchoukine's estimate of the Rājput schools.

C584 Pali *Kaṇṇikā* = Circular Roof-Plate. *Journal of the American Oriental Society*, New Haven, L. 3 (Sept. 1930) 238-43.

AKC conducts a fresh examination of nearly all the original texts in which this word can be found, in an attempt to demonstrate its use as an architectural term. This article was reprinted, as an appendix to "The Symbolism of the Dome", in *Coomaraswamy 1: Selected Papers, Traditional Art and Symbolism* ([1977])—A82—pp. 459-64, and in *Fundamentals of Indian Art* ([1985])—A88—pp. [25]-30.

C585 The Parts of a Vīnā. *Journal of the American Oriental Society*, New Haven, L. 3 (Sept. 1930) 244-53, 2 text illus., 1 pl.

Citing and illustrating sculptured and painted representations of the old Indian harp-vīṇā, to show how it differed from the modern vīṇā; and noting another Indian stringed instrument, "a kind mandolin". AKC provides a restored sketch, and an explanatory list in alphabetical order of the terms (24) in the Sanskrit, Pāli, and Prakrit literature used to designate the harp-vīṇā's various components. Addenda to this article is printed as "The Old Indian *Vīṇā*" in the issue for March 1931—C602; and corrigendum and further addenda, with the title "Upavīṇā', are printed in the issue for September 1931—C614.

C586 [A review of] *Le Buddha paré: son origine indienne. Çakyamuni dans le Mahāyānisme moyen.* Par Paul Mus. *Journal of the American Oriental Society*, New Haven, L. 3 (Sept. 1930) 263-4.

(In English.) AKC praises "this very detailed and learned discussion" of the crowned Buddha type, and gives a summary of Mus' thesis.

C587 [A review of] *Études cambodgiennes, XIX. La date du Bàyon.* Par G. Coedès. *Journal of the American Oriental Society*, New Haven, L. 3 (Sept. 1930) 264-5.

(In English.) AKC discusses George Coedès' attribution of monuments to Jayavarman VII.

C588 [A review of] *Pallava Architecture, Part III*. By A.H. Longhurst. *Journal of the American Oriental Society*, New Haven, L. 3 (Sept. 1930) 266.

AKC offers some minor criticisms of this, the concluding volume of Longhurst's "excellent monograph".

C589 [A review of] *Pratimā-Māna-Lakṣaṇam*. Edited by Phanindra Nath Bose. *Journal of the American Oriental Society*, New Haven, L. 3 (Sept. 1930) 266-7.

AKC lists other *Śilpa-śāstras* dealing with canonical proportions for images, because "the author is somewhat mistaken in his view of the unique character of the text" (p. 267).

C590 An Indian Bronze Bowl. *Ostasiatische Zeitschrift*, Berlin, N.S. VI. 5 (Sept./Oct. 1930) 247-9, 3 text illus., 1 pl. (numbered: 33).

On a rare, chased vessel belonging to Nasli M. Heeramaneck (New York), tentatively assigned here by AKC to the late Gupta period, with a suggested provenance of western India. (See also "A Bronze Vessel from Central Asia", by W. Norman Brown, in *Journal of the Indian Society of Oriental Art*, Calcutta, II. 1 (June 1934) 83-6, reprinted in *India and Indology: Selected Articles*, by W. Norman Brown, edited by Rosane Rocher (Delhi: Motilal Banarsidass [1978]), pp. [268]-269.)

C591 [A review of] *Bihzād and His Painting in the Zafar-Nāmah, MS*. By Thomas W. Arnold. *International Studio*, New York, XCVII. 401 (Oct. 1930) 98.

AKC points out, *inter alia*, that Arnold has overlooked a work by this 16th century Persian painter in the collections of the Museum of Fine Arts, Boston.

C592 [A review of] *La Miniature persane du XIIe au XVIIe siecle*, par Armenag Bey Sakisian. *American Journal of Archaeology*, New York, Second Series, XXXIV. 4 (Oct./ Dec. 1930) 516-18.

(In English.) Also reviewed by AKC (briefly) in *Journal of the American Oriental Society*, New Haven, for March 1930—C571.

C593 A Trinity of Fortune. *Pennsylvania University Museum Bulletin*, Philadelphia, II. 1 (Nov. 1930) 15-18, 2 pls. (numbered: VI-VII).

On a sculptured relief of *circa* AD 8th century, in the Museum collections, that depicts three Indian deities: Gaṇeśa, Śrī-Lakṣmī, and Kubera—respectively patrons of Success, Fortune, and Wealth—compared with an almost identical example owned by Nasli M. Heeramaneck of New York.

C594 A Persian Stucco Frieze, and Other Fragments. *Bulletin of the Museum of Fine Arts*, Boston, XXVIII. 170 (Dec. 1930) 104-7, 4 text illus.

On the recent acquisition by the Museum of a 13th-14th century example from Sāwa in central Persia; three other stucco pieces of about the same date are also discussed.

C595 Two Leaves from a Seventeenth-Century Manuscript of the Rasikapriyā. *Metropolitan Museum Studies*, New York, III. 1 (Dec. 1930) 14-21, 4 text illus.

Four pages from this illustrated Hindī treatise in verse on rhetoric and literary analysis by Keśava Dās are reproduced together with a translation and commentary.

1931

C596 Identification of "Eine Götterstatue aus der Spätzeit". *Acta Orientalia*, Lund, IX. 2 (1931) [374].

AKC identifies a late Javanese relief figure as representing the deified Hindu sage Agastya, with reference to an article by H.P. Blok in an earlier issue.

C597 Early Indian Architecture: III. Palaces. *Eastern Art*, Philadelphia, III. (1931) [180]-[216], 20 pls. (numbered: XCII-CXI, also counted as pages) containing 84 illus.

A paper read by AKC at the Twentieth Annual Meeting of the College Art Association at the Metropolitan Museum of Art, New York, on 1 April 1931. Chiefly on the structural elements of the *prāsāda*, considered here "primarily as a king's palace or the mansion of a wealthy merchant" (p. 181). "The foregoing account of palaces and windows does not pretend to be exhaustive; more material could and should be accumulated from the Epics, from the *kāvya* literature, and from archaeological sources. The palace architecture represented in the paintings of Ajaṇṭā requires a special study, for which the present discussion will provide introductory material. I have not discussed the subject of paintings on palace walls, and the use of statuary in palaces" (p. 205). The captions under illustrations 3 and 6 of Plate XCII are transposed. This article was reprinted, as a separate, in 1975 by Munshiram Manoharlal Pvt., Ltd., New Delhi—A81, and in *Essays in Early Indian Architecture*, edited by Michael W. Meister (1992)—A92. These reprints do not correct the transposed captions on Plate XCII.

C598 An Early Passage on Indian Painting. *Eastern Art*, Philadelphia, III. (1931) 218-19.

A translation by AKC of a passage, illustrating the functioning of aesthetic intuition, in the *Atthasālinī* of Buddhaghoṣa; together with an introduction and notes. Corrigenda and addendum are printed with "Further References to Painting in India" (1930/32)—C622—p. 126. This article was reprinted, incorporating the addendum (but not the corrigenda), as Chapter XIII of *Figures of Speech or Figures of Thought* (1946)—A71.

C599 Two Western Indian Manuscripts. *Bulletin of the Museum of Fine Arts*, Boston, XXIX, 171 (Feb. 1931) 4, 6-11, 8 text illus.

On illustrations contained in some recent acquisitions by gift from Denman W. Ross. The first manuscript, in order of discussion here, is of the 15th century and "consists of devotional Vaishnava poetry . . . the *Bāla-gopāla stuti* ('Praise of the youthful Krishna') of Bilvamaṅgala, a distinguished South Indian poet who flourished about A.D. 1300" (p. 4). The second, of *circa* 1600, is "an incomplete text of the *Kumārasambhava* of Kālidāsa . . . unique as containing almost the only known and in any case the earliest examples of the illustration of any work by Kālidāsa" (p. 10).

C600 Islamic Art in Brief. *International Studio*, New York, XCVIII. 405 (Feb. 1931) 64-5.

A review of *A Handbook of Mohammedan Art*, by M.S. Dimand. AKC comments, "this is the first general history of Mohammedan art to appear in English . . . the careful definition of 'arabesque' is welcome. . . . Calligraphy is too briefly dealt with . . . Perhaps the best and most useful section of the book is that on ceramics".

C601 [A review of] *Histoire de l'Extrême-Orient*, by R. Grousset. *American Journal of Archaeology*, New York, Second Series, XXXV. 1 (Jan./Mar. 1931) 114-15.

"Although naturally in the main a compilation, by selection and synthesis these volumes make a genuinely original contribution to the literature of the history of the world" (p. 115).

C602 The Old Indian *Vīṇā*. *Journal of the American Oriental Society*, New Haven, LI. 1 (Mar. 1931) 47-50, 1 pl. (facing p. 50).

Addenda to "The Parts of a Vīnā" (1930)—C585, with reference to "The Sumerian Harp of Ur", by Francis W. Galpin, in *Music & Letters*, London, for April 1929, and quoting a letter from Jakob Kunst to AKC on the Javanese bow-harp.

C603 [A review of] *La sculpture de Mathurā*. By J. Ph. Vogel. *Journal of the American Oriental Society*, New Haven, LI. 1 (Mar. 1931) 54-8.

AKC commends this "highly meritorious and very welcome volume" (p. 55). In the course of this review AKC briefly considers the propriety of making aesthetic judgements. This review was reprinted, slightly expanded and revised, as "An Introduction to the School of Mathura", in *International Studio*, New York, XCIX. 411 (Aug. 1931) 68-9.

C604 [A review of] *Early Indian Sculpture*. By Ludwig Bachhofer. *Journal of the American Oriental Society*, New Haven, LI. 1 (Mar. 1931) 58-9.

Bachhofer's work represents "a very real advance in method . . . stylistic problems are now discussed seriously . . . and not, as for example in the late Vincent Smith's *History of Fine Art in India and Ceylon*, merely naively" (p. 59). A more detailed discussion by AKC of Bachhofer's book was printed in *Rupam*, Calcutta, for April/July/October 1930—C574.

C605 A Relief and Inscription from Kashmir. *Pennsylvania University Museum Bulletin*, Philadelphia, II. 6 (Apr. 1931) 202-6, 1 pl. (numbered: XII).

On a 16th century equestrian portrait of an armed warrior, "of high interest as a rare and almost uniquely complete representation of contemporary military equipment" (p. 206).

C606 A Stucco Head from Central Asia. *Bulletin of the Museum of Fine Arts*, Boston, XXIX. 173 (June 1931) 39-43, 4 text illus.

On an AD 4th or 5th century sculptured female head, presented to the Museum by Denman W. Ross; incorporating a review of *The Afghan Stuccos of the N.R. F. Collection*, by Josef Strzygowski.

C607 The "Webbed Finger" of Buddha. *Indian Historical Quarterly*, Calcutta, VII. 2 (June 1931) [365]-366.

On the problem of the *jālalakkhaṇa*: its mistaken interpretation as a technical device of sculptors, and on the original meaning of the word *jāla* (as employed by Kālidāsa and Buddhaghoṣa), with reference to an article of this title, by J.N. Banerjea, in the issue for December 1930, and to the views of Alfred Foucher and W. Stutterheim. Addenda to this article is printed on a slip inserted in the issue for September 1931, at page 681.

C608 [A review of] *Die Kultur um den Persischen Golf und ihre Ausbreitung*. Von Amelia Hertz. *Indian Historical Quarterly*, Calcutta, VII. 2 (June 1931) 421-2.

(In English.) AKC discusses Hertz's argument "that the Mesopotamian and the Indus Valley cultures were both of Elamite origin", and remarks on the connection Indian mathematics and geometry have with developments in ancient Mesopotamia and Susa I.

C609 *Ratha-Chidra. Journal of the American Oriental Society*, New Haven, LI. 2 (June 1931) 172.

(In English.) But see *Elements of Buddhist Iconography* (1935)—A60—p. 75, note 65, where AKC advises that the present explanation of this Sanskrit term should be discarded.

C610 [A review of] *Kathakali* . . ., and *Diagrams of Hand Poses in Kathakali* . . . By Vasudava Poduval. *Journal of the American Oriental Society*, New Haven, LI. 2 (June 1931) 180.

Printed in ten lines; "a useful supplement to . . . [A.] Meerwarth's 'Les Kathakalis du Malabar'".

C611 [A review of] *The Commerce Between the Roman Empire and India*. By E.H. Warmington. *Journal of the American Oriental Society*, New Haven, LI. 2 (June 1931) 180-2.

"Cultural influences (religion, art, literature) are dealt with, but very much less than is trade (in the narrower sense of the word)" (p. 181). In this connection AKC cites a number of reference sources not noticed by Warmington.

C612 Two Examples of Muḥammadan Metal Work. *Bulletin of the Museum of Fine Arts*, Boston, XXIX. 174 (Aug. 1931) 70-2, 5 text illus.

Notes on an AD 14th century Egyptian brass bowl with gold, silver, and copper overlay, and an iron tomb key of AD 1386 from Persia, both in the Museum collections.

C613 The Persian Wheel. *Journal of the American Oriental Society*, New Haven, LI. 3 (Sept. 1931) 283-4.

On the water-wheel used for irrigation and citing some early references to this device in the Indian literature.

C614 Upavīṇā. *Journal of the American Oriental Society*, New Haven, LI. 3 (Sept. 1931) 284-5.

(In English.) Mainly on this Sanskrit term, which AKC renders as "plectrum", being corrigendum and addenda to "The Parts of a Vīnā" in the issue for September 1930—C585.

C615 A Yakshi Bust from Bharhut. *Bulletin of the Museum of Fine Arts*, Boston, XXIX. 175 (Oct. 1931) 81-3, 3 text illus.

A detailed description of part of a *circa* 150 BC sculpture of the *śālabhañjikā* (or "woman and tree") type, in the Museum collections. This article is summarized in *Art News*, New York, XXX. 3 (24 Oct. 1931) 19.

C616 Vaḍḍhamāna. *Journal of the Royal Asiatic Society*, London (Oct. 1931) 865.

(In English.) A note printed in twelve lines suggesting "the proper rendering as 'powder-box'", An earlier discussion of this term occurs in "Notes on Indian Coins and Symbols" (1927/28)—C515; a later discussion is included with "Some Pāli Words" (1939)—C760—s.v.

C617 A Rajput Painting. *Bulletin of the Fogg Art Museum*, Cambridge, Mass., I. 1 (Nov. 1931) 14-16, 1 text illus.

On an example of *circa* 1600, representing the musical mode Rāginī Bibhasa (or, Vibhāsa), presented to the Museum by Denman W. Ross.

C618 Origin of the Lotus-Capital. *Indian Historical Quarterly*, Calcutta, VII. 4 (Dec. 1931) 747-50.

With reference to "Origin of the Bell-Capital", by Achyuta Kumar Mitra, in the issue for June. "Mr. Mitra's theory requires . . . that Aśoka should have sent his architects to the ruins of Persepolis, burnt down more than sixty years earlier, there to obtain material for the construction of 'period architecture' in India" (p. 750).

C619 The Guḍimallam Liṅgam. *Indian Historical Quarterly*, Calcutta, VII. 4 (Dec. 1931) 750.

A note on the evidence for assigning this Śiva-liṅgam to the early date of 1st or 2nd century BC, with reference to dates proposed by T.A. Gopinatha Rao and A.H. Longhurst: ". . . in any case, its Śuṅga style is unmistakable".

1932

C620 One Hundred References to Indian Painting. *Artibus Asiae*, Ascona, IV. 1 (1930/32) 41-57.

A collection of citations (consecutively numbered and arranged in approximate chronological order) from the *Upaniṣads*, Pāli and Sanskrit Buddhist literature, Jaina *sūtras*, the *Mahābhārata*, the *Jātakas*, Hindī and Sinhalese vernacular, Chinese (one reference), and other sources, mainly not noticed before, that "not only add to the already collected evidences of the prevalence of painting in India during the historical period . . . but in several instances throw light on the technique, terminology, and special applications" (pp. 41-2).

C621 [A review of] H[einrich]. Zimmer: *Kunstform und Yoga im indischen Kultbild. Artibus Asiae*, Ascona, IV. 1 (1930/32) 78-9.

(In English.) "No more valuable book for the understanding of Indian art, the answering of the fundamental problem 'Why is it what is?' has yet been published" (p. 78). An excerpt from AKC's review is printed as part of the preface to this work's first appearance in English, *Artistic Form and Yoga in the Sacred Images of India*, translated and edited by Gerald Chapple and James B. Lawson (Princeton: Princeton University Press [1984]), pp. xviii-xix.

C622 Further References to Painting in India. *Artibus Asiae*, Ascona, IV. 2/3 (1930/32) 126-9.

Twenty-two supplementary citations to "One Hundred References to Indian Painting" (1930/32)—C620. These references are also to be regarded as additional to those collected in "Ābhāsa" (1932)—C634, "Reactions to Art in India" (1932)—C635, and "Aesthetic of the Śukranītisāra" (1932)—B36. AKC incorporates, on page 126, three corrections to his translation of the *Atthasālinī* text that was published as "An Early Passage on Indian Painting" (1931)—C598.

C623 The "Mystery" of Mahādeva. *Indian Art and Letters*, London, N.S. VI. 1 (1932) 10-13.

AKC introduces, and translates, some songs treating of an episode of Kṛṣṇa's childhood, by the 16th century Hindī poet Sūr Dās. A separately paginated offprint seen (April 1991) among The Coomaraswamy Papers in the Firestone Library, Princeton University.

C624 War—in India and Outside. [Letter]. *Nation*, New York, CXXXIV. 3,477 (24 Feb. 1932) 228-9.

Dated Boston, 29 Jan. [1932]. On India's movement for independence, and the British

Government's "reign of terror", i.e. Lord Willingdon's Ordinances. This letter was reprinted in *Selected Letters of Ananda K. Coomaraswamy* (1988)—A89—p. 333.

C625 Viṣṇudharmottara, Chapter XLI. *Journal of the American Oriental Society*, New Haven, LII. 1 (Mar. 1932) 13-21.

A translation by AKC ("even with the help of Professor Norman Brown I have not been able to solve all the problems") of this chapter, "probably of late Gupta date", that deals with painting; with reference to "a version, by no means satisfactory, of this and other chapters of the Viṣṇudharmottara . . . published by Stella Kramrisch [Calcutta, 1928]" (p. 13). An extended commentary by AKC is subjoined. Corrigendum to this translation is printed in *The Transformation of Nature in Art* (1934)—A56a—p. 192, note 24.

C626 [A review of] *Indische Kunst und Triumphalbild.* Von Albert Ippel. *Journal of the American Oriental Society*, New Haven, LII. 1 (Mar 1932) 83.

(In English.) AKC discusses Ippel's thesis which concerns the contacts between Western and Indian art before Gandhāra.

C627 [A review of] *Les collections khmères du Musée Sarrault* [*sic*, for Musée Albert Sarraut] *à Phnom Penh.* Par George Groslier. *Journal of the American Oriental Society*, New Haven, LII. 1 (Mar. 1932) 83-4.

(In English.) "M. Groslier . . . is the true creator and organiser of the Musée . . . The volume will be indispensible [*sic*] to all students of Khmer art". Also reviewed by AKC (differently) in *American Journal of Archaeology*, New York, for April/June 1932—C631.

C628 [A review of] *L'Attelage et le cheval de selle à travers les âges: contribution à l'histoire de l'esclavage.* Par Ct. Lefebure des Noëttes. *Journal of the American Oriental Society*, New Haven, LII. 1 (Mar. 1932) 84-6.

(In English.) AKC judges this work "extremely defective in parts relating to India . . . we have a right to expect something better than this from an encyclopaedic work purporting to be authoritative". AKC adds a note on the question of whether the invention of stirrups should be credited to China or India, and further on evidence for the equestrienne in Indian iconography.

C628a Introduction to the Art of Eastern Asia. *Open Court*, Chicago, XLVI. 910 (Mar. 1932) [185]-[216], 11 text illus.

This issue also bears the title: The New Orient Society Monograph Series No. 2. Reprinted separately, in a considerably expanded form, by the Open Court Publishing Company, in

1932—A55, and, in this expanded form, but with the omission of the bibliography, footnotes, and illustrations, as "The Philosophy of Ancient Asiatic Art", in *The Hindu View of Art*, [Second Edition], by Mulk Raj Anand (Bombay: Asia Publishing House [1957]), Appendix One, pp. [91]-110, and again, with the original title, and the footnotes, but omitting the illustrations and bibliography, in *Coomaraswamy 1: Selected Papers, Traditional Art and Symbolism* ([1977])—A82—pp. 101-27.

C629 A Vaishnava Relief. *Bulletin of the Museum of Fine Arts*, Boston, XXX. 178 (Apr. 1932) 37-9, 1 text illus.

On the iconography of a *circa* AD 12th century marble sculpture, "probably of Rajputana origin", recently presented to the Museum by Nasli M. Heeramaneck. AKC discusses in detail the idea, represented in this piece, of the Creator reclining on the Cosmic waters.

C630 Oriental Aesthetics. *Parnassus*, New York, IV. 4 (Apr. 1932) 26.

A summary, by AKC(?), of his paper of this title that was read on 31 March at the 21st Annual Meeting of the College Art Association held at the Metropolitan Museum of Art, New York. A general introduction; intended at the same time as "a contribution to the history of aesthetics".

C631 [A review of] *Les Collections Khmères du Musée Sarrault* [*sic*, for Musée Albert Sarraut] *à Phnom-Penh, Ars Asiatica XVI*. By G. Groslier. *American Journal of Archaeology*, New York, XXXVI. 2 (Apr./June 1932) 214-15.

Also reviewed by AKC (differently) in *Journal of the American Oriental Society*, New Haven, for March 1932—C627.

C632 A Bengali Painting. *Bulletin of the Museum of Fine Arts*, Boston, XXX. 179 (June 1932) 49, 1 text illus.

A brief note on an early 18th century example, recently acquired by the Museum, depicting women bringing offerings to Kṛṣṇa.

C633 An Early Rajput Painting. *Bulletin of the Museum of Fine Arts*, Boston, XXX. 179 (June 1932) 50-1, 1 text illus.

A description of a late 16th century miniature, recently acquired by the Museum, showing Rādhā being led by a confidante to the waiting Kṛṣṇa; together with the text and translation into English of the superscription.

C634 Ābhāsa. *Journal of the American Oriental Society*, New Haven, LII. 3 (Sept. 1932) 208-12.

On this Sanskrit word which in *Śilpa* contexts means "painting"; together with notes "on the psychological conception of the relation of painting to sculpture and relief, and on the idea of the third dimension in painting" (p. 210). This article was reprinted, in a revised and expanded form, as Chapter VI of *The Transformation of Nature in Art* (1934)—A56a.

C635 Reactions to Art in India. *Journal of the American Oriental Society*, New Haven, LII. 3 (Sept. 1932) 213-20.

"The purpose of the[se] . . . notes is to bring together, mainly from the general, non-technical literature, a few passages in which the reaction of the public to works of art is reported, partly as a contribution to the vocabulary of criticism, but more with a view to showing how art was actually regarded by those for whom it was made" (p. 213). This article was reprinted, unaltered, as Chapter III of *The Transformation of Nature in Art* (1934)—A56a.

C636 [A review of] *The Shāh Nāmah of Firdausī* . . . Described by J.V.S. Wilkinson, with an introduction on the paintings by Lawrence [*sic*] Binyon. *Journal of the American Oriental Society*, New Haven, LII. 3 (Sept. 1932) 254-5.

AKC objects to Laurence Binyon's "needless assumption" that the "vertical projection or perspective *à cheval*", employed in Persian painting, is specifically Chinese.

C637 Maha-Pralaya and Last Judgement. *Cultural World*, Los Angeles, III. 4 (Dec. 1932) 14-16.

Concerning some eschatological ideas as they are expressed in the Vedic and Christian traditions, with particular reference to the End of Time (*mahā-pralaya*) and "the voyage of the individual after death". This article was reprinted, incorporating Sanskrit equivalents of English terms, and with the addition of footnotes, and other changes, in *Indian Historical Quarterly*, Calcutta, IX. 1 (Mar. 1933), "Haraprasad [Sastri] Memorial Number", pp. [18]-21, and, omitting the second paragraph, but otherwise almost identical to that in *Cultural World*, in *Blackfriars*, Oxford, XIV. 159 (June 1933) 494-7.

1933

C638 Versions from the Vedas. *Indian Art and Letters*, London, N.S. VII. 1 (1933) 19-26.

Some general observations on the "difficult art" of translation preface specimen versions of *Ṛg Veda Saṁhitā* X. 72, 90, 129 (the Creation Hymn), *Bṛhadāraṇyaka Upaniṣad* I. 2. 1-

7, and *Māitri Upaniṣad* VI. 1-4, 35 and VII. 11. These renderings are almost identical with those printed in *A New Approach to the Vedas* (1933)—A57a.

C639 Hindu Sculpture. *League*, New York, V. 3 (Spring 1933) 4-6, 19-20, 6 text illus.

AKC provides an outline of what is required for a proper appreciation of Indian art. This article was reprinted, with the omission of the illustrations, in *Calcutta Review*, Calcutta, XLVIII. 2 (Aug. 1933) [143]-146.

C640 Hindu Sculptures at Zayton. *Ostasiatische Zeitschrift*, Berlin, N.S. IX. 1/2 (Jan./Apr. 1933) [5]-11, 5 text illus., 3 pls.

On archaeological evidence, dating from AD 1200-1400, at the Chinese port of Ch'üan-chou (medieval Zayton), that indicates the existence of long-established and direct relations between China and Ceylon and South India. This article was prepared by AKC at the request of Gustave Ecke (who was the first to study and photograph the reliefs). See also *The Twin Pagodas of Zayton; a Study of Later Buddhist Sculpture in China*, by Gustave Ecke (Cambridge, Mass.: Harvard University Press, 1935), p. 22, for excerpts from a letter by AKC to Ecke.

C641 A Relief from Persepolis. *Bulletin of the Museum of Fine Arts*, Boston, XXXI. 184 (Apr. 1933) 22-5, 2 text illus. (one is printed on the front cover, i.e. p. [21]).

On a sculpture dated 486-465 BC that "appears to have come from the residential palace built by Xerxes" (p. 23), now in the Museum collections, with respect to the view expressed by Anton Moortgat "that Achaemenid art did not borrow its stylistic idiom from contemporary Greece, but derived its idiosyncrasy from indigenous Asiatic sources" (p. 24). Includes an outline of the political history of the Achaemenids. This article was reprinted, in part, under the heading "Boston Persepolis Relief Discussed by Coomaraswamy", in *Art News*, New York, XXXI. 31 (29 Apr. 1933) 8.

C642 On Translation: Māyā, Deva, Tapas. *Isis*, Bruges, XIX. 1 (Apr. 1933) [74]-91.

Suggestions raisonnées as to the rendering into English of these Sanskrit terms, together with notes on what in AKC's view are the inadequacies of existing translations of Vedic texts, and, in the form of an "Appendix", offering sample versions in English of passages from the *Bṛhadāraṇyaka Upaniṣad* and the *Pañcaviṁśa Brāhmaṇa*.

C643 Talking It Over with Unusual Bostonians. No. 5—Ananda K. Coomaraswamy. *Boston Herald*, Boston, CLXXIII. 92 (2 Apr. 1933) Sect. B, "Magazine Features", p. 2, 1 text illus.

An interview, conducted by Elizabeth Borton, with AKC's replies given in quotation marks as his direct words. Chiefly concerning the Indian dance. The illustration reproduces a portrait photograph of AKC taken by Zlata Llamas, i.e. pseud. of Doña Luisa (Mrs A.K.) Coomaraswamy.

C644 Hindu Theatre. *Indian Historical Quarterly*, Calcutta, IX. 2 (June 1933) 594.

Some notes on architectural terms, with reference to an article of this title, by D.R. Mankad, in the issue for September 1932.

C645 [A review of] *Somanātha and other Mediaeval Temples in Kāṭhiāwāḍ*. By Henry Cousens. *Journal of the American Oriental Society*, New Haven, LIII. 2 (June 1933) 187.

AKC calls this "another of Mr. Cousens' sketchy compilations".

C646 [A review of] *Catalogue of the South Indian Metal Images in the Madras Government Museum.* By F.H. Gravely and T.N. Ramachandran. *Journal of the American Oriental Society*, New Haven, LIII. 2 (June 1933) 187-8.

"The authors and the Museum are to be congratulated . . ." (p. 187). AKC discusses briefly the dating and the stylistic development of this group.

C647 The Painter's Art in Ancient India: Ajaṇṭā. *Journal of the Indian Society of Oriental Art*, Calcutta, I. 1 (June 1933) 26-9.

AKC exploits the various contemporary technical and general literary sources of information relative to painting in India during the lst millennium AD, to assemble a verbatim account of the conception and execution of the frescoes at Ajaṇṭā as well as the reactions to them of various classes of people.

C648 [A review of] *Annual Bibliography of Indian Archaeology for the Year 1930* [*and 1931*], edited by Professor J.Ph. Vogel and others at the Kern Institut, Leyden. *American Journal of Archaeology*, New York, Second Series, XXXVII. 3 (July/ Sept. 1933) 526-7.

"The standards of this invaluable Bibliography are maintained".

C649 [A review of] *The Civilizations of the East, Vol. II, India*, by

R. Grousset. *American Journal of Archaeology*, New York, Second Series, XXXVII. 3 (July/Sept. 1933) 527.

"A readable and well documented handbook".

C650 [A review of] *The Meaning of Meaning*. By C.K. Ogden & I.A. Richards [and] *Mencius on the Mind*. By I.A. Richards. *Journal of the American Oriental Society*, New Haven, LIII. 3 (Sept. 1933) 298-303.

"These two volumes . . . are of fundamental importance to Orientalists, who are necessarily concerned with intricate problems of translation and interpretation" (p. 298).

C651 [A review of] *The Secret of the Golden Flower: A Chinese Book of Life*. Translated by Richard Wilhelm, with a commentary by C.G. Jung. *Journal of the American Oriental Society*, New Haven, LIII. 3 (Sept. 1933) 303-5.

"The late Professor Wilhelm . . . translates from the point of view of the student primarily interested in the meaning of the text . . . he treats the inner content of his subject seriously. . . . Jung's explanations, however admirable in themselves . . . represent a Taoism in which the Tao is left out."

C652 [A review of] *The Story of Kāḷaka: Texts, History, Legends, and Miniature Paintings of the Jain Hagiographical Work the Kālakācāryakathā*. By W. Norman Brown. *Journal of the American Oriental Society*, New Haven, LIII. 3 (Sept. 1933) 305-7.

"[A] most admirable monograph . . . The additions to our knowledge of Western Indian painting are very welcome" (pp. 305, 306). AKC makes several observations on the stylistic peculiarities of this school, and as well contributes some additional information on *sthāpanācārya* ("the symbolic representation of the Guru").

1934

C653 Khwājā Khaḍir and the Fountain of Life, in the Tradition of Persian and Mughal Art. *Ars Islamica*, Ann Arbor, I. 2 (1934) [172]-182, 3 pls.

On the nature, the origin, and the wide diffusion of this figure, a prophet and guardian of the water of immortal life, who "is the object of a still surviving popular cult common to Muslims and Hindus" (p. 173). AKC refers to Indian iconographic sources, to Indian and Persian legends and folktales, to the sources of the Islamic legend, and, briefly, to some European parallels. This article was reprinted, in a French translation, as "Khwâjâ Khadir et la Fontaine de Vie", in *Études Traditionnelles*, Paris, XLIII. 224/225 (Aug./Sept. 1938) [304]-318, 2 pls., and, with the omission of the plates, as "Khāwāj [*sic*] Khadir and the Fountain of Life, in the Tradition of Persian and Mughal Art", in *Studies in Comparative Religion*, Bedfont, Middx., IV. 4 (Autumn 1970) 221-30, and again in *What Is Civilisation? and Other Essays* ([1989])—A90—pp. [157]-167.

C654 *Kha* and Other Words Denoting "Zero" in Connection with the Metaphysics of Space. *Bulletin of the School of Oriental Studies*, London, VII. 3 (1934) [487]-497.

AKC purports "to exhibit the metaphysical and ontological implications of . . . terms which were later on actually used by Āryabhata and Bhāskara, etc., to designate 'zero', 'one', and some higher numbers" (p. [487]). This article was reprinted, as "*Kha* and Other Words Denoting 'Zero', in Connection with the Indian Metaphysics of Space", in *Coomaraswamy 2: Selected Papers, Metaphysics* ([1977])—A82—pp. 220-30, and, in a French translation by Gérard Leconte, as "*Kha* et autres mots signifiant 'zéro' dans leurs rapports avec la métaphysique de l'espace", in *Le Temps et l'Eternité*, by Ananda K. Coomaraswamy (Paris: Dervy-Livres [1976]), pp. 117-31.

C655 [Letter to Robert Lachmann, 7 December 1933]. *Zeitschrift für Vergleichende Musikwissenschaft*, Berlin, II. 2/3 (1934) 57-8.

(In English.) Quoted in a note, "Die Vina und das indische Tonsystem bei Bharata", by Robert Lachmann, pp. 57-60. AKC points out "that the old Indian Vīṇā was . . . actually a harp", with reference to an article, "Das indische Tonsystem bei Bharata und sein Ursprung", by Robert Lachmann and Erich M. von Hornbostel, in the first issue of this periodical (1933).

C656 Die Vīṇā und das indische Tonsystem bei Bharata. *Zeitschrift für Vergleichende Musikwissenschaft*, Berlin, II. 4 (1934) 83-4.

(In English.) Printed under the general heading: Diskussionen. Another reply to Robert Lachmann.

C657 [A review of] *Asiatische Miniaturmalerei im Anschluss an Wesen und Werden der Mogulmalerei*. Von Prof. J. Strzygowski, unter Mitarbeit von H. Glück, E. Wellesz und Str. Kramrisch. *Pantheon*, Munich, VII. 1 (Jan. 1934) VIII.

"Besonders wertvoll ist der Abschnitt über Raum und Modellierung in der klassischen indischen Malerei". AKC points out among other things that when Strzygowski deals with the later symbolic expressions of Indian art he tends not to trace them to their earlier (Vedic) formulae; and furthermore "im ganzen macht sich in dem gesamten Werk ein gewisser Mangel an genügender Beweisführung geltend, vor allem in dem Teil, der Indien behandelt". Nevertheless AKC commends the work of Strzygowski because "er befasst sich mit wirklichen Fragen der Kunstgeschichte, —nicht mit jenen unwirklichen, die so oft—einzig um des Antwortens willen—von Kunsthistorikern aufgeworfen werden".

C658 Understanding the Art of India. *Parnassus*, New York, VI. 4 (Apr. 1934) 21-6, 30, 3 text illus.

This article differs entirely from that of the same title printed in *Blackfriars*, Oxford, for April 1935 (and simultaneously in *Calcutta Review*, Calcutta)—C671. On the futility of approaching Indian (and medieval Christian) art apart from any consideration of the meaning of symbols that are the *raison d'être* of the art itself. Corrigenda is printed in the issue for May 1934, p. 31. This article was reprinted, incorporating the corrigenda, in *Sources of Wisdom* ([1981])—A85—pp. 137-58.

C659 [A review of] *Indian Sculpture*. By Stella Kramrisch. *Journal of the American Oriental Society*, New Haven, LIV. 2 (June 1934) 219-21.

AKC provides an epitome of Kramrisch's discussion, with copious quotations; ". . . within its chosen limits probably the best existing introduction to the subject" (p. 219).

C660 [A review of] *Journal of the Indian Society of Oriental Art*. Vol. I, Pts. 1 and 2, Calcutta 1933. *Journal of the American Oriental Society*, New Haven, LIV. 2 (June 1934) 222.

Greeting the successor to *Rupam*, and calling attention to some important articles.

C661 [A review of] *Zeitschrift für Vergleichende Musikwissenschaft*, ed. by Robert Lachmann. Vol. I, Berlin, 1933. *Journal of the American Oriental Society*, New Haven, LIV. 2 (June 1934) 223.

Calling attention to the inaugural issue of the *Zeitschrift*, and commending the work in Oriental and comparative musicology of Robert Lachmann and Erich M. von Hornbostel.

C662 An Eleventh Century Silver Salver from Persia. *Bulletin of the Museum of Fine Arts*, Boston, XXXII. 192 (Aug. 1934) 56-8, 7 text illus. (one is printed on the front cover, i.e. p. [55]).

A description of a recent acquisition by the Museum. The tray bears an inscription in Kufic lettering, and is "ostensibly the only dated and authentic record we possess of Alp Arslān", the second of the "Great Seljūqs", for whom it was made "in the year equivalent to A.D. 1066-7".

C663 The Technique and Theory of Indian Painting. *Technical Studies in the Field of the Fine Arts*, Cambridge, Mass., III. 2 (Oct. 1934) [59]-89, 2 pls. (one facing p. [59]; a detail of which is also reproduced on the front cover of this issue).

An annotated translation by AKC of pasages from the AD 12th century *Abhilashitārthachintāmaṇi* ("Wishing-stone of All Desirable Information"), of the Chālukya Emperor Someśvara III (Bhūlokamalla). AKC says *inter alia* that the texts "prove beyond question the continuity of the technical tradition in Indian painting at least from the Gupta period until almost the present day" (p.[59]). AKC provides additional information and corroborative evidence that Indian wall-painting was not fresco, but tempera; that portrait painting on wooden panels was not executed with liquid paint, but was a pastel art; and that medieval Indian painting was not a reflection of what is merely seen (this matter is treated to a further discussion in note 23, on "imitation", which occupies pages 79-84). This article was reprinted in the *Journal of the Uttar Pradesh Historical Society,* Lucknow, XXIII. 1/2 (1950) 5-34, 1 pl. (facing p. 5). See also C762.

C664 [A review of] *Geschichte der indischen Miniaturmalerei.* Von Hermann Goetz. *Journal of the American Oriental Society*, New Haven, LIV. 4 (Dec. 1934) 440-2.

(In English.) "Only the briefest, and rather derogatory mention . . . is made of the older Indian (Western Indian, Bengali, etc.) schools . . . But in this volume . . . the author has brought together criticisms and appreciations of no less value for the historian of culture than for the student of the history of art" (pp. 441, 442).

1935

C665 Two Vedântic Hymns from the *Siddhântamuktâvalī. Bulletin of the School of Oriental Studies*, London, VIII. 1 (1935) [91]-99.

A technical translation into English, employing Scholastic Christian terminology, of two 16th century Sanskrit texts of Prakāśânanda; together with introduction and commentary by AKC. The chief subject of the first hymn is interpreted by AKC as the differentiation of "the two selves", i.e. the spiritual or intellectual essence from the psycho-physical and sensitive existence; and the subject of the second as having to do with the doctrine of

Gnosis. On pages 95-6 AKC discusses at length the translation of *ātman* by "Essence", an experimental rendering that he adopts for the purposes of the present work.

C666 A Passage on Vīṇā-Playing. *Zeitschrift für Vergleichende Musikwissenschaft*, Berlin, III. 3/4 (1935) 88.

An English translation by AKC, with the claim that his version is an improvement on that by D.T. Suzuki in *The Laṅkâvatāra Sūtra* (1932), pp. 4-5.

C667 The Tree of Jesse and Oriental Parallels. *Parnassus*, New York, VI. 8 [*i.e.* VII. 1] (Jan. 1935) 18-19, 2 text illus.

A discussion of Chapter V of Arthur Watson's "admirable and long awaited monograph", *The Early Iconography of the Tree of Jesse.* AKC (l) adduces analogues (that, as he points out, need not, and generally do not, imply borrowing) from Zoroastrian, Judaic, and Vedic sources, and (2) makes some general observations on how symbols can survive, re-emerge, and be transmitted over several millennia. This article also incorporates addenda to "The Tree of Jesse and Indian Parallels or Sources" in *Art Bulletin*, New York, for June 1929—C549.

C668 The Life of Symbols. *Modern Review*, Calcutta, LVII. 2 (Feb. 1935) 224-6.

A translation into English by AKC of the "Schlusswort" to *Die ionische Säule, Bauform oder Symbol?*, by Walter Andrae. This translation was reprinted as Chapter XVIII, "Walter Andrae: On the Life of Symbols", in *Figures of Speech or Figures of Thought* (1946)—A71. Portions of the translation were incorporated by AKC in his review of Andrae's book in *Art Bulletin*, New York, for March 1935—C670.

C669 Mediaeval Aesthetic I. Dionysius the Pseudo-Aeropagite [*sic*], and Ulrich Engelberti of Strassburg. *Art Bulletin*, New York, XVII. 1 (Mar. 1935) 31-47.

Comprises translations by AKC of (1) *De Divinis Nominibus*, IV. 5, by Dionysius, and (2) the same text as rendered by Ulrich in his *Summa de Bono*. An introduction, that comprises four paragraphs, precedes the translations. A short list of "the chief available works in which an account of Scholastic aesthetic is to be found" is included on page 32. "The present article is the first of a series in which it is intended to make more readily accessible to modern students of mediaeval art the most important sources for the corresponding aesthetic theory" (p. 31). But in all only two instalments of the projected series were published—see C731. AKC had intended translations of *Opusculum de Reductione Artium ad Theologiam*, by St Bonaventura, and *De Tribus Diebus*, VI. 4-13, by Hugo of St Victor, for future instalments, but these did not materialize. This article was reprinted, in a revised form, together with the second instalment, retaining only the third of the introductory paragraphs, and including additionally AKC's discovery of the source of Dionysius's passage in Plato, excerpted from the "The Source of, and a Parallel to, Dionysius on the

Beautiful" (1936)—C684, to form Chapter II, "The Mediaeval Theory of Beauty", in *Figures of Speech or Figures of Thought* (1946)—A71. This revised version in turn was reprinted, with the first two introductory paragraphs restored, in *Coomaraswamy 1: Selected Papers, Traditional Art and Symbolism* ([1977])—A82—pp. 189-228.

C670 [A review of] *Die ionische Säule, Bauform oder Symbol?* By E[*sic*, for W]. Andrae [and] *Greek Geometric Art, its Symbolism and its Origin*. By A. Roes. *Art Bulletin*, New York, XVII. 1 (Mar. 1935) 103-7.

On the significance of some "indications of a new orientation in archaeological research", as exemplified in the work of Andrae and Roes, where the need to study "the meaning or inner life of formal motifs [is recognized] as affording the only effective clue to their 'history'" (pp. 103, 106). Incorporating a translation into English (by AKC) of passages excerpted from the "Schlusswort" to *Die ionische Säule*. (AKC had translated the "Schlusswort", in its entirety, as "The Life of Symbols", in *Calcutta Review*, Calcutta, for February 1935—C668.) The review of Andrae (only) was reprinted, as "Walter Andrae's *Die ionische Säule: Bauform oder Symbol?*: A Review", in *Coomaraswamy 1: Selected Papers, Traditional Art and Symbolism* ([1977])—A82—pp. 341-9.

C671 Understanding the Art of India. *Blackfriars*, Oxford, XVI. 181 (Apr. 1935) 247-52.

Originally a radio broadcast given by AKC in Boston on 13 January 1935. A résumé of the traditional doctrine about art, and of the history of Indian art in particular. This article was printed simultaneously in *Calcutta Review*, Calcutta, LV. 1 (Apr. 1935) [1]-6, and reprinted as Chapter 18 of *Introduction to Indian Art* ([1969])—A45c. The broadcast is summarized, under the heading "Dr. Coomaraswamy Gives Radio Talk on Art of India", in *Art News*, New York, XXXIII. 9 (9 Feb. 1935) 13.

C672 An Illustrated Jaina Manuscript. *Bulletin of the Museum of Fine Arts*, Boston, XXXIII. 197 (June 1935) 36-40, 8 text illus.

AKC discusses the iconography of several unique miniatures belonging to a 16th century manuscript of the *Kalpasūtra* and the *Kālakācāryakathā*, a recent acquisition by the Museum. The illustrations depict the Nativity and childhood exploits of Mahāvīra, as well as other Jaina themes.

C673 [A review of] *On the Iconography of the Buddha's Nativity*. By A. Foucher. *Indian Historical Quarterly*, Calcutta, XI. 2 (June 1935) 357-60.

"Foucher's eloquent study . . . is unfortunately marred by a complete neglect of the Vedic sources of its formulae" (pp. 357-8). This review was reprinted in the *Journal of the American Oriental Society*, New Haven, LV. 3 (Sept. 1935) 323-5.

C674 The Intellectual Operation in Indian Art. *Journal of the Indian Society of Oriental Art*, Calcutta, III. 1 (June 1935) [1]-12.

Concerning "the initial procedure of the Indian imager": a method of visualization that emphasizes contemplation, and "self-identification . . . with the imagined form" (pp. [1], 8). Incorporating, on pages 2-7, a translation (by AKC) of a medieval Buddhist canonical prescription, the *Kiṃcit-Vistara-Tārā Sādhana*. AKC concludes with comments on (1) the Western "fetishistic" attitude to Oriental art, and (2) the so-called maṇḍalas of C.G. Jung's patients. This article was reprinted, in a revised form, as Chapter X of *Figures of Speech or Figures of Thought* (1946)—A71, and, incorporating addenda, in *Coomaraswamy 1: Selected Papers, Traditional Art and Symbolism* ([1977])—A82—pp. 131-46.

C675 A Study of the Kaṭha-Upaniṣad (IV.1). *Indian Historical Quarterly*, Calcutta, XI. 3 (Sept. 1935) [570]-584.

In the main, an analysis of the distinction "between the profane and extroverted and the contemplative or introverted consciousness" (p. 571), in connection with what AKC considers an imperfect rendering of this verse in *The Kaṭha Upaniṣad: An Introductory Study in the Hindu Doctrine of God and of Human Destiny*, by Joseph Nadin Rawson. This article was reprinted, in a French translation (by Gérard Leconte), as "Une étude sur la Katha Upanishad", in *Études Traditionnelles*, Paris, LXXVIII. 456/457 (Apr./May/June/July/Aug./Sept. 1977) 76-93. AKC continues his discussion of Joseph Rawson's work, in "Notes on the Kaṭha Upaniṣad", in *New Indian Antiquary*, Bombay, for April 1938—C733.

C676 Chāyā. *Journal of the American Oriental Society*, New Haven, LV. 3 (Sept. 1935) 278-83.

(In English.) A discussion of the variant meanings of this word (primarily "shadow", secondarily "reflection" and "likeness") as it occurs in the *Ṛg Veda*. AKC explains that "shadow" is at once the manifested likeness of deity and man's temporal refuge. Parallels are adduced from Christian tradition, "not with a view to demonstrating 'influences', but to remind the student that in Vedic doctrine there is nothing unique, and that the voice of tradition is everywhere the same" (p. 283). This article was reprinted, in a French translation (by Gérard Leconte), in *Études Traditionnelles*, Paris, LXXVI. 450 (Oct./Nov./Dec. 1975) 145-51.

C677 [A review of] *The Spirit of Man in Asian Art*. By Laurence Binyon. *Journal of the American Oriental Society*, New Haven, LV. 3 (Sept. 1935) 325-9.

". . . for the general reader the best available introduction to the inner life of Asiatic peoples as it has found expression in art" (p. 325). AKC nevertheless has some reservation about Binyon's view of Rājput painting; he also expresses surprise at the omission of any reference to the art of South-East Asia.

C678 What Is Common to Indian and Chinese Art? *Usha*, Lahore, II. 1 (Nov. 1935) [1]-18.

A lecture given by AKC at Harvard University, before the Summer Seminar on Far Eastern Studies, 25 July 1932. This printed version of the lecture incorporates adaptations for Indian readers. After remarking that, with respect to the Chinese and Indian adherence to First Principles of the metaphysical tradition, these civilizations are truly commensurable and comparable, AKC then proceeds to a comparative discussion of Chinese and Indian aesthetics. He highlights his methodology, by which he intends to demonstrate that "induction from First Principles", in contrast to the Western habit of "deduction from observed fact", is the only method "by which oriental civilizations . . . can be made intelligible" (p. 18). An editorial note on page iii of this issue explains: "We received the article . . . a very long time ago and much regret that we could not publish it earlier. We are grateful to Mr. Ananda Coomarswamy [*sic*] for having sent this most valuable article exclusively for the 'Usha'". The text of the lecture in its original form, but with omissions, is printed in *Studies in Comparative Religion*, Bedfont, Middx., VII. 2 (Spring 1973) 75-91; see also the Autumn issue of the same periodical, page 247, for a note by Marco Pallis on "certain references to Buddhism of a disparaging kind" that are contained in the lecture. A mimeograph copy of the text of the original lecture seen (May 1991) at the Freer Gallery of Art Library, Washington, D.C.

C679 Sacred and Profane Science. *Visva-Bharati Quarterly*, Santiniketan, Bengal, N.S. I. 3 (Nov. 1935/Jan. 1936) [11]-24, 1 text illus.

A translation by AKC of Chapter IV of *La Crise du Monde moderne* (1927), by René Guénon. Supplementary footnotes are supplied by AKC on pages [11], 12, 15, 16, 19, 21, 22, 23, 24. AKC's note on page [11] incorporates his brief appraisal of Guénon's *oeuvre* (the first paragraph of which was used by Luzac & Co. (London) for the blurb on the dust-jackets of their editions of Guénon's *East and West* (1941) and *Crisis of the Modern World* (1942)). AKC has also inserted throughout the text Sanskrit equivalents of English terms. AKC wrote to Rabindranath Tagore on 6 May 1935: "I have been anxious to call the attention of Indian readers to the remarkable work of René Guénon" (in *Ananda Coomaraswamy—The Bridge Builder: A Study of a Scholar-Colossus. Supplement 2*, by S. Durai Raja Singam ([Petaling Jaya, Malaysia, 1981]), p. [40]).

C680 Angel and Titan: An Essay in Vedic Ontology. *Journal of the American Oriental Society*, New Haven, LV. 4 (Dec. 1935) 373-419.

"The leading idea to be developed . . . is that the Devas and Asuras, Angels and Titans, powers of Light and powers of Darkness in RV. [i.e. *Ṛg Veda Saṁhitā*], although distinct and opposite in operation, are in essence consubstantial . . . account is taken only of the masculine powers; in connection with the corresponding feminine powers [see *The Darker Side of Dawn* (1935)—A58]; the two papers should be read together" (pp. 373-4). In his analysis of the nature of this identity, AKC attempts to demonstrate "that neither the

Vedic ontology nor the formulae in which it is communicated are peculiar to RV., but can as well be recognized in all the extra-Indian forms of the 'universal and unanimous tradition'" (pp. 418-19). AKC also discusses *passim* the notion of the typically ophidian nature of the First Principle. In a footnote on page 386 (and repeated on page 400) AKC has: "see my 'Vedic Doctrine of Exemplarism' to appear in the James Haughton Woods Memorial Volume"; this article, with the title shortened to "Vedic Exemplarism", was published instead in *Harvard Journal of Asiatic Studies*, Cambridge, Mass., for April 1936—C686.

C681 "The Conqueror's Life" in Jaina Painting: Explicitur Reductio haec Artis ad Theologiam. *Journal of the Indian Society of Oriental Art*, Calcutta, III. 2 (Dec. 1935) [127]-144, 6 pls. (numbered: XXXIII-XXXVIII) containing 14 illus. (pls. XXXIV and XXXVI are coloured and tipped in).

"The purpose of the present article [is] to call attention to certain characteristics of the Jaina formulation, as to which there can be said what is also true of Indian iconography generally, *viz.* (1) that the formulation is in hardly any detail a private property of the sect that makes use of it, and (2) that ultimate explanations can only be found in the Vedic metaphysical tradition and/or cognate traditions" (p. 128). A separately paginated offprint of this article is in the compiler's possession.

C682 An Approach to Indian Art. *Parnassus*, New York, VII. 7 (Dec. 1935) 17-20, 1 text illus.

A reprint from *Loan Exhibition of Early Indian Sculptures Paintings and Bronzes* ([1935])—B41. Also printed, in a reduced form, as "For an Exhibition of Indian Art", in *Calcutta Review*, Calcutta, LVIII. 3 (Mar. 1936) [263]-266.

1936

C683 L'idée de "création éternelle" dans le Rig-Vêda. *Études Traditionnelles*, Paris, XLI. 193 (Jan. 1936) [11]-17.

This article was reprinted, in English, restoring a reference to A.A. Macdonell inadvertently omitted in the French translation (while at the same time omitting a reference to St Augustine), as "Eternal Creation in the Rig Veda", in *Vedanta Kesari*, Mylapore, XXIII. 9 (Jan. 1937) [342]-344.

C684 The Source of, and a Parallel to, Dionysius on the Beautiful. *Journal of the Greater India Society*, Calcutta, III. 1 (Jan. 1936) [36]-42.

On the concept found throughout the Vedic tradition of a coincidence or identity *in divinis* of the beautiful, the good, being, light, and sound. The discussion is with particular reference to *Chāndogya Upaniṣad*, IV. 15, which AKC attempts to demonstrate is in complete agreement with the doctrine of Dionysius, as well as, generally, with the entire Platonic and Scholastic doctrine of beauty. The translation here by AKC of Dionysius, *De Divinis Nominibus*, IV. 5— "evidently derived, and partly verbatim from Plato, *Phaedrus* [*sic*, for *Symposium*], 210-11" (p. [36])—is almost identical to that printed with "Mediaeval Aesthetic I. Dionysius the Pseudo-Aeropagite [*sic*], and Ulrich Engelberti of Strassburg" (1935)—C669. On page 41, AKC announces that his "Vedic Exemplarism" will "appear this year in the *James Haughton Woods Memorial Volume*". The essay was published instead in the *Harvard Journal of Asiatic Studies* for April 1936—C686. This article was reprinted, in a French translation, revised and expanded, as "Beauté, Lumière et Son" (1937)—C699.

C685 An Indian Crocodile. *Bulletin of the Museum of Fine Arts*, Boston, XXXIV. 202 (Apr. 1936) 26-8, 4 text illus.

A description of a unique 3rd century BC Maurya sculpture, recently acquired by the Museum; with notes on the symbolism of the *makara* (crocodile), and the cult of Kāmadeva (the Indian Eros). Addendum to this article is printed with AKC's review of *Frühchinesische Bronzen und Kulturdarstellungen*, by Carl Hentze, in *Art Bulletin*, New York, for March 1940—C769—p. 52.

C686 Vedic Exemplarism. *Harvard Journal of Asiatic Studies*, Cambridge, Mass., I. 1 (Apr. 1936) 44-64.

A detailed exposition, employing parallels drawn from Neo-Platonic and Scholastic sources, of the concept of the relation of macrocosm to microcosm, or of unity to multiplicity. In addition, "the concluding paragraphs . . . assemble certain . . . Vedic texts in which the doctrine is explicit or implicit that the utterance of a name is of creative efficacy" (p. 60). Addenda and corrigenda to this article are printed in the same volume of this periodical, on page 281. Reprinted, with further revisions and addenda, in *Coomaraswamy 2: Selected Papers, Metaphysics* ([1977])—A82—pp. 177-97, and, in a French translation (by Gérard Leconte), as "L'exemplarisme védique", in *Études Traditionnelles*, Paris, LXXVII. 452/453 (Apr./May/June/July/Aug./Sept. 1976) 49-78.

C687 Vedic "Monotheism". *Journal of Indian History*, Madras, XV. 1 (Apr. 1936) [84]-92.

The present article represents AKC's text in its final form which had arrived too late for inclusion in B43; this revised text "is published here with the Editor's apologies to, and with the approval of, the author" (p. [84]). Corrigenda is printed with "'Pantheism', Indian and Neo-Platonic" (an article intended by AKC to be read as a postscript to "Vedic 'Monotheism'"), in the issue for December 1937—C723—p. [249]. This article was reprinted, with further revisions and extensive addenda, in *Coomaraswamy 2: Selected Papers, Metaphysics* ([1977])—A82—pp. 166-76.

C688 The Love of Art. *Parnassus*, New York, VIII. 4 (Apr. 1936) 22-3.

Originally delivered by AKC as a radio broadcast in Boston, 12 April 1936. AKC suggests that the cultural activities of "lovers of art" actually "represent very little more than palliative measures applied to symptoms of what is really a fundamental spiritual deficiency in ourselves" (p. 22). This article was reprinted in *Blackfriars*, Oxford, XVII. 195 (June 1936) 434-9, in *Good Work*, Buffalo, XXIII. 3 (Pentecost 1960) 67-70, and again in the same periodical, XXVIII. 2 (Spring 1965) 37-40, and in *Temenos*, London, 13 (1992) 55-60.

C689 [*Entry deleted*].

C690 The Appreciation of the Unfamiliar Arts. *Visva-Bharati Quarterly*, Santiniketan, Bengal, N.S. II. 1 (May/July 1936) [17]-21.

Originally delivered by AKC as a radio broadcast in Boston, 9 January 1936. This article was reprinted in *Coomaraswamiana* (1960)—A76—pp. [121-35], and in *Visva-Bharati Quarterly*, "Silver Jubilee Number", XXV. 3/4 ([Aug. 1960]) [43]-49.

C691 Sri Ramakrishna and Religious Tolerance. *Prabuddha Bharata*, Mayavati, India, XLI. 6 (June 1936) 268-74.

A lecture delivered on the occasion of the centennial celebrations of Sri Rāmakrishna's birth, held under the auspices of the Ramakrishna-Vivekananda Center, at Town Hall, New York, on 8 March 1936. This article was reprinted in *Coomaraswamiana* (1960)—A76—pp. [151-62], and in *Coomaraswamy 2: Selected Papers, Metaphysics* ([1977])—A82—pp. 34-42. A French translation is printed, as "Shrî Râmakrishna et la tolérance religieuse", in *Études Traditionnelles*, Paris, XLI. 199 (July 1936) [251]-264.

C692 Rebirth and Omniscience in Pāli Buddhism. *Indian Culture*, Calcutta, III. 1 (July 1936) [19]-33.

AKC offers a "brief criticism of some of Mrs. Rhys Davids' interpretations . . . with reference: (1) to [her] *Kindred Sayings*, II . . . and (2) her 'Rebirth in the Pali Scriptures' published in the *Calcutta Review*, September 1930. By way of parenthesis, let me say that I have nearly completed a much longer study of the doctrine of *Death, Resurrection, and Reincarnation*" (p. [19]). This work-in-progress remained unfinished at the time of AKC's death; for another comment from AKC concerning this uncompleted book, see *Am I My Brother's Keeper?* ([1947])—A72a—p. 110. Corrigendum to this article is printed in the issue for April 1937—C704.

C693 Two Passages in Dante's *Paradiso*. *Speculum*, Cambridge, Mass., XI. 3 (July 1936) 327-38.

AKC selects XVIII. 110-11 and XXVII. 136-8 for exegesis because they have "presented difficulties to commentators relying only on European sources". AKC uses Vedic and Sanskrit texts "for parallels to or even explanations . . . of particular idioms of thought employed by Dante" (p. 332). This article was reprinted, with addenda, in *Coomaraswamy 2: Selected Papers, Metaphysics* ([1977])—A82—pp. 241-55.

C694 The Nature of "Folklore" and "Popular Art". *Quarterly Journal of the Mythic Society*, Bangalore, XXVII. 1/2 (July/Oct. 1936) [1]-12.

On the distinction in India of folk art (*deśī*, "byway") from the "intellectual arts that are the very means of enlightenment" (*mārga*, "highway"), and on the "apparent parallel" this offers to the modern disparagement of superstition and folk art and the reverence paid to "learning" and the "fine arts". AKC also discusses how, regardless of its *deśī* character, folk art may be entrusted with the preservation of scriptural formulae, especially at "the period of dissolution of cultures that takes place at the close of a cycle". Includes (p. 4) a critical note on the harmonium in India. This article was reprinted in *Indian Art and Letters*, London, N.S. XI. 2 (Second Issue for 1937) 76-84, and, with additions to the notes, but omitting the note on the harmonium, as Chapter VIII of *Why Exhibit Works of Art?* (1943)—A67. An excerpt was printed in *Modern Review*, Calcutta, LXI. 4 (Apr. 1937) 455-6. The entire article was reprinted, in a French translation, as "La Nature du 'Folkore' et de l' 'Art Populaire'", in *Études Traditionnelles*, Paris, XLII. 210 (June 1937) [206]-218.

C695 A Note on the Aśvamedha. *Archiv Orientální*, Prague, VIII. 2 (Aug. 1936) 306-17.

An examination of the symbolism of the Indian rite of horse sacrifice, with special reference to the role of the queen and to the ceremony's relationship with Vedic religion. The first six paragraphs consider how modern interpretations of sexual symbolism in religious rites have been "contaminated" through the conventional propriety of scholars such as J. Eggeling, A.B. Keith, and R.T.H. Griffith. In a footnote, on page 308, AKC comments briefly on what he sees as the shortcomings of C.G. Jung's understanding of the nature of tradition and metaphysics.

C696 Nirukta=Hermeneia. *Visva-Bharati Quarterly*, Santiniketan, Bengal, N.S. II. 2 (Aug./Oct. 1936) [11]-17.

On the Indian, and traditional, science of interpretation based upon the hypothesis of an essential (not accidental) connection of sounds with meanings (hermeneutics), as exemplified in *Chāndogya Upaniṣad*, VII. 3.3. AKC expresses the opinion that the theory is neglected by modern scholars. Addendum is printed in the issue for February/April 1937—C702. This article was reprinted, incorporating the addendum, in *Coomaraswamy 2: Selected Papers, Metaphysics* ([1977])—A82—pp. 256-63. Also reprinted, in a French translation, in *Études Traditionnelles*, Paris, XLI. 203 (Nov. 1936) [405]-415; the addendum is printed in the same periodical, XLII. 206 (Feb. 1937) 60-1.

1937

C697 What Is the Use of Art Anyway? *American Review*, New York, VIII. 3 (Jan. 1937) 321-35.

Originally two separate broadcasts, "What Use Is Art Anyway?" and "Art for Art's Sake?", given by AKC in Boston on 14 and 21 January 1937 (respectively), as part of a series of six radio talks sponsored by the Museum of Fine Arts, Boston, from 14 January to 18 February. The other speakers in the series were Graham Carey and John Howard Benson. AKC's two broadcasts were reprinted under their respective titles in *What Use Is Art Anyway* (1937)—B46, and in the form of the present article, in *Essays in Value*, edited by Irving Hamilton White, George B. Franklin, Edward A. Post, George M. Sneath, Austin Warren, and John M. Williams (New York: D. Appleton-Century Company Incorporated [1938]), pp. 395-405, as Chapter IV of *Why Exhibit Works of Art?* (1943)—A67, in *Catholic Art Quarterly*, Boston, XX. 1 (Christmas 1956) 3-5, and in the same periodical, XX. 2 (Easter 1957) 39-43, in *Epiphany*, San Francisco, II. 4 (Summer 1982) 24-31, 3 text illus., and, as "The Use of Art", in *Parabola*, New York, XVI. 3 (Fall 1991) 4-10.

C698 Indian Bronzes. *Parnassus*, New York, IX. 1 (Jan. 1937) 21-3, 4 text illus.

A slightly expanded version of "An Introduction to Bronze Statuettes of India and Farther India" (1937)—B44, but with fewer illustrations, and omitting the descriptive list of sculptures.

C699 Beauté, Lumière et Son. *Études Traditionnelles*, Paris, XLII. 206 (Feb. 1937) [51]-60.

A revised and expanded version, in French, of "The Source of, and a Parallel to, Dionysius on the Beautiful" (1936)—C684. This article was reprinted, in English, with the title "Beauty, Light and Sound", in *What Is Civilisation? and Other Essays* ([1989])—A90—pp. [42]-49. A few excerpted passages, in an earlier and *ad hoc* English translation, appeared in *Introduction to the Study of Musical Scales*, by Alain Daniélou (London: The India Society [1943]), pp. 14-15.

C700 Mahābhārata, Itihāsa. *Annals of the Bhandarkar Oriental Research Institute*, Poona, XVIII. 2 (Mar. 1937) [211]-212.

On the proper use of the Sanskrit term *itihāsa*, and warning against the modern tendency towards literal and historical interpretation of what in reality are not temporal events.

C701 The Parts of a Vīṇā. *Journal of the American Oriental Society*, New Haven, LVII. 1 (Mar. 1937) 101-3.

An English rendering by AKC, together with a brief commentary, of *Jaiminīya Brāhmaṇa*, II. 69-70; affording additional information to "The Parts of a Vīṇā" in the issue for September 1930—C585, "The Old Indian *Vīṇā*" in the issue for March 1931—C602, and "Upavīṇā" in the issue for September 1931—C614.

C702 Nirukta=Hermeneia (Addendum). *Visva-Bharati Quarterly*, Santiniketan, Bengal, N.S. II. 4 (Feb./Apr. 1937) [101].

See C696.

C703 The Vedic Doctrine of "Silence". *Indian Culture*, Calcutta, III. 4 (Apr. 1937) [559]-569.

An explication of the metaphysical significance of "silence", in connection with rites, myths, and mysteries, citing specific details from Vedic tradition, together with parallels drawn from Christian doctrine. This article was reprinted, with addenda, in *Coomaraswamy 2: Selected Papers, Metaphysics* ([1977])—A82—pp. 198-208.

C704 Anattā=Nāma-Rūpa. *Indian Culture*, Calcutta, III. 4 (Apr. 1937) 760-1.

Corrigendum to "Rebirth and Omniscience in Pāli Buddhism" in the issue for July 1936—C692.

C705 Christianity and Hinduism. [Letter]. *Asia*, New York, XXXVII. 5 (May 1937) [396].

A rejoinder to A.B. Keith's letter of criticism (printed on this page) in connection with AKC's radio broadcast talk, "The Indian Doctrine of Man's Last End", which is included in this issue—C706 *n*. Both letters are reprinted in *Coomaraswamiana* (1960)—A76—pp. [182-3], and again (but with Keith's letter slightly reduced) in *Selected Letters of Ananda K. Coomaraswamy* (1988)—A89—pp. 108-9.

C706 The Indian Doctrine of Man's Last End. *Vedanta Kesari*, Mylapore, XXIV. 1 (May 1937) [26]-30.

The text of AKC's broadcast talk on station W1AXL in Boston, 4 December 1936; also read at a meeting of the American Oriental Society at Cleveland, Ohio, on 1 April 1937 (an abstract is printed in 14 lines in the *Journal of the American Oriental Society* for June 1937, p. 244). On what is meant by the Hindu doctrine of "deification", and whether or not this differs from the Christian mystical (chiefly Eckhartian) "deification". This article was also printed, in a reduced form, in *Asia*, New York, XXXVII. 5 (May 1937) 380-1, in *Coomaraswamiana* (1960)—A76—pp. [175-82], and in *Sources of Wisdom* ([1981])—A85—pp. 180-6.

C707 The Virgin Suckling St. Bernard. *Art Bulletin*, New York, XIX. 2 (June 1937) 317-18.

A note on the history and metaphysical significance of this motif, with reference to its occurrence as the subject of a 14th century Majorcan painting, and in connection with "The Madonna of Humility", by Millard Meiss, in the issue for December 1936. This article was reprinted, in a French translation, expanded to include a reference to Nicholas de Cusa on divine "adoption" or "filiation", as "La Vierge allaitant saint Bernard", in *Études Traditionnelles*, Paris, XLII. 216 (Dec. 1937) [415]-418, and again in the the same periodical, XCI. 508/509 (Apr./May/June/July/Aug./Sept. 1990) 54-7. This expanded version was reprinted, in English, in *Studies in Comparative Religion*, Bedfont, Middx., IV. 3 (Summer 1970) 137-9. AKC continues the discussion of this motif in "La Voie lactée" (1938)—C736.

C708 The Rape of a Nāgī: An Indian Gupta Seal. Part I. *Bulletin of the Museum of Fine Arts*, Boston, XXXV. 209 (June 1937) 38-41, 4 text illus.

On the iconography and significance of this motif, which represents the concept of the Psyche caught up by and assimilated to the Spirit. This article, combined with the second part—C714, was reprinted, with addenda, and retaining the illustrations, in *Coomaraswamy 1: Selected Papers, Traditional Art and Symbolism* ([1977])—A82—pp. 331-40.

C709 Janaka and Yājñavalkya. *Indian Historical Quarterly*, Calcutta, XIII. 2 (June 1937) [261]-278.

On *Bṛhadāraṇyaka Upaniṣad*, IV. 1-4, the dialogue between Yājñavalkya and his pupil King Janaka of Videha, and IV. 5, the dialogue between Yājñavalkya and his two wives Maitreyī and Kātyāyanī, considering the metaphysical identities of these "characters" and the significance of their conversations. Includes as well, on pages 274-8, a discussion of the "Vrātya problem", with reference to *Atharva Veda Saṁhitā*, XV, and *Pañcaviṁśa Brāhmaṇa*, XVII. 1-4. Incorporating notes on the Indian view of what it means to be "perfect", and some general criticism of the shortcomings of modern scholars when dealing with "magical efficacies" and "superstitions" (i.e. footnotes 7 and 22, respectively).

C710 [A review of] *Gayā and Buddha-Gayā*. By Benimadhab Barua. *Journal of the American Oriental Society*, New Haven, LVII. 2 (June 1937) 191-3.

"Barua's neglect of all but the oldest literature, taken together with the poverty and incompleteness of the illustrations, justify us in saying that these volumes are very far from important contributions to our knowledge of early Indian art" (p. 193).

C711 The Origins of Art. *Science and Culture*, Calcutta, II. 12 (June 1937) 625-8.

A translation by AKC from the French of Élie Lebasquais in *Études Traditionnelles*, Paris, XLI. 197 (May 1936) [168]-175. AKC contributes four supplementary footnotes; these are marked: (Tr.). This translation was reprinted, with minor changes and omissions (including the omission of AKC's name as the translator), in *Studies in Comparative Religion*, Bedfont, Middx., XIV. 3/4 (Summer/Autumn 1980) 135-9.

C712 Is Art a Superstition or a Way of Life? *American Review*, New York, IX. 2 (Summer [incl. the issue for May] 1937) 186-213.

A lecture given at the Metropolitan Museum of Art, New York, in April, and at Harvard University (Summer School), Cambridge, Mass., in July. Reprinted as a John Stevens Pamphlet (1937)—A63, and, together with a postscript replying to a review by Richard Florsheim, as Chapter III of *Why Exhibit Works of Art?* (1943)—A67.

C713 [A review of] *Schönheit: ein Versuch.* By Theodor Haecker. *Criterion*, London, XVI. 65 (July 1937) 739-41.

AKC says this treatment of the theory of beauty "in so far as it is traditional is also authoritative", but that Haecker introduces his own prejudices when he comes to deal with categories of art.

C714 The Rape of a Nāgī: An Indian Gupta Seal. Part II. *Bulletin of the Museum of Fine Arts*, Boston, XXXV. 210 (Aug. 1937) 56-7.

On the methodology of symbolic exegesis, and contending against the modern art-historian who in AKC's view is preoccupied with aesthetics and with stylistic rather than iconographic interpretation. This article was characterized by René Guénon as "une excellente réponse à certains négateurs du symbolisme" (*Études Traditionnelles*, Paris, XLII. 214/215 (Oct./Nov. 1937) 359), and by Roger Lipsey as AKC's "strongest deposition apropos of symbolism" ("Signature and Significance: A Study of the Life and Writings of Ananda K. Coomaraswamy" (1974)—E116 *n.*—p. 740). Reprinted, combined with the first part—C708, in *Coomaraswamy 1: Selected Papers, Traditional Art and Symbolism* ([1977])—A82—pp. 331-40.

C715 La Doctrine tantrique de la "bi-unité" divine. *Études Traditionnelles*, Paris, XLII. 212/213 (Aug./Sept. 1937) [289]-301.

On "la notion . . . d'une polarité bisexuelle dans la Divinité", and indicating "qu'un symbolisme de cette sorte a été employé universellement dans la Tradition orthodoxe et unanime; et, plus précisément . . . de montrer en quelle manière similaire il a été utilisé dans les formes hindoue et chrétienne de la Tradition révélée" (pp. 290, 301). This issue of *Études Traditionnelles* is sub-titled: *Numéro spécial sur le tantrisme hindou*. This article was reprinted, in English, as "The Tantric Doctrine of Divine Biunity", in *Annals of the Bhandarkar Oriental Research Institute*, Poona, XIX. 2 (Jan. 1938) [173]-183, and, with addenda, in *Coomaraswamy 2: Selected Papers, Metaphysics* ([1977])—A82—pp. 231-40.

C716 [A review of] *Barabuḍur*. By Paul Mus, with a Preface by George Coedès. *Journal of the American Oriental Society*, New Haven, LVII. 3 (Sept. 1937) 336-43.

"This is a book as monumental as the subject with which it deals . . . and must be considered as no less epoch making than the earlier work of Foucher" (p. 336). AKC commends Mus' monograph for its "method in which the researcher no longer envisages Buddhism as an isolated and revolutionary phenomenon, but in its setting, and no longer considers the texts alone or the art alone, but each as an alternative expression of the same underlying theses. This amounts to a veritable bringing to life of the 'dry bones' of what might otherwise have been a merely statistical archaeology" (p. 343). On pages 340-3, AKC summarizes and comments upon what Mus has to say apropos of the symbolism of the domed stūpa.

C717 Uday Shankar's Indian Dancing. *Magazine of Art*, Washington, D.C., XXX. 10 (Oct. 1937) 611-13, 645, 4 text illus.

On the Indian dance as intrinsically mimetic and sacerdotal. (Shankar undertook dance-tours of North America in January and December 1937.)

C718 The Time-Factor in Indian Wall Painting. *Technical Studies in the Field of the Fine Arts*, Cambridge, Mass., VI. 2 (Oct. 1937) [106]-108.

Printed under the general heading: Notes. On literary evidence for the collaboration of several artists in the execution of a single work, and the "importance [of this] in forming estimates of the rate at which the work may have been done" (p.[106]), in connection with "The Mural Paintings in the Brihadisvara Temple at Tanjore—An Investigation into the Method", by S. Paramasivan, in the issue for April.

C719 The "Four Causes" in the Bhagavad Gītā. *Journal of the American Oriental Society*, New Haven, LVII. 4 (Dec. 1937) 415-16.

AKC compares *Bhagavadgītā*, XVIII. 14-15 with *Bṛhadāraṇyaka Upaniṣad*, IV. 4, 2, and with the four Aristotelian causes.

C720 [A review of] *The Cultural Heritage of India*. A symposium by some 100 authors . . . [and] *The Legacy of India*. Edited by G.T. Garratt, with an Introduction by the Marquis of Zetland. *Journal of the American Oriental Society*, New Haven, LVII. 4 (Dec. 1937) 426-8.

In the first, "the unanimity of the several authors' points of view produces a remarkable effect of unity in the book itself . . . Many of the articles are admirable" (p. 426). AKC singles out as an especially important contribution Swami Nirvedananda's "Sri Ramakrishna and Spiritual Renaissance". The second book under review "falls behind the *Cultural Heritage* in total achievement" (p. 427). AKC calls attention to A.H. Fox Strangways' "Music", and Walter Eugene Clark's "Science", as being "of outstanding value", and quotes with approval Garratt's unfavourable opinion of (1) Rudyard Kipling and (2) the English translations of Rabindranath Tagore's poems.

C721 [A review of] *Gaṇeśa*. By Alice Getty. With an Introduction by A. Foucher. *Journal of the American Oriental Society*, New Haven, LVII. 4 (Dec. 1937) 428-9.

"If not absolutely exhaustive, this excellent volume assembles almost all that is known of the rather mysterious elephant-headed Indian deity" (p. 428).

C722 The Pilgrim's Way. *Journal of the Bihar and Orissa Research Society*, Patna, XXIII. 4 (Dec. 1937) [452]-471.

On the metaphysical implications of wayfaring, together with a discussion, and translation (by AKC), of a relevant passage in the *Aitareya Brāhmaṇa*, VII. 15. (This issue of the *Journal* is also called the "[Kashi Prasad] Jayaswal Commemoration Volume".) A separately paginated offprint seen (May 1991) in the Freer Gallery of Art Library, Washington, D.C. Reprinted in *What Is Civilisation? and Other Essays* ([1989])—A90—pp. [107]-114. AKC continues the subject of this article with "The Pilgrim's Way, a Buddhist Recension" in the issue for September 1938—C740.

C723 "Pantheism", Indian and Neo-Platonic. *Journal of Indian History*, Madras, XVI. 3 (Dec. 1937) [249]-252.

An elucidation of this term, together with a protest against its ascription by modern scholars to Indian and neo-Platonic philosophies. AKC intended this article to be read as a postscript to his "Vedic 'Monotheism'" in the issue for April 1936—C687. A slip containing corrigenda and addenda is inserted at p. [249]. Reprinted in a French translation as, "Du prétendu 'panthéisme', dans l'Inde et dans le néo-platonisme", in *Études Traditionnelles*, Paris, XLIII. 226 (Oct. 1938) [355]-359.

1938

C724 Tathāgata. *Bulletin of the School of Oriental Studies*, London, IX. 2 (1938) [331].

(In English.) On the Vedic origins of this Sanskrit word "and with reference to the Buddha *post adventum*", in connection with "Tathāgata and Tahāgaya", by E.J. Thomas, in the *Bulletin*, VIII. 2/3 (1935/37).

C725 The Philosophy of Mediaeval and Oriental Art. *Zalmoxis: Revue des Études Religieuses*, Paris & Bucharest, I. (1938 [*i.e.* Spring 1939?]) [20]-49.

Originally a lecture given by AKC at The Art Institute, Chicago, 4 January 1938, and at the Fogg Art Museum, Cambridge, Mass., 11 April. A comprehensive exposition of the traditional doctrine of art, relying "for greater convenience . . . chiefly upon mediaeval sources", e.g. St Thomas Aquinas, St Augustine, St Bonaventura, Eckhart, Dante, *et al.* "At every step . . . the principles of Mediaeval and Oriental art are identical" (p. [20]). This article was reprinted, in an amended form, and with addenda, in *Coomaraswamy 1: Selected Papers, Traditional Art and Symbolism* ([1977])—A82—pp. 43-70.

C726 Le Symbolisme de l'épée. *Études Traditionnelles*, Paris, XLIII. 217 (Jan. 1938) [11]-17.

An exposition of symbolic weapons, in particular the "derivation" of the sword from a "root" or archetype in lightning. By way of parallel citations, AKC attempts to demonstrate an immemorial and universal distribution of this symbolism. Reprinted, in English, with C732.

C727 Nirmāṇa-Kāya. *Journal of the Royal Asiatic Society*, London (Jan. 1938) [81]-84.

(In English.) Printed under the general heading: Miscellaneous Communications. On the Vedic prototypes of this expression (meaning "a body of artifice"), used in the concept of "the Buddha's iconometric manifestation in the world" (p. 84).

C728 Ethics and Dogma. [Letter]. *New English Weekly*, London, XII. 14 (13 Jan. 1938) 279.

Apropos of various articles in recent issues: on the need for a revival of Christian dogma. This letter was reprinted in *Selected Letters of Ananda K. Coomaraswamy* (1988)—A89—p. 275. The first of AKC's 38 contributions to this periodical; four letters from AKC to *The New English Weekly*, that were not used, are printed for the first time in *Selected Letters of Ananda K. Coomaraswamy*, pp. 106, 202, 394, 396.

C729 Sankaracharya: An Introduction to Vedanta [I]. *Hindu*, Madras (17 Jan. 1938) 6-7.

The first of two instalments. The text of AKC's lecture of this title delivered before the Phi Beta Kappa Iota Chapter of Massachusetts, at Radcliffe College, Cambridge, Mass., on 15 November 1937, and again on 20 November at Wheaton College, Norton, Mass. An exposition of the Vedanta of Śaṅkara, employing parallels drawn from the Christian tradition (chiefly from the sermons of Meister Eckhart). The two instalments were reprinted together, as "The Vedânta and Western Tradition", in *American Scholar*, New York, VIII. 2 (Spring/Apr. 1939) 223-47, and in *Coomaraswamy 2: Selected Papers, Metaphysics* ([1977])—A82—pp. 3-22. Three paragraphs were excerpted to form the "Preface" to *The Vedas: Essays in Translation and Exegesis* (1976)—A57b.

C730 Sankaracharya: An Introduction to Vedanta [II]. *Hindu*, Madras (24 Jan. 1938) 4-5.

C731 Mediaeval Aesthetic II. St. Thomas Aquinas on Dionysius, and a Note on the Relation of Beauty to Truth. *Art Bulletin*, New York, XX. 1 (Mar. 1938) 66-77.

"The first part . . . is a translation [by AKC] of St. Thomas Aquinas' own commentary on Dionysius, *De divinis nominibus*, cap. IV, lect. 5 . . . The second part takes up the scholastic thesis of the essentially intellectual quality of beauty, as being, not indeed logically the same thing as truth, but as being the means by which truth is made apparent as such" (p. 66). This second part of the article was reprinted, with the omission of the footnotes, as "Mediaeval Aesthetic. On the Relation of Beauty to Truth", in *Art Notes*, London, II. 4 (Mar./Apr. 1939) 55-7, and, with the footnotes restored, as Chapter V, "Beauty and Truth", of *Why Exhibit Works of Art?* (1943)—A67. The entire article was reprinted, but with the second part reduced and almost completely rewritten, combined with "Mediaeval Aesthetic I" (1935)—C669, as Chapter II of *Figures of Speech or Figures of Thought* (1946)—A71, and again in *Coomaraswamy 1: Selected Papers, Traditional Art and Symbolism* ([1977])—A82—pp. 189-228.

C732 Symbolism of the Dome. *Indian Historical Quarterly*, Calcutta, XIV. 1 (Mar. 1938) [1]-56, 1 text illus.

A detailed discussion of the principles of sacred architecture, in the course of which AKC explains the underlying theses of Indian domed constructions, taking into account formal and teleological correspondences between the dome, the human skull, the firmament, and the cosmic axis. "It is precisely in the notion of a vertical egress that we shall find an explanation of the symbolism of our domes" (p. 14). AKC also attempts to demonstrate the universality of the correlation of human constructions with supramundane prototypes, by citing parallels from the Greek, Roman, Norse, Christian, and Islamic traditions. An English translation of "Le Symbolisme de l'épée" (1938)—C726—is incorporated on pages 23-9. A list of corrigenda, printed in 89 lines, together with two postscripts, forming a four-page leaflet, was laid in a subsequent issue of *The Indian Historical Quarterly* or circulated privately by AKC, or both. The leaflet is preserved among The Ananda Coomaraswamy Papers in the Firestone Library at Princeton University, Princeton, New Jersey. This article was reprinted, incorporating roughly one quarter of the corrigenda (but omitting the two postscripts), and including additionally, in the form of an appendix, "Pali *Kaṇṇikā* = Circular Roof-Plate" (1930)—C584, in *Coomaraswamy 1: Selected Papers, Traditional Art and Symbolism* ([1977])—A82—pp. 415-64. The version printed in *The Indian Historical Quarterly* was published separately as *Symbolism of Indian Architecture* (1983)—A86. Further corrigenda is printed with "Some Pāli Words" (1939)—C760—p. 136, fn.1.

C733 Notes on the Kaṭha Upaniṣad . . . First Vallī. *New Indian Antiquary*, Bombay, I. 1 (Apr. 1938) [43]-56.

A paper in three instalments (a sequel to C675), comprising a discussion of "several crucial passages [that] appear to have been radically misunderstood even by Śaṅkara and *a fortiori* by modern translators" (p. [43]), with particular reference *passim* to *The Kaṭha Upaniṣad: An Introductory Study in the Hindu Doctrine of God and of Human Destiny*, by Joseph Nadin Rawson. AKC emphasizes that "Death . . . throughout the Brāhmaṇas and Upaniṣads, as also in [the Ṛgveda, is] one of the highest names of God" (p. [43]), and explains how in this story of Naciketas and Death, the former is the *śrāvaka* and *śiṣya*, and the latter the Guru. Recurrent terms and passages are adduced in other Hindu texts, as are parallels from Neo-Platonic, Hermetic, Christian, Islamic, and Buddhist tradition. The word *sṛṅkā* is treated to a lengthy discussion on pages 51-5.

C734 Uṣṇīṣa and Chatra: Turban and Umbrella. *Poona Orientalist*, Poona, India, III. 1 (Apr. 1938) 1-19.

On the general character, iconographic development, and symbolism of these insignia of royal power, as they are associated with the Buddha image, and analogically with the sun, the firmament, and the Axis of the Universe. "What has been said about umbrellas will apply for the most part also to canopies and baldachins, and partly to arches, especially *arcs de triomphe*" (p.18).

C735 The Yakṣa of the Vedas and Upaniṣads. *Quarterly Journal of the Mythic Society*, Bangalore, XXVIII. 4 (Apr. 1938) [231]-240.

By way of an examination of the scriptural tradition, AKC attempts to demonstrate "that *yakṣa* is virtually synonymous, or rather coincident in reference with Brahman, Ātman, Puruṣa, Mṛtyu, Agni, Prajāpati, Manas, etc., and designates that single spiritual principle which assumes a multiplicity and diversity of aspects by its immanence in all things" (p. 239). Reprinted, in a revised form, in *Yakṣas: Essays in the Water Cosmology* (1993)—A51b—pp. [9]-24.

C736 La Voie lactée. *Études Traditionnelles*, Paris, XLIII. 221 (May 1938) [175]-176.

A sequel to "The Virgin Suckling St. Bernard" (1937)—C707. AKC adduces an analogous motif of "adoption by suckling" in the Greek legend of the origin of the Milky Way, with reference to "*The Origin of the Milky Way* in The National Gallery", by Erna Mandowsky, in *Burlington Magazine*, London, for February 1938.

C737 Notes on the Kaṭha Upaniṣad . . . Second [and Third] Vallī. *New Indian Antiquary*, Bombay, I. 2 (May 1938) [83]-108.

The second of three instalments. Incorporating on pages 93-4 a brief digression on "the unreliability of all conceptions of reality based on sense-perception".

C738 Notes on the Kaṭha Upaniṣad . . . Fourth [Fifth, and Sixth] Vallī. *New Indian Antiquary*, Bombay, I. 3 (June 1938) [199]-213.

The last of three instalments. Incorporating brief digressions on the traditional doctrines of "seeing", "vision", or "perception", pages [199]-201, and of "light", pages 208-9.

C739 The Two Reliefs from Bharhut in the Freer Gallery. *Journal of the Indian Society of Oriental Art*, Calcutta, VI. (June/Dec. 1938) [149]-162, 2 pls. (numbered: XXXIV-XXXV).

In the main, on the significance of the form of the stūpa (with reference to its representation in a relief on a railing cross-bar), with an attempt to demonstrate the equivalence of dome to umbrella and of both to cranium. AKC says of the stūpa, that in representing the "complete extinction" of the Wake, it is thus a representation of the "whole" Buddha cosmic and supra-cosmic, immanent and transcendent. AKC also includes some general observations (pp. 159-60) on the nature of "the simultaneously aesthetic and intellectual experience" to be obtained from works of art. Concerning the other Bharhut relief, AKC discusses, among other things, evidence which indicates that this is not, as has been supposed, a doublet of the "Pasenajit Pillar". This issue of the *Journal* is dedicated to the memory of the Bengali painter Gaganendranath Tagore, 1867-1938.

C740 The Pilgrim's Way, a Buddhist Recension. *Journal of the Bihar and Orissa Research Society*, Patna, XXIV. 3 (Sept. 1938) [118]-119.

Further to "The Pilgrim's Way", printed in the issue for December 1937—C722. This article was reprinted (as "Addendum" to "The Pilgrim's Way") in *What Is Civilisation? and Other Essays* ([1989])—A90—pp. 115, 120 (note 22).

C741 The Inverted Tree. *Quarterly Journal of the Mythic Society*, Bangalore, XXIX. 2 (Oct. 1938) [111]-149.

On the traditional doctrine of an arborescent Axis of the Universe. AKC attempts to demonstrate the consistency and meaning of the symbolism of the Tree of Life, by employing documentation culled from various Indian scriptural texts, as well as from Dante, the *Zohar*, and the apocryphal *Acts of Peter*. An errata slip, containing two items printed in four lines, is inserted at page [111]. A separately paginated offprint seen (April 1973) in the Hettiaratchi Collection, at the University of Sri Lanka, Peradeniya. This article was reprinted, incorporating corrigenda and addenda, in *Coomaraswamy 1: Selected Papers, Traditional Art and Symbolism* ([1977])—A82—pp. 376-404, and again, in a French translation (by Gérard Leconte), separately as *L'Arbre inversé* (Milan: Archè, 1984)—A87.

C742 Note on a Review by Richard Florsheim of *Is Art a Superstition or a Way of Life?* by Ananda K. Coomaraswamy . . . *Art Bulletin*, New York, XX. 4 (Dec. 1938) [443].

AKC's explanation of why his criticism of current artistic doctrine and of modern manufacture should not be seen as medievalist. He says he is not advocating a return to a past order of things but rather "a return to first principles". Florsheim's review was printed in the issue for March. This note was reprinted as "Postscript" to Chapter III of *Why Exhibit Works of Art?* (1943)—A67, and in *Selected Letters of Ananda K. Coomaraswamy* (1988)—A89—pp. 47-8.

C743 [A review of] *What Was the Original Gospel in Buddhism?* By Mrs. [C.A.F.] Rhys Davids. *Journal of the American Oriental Society*, New Haven, LVIII. 4 (Dec. 1938) 679-86.

"This volume conveniently summarizes the conclusions Mrs. Rhys Davids has reached as to the nature of the 'original' Buddhist teaching . . . it is largely the result of her work that Buddhism is now seen to have been far less heterodox than was once thought" (p. 679). In the course of this review AKC discusses *inter alia* the *anattā* doctrine (the Buddha's *via negativa*), argues from scriptural evidence that "the two selves" are clearly distinguished in Buddhism, examines the notion of "reincarnation", and concludes with some remarks on the *philosophia perennis*. This review was reprinted, in a French translation, with the title "Le Bouddhisme originel", in *Études Traditionnelles*, Paris, XLIV. 233 (May 1939) [162]-174. See also C751, 765.

1939

C744 Svayamātṛṇṇā: Janua Coeli. *Zalmoxis: Revue des Études Religieuses*, Paris & Bucharest, II. 1 (1939) [3]-51, VII numbered pls.

(In English.) A paper read by AKC at the 150th Meeting of the American Oriental Society held at Dropsie College, Philadelphia, 20 April 1938. An abstract is printed in the *Journal of the American Oriental Society*, New Haven, LVIII. (1938) 534. On solar symbolism, comprising "a fairly complete account of the Indian doctrine of the Sundoor at World's End [and calling attention] to the universality of the doctrine as it is similarly developed in the Chinese, Siberian, Egyptian and Hebrew traditions (p. 11). AKC explicates the symbolism of the superstructure of the Vedic altar, with particular reference to the three perforated bricks (*svayamātṛṇṇā*) which constitute one of its essential parts. On page 38 AKC announces, "we propose to treat in detail the doctrine of the 'Bridge' upon another occasion". While AKC did not, however, publish an essay on this motif, he did assist Doña Luisa (Mrs A.K.) Coomaraswamy in the preparation of her paper "The Perilous Bridge of Welfare", that was printed in the *Harvard Journal of Asiatic Studies*, Cambridge, Mass., VIII. 2 (Aug. 1944) 196-213. The present paper was reprinted, incorporating corrigenda and addenda, and retaining the illustrations, in *Coomaraswamy 1: Selected Papers, Traditional Art and Symbolism* ([1977])—A82—pp. 465-520. A separately paginated offprint seen (April 1991) in the collection of Dr Rama P. Coomaraswamy, Greenwich, Conn.

C745 Le Corps parsemé d'yeux. *Zalmoxis: Revue des Études Religieuses*, Paris & Bucharest, II. 1 (1939) [153]-155.

(In English.) Printed under the general heading: Mélanges. AKC discusses this symbolism of the divine omniscience and omnipresence, its employment in the representation of solar deities and other divine forms in the Vedic and Christian traditions, and its connection with "the whole doctrine of the Spirit and of Light" (p. [153]); with reference to an article of this title, by Raffaele Pettazzoni, in *Zalmoxis*, I. (1938). AKC concludes with a brief discussion of the traditional theory of vision. This article was reprinted, with addenda, and with the addition of a plate, in *Coomaraswamy 1: Selected Papers, Traditional Art and Symbolism* ([1977])—A82—pp. 371-5.

C746 [A review of] "Documents recueillis aux Indes sur les 'Yoguis' par l'enregistrement simultané du pouls, de la respiration et de l'électrocardiogramme", by Charles Laubry and Thérèse Brosse, in *Presse Médicale*, Paris, 83 (14 Oct. 1936). *Études Traditionnelles*, Paris, XLIV. 229 (Jan. 1939) 39.

AKC questions the authors' notion of a Western, therapeutic application of yogic practices.

C747 Eckstein. *Speculum*, Cambridge, Mass., XIV. 1 (Jan. 1939) 66-72.

On the Biblical expression that Christ "is become the head of the corner", and discussing other allusions to Christ as "corner-stone" and "diamond", and how the German word *eckstein* combines both these allusions, with reference to *Consider the Lilies How They*

Grow: An Interpretation of the Symbolism of Pennsylvania German Art, by John Joseph Stoudt. AKC argues by recourse to etymology and by an examination of architectural symbolism from Egyptian, Hebrew, and Indian traditions, that "corner-stone" should, in order to bring out its true meaning, be rendered as "summit-" or "key-stone". AKC also investigates "that . . . complex of ideas in which . . . notions of adamantine quality and of polar or solar axis of the universe are inseparably connected" (p. 71). This article was reprinted in *What Is Civilisation? and Other Essays* ([1989])—A90—pp. [168]-177. A French translation, by Pierre Dumas (who adds a prefatory note), is printed in *Études Traditionnelles*, Paris, LXXV. 441 (Jan./Feb. 1974) 3-15. See also "La Pierre angulaire", by René Guénon, in *Études Traditionnelles*, XLV. 244 (Apr. 1940) [157]-164, and continued in 245 (May 1940) [202]-210, in which article Guénon makes use of previously unpublished addenda to "Eckstein" supplied him by AKC.

C748 Re-incarnation. [Letter]. *New English Weekly*, London, XIV. 12[/13] (5 Jan. 1939) 195.

That "'re-incarnation' has not been taught in India". AKC concludes by suggesting to the editor of *The New English Weekly* that he "pay some attention to [René] Guénon (also [Albert] Gleizes)".

C749 "Art Is Expression". [Letter]. *Nation*, New York, CXLVIII. 7 (11 Feb. 1939) 187.

Dated Boston, 3 Feb. On the proposition that art is primarily the expression of emotion, in connection with a review by Eliseo Vivas of *The Principles of Art*, by R.G. Collingwood, in the issue for 21 January. This letter was reprinted, with an amendment to AKC's quotation from Quintilian, in *Selected Letters of Ananda K. Coomaraswamy* (1988)—A89—pp. 381-2, but described there erroneously as (1) addressed to the editor of *The New English Weekly*, London, and (2) dated 3 February 1941.

C750 "Mahâtmâ". *Études Traditionnelles*, Paris, XLIV. 231 (Mar. 1939) [82]-86.

(In French.) On this word's metaphysical designation: an explication of its several meanings historically, and its application to Mohandas Karamchand Gandhi. Reprinted, in English, in *Calcutta Review*, Calcutta, LXXI. 1 (Apr. 1939) [1]-4, and again in *What Is Civilisation? and Other Essays* ([1989])—A90—pp. [90]-93. An extensively revised, and slightly reduced, version of this article is printed (in English) in *Mahatma Gandhi: Essays and Reflections on His Life and Work*, edited by S. Radhakrishnan (1939)—B48.

C751 Communication from Mrs. Rhys Davids. [Letter]. *Journal of the American Oriental Society*, New Haven, LIX. 1 (Mar. 1939) 110-11.

Under the general heading: Brief Communications. A rejoinder from AKC is printed under a letter from C.A.F. Rhys Davids, who points out that AKC has misquoted her in his review of *What Was the Original Gospel in Buddhism?* in the issue for December 1938—C743. An excerpt from AKC's letter was reprinted in *Selected Letters of Ananda K. Coomaraswamy* (1988)—A89—pp. 136-7.

C752 Le Bouddhisme originel. *Études Traditionnelles*, Paris, XLIV. 233 (May 1939) [162]-174.

A reprint in French of AKC's review of *What Was the Original Gospel in Buddhism?*, by C.A.F. Rhys Davids, in *Journal of the American Oriental Society*, New Haven, for December 1938—C743.

C753 [Letter on abstract art]. *Art Notes*, London, II. 5/6 (May/Aug. 1939) 87.

Printed under the general heading: Letters to the Editor. Dated Boston, Mass., 26 Mar. A reply to an editorial, "Is Abstract Art Wrong?", in the issue for March/April, with a rejoinder from the editor appended. AKC's letter (only) was reprinted, omitting a passage from the fourth paragraph, and with other changes, and erroneously described as a contribution to *Art News* (New York), in *Selected Letters of Ananda K. Coomaraswamy* (1988)—A89—pp. 378-80.

C754 First Understand Your Own Religion. [Letter]. *New English Weekly*, London, XV. 3 [*i.e.* 4] (11 May 1939) 67.

On sexual symbolism in Christianity and Hinduism, with reference to a review by Ronald Duncan of *The True India*, by C.F. Andrews, in the issue for 30 March. This letter was reprinted in *Selected Letters of Ananda K. Coomaraswamy* (1988)—A89—pp. 361-2.

C755 [A review of] *Shaker Furniture*. By Edward Deming Andrews and Faith Andrews; *Consider the Lilies How They Grow; an Interpretation of the Symbolism of Pennsylvania German Art*. By John Joseph Stoudt; *Handicrafts of the Southern Highlands*. By Allen H. Eaton; *Art and Life in New Guinea*. By Raymond Firth; *L'Art des Iles Marquises*. By Willowdean C. Handy; *The Art of Enjoying Art*. By A. Philip MacMahon. *Art Bulletin*, New York, XXI. 2 (June 1939) 200-6.

AKC's review of *Shaker Furniture* was reprinted as Chapter VI of *Figures of Speech or Figures of Thought* (1946)—A71, and, as "Shaker Furniture", in *Good Work*, Cambridge, Mass., XXVIII. 3 (Summer 1965) 69-71, and again with this title, in *Coomaraswamy 1: Selected Papers, Traditional Art and Symbolism* ([1977])—A82—pp. 255-9, 1 pl. (facing p. 255). The reviews of *Art and Life in New Guinea* and *L'Art des Iles Marquises* were reprinted together to form Chapter XVI, "Notes on 'Savage' Art", of *Figures of Speech or Figures of Thought* (1946)—A71.

C756 An Indian Ivory. *Bulletin of the Museum of Fine Arts*, Boston, XXXVII. 221 (June 1939) 51, 1 text illus.

On the Museum's recent acquisition of a late 18th century carved panel of Punjabi origin, depicting an idealized likeness of a woman, probably a princess.

C757 The Traditional Conception of Ideal Portraiture. *Journal of the Indian Society of Oriental Art*, Calcutta, VII. (June/Dec. 1939) [74]-82.

On the theory and practice in Asia and in medieval Europe of the portrayal of the "type", or "spiritual-essence", of a man, rather than a likeness based on the individual peculiarities of his outer appearance. This article was reprinted, slightly expanded and revised, and with the quotations in English translation from Louis Bréhier's *L'Art Chrétien* restored to their original French, in *Twice A Year*, New York, III/IV. (Fall-Winter 1939/Spring-Summer 1940) 244-52, and, with further slight expansions and the addition of a plate, as Chapter VII of *Why Exhibit Works of Art?* (1943)—A67. Also reprinted, in a reduced form, as "The Interior Image", in *Parabola*, New York, XI. 2 (May 1986) 14-19, 2 text illus.

C758 L'Ordination bouddhique est-elle une initiation? *Études Traditionnelles*, Paris, XLIV. 235 (July 1939) [242]-248.

A translation into French of the article s.v. *dikkhita* in "Some Pāli Words" (1939)—C760—pp. 144-9.

C759 Art and Principles. *Examiner*, Bethlehem, Conn., II. 3 (Summer [*i.e.* July] 1939) 273-4.

AKC's is the last of four replies printed under the general heading "Art, Reality, and Romanticism" (pp. 266-83), in response to a review by E.P. Richardson, entitled "The Noble Savage Redivivus", of *Work*, by Ade de Bethune, *Pattern* and *Thoughts and Things*, by Graham Carey, *Is Art a Superstition, or a Way of Life?*, by Ananda K. Coomaraswamy—A63, and *Work and Culture*, by Eric Gill, in the issue for Spring 1939. The other replies are from John Howard Benson and the first two authors named: a rejoinder from Richardson follows (pp. 274-83). A letter from Eric Gill, commenting on the discussion, is printed in the issue for Autumn 1939, pp. 399-402. See also E19.

C760 Some Pāli Words. *Harvard Journal of Asiatic Studies*, Cambridge, Mass., IV. 2 (July 1939) 116-90.

A discussion of 52 Pāli words, in the form of separate articles, arranged according to the Devanāgarī alphabet, "with particular reference to their treatment in the P[āli] T[ext] S[ociety's Pāli-English] Dictionary and to their translation in the now completed Nikāya volumes of the PTS . . .The discussions of *Attha* (*artha*), *Rasa*, *Vyañjana* and *Sahājanetta* amount to a first essay in the study of Buddhist rhetoric, and should be read together"

(p. 116). "I have long had in mind to compile a vocabulary of the Sanskrit and Pāli terminology of archery" (p. 140); there is however no evidence that AKC ever published this projected glossary. Of the more extended, or more substantial, discussions contained in this paper, other than those already mentioned above, the following may be noted: s.v. *jhāna, samādhi* (pp. 138-9), s.v. *dikkhita* (pp. 144-9, on the question of whether Buddhist ordination can be equated with initiation), s.v. *nibbāyati, nibbāna* (pp. 156-63), s.v. *pāsa* (pp. 166-7, on "the general symbolic equivalence of the eye of the needle and loop of the noose"), s.v. *samudda* (pp. 184-8, on symbolism relating to the Pilgrim's "Way", and "Wayfaring"), and s.v. *suññatā* (pp. 189-90). The articles s.v. *dikkhita* and s.v. *nibbāyati, nibbāna* were reprinted separately—C758, 773. A reply to this article from C.A.F. Rhys Davids was printed, under the general heading "Brief Notes", in the *Harvard Journal of Asiatic Studies*, IV. 3/4 (Dec. 1939) 373-4, and corrigenda from AKC is also printed in that same issue on page 403. The entire article was reprinted, incorporating the corrigenda, and after editorial scrutiny from Isaline Blew Horner, in *Coomaraswamy 2: Selected Papers, Metaphysics* ([1977])—A82—pp. 264-329.

C761 De la "Mentalité primitive". *Études Traditionnelles*, Paris, XLIV. 236/237/238 (Aug./Sept./Oct. 1939) [277]-300, 1 pl. (facing p. 292).

A consideration of the type of mentality that manifests itself in traditional societies, and of its treatment by anthropologists; with critical reference to Lucien Lévy-Bruhl's *La Mentalité primitive* and *L'Expérience mystique et les symboles chez les primitifs*, and also to R.R. Schmidt's *Dawn of the Human Mind.* Includes notes on the symbolism of the "safety-pin", and on the doctrine of a "spiritual paternity". This article was reprinted, in English, as "Primitive Mentality", in *Quarterly Journal of the Mythic Society*, Bangalore, XXXI. 2 (Oct. 1940) [69]-91, 1 pl. (a separately paginated offprint seen (May 1991) in the Freer Gallery of Art Library, Washington D.C.), and, in a revised and expanded form, as Chapter XV of *Figures of Speech or Figures of Thought* (1946)—A71, and again, in *Coomaraswamy 1: Selected Papers, Traditional Art and Symbolism* ([1977])—A82—pp. 286-307, 1 pl.

C762 Abhilaṣitārthacintāmaṇi and Śilparatna. *New Indian Antiquary*, Bombay, II. 6 (Sept. 1939) [420].

Printed under the general heading: Miscellanea. A brief note, with reference to statements by G.H. Khare and V. Raghavan in the issue for March. AKC points out that in his "The Technique and Theory of Indian Painting" (1934)—C663—he has called attention to Someśvara's work as the basis of Śrī Kumāra's, and also published there a new translation of Someśvara (on painting).

C763 Ornament. *Art Bulletin*, New York, XXI. 4 (Dec. 1939) [375]-382.

A detailed etymological and semantic analysis of the Sanskrit, Latin, Greek, Chinese, and English words that have been used to express the notion of an ornamentation or decoration; arguing that ornament had an altogether other value than that ascribed to it nowadays. This article "was suggested by and makes considerable use of" the work of Jan Gonda (p. 376). Reprinted as Chapter III of *Figures of Speech or Figures of Thought* (1946)—A71, and, incorporating addenda, in *Coomaraswamy 1: Selected Papers, Traditional Art and Symbolism* ([1977])—A82—pp. 241-53. Also reprinted, reduced (by Ade Bethune), in *Christian Social Art Quarterly*, Burlington, Vt., IV. 2 (Easter 1941) 19-23.

C764 Note on the Iconography of the Cock on the Column. *Art Bulletin*, New York, XXI. 4 (Dec. 1939) 402.

On the cock as a solar symbol, and the motif's occurrence in India and elsewhere, in connection with "The Iconography of the Cock on the Column", by S.A. Callison, in the issue for June.

C765 The Reinterpretation of Buddhism. *New Indian Antiquary*, Bombay, II. 9 (Dec. 1939) [575]-590.

An examination of the work of C.A.F. Rhys Davids, with reference to her *What Was the Original Gospel in Buddhism?*, *To Become or Not to Become*, and *A Manual of Buddhism*, and giving particular attention to her treatment of the *ātman* problem. An expansion of the discussion contained in AKC's review of *What Was the Original Gospel in Buddhism?* in *Journal of the American Oriental Society*, New Haven, for December 1938—C743.

C766 The Ivory Shelter. [Letter]. *New English Weekly*, London, XVI. 9 (14 Dec. 1939) 139.

On the concept of vocation as a principle of the traditional social order, in connection with an article with this title by Maurice B. Reckitt in the issue for 2 November. Reprinted in *Selected Letters of Ananda K. Coomaraswamy* (1988)—A89—pp. 302-3.

1940

C767 [A review of] *Peaks and Lamas* by Marco Pallis. *Asia*, New York, XL. 2 (Feb. 1940) 111.

Printed under the general heading: Asia Book-Shelf. "This is one of those very rare books which it is almost impossible to overpraise". In a letter to George Sarton, 13 August 1939, AKC refers to Pallis's book "as a model of *method* [AKC's emphasis] to be followed in scientific investigations that require intimate relations with alien peoples. I remark especially the concept of translation as interpreted on pp. 80-81" (*Selected Letters of Ananda K. Coomaraswamy* (1988)—A89—p. 41). This review was reprinted, in French, with the omission of the last two paragraphs, in *Études Traditionnelles*, Paris, XLV. 246 (June 1940) [258].

C768 [Prefatory note to "Man and Woman" by Julius Evola]. *Visva-Bharati Quarterly*, Santiniketan, Bengal, N.S. V. 4 (Feb./Apr. 1940) [305]-306.

A brief critical discussion by AKC of Evola's thesis, precedes a translation by Doña Luisa (Mrs A.K.) Coomaraswamy (signing herself "Zlata Llamas Coomaraswamy") of Chapter I, "Uomo e Donna", of *Rivolta contra il mondo moderno*, by Julius Evola. The translation itself, pp. 306-19, which incorporates *passim* additional footnotes signed: (Tr.), was almost certainly undertaken in collaboration with AKC. "Commended by Dr. A.K. Coomaraswamy, we gladly introduce the above paper to our readers . . ." (*note by the Editor*, p. 306, who nevertheless declines to endorse Evola's thesis).

C769 [A review of] Carl Hentze, *Frühchinesische Bronzen und Kulturdarstellungen* [and] A. Salmony, *Carved Jade of Ancient China. Art Bulletin*, New York, XXII. 1 (Mar. 1940) 52-5.

In the course of this review, AKC discusses (1) the symbolism of the T'ao-t'ieh mask, i.e. the daimon-mask, "cognate and equivalent of the Indian *kīrti-mukha* ('glory-face') or *siṁha-mukha* ('lion-face') which is really the full face of a *makara*, the *kāla-makara* of Java" (p. 52), (2) the serrate, or toothed motif (which AKC connects with the "jaws of death"), (3) symbolic weapons, and (4) annular symbolism. AKC also adds some general observations on what in his view are the shortcomings of modern scholarship in the field of comparative religion.

C770 The Sun-Kiss. *Journal of the American Oriental Society*, New Haven, LX. 1 (Mar. 1940) 46-67.

On the essential character and archetypal significance of the Sun-kiss or Kiss of Life, where the Sun is seen as the Life or Spiritual-essence of all things. AKC infers a world-wide distribution of similar "kisses" by citing parallels from Indian and North American Indian myth and ritual. A discussion of the symbolism of the "king-post" is incorporated, pp. 58-60. This article was reprinted, in French, in two parts, as "Le Baiser du Soleil", in *Études Traditionnelles*, Paris, XLVII. 253 (Aug. 1946) [303]-311, and 254 (Sept. 1946) [351]-365.

C771 Eastern Words on Western Worries. [Letter]. *New English Weekly*, London, XVI. 23 (28 Mar. 1940) 344.

On (1) minding one's own business, with reference to "Mysticism: The Yellow Peril", by Lawrence Durrell, in the issue for 25 January, and (2) suggesting to T.S. Eliot that he employ "Anti-Christian" to express the antithesis of Christian. This letter was reprinted in *Selected Letters of Ananda K. Coomaraswamy* (1988)—A89—pp. 59-61.

C772 An Indian Enamel. *Bulletin of the Museum of Fine Arts*,

Boston, XXXVIII. 226 (Apr. 1940) 24-8, 10 text illus. (one is printed on the front cover of this issue, i.e. p. [23]).

On the Museum's recent acquisition of a late 16th century pendant (jewelled on the obverse) of Rājputāna origin, illustrating the "Ten Avatārs of Viṣṇu". AKC discusses (1) the Indian technique of inlaying jewels on a metal ground, (2) the champlevé technique, and concludes with an interpretation of the inconography of this Vaiṣṇava theme.

C773 Nirvâna, Nibbâna. *Études Traditionnelles*, Paris, XLV. 244 (Apr. 1940) [139]-147.

(In French.) A translation of the article s.v. *nibbāyati, nibbāna* in "Some Pāli Words" (1939)—C760—pp. 156-63. "Notre objet principal est cependant de bien marquer que *nibbâna*, et *a fortiori parinibbâna*, est toujours une mort, c'est-à-dire une transformation, et d'expliquer en quel sens on peut dire que la mort est un *summum bonum*, qu'elle coincide avec une régénération et qu'elle est un pouvoir de résurrection" (p. 142).

C774 Ākiṁcañña: Self-Naughting. *New Indian Antiquary*, Bombay, III.1 (Apr. 1940) [1]-16.

An exposition of the "metaphysical doctrine of the transcending of individuation . . . mainly based, as the title implies, on Christian and Buddhist sources" (pp. [1], 7). This article was reprinted, incorporating addenda, in *Coomaraswamy 2: Selected Papers, Metaphysics* ([1977])—A82—pp. 88-106. The final "a" in the first word of the title takes a macron; this was omitted in error by the *New Indian Antiquary*; the error is repeated in the 1977 reprinting.

C775 "Peach Path". [Letter]. *New English Weekly*, London, XVII. 1 (25 Apr. 1940) 16.

On the traditional theory of the relationship of Church and State, with reference to a review by Hugh Gordon Porteus of a book with this title by Ching-ch'iu Kuo. AKC suggests to Porteus that he read Julius Evola's *Rivolta contra il mondo moderno*. This letter was reprinted in *Selected Letters of Ananda K. Coomaraswamy* (1988)—A89—p. 364.

C776 True Philosophy of Art. [Letter]. *New English Weekly*, London, XVII. 19 (29 Aug. 1940) 216.

A reply to a review by Herbert Read of *The Christian and Oriental or True Philosophy of Art* (1939)—A65—in the issue for 11 July. This letter was reprinted in *Selected Letters of Ananda K. Coomaraswamy* (1988)—A89—pp. 389-91, where it is misdated 3 October 1940.

C777 The Philosophy of Art. [Letter]. *New English Weekly*, London, XVII. 24 (3 Oct. 1940) 272.

Replying to a further comment from Herbert Read in the issue for 8 August on *The Christian and Oriental or True Philosophy of Art* (1939)—A65. AKC takes exception to Read's notion of "beauty". This letter was reprinted in *Selected Letters of Ananda K. Coomaraswamy* (1988)—A89—p. 392.

1941

C778 Four Comments. [Letter]. *New English Weekly*, London, XVIII. 21 (13 Mar. 1941) 247-8.

Apropos of matters touched on in recent issues: (1) the clergy and war, with reference to a statement by the Bishop of Ely in the issue for 19 December 1940, (2) the traditional doctrine of art and manufacture, with reference to a remark by Herbert Read in the issue for 16 January, (3) the traditional theory of government, with reference to an editorial of 23 January, and (4) the relations between England and India. The first three comments (only) were reprinted in *Selected Letters of Ananda K. Coomaraswamy* (1988)—A89—pp. 57, 303 (repeated on p. 399), and 319, respectively.

C779 [A review of] *A Pillared Hall from [a Temple at] Madura [India, in the Philadelphia Museum of Art]*, by W. Norman Brown. *American Journal of Archaeology*, New York, Second Series, XLV. 2 (Apr./June 1941) 322.

"Professor Brown's handbook is an admirable piece of work."

C780 [Letter]. *Art Bulletin*, New York, XXIII. 2 (June 1941) [173].

A critical examination of Meyer Schapiro's use of the word "style" in his review of *A Survey of Persian Art*, edited by Arthur Upham Pope, in the March issue. A rejoinder from Schapiro is printed on the same page. AKC's letter (only) was reprinted in *Selected Letters of Ananda K. Coomaraswamy* (1988)—A89—pp. 278-80.

C781 *Līlā. Journal of the American Oriental Society*, New Haven, LXI. 2 (June 1941) 98-101.

On this Sanskrit term with reference to "the divine manifestation and activity thought of as a 'sport', 'playing', or 'dalliance'" (p. 98), and further, that the "play" of a flame or vibrant light is an adequate symbol of the manifestation of the Spirit, with an attempt to demonstrate the universality of these notions by adducing parallels from the Hebrew, Indian, Greek, and Christian traditions. A "Correction" is printed in the issue for September, page 194. AKC continues the subject of this article in "Play and Seriousness" (1942)—C798. Reprinted, incorporating extensive addenda (but omitting the corrigendum), in

Coomaraswamy 2: Selected Papers, Metaphysics ([1977])—A82—pp. 148-55. A French translation (by Gérard Leconte) is printed in *Études Traditionnelles*, Paris, LXXVI. 447 (Jan./Feb./Mar. 1975) 13-21. A Spanish translation (by Agustin Lopez) is printed in *Axis Mundi*, Arenas de San Pedro, 7 (Spring 1996) 69-76.

C782 Religion, Myth and Reality. [Letter]. *New English Weekly*, London, XIX. 13 (17 July 1941) 135-6.

AKC's answer to the euhemerists, with reference to a letter by W.S. Ferrie in the issue for 22 May. Reprinted in *Selected Letters of Ananda K. Coomaraswamy* (1988)—A89—pp. 420-1.

C783 An Ivory Casket from Southern India. *Art Bulletin*, New York, XXIII. 3 (Sept. 1941) [207]-212, 1 pl. (facing p. [207]).

On the iconography of Śiva's dance in the Devadāruvana, as represented on the panels of a 17th century casket.

C784 Why Exhibit Works of Art? *Journal of Aesthetics and Art Criticism*, New York, I. 2/3 (Fall 1941) 27-41.

The text of an address delivered as part of a symposium, "The Art Museum in a Democracy", at the 36th Annual Meeting of the American Association of Museums at Columbus, Ohio, on 15 May, and also at Newport, R.I., in October. On the idea of the museum militant: that the art museum should "offer an education in agreement with the innermost nature and eloquence of the exhibits themselves, [and] that this will not be an education in sensibility, but an education in philosophy, in Plato's and Aristotle's sense of the word . . . nothing will have been accomplished unless men's lives are affected and their values changed by what we have to show . . . It may be that the understanding of the ancient works of art and of the conditions under which they were produced will undermine our loyalty to contemporary methods of manufacture . . . all education implies revaluation" (pp. 39-40). Incorporating a résumé of the traditional doctrine of art, mainly with reference to the writings of Plato, and including a discussion of the ontological significance of the terms "aesthetic", "form", "art", "ornament", "inspiration", and "nature". This address was reprinted, in two parts, in *Blackfriars*, Oxford, XXIII. 270 (Sept. 1942) 358-63, and 271 (Oct. 1942) 382-6, and, reduced, in *Catholic Art Quarterly*, Collegeville, Minnesota, VI. 3 (Pentecost 1943)13-17, in full as Chapter I of *Why Exhibit Works of Art?* (1943)—A67, and again in full in *Catholic Art Quarterly*, XVIII. 4 (Michaelmas 1955) 116-23, and in *Studies in Comparative Religion*, Bedfont, Middx., V. 3 (Summer 1971) 173-83. Also reprinted, in a French translation, as "Pourquoi exposer des oeuvres d'art?", in *Études Traditionnelles*, Paris, LII. 296 (Dec. 1951) [361]-377.

C785 The "E" at Delphi. *Review of Religion*, New York, VI. 1 (Nov. 1941) [18]-19.

A note on the injunction to "Know thyself", with reference to Plutarch's possible explanations. AKC connects the inscription at the temple of Apollo with rites of initiation, and cites parallels to this in the Upaniṣads, Plato, Christian scripture, and Jalāl al-Dīn Rūmī. This article was reprinted, incorporating addenda, in *Coomaraswamy 2: Selected Papers, Metaphysics* ([1977])—A82—pp. 43-5.

C786 The Nature of Myth. [Letter]. *New English Weekly*, London, XX. 5 (20 Nov. 1941) 44.

Calling attention to *Das verlorene Paradies*, by Edgar Dacqué, and reproducing an abstract of this by P.L. Krieger from *Philosophic Abstracts*, New York (Fall 1941). This letter was reprinted in *Selected Letters of Ananda K. Coomaraswamy* (1988)—A89—pp. 421-2. (AKC refers again to Dacqué's book in *Figures of Speech or Figures of Thought* (1946)—A71—p. 122, and in "Does 'Socrates Is Old' Imply that 'Socrates Is'?", *Coomaraswamy 2: Selected Papers, Metaphysics* ([1977])—A82—p. 417.)

C787 [A review of] G.H. Hardy, *A Mathematician's Apology. Art Bulletin*, New York, XXIII. 4 (Dec. 1941) 339.

Chiefly a consideration of Hardy's assertion that "the mathematician's patterns, like the painter's or the poet's, must be beautiful". This review was reprinted as Chapter IX of *Why Exhibit Works of Art?* (1943)—A67.

1942

C787a Measures of Fire. *O Instituto*, Coimbra, Portugal, C. (1942) [386]-395.

Dated Boston, July 1941. On the Indian, and universal, doctrine of fire as the identity of all things, with special reference to *Fire in the Cosmological Speculations of Heracleitus*, by William C. Kirk. This article was reprinted, incorporating addenda, in *Coomaraswamy 2: Selected Papers, Metaphysics,* edited by Roger Lipsey ([1977])—A82—pp. 159-65.

C788 Eastern Religions and Western Thought. *Review of Religion*, New York, VI. 2 (Jan. 1942) [129]-145.

A review of *Eastern Religions and Western Thought*, by S. Radhakrishnan. AKC imputes to Radhakrishnan an "essentially . . . European rather than an Indian mentality . . .[he would not] recognize the deduction that a single page of a *Purāṇa* is worth all the writings of [Rabindranath] Tagore . . . It seems to us that Radhakrishnan has forgotten what it is to be a Hindu, and has become an 'Orientalist'" (pp. 134-5, 140). AKC examines *inter alia* Radhakrishnan's treatment of such subjects as "reincarnation", "caste", "vocation", the doctrine of "the two selves", "*māyā*", and "tolerance", rejecting much that he has to say on the grounds that he ignores Hindu doctrine and instead bases his exposition on modern Western philosophical, historical, and sociological theory. AKC stresses throughout the accord which exists between the many forms of tradition, East and West, and how the texts of any one tradition can be used in the exegesis of those of another independently of time or place. This review was originally submitted to *Isis*, but the German invasion of Belgium (10 May 1940) prevented it being published in that periodical.

C789 Ātmayajña: Self-Sacrifice. *Harvard Journal of Asiatic Studies*, Cambridge, Mass., VI. 3/4 (Feb. 1942) 358-98.

An examination of the Vedic rites of sacrifice: "here we have . . . proposed to emphasize that the Dragon, or Giant—by whatever name, whether we call him Ahi, Vṛtra, Soma, Prajāpati or Puruṣa, or Osiris or Dionysos or Ymir—is always himself the Sacrifice, the sacrificial victim, and that the sacrificer, whether divine or human, is always himself this victim, or else has made no real sacrifice" (p. 387). Footnotes 33 and 34 discuss the symbolism of "mountains" and "caverns", "ingestion" ("swallowing" or "being swallowed up"), and "buried treasure". There are three appendices: I. On Peace—II. Śesa, Ananta, Anantaram—III. Nakula. Reprinted, incorporating addenda, in *Coomaraswamy 2: Selected Papers, Metaphysics* ([1977])—A82—pp. 107-47.

C790 [A review of] Eric Gill: *Autobiography*. *Journal of Aesthetics and Art Criticism*, New York, II. 5 (Spring 1942) 72-3.

"This is not just another book by an 'artist' about himself and his feelings and failings. It is not to exhibit himself, but to talk 'shop' that [Gill] occupies the stage" (p.72).

C791 [A review of] *Manuscript Illustrations of the Uttarādhyayana Sūtra*, by W. Norman Brown. *American Journal of Archaeology*, New York, Second Series, XLVI. 2 (Apr./June 1942) 311.

"So far as a piece of research can be considered 'complete' this excellent volume completes Professor Brown's series of studies on the Western Indian style of miniature painting."

C792 [A review of] *The Gesture Language of the Hindu Dance* by La Meri, with foreword by Ananda K. Coomaraswamy [B52] and introduction by Henry R. Zimmer. *Asia*, New York, XLII. 5 (May 1942) 309-10.

"Madame La Meri rightly stresses the religious inspirations from which 'the most complete dance-form existing today' has never—as we, whose arts are 'secular', should express it—been 'emancipated'" (p. 309).

C793 Hindu Doctrine and Reincarnation. [Letter]. *Light: A Journal of Spiritualism*, London, LXII. 3,201 (21 May 1942) 163.

Printed under the general heading: Our Post Bag. Apropos of "Reincarnation", by C.A. F. Rhys Davids, and "Of Rebirth", by C[harles]. R[ichard]. C[ammell]., in the issue for 8

January, with particular reference to the remark, "In India it is a cardinal point of Hindu Dogma". This letter was reprinted, with minor omissions, and, in line 25, "casually" for: causally, in *Selected Letters of Ananda K. Coomaraswamy* (1988)—A89—p. 119.

C794 An Indian Image of Brahmā. *Bulletin of the Museum of Fine Arts*, Boston, XL. 239 (June 1942) 40-1, 2 text illus. (one is printed on the front cover of this issue, i.e. p. [39]).

An explanation of the concept and iconography of the chief member of the Hindu Trinity in connection with a stone sculpture from South India, assigned to the Vijayanagar Period, and recently acquired by the Museum.

C795 Horse-Riding in the Ṛgveda and Atharvaveda. *Journal of the American Oriental Society*, New Haven, LXII. 2 (June 1942) 139-40.

AKC cites passages containing explicit references to horse-riding in refutation of Arthur Berriedale Keith's claim that no such references occur; together with a note on the "horse and chariot" as a traditional symbol of the psycho-physical complex.

C796 What of India? *New English Weekly*, London, XXI. 16/18 (20 Aug. 1942) 140-1.

On the question of British rule: "whatever the outcome of the present war, it is clear that the days of European exploitation of Asia are over" (p. 140). This article was reprinted in *Selected Letters of Ananda K. Coomaraswamy* (1988)—A89—pp. 338-41.

C797 Truth and Value. [Letter]. *New English Weekly*, London, XXI. 19 (27 Aug. 1942) 155-6.

That they belong to different departments of knowledge. Reprinted in *Selected Letters of Ananda K. Coomaraswamy* (1988)—A89—pp. 199-201.

C798 Play and Seriousness. *Journal of Philosophy*, New York, XXXIX. 20 (24 Sept. 1942) 550-2.

The second of two items printed under the general heading: Comments and Criticism. With reference to an article of this title, by Kurt Riezler, in the issue for 11 September 1941, and continuing the discussion of the subject of "*Līlā*"—C781. Reprinted in *Coomaraswamy 2: Selected Papers, Metaphysics* ([1977])—A82—pp. 156-8.

C799 [Note on *The Overthrow of Satan by St Michael*]. *Catholic Art Quarterly*, Collegeville, Minn., V. 3 (Michaelmas 1942) 30-1.

Printed under the general heading: Who's Who and What? AKC comments (briefly) on the iconography of a painting with this title, by Constance Mary Rowe (Sister Mary of the Compassion, O.P.). AKC writes, "I thought highly of the picture and had it photographed with the *Catholic Art Quarterly* in view". The painting is reproduced, in black-and-white halftones, on page [17] of this issue.

C800 Some References to Pictorial Relief. *Art Quarterly*, Detroit, V. 4 (Autumn 1942) 338-9.

"The object of the present note is to call attention to two late Classical [i.e. Longinus and Sextus Empiricus] and several Indian references [i.e. Asaṅga, Kālidāsa, Bhoja, *et al.*] in which the representation of relief in painting is spoken of in almost identical terms" (p. 338). This article was reprinted as Chapter XIV of *Figures of Speech or Figures of Thought* (1946)—A71.

C801 On Being in One's Right Mind. *Review of Religion*, New York, VII. 1 (Nov. 1942) [32]-40.

The first part of this article comprises a discussion of the notion expressed by the Greek term *metanoia* which, "usually rendered by 'repentance', is literally 'change of mind', or intellectual metamorphosis" (p. [32]); the second part deals with the universal doctrine and traditional distinction of "the two minds" (i.e. mortal and immortal). AKC remarks elsewhere, "although in fact by one author, this article is in effect a product of the collaboration of Christian, Platonist and Hindu, expounding a doctrine held in common" ("Paths that Lead to the Same Summit" (1944)—C840—p. 30). Reprinted, with corrections, in *Studies in Comparative Religion*, Bedfont, Middx., XVI. 3/4 ([mid-1986]) 207-13, and again in *What Is Civilisation? and Other Essays* ([1989])—A90—pp. [33]-41. Also reprinted, with the omission of the footnotes, the quotations in Greek script romanized, and the German motto from Eckhart put into English, and with minor excisions of textual matter, in *Revision*, Cambridge, Mass., V. 2 (Fall 1982) 63-7.

C802 Myth and Literature. [Letter]. *New English Weekly*, London, XXII. 3 (5 Nov. 1942) 24.

With reference to "Creative Myth", by Ross Nichols, in the issue for 24 September. Reprinted in *Selected Letters of Ananda K. Coomaraswamy* (1988)—A89—pp. 422-3; the first half of this letter, as originally drafted by AKC but not used by *The New English Weekly*, is printed on page 202.

C803 The Indian Question. [Letter]. *New English Weekly*, London, XXII. 4 (12 Nov. 1942) 35.

Replying to three questions concerning his article "What of India?"—C796—put to him by A.S. Elwell-Sutton in a letter in the issue for 3 September. Reprinted in *Selected Letters of Ananda K. Coomaraswamy* (1988)—A89—pp. 342-4, together with Elwell-Sutton's letter (pp. 341-2).

C804 [Letter]. *Art Bulletin*, New York, XXIV. 4 (Dec. 1942) 383-4.

Concerning the symbolism of the ass's jaw-bone, in connection with "Cain's Jaw-Bone that Did the First Murder", by Meyer Schapiro, in the September issue.

C805 The Japanese Emperor. [Letter]. *Asia and the Americas*, New York, XLII. 12 (Dec. 1942) 726.

On Hirohito, and the war with Japan, in the light of the traditional Asiatic theory of kingship, in connection with "What of Postwar Japan?", by Willis Church Lamott, in the October issue. Reprinted in *Selected Letters of Ananda K. Coomaraswamy* (1988)—A89—pp. 322-3.

C806 *Sarpabandha. Journal of the American Oriental Society*, New Haven, LXII. 4 (Dec. 1942) 341-2.

A note on this Sanskrit word ("snake-fetter") in connection with the imagery of "bonds" and "knots" (denoting attachment to pleasure and pain).

C807 Mind and Myth. *New English Weekly*, London, XXII. 10 (24 Dec. 1942) 83.

Printed under the general heading: Views and Reviews. On (1) the distinction between instinct (i.e. appetites and wants) and intellect, and the necessary regulation of the former by the distinterested Mind or higher principle; and (2) that no distinction ought to be made between myth and "folklore", because the materials of both are essentially metaphysical. In this connection AKC points out that Ross Nichols in his review of *Monkey*, Arthur Waley's translation of Wu Ch'êng-ên's *Hsi Yu Chi*, in the issue for 8 October, is mistaken in calling such a work "a mine of *popular* fancy". AKC includes a brief discussion of the symbolism of the "bridge", with reference to an episode in *Monkey*. This article was reprinted in *Selected Letters of Ananda K. Coomaraswamy* (1988)—A89—pp. 414-17, in *What Is Civilisation? and Other Essays* ([1989])—A90—pp. [121]-124, and in *The Door in the Sky* ([1997])—A95—pp. 3-5.

1943

C808 The Symbolism of Archery. *Ars Islamica*, Ann Arbor, X. (1943) [105]-119.

On the metaphysical implications of archery, with separate considerations of the "bow" and "arrow", the "bowstring", the "grip", "shooting", and the "target". The exposition is based on the Indian literature, and the actual practice of archery in modern Turkey (using

Joachim Hein's account of the *Telkhiṣ Resāil er-Rümat* of Muṣṭafā Kānī) and Japan (quoting at length from *Toyō kyūdō Kikan*, by William Acker and Toshisuke Nasu). A number of analogous, and combined, symbols are also discussed, e.g. "wings", the "bridge", the "thread", and the notion of "penetration". This article was reprinted in *Studies in Comparative Religion*, Bedfont, Middx., V. 2 (Spring 1971) 72-91, in *What Is Civilisation? and Other Essays* ([1989])—A90—pp. [135]-156, and, in French, in two instalments, as "Le Symbolisme du tir à l'arc", in *Études Traditionnelles*, Paris, XLVI. 247 (Oct./Nov. 1945) [30]-34, and 248 (Dec. 1945) [64]-78. "The Symbolism of Archery" was originally to have appeared in 1940 in a special number of *Études Traditionnelles* devoted to the "Symbolism of Games"; but, following the German occupation of Paris in June of that year, the periodical was suspended; it resumed publication in 1945 with the issue for October/November.

C809 Caste and Vocation. [Letter]. *Nation*, New York, CLVI. 5 (30 Jan. 1943) 179-80.

Dated Boston, 5 Jan. [1943]. On Reinhold Niebuhr's review of *Warning to the West*, by Krishnalal Shridharani, in the issue for 2 January. A rejoinder from Niebuhr is printed on page 180. AKC's letter (only) was reprinted, in part, in *Selected Letters of Ananda K. Coomaraswamy* (1988)—A89—pp. 306-7.

C810 Am I My Brother's Keeper? *Asia and the Americas*, New York, XLIII. 3 (Mar. 1943) 135-8.

On the problems of inter-cultural relations; in particular the modern West's "proselytizing fury" (René Guénon's phrase) and the effect of Western contact with traditional culture. See also the ensuing correspondence, "Rebuke to the West", in the issue for June—C820. Eric Schroeder recalls AKC as saying that this article was written "at white heat" ("Memories of the Person"—E179, p. 79). AKC intended the present article to serve as the preface to his projected series on modern "bugbears"—see the prospectus for the series printed with "The Bugbear of Democracy, Freedom and Equality"—C900, p. 134. Reprinted, slightly expanded, and with the addition of notes, as [Chapter] I of *Am I My Brother's Keeper?* ([1947])—A72a, and again in *Jubilee*, New York, [IV.] (Jan. 1957) 37-40.

C811 [*Entry deleted.*]

C812 Ars Sine Scientia Nihil. *Catholic Art Quarterly*, Collegeville, Minn., VI. 2 (Easter 1943) 12-14.

(In English.) On this fundamental axiom enunciated by the Parisian Master Jean Mignot in connection with the building of Milan Cathedral in 1398. AKC presents homologous statements of Dante, Guido d'Arezzo, St Augustine, and Plato. Reprinted, revised and slightly expanded, as Chapter IV of *Figures of Speech or Figures of Thought* (1946)—A71, and, incorporating further addenda, in *Coomaraswamy 1: Selected Papers, Traditional*

Art and Symbolism ([1977])—A82—pp. 229-32. Another version of this article, with the text editorially rearranged, with some minor omissions, and with the words in Greek script romanized, was printed in *Catholic Art Quarterly*, Buffalo, N.Y., XVI. 2 (Easter 1953) 70-2.

C813 Eastern Wisdom and Western Knowledge. *Isis*, Cambridge, Mass., XXXIV. 96 (Spring 1943) 359-63.

An introduction to the writings of René Guénon: "the leading living exponent of a traditional wisdom that is no more essentially Oriental than it is Occidental" (p. 363); "[he] is not an 'Orientalist' but what the Hindus would call a Guru" (p. 359). AKC includes a discussion, with reference to Guénon's *East and West*, of the problem of relations between Orient and Occident, which Guénon and AKC see as really one of tradition versus anti-tradition. This article was reprinted, in French, as "Sagesse orientale et savoir occidental", in *Études Traditionnelles*, Paris, LII. 293/294/295 (July-Aug./Sept./ Oct.-Nov. 1951) [197]-208 (this issue of *Études* bears the subtitle, "Numéro spécial consacré à René Guénon", whose death had occurred on 7 January), and, in English, in a slightly expanded and revised form, as [Chapter] IV of *Am I My Brother's Keeper?* ([1947])—A72.

C814 *Saṁvega*, "Aesthetic Shock". *Harvard Journal of Asiatic Studies*, Cambridge, Mass., VIII. 3 (Apr. 1943) 174-9.

On this Pāli word with reference "to the experience that may be felt in the presence of a work of art, when we are struck by it" (p. 178). This article was reprinted, as Chapter XII of *Figures of Speech or Figures of Thought* (1946)—A71, in *Aperture*, New York, XVI. 3 (1972) [2-7], and, incorporating addenda, in *Coomaraswamy 1: Selected Papers, Traditional Art and Symbolism* ([1977])—A82—pp. 179-85.

C815 Prāṇa-citi. *Journal of the Royal Asiatic Society*, London (Apr. 1943) [105]-109.

(In English.) A commentary on *Atharva Veda*, X. 2, 8c, d, and 26c, d; passages that had been dismissed by W.D. Whitney as "extremely obscure". The significance of the "breaths", and their "piling", is discussed in connection with the idea of the "Internal Agnihotra".

C816 Education and Vocation. [Letter]. *New English Weekly*, London, XXII. 24 (1 Apr. 1943) 211-12.

A critique of modern education, with reference to a letter by Hilderic Cousens in the issue for 7 January. Reprinted in *Selected Letters of Ananda K. Coomaraswamy* (1988)—A89—pp. 291-3.

C817 The Blowpipe in Persia and India. *American Anthropologist*, Menasha, Wis., N.S. XLV. 2 (Apr./June 1943) 311-12.

AKC cites evidence located in the *Mathnawī* of Jalāl al-Dīn Rūmī, and in the Indian text *Taittirīya Saṁhitā.*

C818 Understanding and Reunion. *Asia and the Americas*, New York, XLIII. 5 (May 1943) 270.

A brief statement printed in 21 lines, contrasting the Oriental and traditional culture and way of life with the modern Western and anti-traditional one. Reprinted, with minor alterations, as the third paragraph of "Understanding and Reunion: An Oriental Perspective" (1945)—B64.

C819 Symptom, Diagnosis, and Regimen. *College Art Journal*, New York, II. 4 (May 1943) 121-4.

AKC examines the "symptomatic abnormalities" that index a "morbid condition" of contemporary art, and prescribes a remedy. Reprinted, with minor additions, as Chapter XVII of *Figures of Speech or Figures of Thought* (1946)—A71, and in *Good Work*, Boston, XXIV. 2 (Spring 1961) 49-51, and again in *Coomaraswamy 1: Selected Papers, Traditional Art and Symbolism* ([1977])—A82—pp. 316-19. This paper was intended for a symposium, "Art and Reality", to have been held under the auspices of the College Art Association at Baltimore in January 1943, that was cancelled because of World War II.

C820 Rebuke to the West. [Letter]. *Asia and the Americas*, New York, XLIII. 6 (June 1943) 389.

A reply to criticism of "Am I My Brother's Keeper?"—C810—from Sidney Lewis Gulick. Gulick's letter to AKC, titled "In Defense of Christian Missions", is printed on the same page. Three letters from AKC to Gulick (but not the present letter) are printed for the first time in *Selected Letters of Ananda K. Coomaraswamy* (1988)—A89—pp. 66-71.

C821 A Buddha Head from Java. *Bulletin of the Museum of Fine Arts*, Boston, XLI. 244 (June 1943) 33-4, 1 text illus.

Of *circa* AD 800, and recently acquired by the Museum. A brief note on its provenance and iconography.

C822 [A review of] *Ancient Vijñaptipatras.* By Hirananda Śastri. *Journal of the American Oriental Society*, New Haven, LXIII. 2 (June 1943) 179.

AKC points to the historical value of these "richly illustrated" Jaina reports or letters, and selects for special comment an illustration of a "Jaina Maṅgala-kalaśa [= chalice] with eyes" which AKC connects with the traditional symbolism of the Fountain and Tree of Life.

C823 Ūnatiriktau and Ātyaricyata [*sic*]. *New Indian Antiquary*, Bombay, VI. 3 (June 1943) [52]-56.

"The two purposes of this article are to show from the occurrences of the dual *ūnātiriktau* that Prajāpati as Progenitor and Ruler is to be regarded as a syzygy of conjoint principles, male and female . . . and to discuss the meaning of *atyaricyata* in [Ṛgveda] X. 90. 5" (p. [52]).

C824 [A review of] *East and West* by René Guénon, translated by W. Massey [and] *The Crisis of the Modern World* by René Guénon, translated by A. Osborne. *Asia and the Americas*, New York, XLIII. 8 (Aug. 1943) 504.

"René Guénon is a gifted and learned writer, primarily an exponent of the universal metaphysical tradition which has been the foundation of every past culture, and which represents the indispensable basis of any civilization deserving to be so called". AKC summarizes Guénon's concept of an "élite", whose urgent and practical task would be that of returning the West to a traditional civilization.

C825 Unesthetic Future? [Letter]. *Common Sense*, New York, XII. 8 (Aug. 1943) 305-6.

With reference to "Flivver Houses", by William Jordy, in the issue for July. AKC points out that the question of whether pre-fabricated houses are socially and aesthetically desirable is one that has been set aside in the interests of "progress" and the manufacturers' profit-motive. The gist of this letter is summarized in the concluding paragraph of AKC's "Introduction" to *It All Goes Together*, by Eric Gill (1944)—B61—p. xiv. Reprinted in *Selected Letters of Ananda K. Coomaraswamy* (1988)—A89—pp. 300-1, with additionally a postscript citing Xenophon.

C826 The Meeting of Eyes. *Art Quarterly*, Detroit, VI. 4 (Autumn 1943) 322-4.

On the iconographical significance of that phenomenon where the eyes in some portraits, e.g. in many of the representations of Christ, "seem to be looking straight at the spectator whether he faces the picture or moves to right or left of it" (p. 322). AKC connects this effect with the universal idea of an immanent and all-seeing God. Reference is made to "The Apparent Direction of Eyes in a Portrait", by W.H. Wollaston, and to the *De visione Dei* of Nicholas de Cusa. This article was reprinted as Chapter V of *Figures of Speech or Figures of Thought* (1946)—A71, and, with the addition of a plate, in *Coomaraswamy 1: Selected Papers, Traditional Art and Symbolism* ([1977])—A82—pp. 233-7.

C827 Why Exhibit Works of Art? [Letter]. *Listener*, London, XXX. 770 (14 Oct. 1943) 445.

A reply to Herbert Read's review of *Why Exhibit Works of Art?* (1943)—A67, in the issue for 29 July.

C828 Henry R. Zimmer (1890-1943). *Review of Religion*, New York, VIII. 1 (Nov. 1943) 16-18.

The second of three tributes printed under this heading (Heinrich Zimmer "Americanized" his name upon arrival in the U.S.A.). "Among Indologists he was one of the comparatively few whose interests are not merely philological or even literary, but philosophical and vital . . . Zimmer's work is stimulating, precisely because he is always alive to the significance of his material; it is never for him a matter of mere curiosity or 'pure' scholarship, but a source of wisdom as pertinent now as it was in the 'mythopoetic' past" (pp. 16, 17). AKC was later to assist Joseph Campbell with the editing of two of Zimmer's posthumous works, *Myths and Symbols in Indian Art and Civilization* (1946)—B71, and *The King and the Corpse* ([1948])—B77.

C829 [A review of] Eric Schroeder, *Persian Miniatures in the Fogg Museum of Art*. *Art Bulletin*, New York, XXV. 4 (Dec. 1943) 380-2.

"This is, probably, the best introduction to Persian painting that has yet appeared . . . [although] Schroeder is inclined to overstress the secular character of Persian painting" (pp. 380, 381).

C830 Art and Instinct [I]. [Letter]. *New English Weekly*, London, XXIV. 10 (23 Dec. 1943) 88.

The first of three letters from AKC in answer to Romney Green. On the traditional doctrine of art, objecting to an assertion that "art is mainly an affair of instinct", with reference to a review by Green of *Child Art to Man Art*, by William Johnstone, in the issue for 16 September. This letter was reprinted in *Selected Letters of Ananda K. Coomaraswamy* (1988)—A89—p. 393.

1944

C831 Sir Gawain and the Green Knight: Indra and Namuci. *Speculum*, Cambridge, Mass., XIX. 1 (Jan. 1944) 104-25.

On this Middle English poem, employing parallels from Indian sources, as well as from Plato, Philo, Meister Eckhart, and Jalāl al-Dīn Rūmī, to explicate metaphysically the meaning of the "decapitation" motif. A separately paginated offprint is in the compiler's possession. Reprinted, in facsimile of the printed article, in *Sophia Perennis*, Tehran, III.

2 (Autumn 1977) 18-39. This issue of *Sophia Perennis* is devoted to the theme of "Tradition and the Arts", to mark the centenary of AKC's birth.

C832 Woman in Hinduism. [Letter]. *New English Weekly*, London, XXIV. 14 (20 Jan. 1944) 116.

On *Woman in the Sacred Scriptures of Hinduism*, by Mildred Worth Pinkham, reviewed (anonymously) in the issue for 16 September 1943. This letter was reprinted in *Selected Letters of Ananda K. Coomaraswamy* (1988)—A89—p. 363.

C833 The Bugbear of Literacy. *Asia and the Americas*, New York, XLIV. 2 (Feb. 1944) 53-7, 1 pl. (facing p. 53).

AKC "essay[s] to show (1) that there is no necessary connection of literacy with culture, and (2) that to impose our literacy . . . upon a cultured but illiterate people is to destroy their culture in the name of our own" (p. 53). This article was reprinted, with the addition of notes, as [Chapter] II of *Am I My Brother's Keeper?* ([1947])—A72a.

C834 Chinese Painting at Boston. *Magazine of Art*, Washington, D.C., XXXVII. 3 (Mar. 1944) 94-9, 6 text illus.

Subtitled: Not a Collection of Curiosities, but the Evidences of a People's Inner Life. On (1) the sense in which Chinese painting can be called religious, (2) that the paintings are the products, then supports, of contemplation, (3) the Chinese painter's identification with nature, and (4) the Taoist spirit in Chinese painting; with reference to the anecdotal literature, and to the "Six Canons" of Hsieh Ho. An editorial note on page [81] explains: "[AKC] wrote this essay for us on the occasion of the extensive exhibition of . . . Chinese paintings opened this month by the Museum [of Fine Arts, Boston]". Reprinted, with the omission of the illustrations, in *Coomaraswamy 1: Selected Papers, Traditional Art and Symbolism* ([1977])—A82—pp. 308-15.

C835 Soul and Spirit. [Letter]. *New English Weekly*, London, XXIV. 21 (9 Mar. 1944) 179-80.

On the traditional doctrine of "the two selves", with reference to a review by Gens of *Renascence*, by "Nicodemus", in the issue for 23 December 1943. Reprinted in *Selected Letters of Ananda K. Coomaraswamy* (1988)—A89—pp. 154-5, where it is mistakenly dated 6 March 1943.

C836 East and West [I]. [Letter]. *New English Weekly*, London, XXIV. 22 (16 Mar. 1944) 188.

On a report of the Pasha of Marrakesh's rejection of modern Western civilization. This letter was reprinted in *Selected Letters of Ananda K. Coomaraswamy* (1988)—A89—pp. 65-6.

C837 Art and Instinct [II]. [Letter]. *New English Weekly*, London, XXIV. 24 (30 Mar. 1944) 204.

A further reply to Romney Green. Reprinted in *Selected Letters of Ananda K. Coomaraswamy* (1988)—A89—pp. 393-4, together with an (undated) letter from AKC on Green's use of the terms "instinct" and "intellect", and objecting to his remarks concerning "human sacrifice", that was not used by *The New English Weekly*, pp. 394-5.

C838 The Iconography of Dürer's "Knots" and Leonardo's "Concatenation". *Art Quarterly*, Detroit, VII. 2 (Spring 1944) 109-28, 4 pls. (containing 18 illus.).

On a wood-engraving by Albrecht Dürer, from the series *Sechs Knoten*, that comprises an interlacing pattern formed by a white, unbroken line on a black ground, and a similar device, a copper-engraving commonly attributed to Leonardo da Vinci, pointing out that Dürer and Leonardo are making use of the traditional symbolism of "weaving" and "embroidery". AKC discusses this symbolism together with various related and combined symbols such as those of "sewing", "knots", the "needle", the "thread" (summarizing the Indian *sūtrātman*, or "thread-spirit", doctrine), the "spider's web", the "spiral", the "labyrinth", the "pin" or "brooch", and considers as well the metaphysical implications of the continuous or one-line technique used in drawing and engraving. Reference is made to representations of these symbols in the work of Dante, Pedro Diaz Morante, Claude Mellan, and in the *Berthold Missal*, American Indian (Mimbres) bowls, the labyrinth at Chartres Cathedral, and as found in artefacts from Greece, India, the New Hebrides, and elsewhere. AKC intended this article to serve as a model of method in any serious investigation of symbols. Reprinted, in an abridged form, as "The One Thread", in *Parabola*, New York, XVII. 2 (May/Summer 1992) 26-33, 6 text illus.

C839 A Note on the Stickfast Motif. *Journal of American Folklore*, Philadelphia, LVII. 224 (Apr. 1944) 128-31.

An explication of the motif of "desire" in the Tar-baby story, from the standpoint of the traditional psychology, and with reference to the work of W. Norman Brown, Ruth I. Cline, and Aurelio M. Espinosa. AKC traces similar stories in the Buddhist (*Saṁyutta Nikāya*) and Jaina literature. "We do *not* mean to imply that [this motif] *must* have originated in India . . . if not in India within the historical period, then in some prehistoric Kulturkreis from which conceptions have been inherited alike in India and elsewhere" (pp. 130-1).

C840 Paths That Lead to the Same Summit. *Motive; A Magazine of the Methodist Student Movement*, Nashville, Tenn., IV. 8 (May 1944) 29-32, 35.

Subtitled: Some Observations on Comparative Religion. AKC discusses the meaning of the multiplicity of religions and of their essential unity. "This . . . article . . . is based upon an address given last year to a large group of schoolteachers in a series entitled 'How to Teach About Other Peoples', sponsored by the New York School Board and the East and

West Association. . . . Our proposition is that the proper objective of an education in Comparative Religion should be to enable the pupil to discuss with other believers the validity of particular doctrines" (pp. 29, 30). Reprinted, slightly expanded and revised, as [Chapter] III of *Am I My Brother's Keeper?* ([1947])—A72.

C841 East and West [II]. [Letter]. *New English Weekly*, London, XXV. 10 (22 June 1944) 92.

On the attitude of Eastern peoples to modern Western civilization, with reference to a comment made by John Bate in the issue for 30 March. This letter was reprinted in *Selected Letters of Ananda K. Coomaraswamy* (1988)—A89—pp. 63-5.

C842 Art and Instinct [III]. [Letter]. *New English Weekly*, London, XXV. 15 (27 July 1944) 132.

Quoting a passage from *Clothing Without Cloth*, by Eric Gill. This letter was reprinted in *Selected Letters of Ananda K. Coomaraswamy* (1988)—A89—pp. 395-6.

C843 A Message. *Voice of India*, Washington, D.C., I. 1 (Sept. 1944) 12.

On the issue of India's political freedom and self-determination, and welcoming the appearance of this periodical.

C844 Causality. [Letter]. *New English Weekly*, London, XXV. 25 (5 Oct. 1944) 200.

Concerning the First Cause, with reference to a letter by Anthony M. Ludovici printed under this heading in the issue for 27 July.

C845 Headless Magicians; and an Act of Truth. *Journal of the American Oriental Society*, New Haven, LXIV. 4 (Oct./Dec. 1944) 215-17.

On the characteristic power of other-worldly magicians to present themselves as headless but still alive, and on the metaphysical implications of the "decapitation" motif; with reference to the inconography of a Buddhist sculpture from Haḍḍa, published by J. Hackin in *La Sculpture indienne et tibétaine au Musée Guimet*, that represents a demon member of Māra's army in the act of removing his own head.

C846 Contra Cartesium. *New English Weekly*, London, XXVI. 9 (14 Dec. 1944) 77.

A three-line aphorism, in blank verse: AKC's answer to René Descartes' "*Cogito, egro sum*". Variant readings of this aphorism are printed in *Homage to Ananda Coomaraswamy: (A Memorial Volume) A Garland of Tributes*, edited by S. Durai Raja Singam (1952)—B85—p. ix, and in "Some Recollections and References to Dr. Ananda Coomaraswamy", by Doña Luisa Coomaraswamy, in *Kalāmanjari*, Colombo, I. 1 (1950/51)—E30—p. 18. A facsimile of a typed letter from AKC to Robert Allerton Parker, dated 10 November 1944, incorporating this aphorism, and adding: "I was inspired by [Thomas] Traherne to write Contra Cartesium", is printed in *Ananda Coomaraswamy—the Bridge Builder*, by S. Durai Raja Singam (1977)—B94—p. [496].

C847 Intention. *American Bookman*, New York, I. 1 (Winter 1944) [41]-48.

An essay taking the form of an open letter addressed to Monroe C. Beardsley and W.K. Wimsatt, Jr., concerning their entry *sub verbo* in the *Dictionary of World Literature*, edited by Joseph T. Shipley (New York, 1943). AKC maintains, in opposition to the view of Beardsley and Wimsatt, that the critic *can* know what was in the artist's mind, and furthermore that judgement and criticism of a work of art must be based upon the ratio of intention to result. Reprinted, as Chapter VIII of *Figures of Speech or Figures of Thought* (1946)—A71, and, incorporating addenda, in *Coomaraswamy 1: Selected Papers, Traditional Art and Symbolism* ([1977])—A82—pp. 266-75.

C848 Gradation and Evolution [I]. *Isis*, Cambridge, Mass., XXXV. 99 (Winter 1944) 15-16.

With reference to a note, "On the Concepts of Gradation and Evolution", by M.F. Ashley Montagu, in the issue for Spring 1943. "The object of the present note is to point out that if the doctrine of special creation is understood as it has generally been interpreted by Christian and other philosophers, then [the traditional doctrine of] Gradation and [the modern biological theory of] Evolution are not irreconcilable alternatives . . ." (p. 15). AKC continued this discussion in the issue for November 1947—C886. Reprinted in *What Is Civilisation? and Other Essays* ([1989])—A90—pp. [70]-72.

1945

C849 Imitation, Expression, and Participation. *Journal of Aesthetics and Art Criticism*, New York, III. 11/12 ([1945]) 62-72.

An analysis (drawing chiefly on St Bonaventura) of these traditional "predications of the essential nature of art", and furthermore, emphasizing how art "is these three in one" (p. 62), with reference to "Imitation and Expression in Art", by Iredell Jenkins, in the issue for Spring 1942. This article was reprinted as Chapter IX of *Figures of Speech or Figures of Thought* (1946)—A71, and, incorporating addenda, in *Coomaraswamy 1: Selected Papers, Traditional Art and Symbolism* ([1977])—A82—pp. 276-85.

C850 "Romanticism Comes of Age". [Letter]. *New English Weekly*, London, XXVII. 9 (14 June 1945) 80.

A brief discussion of the term "imagination", with reference to a review, by Charles Williams, of a book of this title by Owen Barfield, in the issue for 10 May. This letter was reprinted in *Selected Letters of Ananda K. Coomaraswamy* (1988)—A89—pp. 397-8.

C851 "Spiritual Paternity" and the "Puppet-Complex". A Study in Anthropological Methodology. *Psychiatry*, Baltimore, VIII. 3 (Aug. 1945) 287-97.

"The purpose of this article is methodological, and mainly to suggest that the anthropologist is rather too much inclined to consider the peculiarities of 'primitive' peoples—Naturvölker—in isolation, neglecting the possibility or probability that these peculiarities may not be of local origin, but may represent only provincial or peripheral survivals of theories held by some or all of the more sophisticated communities from which the primitive peoples may have declined" (p. 287). AKC discusses (1) the Australian aborigines' "distinction of the mediate from the first cause of conception", with reference to M.F. Ashley Montagu's article "Nescience, Science and Psycho-Analysis", in the issue for November 1941, and (2) what Margaret Mead in *Balinese Character* chooses to call the "puppet-complex", i.e. man thought of as a puppet whose actions are not determined by his own passions, but governed by a superior will, ultimately the Divine Will itself. This latter concept AKC shows is closely connected with the Indian *līlā* and *sūtrātman* doctrines. These discussions are with reference to the traditional Indian and Greek psychology, namely the *Upaniṣads*, *Brāhmaṇas*, *Bhagavadgītā*, Plato, and Philo Judaeus. Also included are notes on the symbolism of the "sun", "food", "fishing" and "fish hooks" (footnotes 7, 63, 74, respectively), and a commentary on the myth of the City of Wooden Automata in the *Kathā Sarit Sāgara* compared with a similar account of an ideal city-state in the *Tripurā Rahasya*. This article was reprinted as [Chapter] VI of *Am I My Brother's Keeper?* ([1947])—A72a. A French translation is printed, as "'Paternité spirituelle' et 'Puppet complex'", in *Études Traditionnelles*, Paris, LXXV. 443/444 (May/June-July/Aug. 1974) 97-119.

C852 Reference Lists of Contributing Authors . . . Ananda K. Coomaraswamy. *Psychiatry*, Baltimore, VIII. 3 (Aug. 1945) 373-7.

At the editor's request AKC has provided a select list of his writings (151 items), in a chronological arrangement, from 1903 to 1945. The list is printed in double columns, with items thought pertinent to readers of *Psychiatry* starred. Reprinted, augmented with the addition of three late items, in *Art and Thought; Issued in Honour of Dr. Ananda K. Coomaraswamy on the Occasion of His 70th Birthday*, edited by K. Bharatha Iyer (1947)—E86—pp. 255-9. In 1942, AKC had assisted Helen E. Ladd, of the Research Seminary in Islamic Art at the University of Michigan, to compile a fuller list of his publications—E104.

C853 "Bengal Lancer". [Letter]. *New English Weekly*, London, XXVII. 21 (6 Sept. 1945) 156.

On Rudyard Kipling, with reference to a remark by Arthur Bryant in the issue for 5 July.

C854 On the Loathly Bride. *Speculum*, Cambridge, Mass., XX. 4 (Oct. 1945) 391-404.

"My intention in the present article is to call attention to certain aspects of the story of the transformation of the 'Loathly Lady' that have hitherto been overlooked, and, in particular, (1) to adduce a number of Oriental parallels, (2) to point out that the Loathly Lady must be identified with the Dragon or Snake whom the hero disenchants by the Fier Baiser, and (3) to point out that the Loathly Lady or Dragon-Woman is the Undine, mermaid soul, the Psyche, whose disenchantment and transformation are brought about by her marriage with the Hero" (p. 393). This article was reprinted, incorporating addenda, in *Coomaraswamy 1: Selected Papers, Traditional Art and Symbolism* ([1977])—A82—pp. 353-70.

C855 Mr. Finlayson's Providential Order of Fairplay. *Trees*, Puncknoll, Dorset, IX. 2 (Oct./Nov./Dec. 1945) 69-71.

Dated Boston, 18 July 1945. On "The Providential Order of Fairplay", by Henry G. Finlayson, in the issue for April/May/June. AKC considers Finlayson's hope of a betterment of "human activities in the sane new world", with reference to (1) the Classical and Oriental theory of Kingship, (2) the vocational society, and (3) the Platonic and Greek conceptions of Justice and Equality. A rejoinder from Finlayson is printed in five lines on page 71. This article was reprinted, with minor omissions and additions, in *Selected Letters of Ananda K. Coomaraswamy* (1988)—A89—pp. 280-3.

C856 Culture and World-Domination. [Letter]. *New English Weekly*, London, XXVII. 25 (4 Oct. 1945) 191-2.

Calling attention to (1) the work of the Indian sociologist Bharatan Kumarappa, and (2) American influence internationally. This letter was reprinted in *Selected Letters of Ananda K. Coomaraswamy* (1988)—A89—pp. 58-9.

C857 [A review of] *The Lady of the Hare; a Study in the Healing Power of Dreams*. By John Layard. *Psychiatry*, Baltimore, VIII. 4 (Nov. 1945) 507-13.

On the significance of a psychoanalytic patient's "dreams of a Hare which she was required to sacrifice . . . of particular interest to anyone who, as I am, is thoroughly distrustful of psycho-analysis, Freud and Jung; I think that Dr. Layard owes much less than he supposes to Jung, and much more than he supposes to his faith in supra-personal spiritual forces" (p. 507). AKC explains, with reference to the terms of the traditional Indian and Platonic psychology, that the Hare represents "the outer man, or self of uncontrolled instinct" (p. 507), and shows how such symbols can be effectively used by psychoanalysts in "the healing of souls to which the traditional philosophies have always been directed" (p. 513). Reprinted, in the form of an article, as "On Hares and Dreams", with additionally an appendix comprising addenda, and the quotes in German from Walter Andrae and Karl von Spiess, and the French of Mircea Eliade, put into English, in *Quarterly Journal of the Mythic Society*, Bangalore, XXXVII. 1 (July 1946) [1]-14, and again in *What Is Civilisation? and Other Essays* ([1989])—A90—pp. [94]-106.

C858 The Artist's Responsibility. [Letter]. *New English Weekly*, London, XXVIII. 8 (6 Dec. 1945) 79.

On the use of the term "art", with reference to an article with this title, by Douglas Newton, in the issue for 1 November. Reprinted in *Selected Letters of Ananda K. Coomaraswamy* (1988)—A89—p. 381. A further letter by AKC on "art" (and "abstraction"), of 12 December, submitted for publication in *The New English Weekly* but not used by them, is printed in *Selected Letters* on pages 396-7.

C859 Comparative Religion [I]. [Letter]. *New English Weekly*, London, XXVIII. 10 (20 Dec. 1945) 100.

In response to a letter by Francis Glendenning in the issue for 25 October: on teaching comparative religion. Reprinted in *Selected Letters of Ananda K. Coomaraswamy* (1988)—A89—p. 105. A further letter by AKC on this subject that was not used by *The New English Weekly*, is printed in *Selected Letters* on page 106.

C860 East and West. *Biosophical Review*, New York, VIII. 1 (Winter 1945), "East-West Issue", pp. 15-18.

On the problem of a traditional East versus an anti-traditional West, and what is required of the West in any move toward a *rapprochement*. This article was reprinted, revised and with the addition of notes, in *The Religious Basis of the Forms of Indian Society* (1946)—A70a, and as [Chapter] V of *Am I My Brother's Keeper?* ([1947])—A72a.

1946

C861 Comparative Religion [II]. [Letter]. *New English Weekly*, London, XXVIII. 14 (17 Jan. 1946) 136.

With reference to an article with this title, by Gens, in the issue for 27 December 1945. Reprinted, with a correction, in *Selected Letters of Ananda K. Coomaraswamy* (1988) A89—pp. 106-8.

C862 The Future of Trade. [Letter]. *New English Weekly*, London, XXVIII. 19 (21 Feb. 1946) 188.

With reference to an editorial that contained remarks on "vocation", and a letter, "Post War Economics", by Montague Fordham, both of which appeared in the issue for 17 January, and, in a postscript, calling attention to a misprint in his letter published in that same issue—C861. Reprinted, with the omission of the postscript, in *Selected Letters of Ananda K. Coomaraswamy* (1988)—A89—p. 58.

C863 Ṛgveda 10. 90. 1 *áty atiṣṭhad daśāṅgulám*. *Journal of the American Oriental Society*, New Haven, LXVI. 2 (Apr./June 1946) 145-61.

An explanation of this passage, with reference to the interpretations and translations of Lucian Scherman, Max Weber, and W. Norman Brown. AKC compares this with related passages in the Brāhmaṇas; and adduces a parallel in Genesis II. 7, to show that "hardly any . . . detail of the ontology and psychology . . . is peculiarly Indian" (p. 155). AKC includes *inter alia* notes on (1) the problems of iconometry and of God, and man, as the measure of all things, (2) the concept of *māyā*, (3) the *scintilla animae*, and (4) the doctrine of the Seven Rays of Agni or the Sun.

C864 [Letters]. *Journal of Aesthetics and Art Criticism*, New York, IV. 4 (June 1946) 248-9.

Printed under the general heading: Letters Pro and Con. Comprises two letters from AKC on the misuse of the term "tradition", in connection with "Note on 'A History of Esthetics'", by Van Meter Ames, in the issue for September 1945. Ames's reply is printed on page 249. The second (only) of AKC's letters is reprinted in *Selected Letters of Ananda K. Coomaraswamy* (1988)—A89—p. 46.

C865 Primordial Images. *Publications of the Modern Language Association of America*, Baltimore, LXI. 2 (June 1946) 601-2.

A reply to "Archetypal Imagery of T.S. Eliot", by Genevieve W. Foster, in the issue for June 1945. AKC challenges her Jungian interpretation of Eliot's symbols (i.e. in *The Waste Land*), and calls attention to the distinction between "*le symbolisme qui sait*" and "*le symbolisme qui cherche*". Foster continues the discussion on pages 602-3. Another letter from AKC to Foster, of 13 May 1946, is printed in *Selected Letters of Ananda K. Coomaraswamy* (1988)—A89—pp. 157-8.

C866 Gradation, Evolution, and Reincarnation. *Main Currents in Modern Thought*, Port Chester, N.Y., IV. 3 (July 1946) 73-4.

Reprinted in *Blackfriars*, Oxford, XXVII. 320 (Nov. 1946) 425-9, with an introduction by Bernard Kelly on page 425, and, slightly revised and with the addition of a postscript, as

[Chapter] VII of *Am I My Brother's Keeper?* ([1947])—A72a, and, with the further addition of end-notes, as [Chapter] VII of *The Bugbear of Literacy* ([1949])—A72b. Also reprinted, without those revisions and additions, in *Vishveshvaranand Indological Series—2: Siddha-Bhāratī . . . or The Rosary of Indology* ([1950])—B82, in *Theosophist*, Madras, LXXIX. 1 (Oct. 1957) 40-5, and again in *Sources of Wisdom* ([1981])—A85—pp. 172-9. A French translation is printed in *Études Traditionnelles*, Paris, XLVIII. 263 (Oct./Nov. 1947) [275]-280.

C867 Effective Demand. [Letter]. *New English Weekly*, London, XXIX. 15 (25 July 1946) 152.

AKC's is the second of two letters printed under this heading. On ancient currencies, with reference to an editorial in the issue for 6 June.

C868 [A review of] *Self-Knowledge* by Swami Nikhilananda. *Asia and the Americas*, New York, XLVI. 8 (Aug. 1946) 380-1.

AKC commends Nikhilananda's "competent exposition of the Vedanta" (p. 381).

C869 Vocation and Procreation. [Letter]. *New English Weekly*, London, XXIX. 17/21 (5 Sept. 1946) 172.

A reply to Anthony M. Ludovici and others: on the decline of the birth rate and the concomitant loss of the sense of vocation. Reprinted in *Selected Letters of Ananda K. Coomaraswamy* (1988)—A89—p. 300.

C870 Vocation and the Birth-Rate. [Letter]. *New English Weekly*, London, XXX. 2 (24 Oct. 1946) 20.

Another (brief) reply to Anthony M. Ludovici.

C871 [A greeting to Jawaharlal Nehru]. *Voice of India*, Washington, D.C., III. 3 (Nov. 1946) 356.

Printed under the general heading: Greetings and Tributes to Pandit Jawaharlal Nehru [on the occasion of his fifty-seventh birthday, 14 November]. Reprinted in *Selected Letters of Ananda K. Coomaraswamy* (1988)—A89—p. 348.

C872 Majorities, Kings and Divine Right. [Letter]. *New English Weekly*, London, XXX. 5 (14 Nov. 1946) 52.

On the traditional doctrine of monarchy, with reference to comments by Paul Derrick in the issue for 10 October. This letter was reprinted in *Selected Letters of Ananda K. Coomaraswamy* (1988)—A89—pp. 320-1.

1947

C873 [Letter to H.G. Rawlinson]. *Indian Art and Letters*, London, XXI. 1 (1947) 57.

An obituary notice, "Dr. A.K. Coomarawamy", by H.G. Rawlinson (pp. 56-7), incorporates an excerpt from a letter from AKC of unspecified date.

C874 Athena and Hephaistos. *Journal of the Indian Society of Oriental Art*, Calcutta, XV. (1947), "A.K. Coomaraswamy Commemoration Volume, Part I", pp. [1]-6.

On Athena and the Titan smith as co-operators, with reference to the Greek doctrine of the complementary faculties of wisdom and method involved in the creation of a work of art (in contrast with their divorce in modern industrial modes of production). This article was reprinted, with the omission of the epigraph from St Thomas Aquinas, in *On the Traditional Doctrine of Art* ([1977])—A83—pp. 19-[24], and in *What Is Civilisation? and Other Essays* ([1989])—A90—pp. [183]-187.

C875 Dr. Coomaraswamy's Talk at His Boston Dinner. *Journal of the Indian Society of Oriental Art*, Calcutta, XV. (1947), "A.K. Coomaraswamy Commemoration Volume, Part I", pp. [10]-12.

The dinner was held at The Harvard Club of Boston, on 22 August 1947, to mark the occasion of AKC's seventieth birthday. Those invited were, A. Graham Carey, Alvan C. Eastman, George H. Edgell, Murray Fowler, Richard B. Gregg, Edward J. Holmes, Werner Jaeger, Joseph L. McNamara, Robert T. Paine, J.M. Plumer, Benjamin Rowland, George Sarton, P.A. Sorokin, Georg Swarzenski, Kojiro Tomita, Robert Ulich, Langdon Warner, H.A. Wolfson, and Leland C. Wyman. In the course of his talk AKC among other things acknowledges the Festschrift *Art and Thought*, edited by K. Bharatha Iyer (1947)—B75, E86 (presented to him in dummy make-up form), pays his respects to four deceased scholars: Denman W. Ross, John Lodge, Lucian Scherman, and James Woods, acknowledges his indebtedness to the American Oriental Society, discusses the traditional concept of a society in which "the social orders [are] integrated on the basis of vocation" and compares "the conditions of making" attained in such a society with those imposed in a modern capitalist one, and announces his retirement plans. ". . . I should like to emphasize that I have never built up a philosophy of my own or wished to establish a new school of thought. Perhaps the greatest thing I have learned is never to think for myself; I fully agree with André Gide that 'Toutes choses sont dites déja [*sic*]', and what I have sought is to understand what has been said, while taking no account of the 'inferior philosophers'. Holding with Heraclitus that the Word is common to all, and that Wisdom is to know the Will of [*sic*] whereby all things are steered, I am convinced with [Alfred] Jeremias that the human cultures in all their apparent diversity are but the dialects of one and the same language of the spirit, that there is a 'common universe of discourse' transcending the differences of tongues" (p. 11). This talk was reprinted, with the addition of a report of the dinner by James Marshall Plumer, as "The Farewell Dinner", in *Homage to Ananda K. Coomaraswamy*, edited by S. Durai Raja Singam ([1948])—B79—pp. 140-6, and, with the further addition of a short prefatory note by Plumer, in *Ananda Coomaraswamy: Remembering and Remembering Again and Again*, edited by S. Durai Raja Singam (1974)—B91—pp. 273-6, and again in *Sources of Wisdom* ([1981])—A85—pp. 11-19. Also reprinted, with the report by Plumer reduced, as "The Last Oration of Dr. Ananda Coomaraswamy", in *Modern Review*, Calcutta, LXXXVI. 8 (Aug. 1949) 131-2, and, without the report, as part of [Chapter] XVI of *Coomaraswamy 3: His Life and Work*, by Roger Lipsey ([1977])—B94a—pp. 252-4, and again, with the omission of a sentence in the fourth paragraph, as "The Seventieth Birthday Address", in *Coomaraswamy 2: Selected Papers, Metaphysics* ([1977])—A82—pp. 433-5.

C876 [A review of] *The Sikhs in Relation to Hindus, Moslems, Christians, and Ahmadiyyas. A Study in Comparative Religion.* By John Clark Archer. *Journal of the American Oriental Society*, New Haven, LXVII. 1 (Jan./Mar. 1947) 67-70.

AKC singles out for discussion Archer's treatment of reincarnation and pantheism, and adds some notes on the traditional doctrines of momentary actuality, and the two "I's".

C877 [A review of] *The Great Religions of the World.* Edited by Edward J. Jurji. *Journal of the American Oriental Society*, New Haven, LXVII. 1 (Jan./Mar. 1947) 71-2.

AKC considers only the contribution on Hinduism, by John Clark Archer, and says that Archer misunderstands the concept of caste.

C878 The "Curse" of Foreign Rule. *United Nations World*, New York, I. 1 (Feb. 1947) 32-4, 4 text illus.

A reprint, in part, with additions and revisions, of "For What Heritage and to Whom Are the English-Speaking Peoples Responsible?" ([1947])—B73, with an introductory comment by the editor: "a great Indic Scholar takes up the cudgels for India against the 'irresponsible and uninstructed mentality' of Rudyard Kipling". A short biographical note on AKC is printed at the foot of page 32. This article was in turn reprinted, in a reduced form, as "Laying Kipling's Ghost", in *United Nations World*, London, I. 9 (June 1949) 338-9, 3 text illus.

C879 [A review of] Shewring, Walter. *Art in Christian Philosophy. Journal of Aesthetics and Art Criticism*, New York, V. 3 (Mar. 1947) 228-9.

"An excellent summary, primarily in the Thomistic terms in which, from the author's point of view, the traditional 'doctrine of art' has been most adequately focussed" (p. 228).

C880 [A review of] *Myths and Symbols in Indian Art and Civilization.* By Heinrich Zimmer. Edited by Joseph Campbell. *Review of Religion*, New York, XI. 3 (Mar. 1947) [285]-290.

"Zimmer's broad scholarship was anything but of that 'objective' and merely analytical sort that deals with living Oriental cultures as one might with a dead body. . . . It had been Zimmer's specialty to study and expound the Purāṇas . . . which so many other Indologists have been inclined to neglect. . . . Zimmer was . . . equipped, with his [wide] knowledge of the language of myth . . . to make the mythological formulae transparent and significant even to the modern reader. . . . I think that Zimmer takes the mythological expressions of the concept of 'reincarnation' too literally and individually" (pp. [285], 286, 287).

C881 "Epoch in World History" . . . From K.S. Shelvankar. *Hindu*, Madras (25 Mar. 1947) 5.

A report, dated New York, 23 March, of the reactions in America to the Asian Relations Conference at New Delhi, quotes AKC's words under the subheading, "Dr. Coomaraswami's [*sic*] Hope". (The title given to the report itself is derived from a comment of Lin Yutang.)

C881a Le Mythe du Bouddha. *Études Traditionnelles*, Paris, XLVIII. 259 (Apr./May 1947) [99]-109.

An excerpt in a French translation from *Hinduism and Buddhism* ([1943])—A68a—pp. 50-7.

C882 I Meet Ananda K. Coomaraswamy [by S. Chandrasekhar]. *Aryan Path*, Bombay, XVIII. 8 (Aug. 1947) [365]-371.

An interview, in which AKC's replies are given in quotation marks as his direct words. On (1) Lord Mountbatten's plan for the partition of Pakistan, (2) the Indian Princes, (3) caste, (4) literacy and education, (5) Indian music and the harmonium, (6) the problems of intercultural contacts, (7) Mohammad Ali Jinnah, Jawaharlal Nehru, and Mohandas Karamchand Gandhi, among other topics. "A Biographical Note" of AKC is printed on pages [365]-366. This interview was reprinted in *Homage to Ananda Coomaraswamy*, edited by S. Durai Raja Singam (1952)—B85.

C883 Renaissance of Indian Culture. *Hindu*, Madras, "Independence Day Number" (15 Aug. 1947) Supplement, p. xv.

An address delivered by AKC at a meeting of the Hindustan Association of Harvard University, 15 August 1947. This address was reprinted, with the addition of a new concluding paragraph, in *Journal of the Indian Society of Oriental Art*, Calcutta, XV. (1947), "A.K. Coomaraswamy Commemoration Volume, Part I", pp. [7]-9, in *Sources of Wisdom* ([1981])—A85—pp. 225-8, and in *Selected Letters of Ananda K. Coomaraswamy* (1988)—A89—pp. 356-8. Also reprinted, with omissions and alterations, as part of an article, "Some Recollections and References to Dr. Ananda Coomaraswamy", by Doña Luisa Coomaraswamy, in *Kalāmanjari*, Colombo, I. 1 (1950/51) 18-23 (AKC's address occupies pages 22-3).

C884 India. [Letter]. *New English Weekly*, London, XXXI. 17/21 (4 Sept. 1947) 156.

AKC reproduces his reply to the question, "What is your message to the new India of our dreams?" that had been put to him by S. Durai Raja Singam. The original reply, dated 15 August 1947 (i.e. Indian Independence Day), is printed, in facsimile of AKC's holograph, in *Ananda Coomaraswamy: Remembering and Remembering Again and Again*, edited by S. Durai Raja Singam (1974)—B91—p. [170]. Also printed, as the concluding paragraph to "Renaissance of Indian Culture", in *Journal of the Indian Society of Oriental Art*, Calcutta (1947)—C883.

C885 An Indian Temple: The Kandarya Mahadeo. *Art in America*, New York, XXXV. 4 (Oct. 1947) 285-92, 1 pl.

On the sacred structure, the human frame, and the universe, as analogical equivalents; with reference to the Kandariya Mahadeva temple at Khajuraho, Madhya Pradesh, and to "the recent publication of Dr. Stella Kramrisch's magnificent work, *The Hindu Temple*" (p. 285). Preceded by an obituary notice of AKC by the periodical's editors and staff (p. [284]). This article was published simultaneously, as "The Hindu Temple", in *Silpi*, Madras, II. 3 (Oct. 1947) [83]-90, 2 pls., and reprinted in *Coomaraswamy 1: Selected Papers, Traditional Art and Symbolism* ([1977])—A82—pp. 3-10, 1 pl. (facing p. 3), and again in *Parabola*, New York, III. 1 ([Feb.?] 1978) 4-9, 3 text illus.

C886 Gradation and Evolution—II. *Isis*, Cambridge, Mass., XXXVIII. 111/112 (Nov. 1947) 87-94.

On the traditional concept of evolution, continuing his discussion of this subject in the issue for Winter 1944—C848. Incorporating, as a footnote (pp. 88-9), some remarks on the doctrine of "adequate symbolism". Addenda on page 94 begins, "A long time having elapsed between the preparation and the publication of the present article, I could now have improved and added to it. For further material on the same theme the reader is asked to refer to my 'Gradation, Evolution, and Reincarnation' [(1946)—C866]". On the first page is an editorial note, signed I. B[ernard]. C[ohen].: "The author completed his reading of the proof a few days before he died". This article was reprinted in *What Is Civilisation? and Other Essays* ([1989])—A90—pp. [73]-85.

C887 Who Is "Satan" and Where Is "Hell"? *Review of Religion*, New York, XII. 1 (Nov. 1947) [36]-47.

On the problem of the existence of Satan, thought of as "a real and single Person", and the notion of his realm as a time and a place, together with notes on the related problems of "dualism" and "theodicy". AKC also considers the doctrine of the "ego" and the traditional distinction of "the two selves", mainly with reference to the Hindu, Judaic, Greek, Christian, and Islamic traditions. This article was reprinted in *Wind and the Rain*, London, V. 1 (Summer 1948) [50]-59, in *Disguises of the Demonic*, edited by Alan M. Olson (1975)—B92, and again in *Coomaraswamy 2: Selected Papers, Metaphysics* ([1977])—A82—pp. 23-33.

1948

C888 [A review of] *Arab Archery: A Book on the Excellence of the Bow and Arrow and the Description Thereof*, translated by Nabih Amin Faris, with Notes and Appendix by Robert Potter Elmer. *Ars Islamica*, Ann Arbor, XIII/XIV. (1948) 198-201.

Of this translation AKC remarks that "the work of both authors inspires confidence" (p. 198). In the course of this review AKC discusses (1) the problem of the shape of Arab bows, (2) the coincidence of practical and transcendent values in archery (and this, according to traditional ways of thinking, as a *sine qua non* in any given procedure), (3) poisoned arrows (of which this book "has nothing to say"), and (4) the modern revival of archery.

C889 Personality and Tradition in Art. *Adyar Library Bulletin*, Madras, XII. 1 (17 Feb. 1948) 31-2.

A reprint of the "Introduction" to *Introduction to Indian Art* (1923)—A45a, preceded by an obituary of AKC by James H. Cousins (pp. [29]-31).

1949

C890 [Excerpts from letters to V. S. Agrawala]. *Journal of the United Provinces Historical Society*, Lucknow, XXII. 1/2 (1949) 6.

An article, "Ananda Coomaraswamy", by Agrawala, pp. [1]-7, incorporates excerpts from two letters of 1939 (on scholarship in the field of Indian art). The second of these is printed in full in *Selected Letters of Ananda K.Coomaraswamy* (1988)—A89—pp. 167-8.

C891 The Common Wisdom of the World. *Bhāratīya Vidyā*, Bombay, IX. (1948 [*i.e.* Aug. 1949]) 120-4.

This issue also bears the title: *Shri K.M. Munshi Diamond Jubilee Volume—Part I.* An assemblage of passages enunciating homological doctrines, culled from the Upaniṣads, the Bible, Chuang Tzu, Plato, Ovid, Buddhist scripture, American Indian oratory, Rūmī, Dante, T.S. Eliot, and other sources. The passages are arranged under eight headings: "He Who Is", "The Fellow-traveller", "Love of Self", "Look Not Back", "Motion-at-Will", "Everlasting Day", "Knowledge Hereafter", and "Causality". "Any extended list of such *dharma-paryāyas* would fill a book" (p. 124). Reprinted in *Sources of Wisdom* ([1981])—A85—pp. 187-92.

1951

C892 Note on the Philosophy of Persian Art. *Ars Islamica*, Ann Arbor, XV/XVI. (1951) [125]-128.

A paper read by AKC at Princeton University's Bicentennial Conference XII, "Near Eastern Culture and Society", at Princeton Inn, 25-27 March 1947. "The problem of meaning in Persian art [is] discussed only in connection with the representations of living things" (p. [125]). Reprinted in *Coomaraswamy 1: Selected Papers, Traditional Art and Symbolism* ([1977])—A82—pp. 260-5.

C893 [Letters to William Rothenstein]. *Art and Letters*, London, N.S. XXV. 1 (1951) 17-20.

Under the heading "Correspondence II Coomaraswamy", seven letters, written by AKC between 18 September 1910 and 14 March 1924, are printed in full in an article by Kenneth Romney Towndrow, "Sir William Rothenstein and His Indian Correspondence", pp. 12-32. Except for that of 18 January 1916, these letters are reprinted in *Selected Letters of Ananda K. Coomaraswamy* (1988)—A89—pp. 370-1, 372-8; a few passages are restored to the letter of 14 March 1924; postscripts belonging to letters of 18 September 1910 and 5 January 1915 are omitted. Three sentences excerpted from the letter of 10 October 1910 are printed in *Imperfect Encounter: Letters of William Rothenstein and Rabindranath Tagore 1911-1941*, edited by Mary M. Lago (Cambridge, Mass.: Harvard University Press, 1972), p. 31.

1971

C894 What Do People Get From Works of Art? A Short Introduction to Coomaraswamy by Roger Lipsey. *Big Rock Candy Mountain*, Menlo Park, Calif., II. 1 ([Summer] 1971) 33-7.

An article which includes, on pages 35-7, passages selected from *Why Exhibit Works of Art?* (1943)—A67—pp. 20-2, 98-9, *Am I My Brother's Keeper?* ([1947])—A72a—pp. 66-7, 73-4, *Hinduism and Buddhism* ([1943])—A68a—pp. 16, 65, and *The Transformation of Nature in Art* (1934)—A56a—p. 92.

1972

C895 "A Figure of Speech or a Figure of Thought?" [Part I]. *Studies in Comparative Religion*, Bedfont, Middx., VI. 1 (Winter 1972) 43-61.

A reprint, in two instalments, of Chapter I of *Figures of Speech or Figures of Thought* (1946)—A71.

C896 "A Figure of Speech or a Figure of Thought?" Part II. *Studies in Comparative Religion*, Bedfont, Middx., VI. 2 (Spring 1972) 104-12.

1973

C897 [Letter to S. Durai Raja Singam, May 1946]. *Span*, New Delhi, XIV. 3 (Mar. 1973) 47.

Forbidding the publication of biographical matter relating to himself. The letter is reproduced here, in facsimile of AKC's typewritten original, as an illustration to Chidananda Dasgupta's article, "Light on the Art of India. Postscript to a Film", pp. [42]-48. See also E48. This letter was first published in *Letters of the Great*, edited by S. Durai Raja Singam ([1954])—B86—p. 35.

C898 The Flood in Hindu Tradition. *Studies in Comparative Religion*, Bedfont, Middx., VII. 4 (Autumn 1973) 203-11.

A reprint of *The Flood in Hindu Tradition* ([1972?])—A79.

1974

C899 The Influence of Greek on Indian Art. *Studies in Comparative Religion*, Bedfont, Middx., VIII. 1 (Winter 1974) 42-50.

A reprint of *The Influence of Greek on Indian Art* ([1908])—A13b.

1977

C900 The Bugbear of Democracy, Freedom and Equality. *Studies in Comparative Religion*, Bedfont, Middx., XI. 3 (Summer 1977) 133-58.

This issue also bears the title: *A.K. Coomaraswamy Centenary Issue.* "In the present article I propose to discuss the prejudices that are aroused in every hundred per cent progressive and democratic-egalitarian mind by the (Portuguese) word 'caste'" (p. 134). This article, written *circa* 1944, and discovered among AKC's papers after his death by his son, Dr. Rama P. Coomaraswamy (see the "Editorial", by F. Clive-Ross, p. 131), was to have formed part of a projected series of articles on modern "bugbears", of which only one was published in AKC's lifetime: "The Bugbear of Literacy" (1944)—C833. "Am I My Brother's Keeper?" (1943)—C810—was intended by AKC to serve as a preface to the series. A prospective list of the topics to be treated in the "bugbear series" is printed on page 134. This article was reprinted as Chapter VIII of *The Bugbear of Literacy* ([1979])—A72c.

C901 One of the Great Creations of Indian Art. *Journal of Tamil Studies*, Madras, XII. (Dec. 1977) [37]-41, 1 text illus.

This issue also bears the title: *Dr. Ananda K. Coomaraswamy's Commemoration Volume.* A brief anthology of excerpts concerning Śiva as Naṭarāja, reprinted from "The Dance of Siva" (1912)—C293, "Medieval and Modern Hinduism" (1923)—C460, *History of Indian and Indonesian Art* (1927)—A50, and "Understanding and Reunion: An Oriental Perspective" (1945)—B64.

C902 Stories from the Collections of Ananda Coomaraswamy. *Journal of Tamil Studies*, Madras, XII. (Dec. 1977) [55]-63.

This issue also bears the title: *Dr. Ananda K. Coomaraswamy's Commemoration Volume.* A hitherto unpublished translation of Tamil folk-tales, prepared by AKC in Tanjore, in 1909, reproduced in facsimile of AKC's handwritten original, with the texts in Tamil script (in another hand?) on facing pages. There is a prefatory note by S. Durai Raja Singam, p. [55], which includes an acknowledgement: "I am specially indebted to Dr. Rama P. Coomaraswamy for gifting the original manuscript".

1979

C903 Fate, Foresight, and Free-Will. *Studies in Comparative Religion*, Bedfont, Middx., XIII. 3/4 (Summer/Autumn 1979) 184-6.

A hitherto unpublished note. Reprinted in *What Is Civilisation? and Other Essays* ([1989])—A90—pp. [86]-89.

1980

C904 Symbols. *Studies in Comparative Religion*, Bedfont, Middx., XIV.1/2 (Winter/Spring 1980) 15-17.

A hitherto unpublished note. A general introduction to "the language of traditional art". Reprinted in *What Is Civilisation? and Other Essays* ([1989])—A90—pp. [125]-127.

C905 The Interpretation of Symbols. *Studies in Comparative Religion*, Bedfont, Middx., XIV. 1/2 (Winter/Spring 1980) 62-7.

An essay printed for the first time. "For the complete appreciation or experiencing of a work of traditional art . . . we need at least as much to *eindenken* as to *einfühlen*, to 'think-in' and 'think-with' at least as much as to 'feel-in' and 'feel-with'" (p. 66). Reprinted in *What Is Civilisation? and Other Essays* ([1989])—A90—pp. [128]-134.

1983

C906 The Religious Basis of the Forms of Indian Society. *Studies in Comparative Religion*, Bedfont, Middx., XV. 1/2 (Winter/Spring 1983) 9-29.

Reprinted, with addenda, from *The Religious Basis of the Forms of Indian Society* . . . ([1946])—A70a.

C907 Indian Art. *Studies in Comparative Religion*, Bedfont, Middx., XV. 3/4 (Summer/Autumn 1983) 181-93.

A hitherto unpublished essay.

1985

C908 Indian Culture and English Influence. *Dilip*, Bombay, XI. 1/2 (Jan./Apr. 1985) 24-31.

Reprinted from *The Religious Basis of the Forms of Indian Society* . . . ([1946])—A70a.

1988

C909 Early Indian Architecture: IV. Huts and Related Temple Types. *Res: Anthropology and Aesthetics*, Cambridge, Mass., XV. (Spring 1988) [5]-26, 27 text illus. (incl. port.).

A hitherto unpublished paper that belongs to the series of articles on Indian architecture that AKC contributed in 1930-31 to *Eastern Art*, Philadelphia—C562, 597. The publication of this instalment was aborted when *Eastern Art* succumbed to the Depression. AKC's typescript and the seventy-six illustrations he submitted (to have been printed on twelve plates) were not returned to him. The present version was edited by Michael W. Meister from AKC's carbon typescript (preserved in the Firestone Library at Princeton University). In this paper AKC points to the direct inheritance from primitive building types of the formal and symbolic elements of later temple architecture. Evidence is adduced from textual references in the Sanskrit, Prakrit, and Pāli literature, and from representations in pre-Gupta relief sculpture, to demonstrate a continuity in architectural morphology and terminology. AKC's descriptions of, and his sources for, the lost illustrations, are "edited here [on pp. 22-6] as part of the record of Coomaraswamy's thinking at the time. I have left his dates . . . although modern scholarship has made some revisions. In instances where one of his figures corresponds to one of those used to illustrate this publication, the present number has been provided as well, within square brackets and in boldface" (*editorial note*, p. 22). Meister also contributes a "Preface", pp. [5]-7, and appends an "Afterword" (i.e. a conversation with Joseph Rykwert), pp. 27-33. Reprinted in *Essays in Early Indian Architecture* (1992)—A92.

D. Miscellaneous

D. Miscellaneous

D1 Publications on Museum Topics by Officers of the Museum, 1917 . . . Ananda K. Coomaraswamy. *Forty-second Annual Report for the Year 1917*. Boston: Museum of Fine Arts, Boston, 1917, p. 150.

The first of 31 selective lists of AKC's publications (368 items), almost certainly partly if not wholly compiled by him, that were printed under this heading (the heading varies) in the issues of the *Annual Report* to 1947, as follows: (43rd) 1918, p. 142; (44th) 1919, p. 169; (45th) 1920, p. 124; (46th) 1921, p. 125; (47th) 1922, p. 129; (48th) 1923, p. 128; (49th) 1924, p. 111; (50th) 1925, p. 94; (51st) 1926, p. 97; (52nd) 1927, pp. 95-6; (53rd) 1928, p. 95; (54th) 1929, pp. 99-100; (55th) 1930, pp. 104-5; (56th) 1931, pp. 99-100; (57th) 1932, p. 92; (58th) 1933, p. 94; (59th) 1934, p. 108; (60th) 1935, pp. 114-15; (61st) 1936, pp.119-20; (62nd) 1937, pp. 112-13; (63rd) 1938, pp. 122-3; (64th) 1939, pp. 117-18; (65th) 1940, p. 117; (66th) 1941, p. 120; (67th) 1942, pp. 80-1; (68th) 1943, pp. 70-1; (69th) 1944, pp. 78-9; (70th) 1945, pp. 81-2; (71st) 1946, pp. 82-3; (72nd) 1947, pp. 89-90. Ardelia Ripley Hall writes of assisting AKC in the preparation of these lists (in the 1930s) in her "The Keeper of the Indian Collection"—E80, pp. 118, 121.

D2 [Editor of words of Indian origin]. *Webster's New International Dictionary of the English Language*. Second Edition. Springfield, Mass.: G. & C. Merriam Company, 1934.

Under the heading "Special Editors", a note on page xix, printed in 7 lines, introduces AKC as the Dictionary's editor for the subject India. A photograph of AKC, numbered: 30, and signed: Llamas, i.e. pseud. of Doña Luisa (Mrs A.K.) Coomaraswamy, is reproduced facing page xvi. S. Durai Raja Singam reprints 149 of the entries for Indian words—"only a fraction of Dr. Coomaraswamy's contribution to the volume"—in his *Ananda Coomaraswamy—the Bridge Builder; a Study of a Scholar-Colossus* (1977)—E192—pp. [380-400], with AKC's draft slips for *pūjā, dharma, nirvāna,* and *mantra,* reproduced on page [376], and a letter, from AKC to G. & C. Merriam Company, dated 15 April 1929 (p. [379]). The slips (only) were also reproduced in E191, page 221.

D3 The Dove and the Crow. *Studies in Comparative Religion*, Bedfont, Middx., XVI. 2/3 [*i.e.* 3/4] ([Summer/Autumn 1984, but published *circa* Summer 1986]) 141-7.

D. MISCELLANEOUS

The byline attributes authorship of this article to AKC (notwithstanding, among other indications, the half a dozen references it includes to works published long after AKC's death, which make such an attribution virtually impossible). In a "Corrigendum" in the next issue the editors offer an apology for this mistaken attribution and identify the real author as: "Father Ian Herring, of the Anglican Church of Saint Peter, Bundona [*sic*, for Bundoora], Victoria, Australia".

E. Appendix: Select List of Material on Ananda K. Coomaraswamy

E. Appendix: Select List of Material on Ananda K. Coomaraswamy

E1 ADAMS, Frank Dawson. The Geology of Ceylon. *Canadian Journal of Research*, Ottawa, I. 5 (Nov. 1929) 425-65; and 6 (Dec. 1929) 467-511.

Includes references to AKC's early career in geology; see especially pages 430-1. Adams had corresponded with AKC preparatory to writing this article.

E2 AGRAWALA, Vasudeva Saran. Ananda Coomaraswamy. *Journal of the United Provinces Historical Society*, Lucknow, XXII. 1/2 (1949) [1]-7, 1 pl. (port.) facing p. [1].

A general account of AKC's life and work, by a former Superintendent of the National Museum of India, New Delhi.

E3 AMUR, G.S. Evolution of Indian Sensibility in Art: Ananda K. Coomaraswamy's View. *Images and Impressions: Essays Mainly on Contemporary Indian Literature*, by G.S. Amur. Jaipur: Panchsheel Prakashan, 1979, pp. 79-87.

Reprinted in E131, pp. [57]-66.

E4 *Ananda Coomaraswamy Centenary 1877-1977*. Colombo: Royal Asiatic Society, Sri Lanka Branch, 1977. [8] pp., frontis. (port.).

A brochure issued in conjunction with a public meeting held in Colombo on 23 September 1977 to mark the centenary; contains a biographical note, tributes, and a select bibliography.

E5 Ananda K. Coomaraswamy. *Études Traditionnelles,* Paris, XLIX. 265 (Jan./Feb. 1948) [10]-12.

(In French.) An obituary, signed: La Rédaction. An earlier announcement of AKC's death appeared in *Études Traditionnelles*, XLVIII. 263 (Oct./Nov. 1947) 280.

E5a Ananda K. Coomaraswamy, 70, Oriental Art Scholar, Is Dead. *Boston Herald*, Boston (10 Sept. 1947) 27, 1 text illus. (port.).

For other prominent obituaries of AKC in the world's press see, for instance, "A. Coomaraswamy, Art Expert, Dead", *New York Times*, New York (10 Sept. 1947) 27; "Dr. A. Coomaraswamy. Research in Indian Art", *The Times*, London (30 Sept. 1947) 6; "Noted Savant Dead. Ananda Coomaraswamy", *Hindu*, Madras (11 Sept. 1947) 6.

E6 ANSHEN, Ruth Nanda. Ananda Coomaraswamy: *Esse Omnium Est Superesse Divinitas. Homage to Ananda Coomaraswamy*, edited by S. Durai Raja Singam (1952)—E189—pp. 222-33.

An epitome of the traditional metaphysic as expounded by AKC.

E7 ARCHER, William George. *Indian Paintings from the Punjab Hills: A Survey and History of Pahari Miniature Painting.* Delhi: Oxford University Press/London & New York: Sotheby Parke Bernet, 1973, *Vol. I*, pp. xxvii-xxx, 21-4, 70-1, 101-2, 183-4, 263-7, 405.

Contains on these pages, a critical survey of AKC's contributions to the study of Indian painting; see particularly page 265, where Archer questions AKC's probity.

E8 *Architecture & Arts in Ceylon*, Colombo, 2 (Sept./Dec. 1965), "Ananda Coomaraswamy Commemoration Issue".

For the more outstanding among the contributions to this special issue see E72, 129a *n*.

E9 ARNHEIM, Rudolf. The Man with the Tables of the Law. *Ananda Coomaraswamy: Remembering and Remembering Again and Again*, edited by S. Durai Raja Singam (1974)—E191—pp. 97-8.

A tribute paid to AKC as the pre-eminent expositor of the traditional doctrine of art.

E10 BAGCHEE, Moni. *Ananda Coomaraswamy: A Study.* [Bharata Manisha Research Series 9]. Varanasi: Bharata Manisha [1977]. xvii, 205 pp.

See also B93.

E11 BAISTROCCHI, Marco. The Last Pillars of Wisdom. *Ananda Coomaraswamy: Remembering and Remembering Again and Again*, edited by S. Durai Raja Singam (1974)—E191—pp. 350-9.

A comparative analysis of the writings of AKC and René Guénon.

E12 BANDARANAYAKE, Senake. Ananda Coomaraswamy and Approaches to the Study of Traditional Sri Lankan Art and Society. *Parokṣa*, edited by Gulam Mohammed Sheikh *et al.* (1984)—E182—pp. 27-37.

Bandaranayake's paper as it was originally presented at a seminar held in New Delhi in 1977—see E182 *n.* A revised version is printed in *P.E.P. Deraniyagala Commemoration Volume*, edited by Thelma T.P. Gunewardana, Lee Rananda Prematilleka, and Roland Silva (Colombo: Lake House Investments Ltd., 1980), pp. [68]-84, 2 pls.

E13 BANERJEE, N.R., editor. *A Catalogue of the Special Exhibition of Paintings and Books in Honour of the Birth Centenary of Ananda K. Coomaraswamy.* New Delhi: National Museum [1976]. 60 pp., 18 pls.

E14 BHATTACHARYYA, D.C. Coomaraswamy on Buddhist Art and Iconography. *Parokṣa*, edited by Gulam Mohammed Sheikh *et al.* (1984)—E182—pp. 62-4.

E15 BLOCK, Marguerite Beck. Ananda K. Coomaraswamy. *Review of Religion*, New York, XII. 1 (Nov. 1947) [51]-53.

An obituary, incorporating an account at first hand of AKC's lecture technique. Reprinted in E189, pp. 150-3.

E16 BROWN, Joseph Epes. Coomaraswamy, the Husbandman. *Homage to Ananda Coomaraswamy*, edited by S. Durai Raja Singam (1952)—E189—pp. 25-8.

On AKC's botanical knowledge and on the significance of his enthusiasm for gardening. AKC was a Fellow of the Linnean Society, for this see *Proceedings of the Linnean Society of London*, London, 113th Session (1900-1) 5.

E17 CAGE, John. Homage to Coomaraswamy. *For the Birds*, by

John Cage, in conversation with Daniel Charles. London & Boston: Marion Boyars [1981], pp. 101, 104-5.

The composer acknowledges an indebtedness to AKC for certain ideas concerning the Hindu and traditional theories of art and aesthetics that he found in *The Dance of Śiva* (1918) and *The Transformation of Nature in Art* (1934). Originally published as *Pour les oiseaux* (Paris: Pierre Belfond, 1976).

E18 CAMMANN, Schuyler. Remembering Again: The Life and Work of Ananda K. Coomaraswamy. *Parabola*, New York, III. 2 (May 1978) 84-91, 4 text illus. (ports.).

On Roger Lipsey's biography—E116, adding personal information.

E19 CAREY, A. Graham. Holes in Oblivion. *Ananda Coomaraswamy: Remembering and Remembering Again and Again*, edited by S. Durai Raja Singam (1974)—E191—pp. 180-4.

Some glimpses of AKC and his entourage in New England, 1935-42.

E20 CHAKRAVARTHY, G.N. Ananda Coomaraswamy's Approach to the Veda. *Ananda Coomaraswamy Centenary Essays*, edited by C.D. Narasimhaiah (1982)—E131—pp. [165]-174.

E21 CHANDRA, Pramod. The Study of Indian Temple Architecture. *Studies in Indian Temple Architecture. Papers Presented at a Seminar Held in Varanasi, 1967*, edited by Pramod Chandra. [New Delhi] American Institute of Indian Studies, 1975, pp. 1-39.

Incorporates an estimate of AKC's work in this field; see particularly pages 27-30.

E22 ———A Tribute to Ananda Coomaraswamy (1877-1947). *From River Banks and Sacred Places* ([1977])—E66—pp. 4-5.

E23 ———Introduction. *Symbolism of Indian Architecture*, by Ananda K. Coomaraswamy. Jaipur: The Historical Research Documentation Programme [1983], pp. [3]-4.

E24 ——— *On the Study of Indian Art*. Cambridge, Mass.: Harvard University Press, 1983, pp. 31-3, 52-3, 57-62, 93-8.

Contains on these pages, a survey and an evaluation of AKC's contribution to the study of Indian architecture, painting, and sculpture.

E25 CHANDRASEKHAR, Sripati. *Ananda K. Coomaraswamy (1877-1947): A Critical Appreciation*. Madras: Blackie & Son Publishers Pvt. Ltd. [1977]. 59 pp.

An expanded version of an address delivered before a meeting of the Indo-American Association held at Madras on 22 August 1977 to mark the centenary of AKC's birth. See also Chandrasekhar's interview with AKC—C882.

E26 CHARI, V.K. The Rasa Theory: Theology or Aesthetics? *The Sacred and the Secular in India's Performing Arts*, edited by V. Subramaniam (1980)—E201—pp. [47]-61.

A critical analysis of AKC's treatment of this fundamental term in the Indian theory of art.

E27 CLARK, Walter Eugene. Foreword. *Elements of Buddhist Iconography*, by Ananda K. Coomaraswamy. Cambridge, Mass.: Harvard University Press, 1935, *recto of leaf following title-leaf*.

On AKC's realization of the importance of Vedic materials in interpreting the later developments of Indian art.

E27a CLIVE-ROSS, F. *See* E197 *n*.

E28 COATTS, Margot. *A Weaver's Life: Ethel Mairet, 1872-1952*. [London] Crafts Council [1983], pp. 14-38, 107-20, 125.

Contains on these pages, an account of AKC and Ethel Mairet (formerly Mrs AKC) in Ceylon and at Broad Campden in Gloucestershire, 1903-11.

E29 ——— *A Weaver's Life: Ethel Mairet 1872-1952. A Selection of the Source Material*. [London] Crafts Council [1984?], pp. 97-103.

Contains on these pages, an inventory of the manuscripts and photographs by AKC, and books and other items from his personal collection, that are preserved in American libraries and museums.

E30 COOMARASWAMY, Doña Luisa. Some Recollections and References to Dr. Ananda Coomaraswamy. *Kalāmanjari*, Colombo, I. 1 (1950/51) 18-23, 2 text illus. (ports.).

A memoir by his widow. For another contribution that concerns AKC contained in this same issue see E204.

E31 ———Introduction (1963). *The Arts & Crafts of India & Ceylon*, by Ananda K. Coomaraswamy. New York: The Noonday Press, 1964, pp. v-vii.

E32 ———Coomaraswamy, Ananda Kentish. *New Catholic Encyclopedia*. New York: McGraw-Hill Book Company, 1967, *Vol. IV*, pp. 296-7, 1 text illus. (port.).

Signed: L. Coomaraswamy.

E33 ———Details of [the] Death of Ananda K. Coomaraswamy as Given in a Letter . . . to S. Durai Raja Singam. *Ananda Coomaraswamy—The Bridge Builder*, by S. Durai Raja Singam (1977)—E192—pp. [546-7].

The letter is dated Needham, Mass., 25 September 1947.

E34 ———& COOMARASWAMY, Rama Ponnambalam. Coomaraswamy: The Man and His Message. *United Asia*, Bombay, I. 2 (Sept. 1948) 177, 1 text illus. (port.).

Reprinted in E192, p. [553].

E35 COOMARASWAMY, Rama Ponnambalam. Who Speaks for the East? *Studies in Comparative Religion*, Bedfont, Middx., XII. 2 (Spring 1977) 85-91.

AKC's son includes *passim* references to his father's life and work; see particularly the footnote on page 89. Reprinted in E87, pp. [3]-8, and in E131, pp. 18-25. See also E129.

E35a ———*Ananda Kentish Coomaraswamy: A Working*

Bibliography, compiled by Dr. Rama P. Coomaraswamy. New Delhi: Department of Culture, Lalit Kala Akademi [1979]. [iv], 67 pp.

"The present bibliography makes no claim to completeness—indeed the important area of book reviews has been entirely omitted. Its aim is to bring together in one place the major essays, and to inform the reader where these may be located" ("Introduction", p. [iii]). Lists 654 items arranged in chronological order, but by haphazard within each year. Includes some unpublished writings of AKC held by Princeton University Library and in the possession of Dr Rama P. Coomaraswamy. There are no annotations, and no index. In Roger Lipsey's life of AKC—E116, this bibliography is referred to *passim* as *A Working Bibliography of Ananda K. Coomaraswamy.*

E36 ———Introduction. *Sources of Wisdom*, by Ananda K. Coomaraswamy. [Colombo] Ministry of Cultural Affairs, Sri Lanka [1981], pp. 5-9.

E37 ———, compiler. *Ananda K. Coomaraswamy: Bibliography/ Index*. [Berwick-upon-Tweed] Prologos Books [1988]. x, 70 pp.

This bibliography was prepared in collaboration with Lester Kanefsky, proprietor of Prologos Books. Lists 913 items (including some "unpublished works") grouped in six sections and arranged chronologically. Within each year though the arrangement is not chronological: AKC's books are entered first, followed by his articles arranged alphabetically by the title of the periodical in which they appeared. Entries are frequently rendered telegraphic if not cryptographic by the compliers' over-reliance on abbreviations. Very lightly annotated. The index is incomplete. Numerous inaccuracies and errors compromise its usefulness as a bibiliography.

E37a ———Preface. *The Door in the Sky: Coomaraswamy on Myth and Meaning*, edited by Rama P. Coomaraswamy. Princeton: Princeton University Press [1997], pp. ix-xxii.

An outline of AKC's thinking about mythology, fairy tales, symbolism, ritual, and the arts. See also A95 *n.*

E38 COORAY, Percival Gerald. *An Introduction to the Geology of Ceylon*. [Colombo] National Museums of Ceylon Publication [1967], pp. 102-3.

Contains on these pages, an appraisal of AKC's work in geology.

E39 CRAWFORD, Alan. Ananda Coomaraswamy and C.R. Ashbee. *Ananda Coomaraswamy: Remembering and Remembering Again and Again*, edited by S. Durai Raja Singam (1974)—E191—pp. 239-44, 5 text illus.

An account of AKC's association with Ashbee and the Essex House Press at Broad Campden, Gloucestershire, 1903-11. See also the references to AKC in Crawford's *C.R. Ashbee: Architect, Designer & Romantic Socialist* (New Haven & London: Yale University Press, 1985), pp. 140-1, 146-7, 158, 263-8, 396, 450, 459, 472, 482, 483.

E40 CROSS, Stephen. E.B. Havell and the Art of India. *Temenos*, London, 10 (1989) [224]-243.

Compares *passim* the early work of Havell and AKC.

E41 ———St. Augustine and the Perennial Philosophy. *Avaloka*, Grand Rapids, Mich., VI. 1/2 (1992) 56-61.

Points out AKC's error in assuming (as he seems to have done) that a statement by St Augustine concerning the *Philosophia Perennis* (in *Retractationes*) had been withdrawn by him.

E42 CROUCH, James S. Ananda Coomaraswamy in Ceylon: A Bibliography. *Ceylon Journal of Historical and Social Studies*, Peradeniya, N.S. III. 2 (July/Dec. 1973 [*i.e.* Dec. 1974]) 54-66.

An annotated list, arranged chronologically, of AKC's pamphlets and articles (96 items) from the period 1900 to 1906 (an early draft of a portion of the present work).

E43 ———Notes on Roger Lipsey's Life of Coomaraswamy. *Journal of Tamil Studies*, Madras, XXVI. (Dec. 1984) [53]-64.

Rectifying factual inaccuracies in E116.

E44 CROWLEY, Aleister. *The Confessions of Aleister Crowley: An Autohagiography*, edited by John Symonds & Kenneth Grant. London: Jonathan Cape [1969], pp. 469, 773-6, 869.

Includes on these pages, a memoir of AKC and Ratan Devī (i.e. Mrs AKC) in New York, 1916.

E45 ———Not Good Enough. *The Scrutinies of Simon Iff*, by Aleister Crowley, edited by Martin P. Starr. Chicago: The Teitan Press, Inc. [1987], pp. 125-50, 178-9 (notes).

A short story, based upon the author's encounters with AKC and Ratan Devī (i.e. Mrs AKC), that first appeared in *International*, New York, XII. 1 (Jan. 1918) 3-9, under the pseudonym "Edward Kelly". See the references to AKC in the editor's introduction, page xv. See also Crowley's review *ad hominem* of AKC's *The Dance of Śiva* (1918) in *Equinox*, Detroit, III. 1 (Mar. 1919) 292-4, under the pseudonym "A Mourner Clad in Green".

E46 CUNNINGHAM, Adrian. The Importance of Coomaraswamy. *Tablet*, London, CCXXXIII. 7,259 (25 Aug. 1979) 825.

A review of A82 and E116.

E47 DAS, Asok Kumar. Ananda Coomaraswamy and the Study of Mughal Painting. *Ananda Coomaraswamy: A Centenary Volume*, edited by Kalyan Kumar Dasgupta (1981)—E50—pp. [38]-48.

E48 DASGUPTA, Chidananda. Light on the Art of India: Postscript to a Film. *Span*, New Delhi, XIV. 3 (Mar. 1973) [42]-48, 7 text illus. (incl. ports.).

The author was producer and co-director (with B.D. Garga) of the U.S.I.S. documentary on AKC, *The Dance of Shiva* (1975). Reprinted, as "Rediscovery of Ananda Coomaraswamy", in *Triveni*, Machilipatnam, XLV. 3 (Oct./Dec. 1976) [10]-18.

E49 DASGUPTA, Kalyan Kumar. Ananda Coomaraswamy and Indian Numismatics. *Journal of the Numismatic Society of India*, Varanasi, XL. 1/2 (1978) 6-8.

E50 ———, editor. *Ananda Coomaraswamy: A Centenary Volume*. Calcutta: Centre of Advanced Study in Ancient Indian History & Culture, Calcutta University, 1981. xvi, 128 pp.

Collects 15 papers by scholars from India and Malaysia, 10 of which were presented at two seminars held under the auspices of the Centre of Advanced Study, Calcutta University, in March 1976 and August 1977. For the more outstanding among these papers see E47, 51, 52, 105, 158.

E51 ———Coomaraswamy and Indian Iconography. *Ananda Coomaraswamy: A Centenary Volume*, edited by Kalyan Kumar Dasgupta (1981)—E50—pp. [55]-68.

E52 DASGUPTA, R.K. Coomaraswamy's Concept of Alaṁkāra. *Ananda Coomaraswamy: A Centenary Volume*, edited by Kalyan Kumar Dasgupta (1981)—E50—pp. [93]-100.

An examination of AKC's approach to Sanskrit poetics.

E53 DENNEY, Reuel. Coomaraswamy and the "Bugbears" of Modern Man. *Literary Criterion*, Mysore, XIII. 3 (1978) [34]-41.

E54 DESAI, Devangana. Reflections on Coomaraswamy's Approach to Indian Art. *Parokṣa*, edited by Gulam Mohammed Sheikh *et al.* (1984)—E182—pp. 60-1.

E55 DESAI, S.K. Ananda K. Coomaraswamy's View of Indian Poetics. *Ananda Coomaraswamy Centenary Essays*, edited by C.D. Narasimhaiah (1982)—E131—pp. [115]-126.

E56 DE SILVA, Lucian. Coomaraswamy, the Student. *Homage to Ananda K. Coomaraswamy*, edited by S. Durai Raja Singam ([1948])—E188—pp. 133-4.

Reminiscences "from one who was his contemporary for four or five years" at University College (London), 1897-1900; excerpted from De Silva's letter that was printed in the *Ceylon Daily News*, Colombo, for 12 September 1947, under the heading "Dr. Ananda Coomaraswamy and His Philosophy of Art". Reprinted in E191, p. 248. For details of the conferral of AKC's doctorate and of the thesis he presented, see "Report of the Examiners upon a Thesis for the D.Sc. Degree for External Students" in *London University Gazette*, London (7 Feb. 1906) 82.

E57 DEVDAS, Nalini. Sri Aurobindo's Views on the Creation and Enjoyment of Art. *The Sacred and the Secular in India's Performing Arts*, edited by V. Subramaniam (1980)—E201—pp. [163]-180.

In part, a comparison of the writings of AKC and Sri Aurobindo; see particularly pages 173-6.

E58 EATON, Gai. Two Traditionalists. *The Richest Vein: Eastern Tradition and Modern Thought*, by Gai Eaton. London: Faber & Faber Ltd. [1949], pp. 183-209 (*i.e.* Pt. II, Chap. 9).

A comparative study of the writings of René Guénon and AKC; see particularly pages 199-209. Reprinted in E191, pp. 335-49.

E59 ELIADE, Mircea. Ananda Coomaraswamy. *Revista Fundatiilor Regale*, Bucharest, IV. 7 (July 1937) 183-9.

(In Romanian.) An omnibus review of AKC's writings. Reprinted, in a slightly expanded and revised form, in *Insula lui Euthanasius*, by Mircea Eliade (Bucharest: Fundatia Regala pentru Literatura si Arta, 1943), pp. 265-75.

E60 ———Some Notes on *Theosophia Perennis*: Ananda K. Coomaraswamy and Henry Corbin. *History of Religions*, Chicago, XIX. 2 (Nov. 1979) 167-76.

In part, a discussion of Roger Lipsey's biography of AKC—E116.

E61 ELIOT, T.S. [A note on AKC]. *Homage to Ananda K. Coomaraswamy*, edited by S. Durai Raja Singam ([1948])—E188—p. 132.

An excerpt, printed in 6 lines, from the poet's letter to K. Bharatha Iyer. Eliot appears to have been invited to contribute to Iyer's Festschrift—E86, but in the event did not. Reprinted in E189, p. xiv, and E191, p. 83.

E62 ETTINGHAUSEN, Richard. *See* E104 *n*.

E63 FERNANDO, Ranjit. Dance of Shiva. [Letter]. *Ceylon Daily News*, Colombo (2 Aug. 1975) 4.

A brief critique of the film of this title on AKC—E48 *n*.

E64 FOWLER, Murray. In Memoriam Ananda Kentish Coomaraswamy. *Artibus Asiae*, Ascona, X. 3 (1947) 241-4.

See also pages 249-[250] in this issue for Fowler's review of AKC's *Time and Eternity* (1947). The obituary was reprinted in E189, pp. 7-14.

E65 ———[Letter to S. Durai Raja Singam, 4 July 1946, on AKC]. *Homage to Ananda K. Coomaraswamy*, edited by S. Durai Raja Singam ([1948])—E188—pp. 125-7.

"The best account of my work" (AKC in a letter of 20 Aug. 1947 to Muhammad Hafiz Syed, quoted in E194, *Part II*, p. [vi]). Reprinted in E191, pp. 154-5.

E66 *From River Banks and Sacred Places: Ancient Indian Terracottas. An Exhibition to Commemorate the One-Hundredth Anniversary of the Birth of Ananda K. Coomaraswamy . . . August 23—December 31, 1977*, introductory remarks by Pramod Chandra [*see* E22] and reprinted essay by Ananda K. Coomaraswamy [*see* B95]. Catalogue by Joyce Paulson. [Boston] Museum of Fine Arts, Boston [1977]. 48 pp., 80 text illus. (incl. port.).

E67 GANGOLY, Ordhendra Coomar. Dr. Ananda Coomaraswamy. *Modern Review*, Calcutta, LXXXII. 10 (Oct. 1947) 309-12, 1 text illus. (port.).

An obituary. Reprinted in E189, pp. 90-100.

E68 ———Ananda K. Coomaraswamy. *Annals of the Bhandarkar Oriental Research Institute*, Poona, XXVIII. (1947/48) [149]-155.

An obituary; differs from the preceding entry.

E69 GILBERT, Katharine Everett. Art: Reminder and Delight. *Aesthetic Studies; Architecture and Poetry*, by Katharine E. Gilbert. [Durham, N.C.] Duke University Press, 1952, pp. [125]-133.

A general discussion of AKC's writings on aesthetics that first appeared as a book review in *Art Bulletin*, New York, XXX. 2 (June 1948) 157-9.

E70 ———Ananda K. Coomaraswamy, a Catholic Eminenter. *Homage to Ananda Coomaraswamy*, edited by S. Durai Raja Singam (1952)—E189—pp. 85-90.

On AKC's knowledge of, and sympathy with, Roman Catholic doctrine; but emphasizing his catholicity.

E71 GILL, Eric. *Autobiography*. London: Jonathan Cape [1940], p. 174.

This page contains Gill's oft-quoted panegyric upon AKC. Another (brief) reference to AKC occurs on page 207. The panegyric (only) is reprinted in E188, p. 3.

E72 GODAKUMBURA, Charles Edmund. Coomaraswamy's Contribution to Culture. *Architecture & Arts in Ceylon* (1965)—E8—pp. 17-20.

A conspectus of AKC's *oeuvre*, by the Archaeological Commissioner of Ceylon (1959-67).

E73 GOSWAMI, B.N. Ananda Coomaraswamy as a Historian of Rajput Painting. *Historians of Medieval India*, edited by Mohibbul Hasan. Meerut: Meenakshi Prakashan [1968], pp. [258]-270.

Reprinted in E191, pp. 75-83.

E73a GRAY, Basil. Obituary—Dr. Ananda Coomaraswamy. *Burlington Magazine*, London, LXXXIX. 536 (Nov. 1947) 320-1.

Another obituary of AKC by Gray is in the *Manchester Guardian*, Manchester, for 1 October 1947, p. 3.

E74 GRIGSON, Geoffrey. The Arts of Ministration and the Arts of Flattery. *Homage to Ananda K. Coomaraswamy*, edited by S. Durai Raja Singam ([1948])—E188—pp. 162-70.

A discussion centred on AKC's *Figures of Speech or Figures of Thought* (1946). Grigson incidentally calls attention to AKC's repudiation of copyright, i.e. the "No rights reserved" notice placed by him in this volume (and in *Why Exhibit Works of Art?* (1943)).

E75 GUDAS, Fabian. Ananda K. Coomaraswamy: The Perennial

Philosophy of Art. *Studies in Comparative Literature*, edited by Waldo Forest McNeir. Baton Rouge: Louisiana State University Press, 1962, pp. 1-28, 273-84 (notes).

"The present essay confines itself to an analysis of the theory of art as taught by the perennial philosophy, with special emphasis on what it has to say on myth and symbol, on folklore, and on the aims and methodology of comparative literature. These are subjects to which Coomaraswamy devoted a great deal of attention in the last fifteen years of his life" (p. 2).

E76 GUÉNON, René. *Études sur l'Hindouisme*. Paris: Éditions Traditionnelles, 1966, pp. 130-1, 133-4, 137-8, 140, 148-9, 159-60, 193-201, 207-9, 216-17, 221, 224-5, 231-3, 235-42, 244-6, 250-72.

Collects on these pages 54 of Guénon's reviews, of books and articles by AKC, published in *Le Voile d'Isis* and *Études Traditionnelles*, Paris, from 1935 to 1948. S. Durai Raja Singam reprints 41 of these, in English, in E194, *Part II:* pp. 129, 142-6, 155, 160, 162, 163, 166, 167, 179, 188, 197-8, 203, 204-5, 207, 211, 219, 222-3, 231-3, 247, 248, 257-9, 260-1, 265, 266-7, 279, 281, 309-10, 316-17, 318-19, 323, 338-9, 356-8, 393, 404-5, 412, 418.

E77 ———*Comptes rendus*. Paris: Villain et Belhomme—Éditions Traditionnelles, 1973, pp. 36, 56, 78, 155, 164-6, 181, 184, 185.

Collects on these pages 12 of Guénon's reviews, of books and articles by AKC, published in *Études Traditionnelles*, Paris, from 1940 to 1947 (additional to those collected in E76). S. Durai Raja Singam reprints 9 of these, in English, in E194, *Part II:* pp. 224-5, 250-1, 278, 280-1, 284-6, 340, 341, 359, 365.

E78 GULICK, Sidney Lewis. Oriental Conceptions of the Self. *Personalist*, Los Angeles, XXVII. (July 1946) 306-13.

On AKC's exposition of the traditional doctrine of "the two selves", with particular reference to this doctrine's treatment in *Hinduism and Buddhism* ([1943]).

E79 GUNAWARDANA, A.J. Ananda Coomaraswamy and the Greater India. *Ananda Coomaraswamy Centenary Essays*, edited by C.D. Narasimhaiah (1982)—E131—pp. [26]-34.

An examination of AKC's "emphasis on [the] theme of unity between India and Sri Lanka".

E80 HALL, Ardelia Ripley. The Keeper of the Indian Collection:

An Appreciation of Ananda Kentish Coomaraswamy. *Ananda Coomaraswamy: Remembering and Remembering Again and Again,* edited by S. Durai Raja Singam (1974)—E191—pp. 106-24.

A colleague's account of AKC's term of office at the Museum of Fine Arts, Boston, 1917-47, together with further biographical data. Includes, as an appendix (pp. 123-4), a list of AKC's contributions to the Museum's *Bulletin*: 61 items are recorded in a chronological arrangement by year of publication (the list is incomplete).

E81 HASTINGS, Somerville. [A memoir of AKC as a student at Wycliffe College (Stonehouse, Glos.) and at University College (London), 1889-1900]. *Ananda Coomaraswamy: Remembering and Remembering Again and Again*, edited by S. Durai Raja Singam (1974)—E191—p. 247.

E82 HERMAN, Arthur L. A.K.C. and the Pertinence of Philosophy. *Ananda Coomaraswamy: Remembering and Remembering Again and Again*, edited by S. Durai Raja Singam (1974)—E191—pp. 84-93.

See also Herman's "A.K. Coomaraswamy and Śaṁkara [*sic*]", in his *The Problem of Evil and Indian Thought* (Delhi: Motilal Banarsidass [1976]), pp. 165-8; other references to AKC occur on pp. 175, 189, 248, 260.

E82a ———Ananda K. Coomaraswamy and the Bugbear of Information. *Triveni* (1977)—E206—pp.[55]-60.

E83 HORNER, Isaline Blew. An Appreciation of a Pali Buddhist Scholar. *Homage to Ananda Coomaraswamy*, edited by S. Durai Raja Singam (1952)—E189—pp. 126-34.

Reprinted in E191, pp. 20-3.

E84 HUXLEY, Aldous. [A note on AKC]. *Homage to Ananda Coomaraswamy*, edited by S. Durai Raja Singam (1952)—E189—p. xv.

See also Huxley's comments on AKC in "A Conversation with Aldous Huxley", by Krishna Bladev Vaid, in *Illustrated Weekly of India*, Bombay, LXXXII. 49 (3 Dec. 1961) [13]-15.

E85 IRWIN, John Conran. "Asokan" Pillars: A Reassessment of the Evidence I[-IV]. *Burlington Magazine*, London, CXV. 848 (Oct. 1973) 706-20; CXVI. 861 (Dec. 1974) 712-27; CXVII. 871 (Oct. 1975) 631-43; CXVIII. 884 (Nov. 1976) 734-53.

Includes *passim* references to AKC's contribution to the Aśokan pillar debate of the 1930s; see particularly part III: pp. 631, 636, 638.

E86 IYER, K. Bharatha, editor. *Art and Thought; Issued in Honour of Dr. Ananda K. Coomaraswamy on the Occasion of His 70th Birthday*. London: Luzac & Company Ltd., 1947. xvi, 259 pp., 51 pls. incl. frontis. (port.).

Comprises 40 essays contributed by scholars from England, France, Germany, India, the U.S.A., and elsewhere. See the editor's introduction, pages xiii-xvi, also Walter Shewring's contribution—E183, and "Bibliography of Ananda K. Coomaraswamy's Writings"—C852 *n.*, the only other items in this Festschrift that are wholly concerned with AKC.

E87 *Journal of Tamil Studies*, Madras, XII. (Dec. 1977), "Dr. Ananda K. Coomaraswamy's Commemoration Volume".

Comprises 8 essays contributed by scholars from India, Malaysia, and the U.S.A. For the more outstanding among these contributions see E35, 177.

E88 *Journal of the Indian Society of Oriental Art*, Calcutta, V. (June/Dec. 1937).

This issue is dedicated to AKC on the occasion of his 60th birthday. See also E169.

E89 *Journal of the Indian Society of Oriental Art*, Calcutta, XV. (1947) and XVI. (1948), "A.K. Coomaraswamy Commemoration Volume[s], Part[s] I[-II]".

For the more outstanding among the contributions to these special issues see E138, 207.

E90 KAMALIAH, K.C. *Ananda Coomaraswamy: Wise Man from the East*. Madras [Printed for the author by Meipporul Achagam] 1977. ix, 141 pp., 1 pl., frontis.(port.).

E90a KANEFSKY, Lester. *See* E37 *n.*

E91 KAPUR, Geeta. On the Vocation of the Artist. *Parokṣa*, edited by Gulam Mohammed Sheikh *et al.* (1984)—E182—pp. 148-53.

An exposition that draws, and reflects extensively, upon AKC's writings.

E92 KEEBLE, Brian. Meister Eckhart and Ananda K. Coomaraswamy. *Eckhart Society Newsletter*, Cambridge, Cambs., 3 (Summer 1989) [1-4].

E92a ———Ananda K. Coomaraswamy: Scholar of the Spirit. *Sophia: A Journal of Traditional Studies*, Oakton, Va., II. 1 (Summer 1996) 71-91, 2 text illus. (one facing p. 71).

The text of a lecture given by Keeble at the Temenos Academy (London) in May 1994. Includes a discussion of (1) the idea of tradition, (2) the doctrine of "the two selves", and (3) the doctrine of the traditional or "normal" view of art, themes that have a fundamental place in AKC's writings.

E93 KELLY, Bernard. Dr. Coomaraswamy on Art. *Blackfriars*, Oxford, XXIV. 282 (Sept. 1943) [345]-348.

E94 ———Ananda K. Coomaraswamy. *Blackfriars*, Oxford, XXVIII. 332 (Nov. 1947) 515-16.

An obituary. Reprinted in E189, pp. 155-7.

E95 ———Notes on the Light of the Eastern Religions with Special Reference to the Works of Ananda Coomaraswamy, René Guénon and Frithjof Schuon. *Dominican Studies*, Oxford, VII. (1954) 254-71.

Reprinted in *Religion of the Heart: Essays Presented to Frithjof Schuon on His Eightieth Birthday*, edited by S.H. Nasr and William Stoddart ([Washington, D.C.: Foundation for Traditional Studies, 1991]), pp. 155-76.

E96 KHANDALAVALA, Karl J. Coomaraswamy's Dicta Analyzed. *Pahari Miniature Painting*, by Karl Khandalavala. Bombay: New Book Company Ltd. [1958], pp. 18-20.

Other (brief) references to AKC occur on pages 61, 63, 64, 65.

E97 ———Foreword [and] List of Plates. *Rajput Painting*, by Ananda K. Coomaraswamy. Second Edition. Delhi: Motilal Banarsidass [1977], Vol. I, pp.[5]-16.

See A34b *n*.

E98 KILPATRIC, G. Wayne. Coomaraswamy's View of the Proper Place of Art in Society. *Bulletin of the Ramakrishna Mission Institute of Culture*, Calcutta, X. 4 (Apr. 1959) [73]-87.

E99 KRISHNAMOORTHY, K. Rasa, Bhava and Sadrsya in Ananda Coomaraswamy's Theory of Indian Art. *Ananda Coomaraswamy Centenary Essays*, edited by C.D. Narasimhaiah (1982)—E131—pp.[67]-78.

E100 KULARATNAM, Karthigesapillai. The Scientist. *Homage to Ananda K. Coomaraswamy*, edited by S. Durai Raja Singam ([1948])—E188—pp. 127-30.

AKC's career in geology, giving an account of his term as Director of the Mineralogical Survey of Ceylon, 1903-6. Reprinted in E189, pp. 168-71. AKC was a Fellow of the Geological Society, for this see *Proceedings of the Geological Society of London, Session 1898-99*, London, LV. (Feb. 1899) iii.

E101 KUMARAPPA, Bharatan. Coomaraswamy and [Mohandas Karamchand] Gandhiji. *Homage to Ananda K. Coomaraswamy*, edited by S. Durai Raja Singam ([1948])—E188—pp. 61-7.

E102 KUNST, Arnold. New Introduction. *Buddha and the Gospel of Buddhism*, by Ananda K. Coomaraswamy. New Hyde Park, New York: University Books [1969], pp. iii-xviii.

E103 KUSPIT, Donald B. [A review of] Ananda K. Coomaraswamy, *Selected Papers, Traditional Art and Symbolism*, Vol. I; *Selected Papers, Metaphysics*, Vol. II;

Roger Lipsey, *His Life and Work*, Vol. III (Bollingen Series, LXXXIX) . . . *Art Bulletin*, New York, LXI. 3 (Sept. 1979) 501-4.

Focussing on AKC's view of modern art.

E104 [LADD, Helen E., compiler]. The Writings of Ananda K. Coomaraswamy. *Ars Islamica*, Ann Arbor, IX. (1942) [125]-142.

A check-list, comprising 494 items printed in double columns, initiated (to mark the occasion of AKC's 65th birthday) by Richard Ettinghausen, who contributes a brief prefatory note. "Compiled . . . with the help of Dr. Coomaraswamy . . . At his suggestion, the bibliography does not pretend to be complete . . . Publications dealing with Islamic subjects are marked with an asterisk" (p.[125]). Reprinted, in a Sinhala translation by K.C. Perera, in *Sanskruti*, Colombo, III. 3 (July/Sept. 1955) 86-131. Ettinghausen's note (only) was reprinted, reduced, and with other changes, in E37, p. vii. See also C373a, 852.

E104a LAGO, Mary. [A review of] *Coomaraswamy. Volume III. His Life and Work.* By Roger Lipsey. *Journal of Asian Studies*, Ann Arbor, XXXIX. 1 (Nov. 1979) 207-9.

E105 LAHIRI, A.N. Coomaraswamy and Indian Coins. *Ananda Coomaraswamy: A Centenary Volume*, edited by Kalyan Kumar Dasgupta (1981)—E50—pp.[111]-118.

E106 LAL, Mukandi. My Guru. *Homage to Ananda Coomaraswamy*, edited by S. Durai Raja Singam (1952)—E189—pp. 302-11.

A memoir of AKC in India and England, 1908-16. Lal assisted AKC in the preparation of *Rajput Painting* (1916).

E107 LEIDECKER, Kurt F. Coomaraswamy, a Modern Plato. *Ananda Coomaraswamy: Remembering and Remembering Again and Again*, edited by S. Durai Raja Singam (1974)—E191—pp. 11-13.

E108 LE MAY, Reginald. Commemoration Address for the Late

Dr. Ananda Coomaraswamy. *Art and Letters*, London, XXVI. 2 (1952) 87-93.

Delivered at the annual meeting of the Royal India, Pakistan and Ceylon Society in London on 1 May 1952. Reference is made to AKC as one of the founders of the India Society, forerunner of the above (see also E168 *n.*, and "The India Society", *The Times*, London, for 11 June 1910, p. 18). This address was reprinted in E190, pp. 23-[34], and E191, pp. 292-8.

E109 LINGS, Martin. *The Eleventh Hour: The Spiritual Crisis of the Modern World in the Light of Tradition and Prophecy.* [Cambridge, Cambs.] Quinta Essentia [1987], pp. 84-92.

Includes on these pages, a comparison of the work of AKC and René Guénon, together with a discussion of the former's paper "Symplegades" (1946).

E110 LIPSEY, Roger W. What Do People Get from Works of Art? A Short Introduction to Coomaraswamy. *Big Rock Candy Mountain*, Menlo Park, Calif., II. 1 ([Summer] 1971) 33-7.

See also C894.

E111 ———Double Portrait, Alfred Stieglitz & Ananda Coomaraswamy. *Aperture*, New York, XVI. 3 (1972) [16-21].

On AKC's friendship with the doyen of American photographers. Reprinted, with revisions, in E116, pp. 155-60.

E112 ———The Two Selves: Coomaraswamy as Man and Metaphysician. *Studies in Comparative Religion*, Bedfont, Middx., VI. 4 (Autumn 1972) 199-211.

Reprinted in E116, pp. 232-45 (*i.e.* Chap. XV).

E113 ———Introduction. *Ananda Coomaraswamy: Remembering and Remembering Again and Again*, edited by S. Durai Raja Singam (1974)—E191—pp. xv-xvi.

Reviewing the "posthumous fortunes" of AKC's writings.

E114 ———The Coomaraswamy Bequest at Princeton University. *Ananda Coomaraswamy: Remembering and Remembering*

Again and Again, edited by S. Durai Raja Singam (1974)—E191—pp. 64-5, 1 text illus. (on p. 67).

(This bequest escaped the *Princeton University Library Chronicle*.) About one half of AKC's library (the other half is in possession of his family) was absorbed into the Marquand (Art) Library and distributed throughout the various printed book divisions of the Firestone Library. His typescripts of notes and completed articles, proofs, correspondence, memorabilia, etc., are segregated as a special collection, The Ananda Coomaraswamy Papers in the Firestone's Department of Rare Books.

E115 ———Coomaraswamy, Ananda Kentish. *Dictionary of American Biography. Supplement Four 1946-1950*, edited by John A. Garraty and Edward T. James. New York: Charles Scribner's Sons [1974], pp. 176-8.

(AKC is not an entrant in the British *Dictionary of National Biography* or the supplementary volume *Missing Persons*, edited by C.S. Nicholls in 1993.)

E116 ———*Coomaraswamy 3: His Life and Work.* Bollingen Series LXXXIX. [Princeton] Princeton University Press [1977]. xvii, 312 pp., 32 pls. incl. frontis. (port.).

Excerpted from Lipsey's otherwise unpublished doctoral dissertation, "Signature and Significance: A Study of the Life and Writings of Ananda K. Coomaraswamy" (New York University, 1974). For a summary (by Lipsey) of the dissertation see *Dissertation Abstracts International*, Section A, XXXV. 2 (Aug. 1974) 969-A, and *Marsyas: Studies in the History of Art*, New York, XVII. (1974/75) 114. See also A82, B94a, E43, and 179 *n*. Lipsey includes a check-list of AKC's writings (651 items) "compiled by Doña Luisa [Mrs A.K.] Coomaraswamy, slightly revised by Roger Lipsey", which occupies 46 unnumbered pages following the last page of the dissertation.

E117 ———*Daedalus: Lectures Commemorating the Birth Centenary of A.K. Coomaraswamy.* Institute of Indian Art History Lecture Series—No. 1. Dharwar: Karnatak University, 1980. xii, 110 pp.

Incorporates *passim* numerous references to the writings of AKC; see particularly pages 83-100, i.e. the last of the four lectures, which discusses *Spiritual Authority and Temporal Power in the Indian Theory of Government* (1942).

E118 ———Traditional Ideas and Modern Art. *Parokṣa,* edited by Gulam Mohammed Sheikh *et al.* (1984)—E182—pp. 145-7.

How from AKC's writings on the traditional philosophy of art there might be derived a new criticism of modern art; excerpted from E117, pp. 3-9.

E119 ———Coomaraswamy, Ananda. *The Encyclopedia of Religion*, general editor Mircea Eliade. New York: Macmillan Publishing Company [1987], *Vol. 4*, pp. 79-80.

E120 LIVINGSTON, Ray Frederick. *The Traditional Theory of Literature.* Minneapolis: University of Minneapolis Press [1962]. 188 pp.

The published version of Livingston's "Ananda K. Coomaraswamy's Theory of Literature. A Thesis Submitted to the Graduate Faculty of the University of Minnesota . . . for the Degree of Doctor of Philosophy, Fall, 1956."

E120a LUTCHMANSINGH, Larry D. Ananda Coomaraswamy and William Morris. *Journal of the William Morris Society*, London, IX. 1 (Autumn 1990) 35-42.

A comparison of their views on the definition of art and its part in life; their most fundamental difference being "the relative absence of a political element in Coomaraswamy's vision" (p. 41).

E121 McGUIRE, William. *Bollingen: An Adventure in Collecting the Past.* [Princeton] Princeton University Press, Bollingen Series [1982], pp. 54, 94, 141, 150, 165, 166, 177, 314.

Contains on these pages, accounts of AKC's contacts with Heinrich Zimmer, Stella Kramrisch, Joseph Campbell, Mircea Eliade, Mai-mai Sze, and concerning Doña Luisa (Mrs A. K.) Coomaraswamy's Bollingen Fellowship (1952-69).

E122 MAIRET, Philip. *Autobiographical and Other Papers*, edited by C.H. Sisson. Manchester: Carcanet [1981], pp. 39-55, 70, 88, 119, 247.

Incorporates on these pages, a memoir of AKC from the period 1910-11 (Mairet was at the time AKC's secretary). See also Mairet's "When A.K.C. Met G[eorge]. B[ernard]. S[haw]." in E191, p. 365.

E122a MEISTER, Michael W. Preface [and] Introduction: The Language and Process of Early Indian Architecture. *Ananda*

K. Coomaraswamy: Essays in Early Indian Architecture, edited by Michael W. Meister. New Delhi: Indira Gandhi National Centre for the Arts/Oxford University Press, 1992, pp. xiv-xv, xvii-xxviii.

On AKC's contribution to the history and symbolic interpretation of Indian architecture. Meister continues his discussion on pages 103-19, 125-31 (reprinted from C909). See also his review of Roger Lipsey's biography of AKC, in *Journal of the American Oriental Society*, New Haven, C. 2 (Apr./June 1980) 151-3.

E122b ——— Introduction: Architecture as Ornament, Essential Form. *Ananda K. Coomaraswamy: Essays in Architectural Theory*, edited by Michael W. Meister. New Delhi: Indira Gandhi National Centre for the Arts/Oxford University Press, 1995, pp. xv-xxiii.

Meister traces the development of AKC's methodology for the study of Indian architectural history and theory, highlighting his central ideas.

E123 MITTER, Partha. *Much Maligned Monsters: A History of European Reactions to Indian Art*. Oxford: Clarendon Press, 1977, pp. 277-86.

Contains on these pages, a critical discussion of AKC as an historian of Indian art.

E124 ——— A Man of Our Time: Ananda Coomaraswamy, the West and Indian Nationalism. *Asian Studies Association of Australia Review*, Canberra, VII. 3 (Apr. 1984) 48-51.

For another contribution that concerns AKC contained in this same issue see E211.

E125 MOHAN, Jag. *Ananda K. Coomaraswamy*. Builders of Modern India Series. New Delhi: Publication Division, Ministry of Information and Broadcasting, Government of India [1979]. xv, 118 pp., frontis.(port.).

E126 ——— Contemporary Relevance of Ananda Coomaraswamy. *Parokṣa*, edited by Gulam Mohammed Sheikh *et al.* (1984)—E182—pp. 164-7.

E127 MOKASHI-PUNEKAR, Shankar. Ananda Coomaraswamy's "The Dance of Shiva". *Journal of the Karnatak University*, Dharwar, XII. (1968) 76-91.

On *The Dance of Śiva* (1918).

E128 MOORE, Alvin, Jr. Foreword. *The Indian Craftsman*, by Ananda K. Coomaraswamy. Second Edition. New Dẹlhi: Munshiram Manoharlal Publishers Pvt. Ltd. [1989], pp.[vii]-xiv.

E129 ——— & COOMARASWAMY, Rama Ponnambalam. Introduction. *Selected Letters of Ananda K. Coomaraswamy*, edited by Alvin Moore, Jr. and Rama Poonambulam [*sic*] Coomaraswamy. Delhi: Indira Gandhi National Centre for the Arts/Oxford University Press, 1988, pp.[xix]-xxxiii.

See also E151.

E129a MOORE, Patrick A., Immersion of Ananda K. Coomaraswamy's Ashes. *Ananda Coomaraswamy: Remembering and Remembering Again and Again*, edited by S. Durai Raja Singam (1974)—E191—pp. 287-8.

Moore accompanied AKC's widow during the ceremony which took place, in accordance with traditional Hindu rites, at the confluence of the Ganges and Jumna rivers at Allahabad in September 1965. A portion of the ashes was also taken to Sri Lanka—see "Ashes of a Savant Arrives [*sic*]", in E8, p. 11.

E130 NAIPAUL, Vidiadhar Surajprasad. Indian Art and Its Illusions. *New York Review of Books*, New York, XXVI. 4 (22 Mar. 1979) 6-14.

In part, concerning the biography of AKC by Roger Lipsey—E116.

E131 NARASIMHAIAH, C.D., editor. *Ananda Coomaraswamy Centenary Essays*. Other Publications—74. [Mysore] University of Mysore, 1982. xxii, 176 pp.

Collects 16 papers by scholars from India, Malaysia, Sri Lanka, and the U.S.A., that were presented at a seminar held by the Department of English at the University of Mysore in

1977. See the references to AKC in the editor's introduction, pages [xi]-xxii, and for the more outstanding among the papers see E3, 20, 35, 55, 79, 99. See also Narasimhaiah's "Not a Man, but a Phenomenon", in E191, pp. 363-5; reprinted as "Ananda K. Coomaraswamy: A Centenary Tribute", in *Literary Criterion*, Mysore, XIII. 2 (1978) [1]-4.

E132 NARAVANE, Vishwanath S. The Perennial Philosophy of Coomaraswamy. *Indian Horizons*, New Delhi, XXVI. 3 (1977) 17-29.

E133 ———*Ananda K. Coomaraswamy*. Twayne's World Leaders Series No. 75. Boston: Twayne Publishers [1978]. 188 pp., frontis.(port.).

E134 NASR, Seyyed Hossein. *Knowledge and the Sacred. The Gifford Lectures, 1981*. [Edinburgh] Edinburgh University Press [1981], pp. 105-7, 124 (notes).

Includes on these pages, a discussion of AKC's part in the modern revival and dissemination of traditional teachings.

E135 ———Ananda Coomaraswamy and the Metaphysics of Art: A Review Essay of His Selected Papers on Traditional Art and Symbolism. *Temenos*, London, 2 (1982) 252-9.

On *Coomaraswamy 1: Selected Papers, Traditional Art and Symbolism* ([1977]).

E136 ———Foreword. *What Is Civilisation? and Other Essays*, by Ananda K. Coomaraswamy. [Ipswich] Golgonooza Press [1989], pp. [vii]-ix.

E137 The Nature and Purpose of Art. *Times Literary Supplement*, London, 2,359 (19 Apr. 1947) 180.

An anonymous review of AKC's *Figures of Speech or Figures of Thought* (1946).

E138 NORMAN, Dorothy. The Last Time I Saw Coomaraswamy. *Journal of the Indian Society of Oriental Art* (1948)—E89—pp.[i]-iv, 1 pl. (port., facing p.[i]).

On taking a series of portrait photographs of AKC in the Summer of 1947, one of which is reproduced; chiefly a report of the conversation Norman had with AKC on that occasion. Reprinted in E191, pp. 68-70. See also B96.

E139 PALLIS, Marco. In Memoriam—A.K.C. *Homage to Ananda Coomaraswamy*, edited by S. Durai Raja Singam (1952)—E189—pp. 102-5.

Reprinted in E191, pp. 1-2.

E140 ——— Coomaraswamy and Buddhism. [Letter]. *Studies in Comparative Religion*, Bedfont, Middx., VII. 4 (Autumn 1973) 247.

On the disparaging references to Buddhism in AKC's essay "What Is Common to Indian and Chinese Art?" (1935), which was reprinted in the issue for Spring 1973. See also Pallis's review of AKC's *Buddha and the Gospel of Buddhism* in *Tomorrow*, London, XII. 3 (Summer 1964) 245.

E141 ——— A Fateful Meeting of Minds: A.K. Coomaraswamy and R. Guénon. *Dilip*, Bombay, V. 1 (Jan./Feb. 1978) 23-30.

Includes an account of René Guénon's recension of the Buddhist material in his *Introduction to the Study of the Hindu Doctrines* and *Man and His Becoming According to the Vedanta*, and AKC's part in bringing this about. In this article Pallis also recalls his contacts with AKC, from 1939 to 1947. Reprinted in *Studies in Comparative Religion*, Bedfont, Middx., XII. 3/4 (Summer/Autumn 1978) 176-88. See also Pallis's "René Guénon et le Bouddhisme" in *Études Traditionnelles*, Paris, LII. 293/294/295 (July-Aug./Sept./Oct.-Nov. 1951) [308]-316.

E142 ——— *A Buddhist Spectrum*. London: George Allen & Unwin [1980], pp. 131-3.

Contains on these pages, a critical examination of AKC's treatment of the *anattā* doctrine; see also page 120.

E143 PARIMOO, Ratan. Coomaraswamy and Indian Art History. *Parokṣa*, edited by Gulam Mohammed Sheikh *et al.* (1984)—E182—pp. 20-4.

Also printed in *Journal of the Oriental Institute*, Baroda, XXXII. 1/2 (Sept./Dec. 1982) [124]-130.

E144 PARKER, Robert Allerton. Introduction. *Am I My Brother's*

Keeper?, by Ananda K. Coomaraswamy. New York: The John Day Company [1947], pp. vii-xiii.

Dated New York, Mar. 1946. In part, on the polemical nature of certain of AKC's later essays, together with a consideration of their import.

E145 PASQUIER, Pierre. Les véhémences de la rosée: Introduction à la correspondance E[dward]. G[ordon]. Craig—A.K. Coomaraswamy. *Revue d'Histoire du Théatre*, Paris, XXXVI. 1 (Jan./Mar. 1984) 7-26.

See also the references to AKC and Craig in *Gordon Craig Archives*, compiled by L.M. Newman (London: The Malkin Press, 1976), pp. 69, 73, and in *Gordon Craig on Movement and Dance*, edited by Arnold Rood (New York: Dance Horizons [1977]), pp. 181-2, 192, 194, 195, 196-8.

E146 PEREIRA, José. The Nataraja Theme: A New Interpretation. *Journal of the Asiatic Society of Bombay*, Bombay, N.S. XXX. 1/2 (1955) [71]-86.

Incorporates *passim* a critical assessment of AKC's essay "The Dance of Siva" (1912).

E147 [*Entry deleted.*]

E148 PERRY, Whitall N. The Man and the Witness. *Ananda Coomaraswamy: Remembering and Remembering Again and Again*, edited by S. Durai Raja Singam (1974)—E191—pp. 3-7.

That AKC and René Guénon possessed "certain peculiar similarities", and moreover that they "personified complementary poles of a single function".

E149 ———Coomaraswamy—the Man, Myth, and History. *Studies in Comparative Religion* (1977)—E197—pp. 159-65.

A sequel to the preceding entry. Reprinted in E206, pp.[23]-30, and E196, pp. 10-17.

E150 ———The Bollingen Coomaraswamy Papers and Biography. *Studies in Comparative Religion*, Bedfont, Middx., XI. 4 (Autumn 1977) 205-20.

A review of A82 and E116.

E151 ———Foreword. *Selected Letters of Ananda K. Coomaraswamy*, edited by Alvin Moore, Jr. and Rama Poonambulam [*sic*] Coomaraswamy (1988)—E129—pp. [ix]-xiii.

E152 ——— The Revival of Interest in Tradition. *The Unanimous Tradition: Essays on the Essential Unity of All Religions*, edited by Ranjit Fernando. Colombo: The Sri Lanka Institute of Traditional Studies, 1991, pp. 3-16.

On René Guénon, AKC (see particularly pp. 11-14), and Frithjof Schuon.

E153 POPE, John A. [A review of] *Why Exhibit Works of Art?* by Ananda K. Coomaraswamy. *Review of Religion*, New York, VIII. 3 (Mar. 1944) 314-19.

In the course of this review Pope also considers the overall import of AKC's *oeuvre*.

E154 PRÉAU, André. A.K. Coomaraswamy et la pensée de l'Inde. *Cahiers du Sud*, Marseilles, XXVIII. 290 ([June/Dec.] 1948) [126]-132.

"Nous croyons rendre à [AKC's] mémoire l'hommage qui convient en parlant ici d'un de ses derniers livres, *Hinduism and Buddhism*". Préau discusses, what he sees as two ideas central to that book, "la notion vêdique du sacrifice et la conception bouddhique du 'soi'" (p.[126]).

E155 [*Entry deleted.*]

E156 RAINE, Kathleen Jessie. Seminal Influence. *The Times*, London (18 May 1978) 22, 1 text illus. (port.).

Chiefly a discussion of the biography of AKC by Roger Lipsey—E116.

E157 RAMAKRISHNAN, R. Dr. Ananda Kentish Coomaraswamy: His Life & Work. *Quarterly Journal of the Mythic Society*, Bangalore, LXX. 1/2 (Jan./June 1979) [53]-76.

E158 RAMAN, K.V. Ananda Coomaraswamy on Early Indian Architecture. *Ananda Coomaraswamy: A Centenary Volume*, edited by Kalyan Kumar Dasgupta (1981)—E50—pp.[49]-54.

An examination of AKC's methodology.

E159 RANGANATHAN, Airavathan. *A Coomaraswamy Spectrum*. Development Education Series No. 5. Madras: Published for the Institute for Development Education by the Christian Literature Society [1981]. v, 41 pp.

E160 RAO, C.V. Ramachandra. *A.K. Coomaraswamy (An Inspirer of Indian Renaissance) & Other Cultural Causerie*. Nellore: Manasa Publications, 1980. xiv, 99 pp.

The eponymous essay occupies pages [1]-54.

E161 RAPHAEL, R. The Metaphysical Basis of Coomaraswamy's Aesthetics. *Indian Horizons*, New Delhi, XXV. 3/4 (1976) 9-21.

E162 ———*Ananda Coomaraswamy: Spiritual Frontiers of Art, Literature and Culture*. Madras: Rayappa Publishers, 1977. viii, 232 pp.

E163 ———Aesthetic Theories of Ananda Coomaraswamy. *Indian Literature*, New Delhi, XX. 6 (Nov./Dec. 1977) 28-50.

E164 RAWSON, Philip. A Professional Sage. *New York Review of Books*, New York, XXVI. 2 (22 Feb. 1979) 15-17, 1 text illus.

In the main, concerning the biography by Roger Lipsey—E116. The illustration is a caricature of AKC by David Levine.

E165 RENOUF, Renée. [A review of] *The Dance of Shiva*, co-produced and directed by Chidananda Dasgupta and B.D. Garga. *Ethnomusicology*, Ann Arbor, XX. 1 (Jan. 1976) 172-6.

Concerning the documentary film on AKC—E48 *n.*

E166 RIEPE, Dale. *The Philosophy of India and Its Impact on American Thought*. Springfield: Charles C. Thomas [1970?], pp. 122-8.

These pages contain an account of AKC in the milieu of American Indology. Other (brief) references to AKC occur *passim.*

E167 ———The Philosophy of A.K. Coomaraswamy and Its Relation to Marx's Critique of Capitalism. *Ananda Coomaraswamy: Remembering and Remembering Again and Again*, edited by S. Durai Raja Singam (1974)—E191—pp. 99-105.

E168 ROTHENSTEIN, William. *Men and Memories; Recollections of William Rothenstein 1900-1922.* London: Faber & Faber [1932], pp. 231, 247, 248, 250.

Contains on these pages, personal reminiscences of AKC in England and India, 1908-11. Reference is made to AKC and Rothenstein's founding, in 1910, of the India Society (p. 231). In Mary Lago's abridged edition (London: Chatto & Windus, 1978) only the matter on page 231 is retained.

E169 ———Introduction. *Journal of the Indian Society of Oriental Art* (1937)—E88—p.[1].

A tribute. Reprinted in E188, p. 29, and E191, p. 281.

E170 ROWLAND, Benjamin. In Memoriam Ananda Kentish Coomaraswamy (1877-1947). *Ars Islamica*, Ann Arbor, XV/XVI. (1951) [259]-261.

Reprinted in E189, pp. 182-7.

E171 ROY, Pabitrakumar. A Return to Rhetoric: Ananda

Coomaraswamy's Philosophy of Art. *Visvabharati Quarterly*, Santiniketan, Bengal, XLII. 3/4 (Nov. 1976/Apr. 1977 [*i.e.* May 1978]) [238]-260.

E172 RYKWERT, Joseph. A.K. Coomaraswamy. *Religion*, London, IX. (Spring 1979) 104-15.

Chiefly a discussion of the biography by Roger Lipsey—E116. See also C909 *n.*

E173 SANBORN, Cyrus Ashton Rollins. Ananda K. Coomaraswamy 1877-1947. *Bulletin of the Museum of Fine Arts*, Boston, XLV. 262 (Dec. 1947) 77.

Signed: A.S. An obituary by the Museum's librarian (1922-52). Reprinted in E189, pp. 160-2, and E191, pp. 159-60.

E174 SANNMUGANATHAN, S. Kalayogi Ananda Coomaraswamy and His Connections with Ceylon. *Homage to Ananda K. Coomaraswamy*, edited by S. Durai Raja Singam ([1948])—E188—pp. 85-9, 1 pl.

Tracing AKC's paternal ancestry. The plate is a genealogical tree.

E175 SASTRI, P.S. Footnoting in Ananda Coomaraswamy. *Literary Criterion*, Mysore, XI. 1 (Winter 1973) [20]-32.

On AKC's somewhat idiosyncratic use of footnotes. Reprinted in E176, pp. 184-99.

E176 ——— *Ananda K. Coomaraswamy.* Indian Writers Series VIII. [New Delhi] Arnold-Heinemann Publishers (India) Private Limited [1974]. 203 pp.

E177 SATCHIDANANDAM, K.R. Platonic Idea and Ananda Coomaraswamy's Interpretation of Indian Art. *Journal of Tamil Studies* (1977)—E87—pp.[31]-36.

E178 SCHERMAN, Lucian. Indische Weisheit. *Journal of the American Oriental Society*, New Haven, LXIII. 4 (Oct. 1943) 241-62.

Marginal notes to AKC's *Hinduism and Buddhism* ([1943]). Reprinted, in an English translation by Hermann Goetz, as "Indian Wisdom", in *New Indian Antiquary*, Bombay, VIII. 1 (Jan. 1946) [7]-30. See also the tribute from Scherman, comparing AKC to Philo Judaeus of Alexandria, in E191, p. 66.

E179 SCHROEDER, Eric. Memories of the Person. *Homage to Ananda Coomaraswamy*, edited by S. Durai Raja Singam (1952)—E189—pp. 65-80.

Schroeder recalls his friendship with AKC, 1937 to 1947. Reprinted in E116, pp. 283-92.

E180 SEN, Amiya Kumar. [Rabindranath] Tagore and Coomaraswamy. *Homage to Ananda Coomaraswamy*, edited by S. Durai Raja Singam (1952)—E189—pp. 246-57, 2 pls.(ports.).

See also "The Two Sages: Tagore and Ananda Coomaraswamy", by K. Chandrasekharan, in *Bhavan's Journal*, Bombay, XXIV. 3 (11 Sept. 1977) 30-7 and 4 (25 Sept. 1977) 63-71.

E181 SHEIKH, Gulam Mohammed. Coomaraswamy and Rajput Painting. *Parokṣa*, edited by Gulam Mohammed Sheikh *et al.* (1984)—E182—pp. 86-96, 8 pls.

E182 ———, SUBRAMANYAN, K.G., & VATSYAYAN, Kapila, editors. *Parokṣa: Coomaraswamy Centenary Seminar Papers*. New Delhi: Lalit Kala Akademi, 1984. xii, 167 pp.

Collects 27 papers on Indian and further Indian art, by scholars from America, India, Sri Lanka, and Thailand, that were presented at a seminar jointly sponsored by the Department of Culture, Government of India and the Lalit Kala Akademi, at New Delhi, 19-20 December 1977. See the references to AKC in the foreword by Kapila Vatsyayan, and for the more outstanding among the papers see E12, 14, 54, 91, 118, 126, 143, 181, 202.

E183 SHEWRING, Walter Hayward Francis. Carmen natalicium. *Art and Thought*, edited by K. Bharatha Iyer (1947)—E86—pp. 1-4.

A eulogy upon AKC, taking the form of a poem in Latin. An English prose version, by Shewring, is printed in E191, pp. 190-1.

E184 ———Ananda K. Coomaraswamy. *Homage to Ananda K. Coomaraswamy*, edited by S. Durai Raja Singam ([1948])—E188—pp. 53-4.

E185 ———Ananda Coomaraswamy and Eric Gill. *Ananda Coomaraswamy: Remembering and Remembering Again and Again*, edited by S. Durai Raja Singam (1974)—E191—pp. 189-90.

E186 ———Introduction. *Who Is This Coomaraswamy?*, by S. Durai Raja Singam ([1980])—E193—pp. 16-19.

E187 [SIBLY, A.]. Dr. Ananda K. Coomaraswamy. *Wycliffe Star*, Stonehouse, Glos., CLXXXII. (Sept. 1947/Apr. 1948) 2-4.

An obituary that contains recollections of AKC as a pupil at Wycliffe College, 1889-97. The *Wycliffe Star* is the magazine of that school. Reprinted in E189, pp. 157-60, and E191, pp. 245-6.

E188 SINGAM, Sabapathipillay Durai Raja, editor. *Homage to Ananda K. Coomaraswamy. A Garland of Tributes.* [Kuala Lumpur: Printed for the editor by the Malayan Printers, 1948]. xii, 192 pp., 39 pls.(incl. ports.).

A Festschrift that comprises 96 messages, tributes, and essays, contributed by scholars from England, India, the U.S.A., and elsewhere. For the more outstanding among the contributions see E56, 61, 65, 71 *n.*, 74, 100, 101, 169 *n.*, 174, 184, 210, 216.

E189 ———, editor. *Homage to Ananda Coomaraswamy: (A Memorial Volume) A Garland of Tributes.* [Kuantan & Singapore: Printed for the editor by Liang Bros. & Co.] 1952. xxiv, 333 pp., 47 pls.(incl. ports.).

A Festschrift that comprises 111 messages, tributes, and essays (15 are reprinted from E188), contributed by scholars from England, India, the U.S.A., and elsewhere. For the more outstanding among the contributions see E6, 15, 16, 61, 64, 67, 70, 83, 84, 94, 100, 106, 139, 170, 173, 179, 180, 187, 207, 209, 210, 216.

E190 ——— *Ananda Coomaraswamy—A New Planet in My Ken.* [Kuala Lumpur: Printed for the author by S. Lazar & Sons, 1963?]. 38 pp., 12 text illus. (incl. ports.).

E191 ———, editor. *Ananda Coomaraswamy: Remembering and Remembering Again and Again.* [Kuala Lumpur: Printed for the editor by Khee Meng Press] 1974. xxxii, 375 pp., 187 text illus. (incl. ports.).

A Festschrift that comprises 162 messages, tributes, and essays (32 are reprinted from E188, and 45 from E189), contributed by scholars from England, India, the U.S.A., and elsewhere. For the more outstanding among the contributions see E9, 11, 19, 39, 56, 58, 61, 65, 73, 80, 81, 82, 83, 107, 108, 113, 114, 122 *n.*, 129a, 138, 139, 148, 167, 169 *n.*, 173, 178 *n.*, 183 *n.*, 185, 187, 207, 210, 214a, 216.

E192 ——— *Ananda Coomaraswamy—the Bridge Builder; a Study of a Scholar-Colossus.* [Kuala Lumpur: Printed for the author by Khee Meng Press] 1977. [632] pp., 158 text illus. (incl. ports.).

See also E33, 34 *n.*

E193 ——— *Who Is This Coomaraswamy? [A Word and Picture Account Containing Pictures Arranged Chronologically with a Life-Sketch of Coomaraswamy and Appropriate Write-Ups for Each Picture*, with an introduction by Walter Shewring [E186]. Kuala Lumpur: Printed for the author by Academe Art & Printing Services, 1980]. 256 pp., approx. 298 text illus. (incl. ports.).

E194 ———, compiler. *Ananda Kentish Coomaraswamy: A Bibliographical Record, being a Comprehensive Bibliography of all His Publications from 1895-1981 . . .* with an introduction by A.K. Saran. *Part I: 1895-1927* [*-Part II: 1928-1982*]. Kuala Lumpur: Privately Published, 1981[-1984]. *Part I*, xlvi, 424 pp.; *Part II*, [xii], 564 pp.

This bibliography is marred by inaccuracies and by being indexless. The entries are not numbered. Its value as a serious instrument of research is further compromised by the compiler's lack of bibliographical know-how, authorial and compositorial errors, omissions, irrelevancies, and second-hand descriptions, as well as other misleading and distracting elements. Includes, in *ad hoc* English translation, some reviews by René Guénon of publications by AKC—for a description of these see E76 and 77.

E195 SMITH, Huston. [A review of] *Coomaraswamy 1* [and 2] *Selected Papers, . . .* edited by Roger Lipsey [and] *Coomaraswamy 3: His Life and Work*, by Roger Lipsey.

Philosophy East and West, Honolulu, XXIX. 3 (July 1979) [347]-356.

E196 *Sophia Perennis*, Tehran, III. 2 (Autumn 1977), "Special Issue on Tradition and the Arts in Honour of the Centenary of Ananda K. Coomaraswamy".

For one of the more outstanding of the contributions to this special issue see E149.

E197 *Studies in Comparative Religion*, Bedfont, Middx., XI. 3 (Summer 1977), "A.K. Coomaraswamy Centenary Issue".

See the editorial on AKC, by F. Clive-Ross, pages 131-2, and Whitall N. Perry's contribution—E149, the only other item here that is wholly concerned with AKC.

E198 STUNKEL, Kenneth R. The Meeting of East and West in Coomaraswamy and Radhakrishnan. *Philosophy East and West*, Honolulu, XXIII. 4 (Oct. 1973) [517]-524.

A discussion with special reference to AKC's review of Sarvepalli Radhakrishnan's *Eastern Religions and Western Thought*—C788.

E199 ——— Some Applications of Ananda Coomaraswamy's Traditionalism. *Triveni* (1977)—E206—pp.[13]-22.

E200 SUBRAMANIAM, V. Ananda K. Coomaraswamy. *Economic and Political Weekly*, Bombay, XII. 35 (27 Aug. 1977) 1533.

Subramaniam evaluates the impact of AKC at popular and sophisticated levels in India and the West.

E201 ———, editor. *The Sacred and the Secular in India's Performing Arts—Ananda K. Coomaraswamy Centenary Essays*. New Delhi: Ashish Publishing House, 1980. xx, 185 pp., 5 pls. (incl. ports.).

"The first part [of this book is] devoted to a direct analysis and criticism of . . . the major thesis and theme of [AKC's] mature years, namely, the close relation or the identity of art and religion" (pp.[vii], viii). See the references to AKC in Subramaniam's introduction, pages [vii]-xi; also his essay "The Kalayogi [i.e. AKC], Art and Religion", pages [xiii]-xx, and postscript, pages 181-5. For the more outstanding among the other contributions to this volume see E26, 57.

E202 SUBRAMANYAN, K.G. The Significance of Coomaraswamy's Ideas in Our Times. *Parokṣa*, edited by Gulam Mohammed Sheikh *et al.* (1984)—E182—pp. 15-19.

E203 SUTTON, Jonathan. Meaning and Symbolism in the Work of Ananda Coomaraswamy. *Sri Lanka Journal of the Humanities*, Peradeniya, VII. 1/2 (1981[*i.e.* 1983]) [1]-28.

Incorporates a lengthy discussion of *Spiritual Authority and Temporal Power in the Indian Theory of Government* (1942).

E204 [SWARNATILAKA, Seneviratne. A note on the *vaka deka*]. *Kalāmanjari*, Colombo, I. 1 (1950/51) 82, 1 pl. (folding).

(In English.) A correction to an illustration in AKC's *Mediaeval Sinhalese Art* ([1908]), page 65, of a device, comprising a double curve, that traditionally formed the foundation of instruction in drawing.

E205 THOMAS, Sharon. Coomaraswamy: A Vision of Unity. *Theosophist*, Madras, XCIX. 3 (Dec. 1977) 84-6, 1 text illus.

E206 *Triveni*, Machilipatnam, XLVI. 2 (July/Sept. 1977), "Ananda K. Coomaraswamy Special Number".

See page 10 for a note by the editor, Bhavaraja Narasimha Rao, concerning the Indian postage stamp issued 22 August 1977 to commemorate the centenary of AKC's birth, and for the more outstanding among the contributions to this special issue see E82a, 149, 199.

E207 [ULICH, Robert]. In Memoriam Ananda K. Coomaraswamy. *Journal of the Indian Society of Oriental Art* (1947)—E89—pp.[13]-17.

The text of Ulich's oration at AKC's funeral. Reprinted in E189, pp.[1]-6, and E191, pp. 284-6.

E208 VATSYAYAN, Kapila. *See* E182.

E209 [WALKER, Roy]. Ananda K. Coomaraswamy. *Vegetarian News*, London, XXVIII. 259 (Spring 1948) 24.

An obituary notice, with a brief comment concerning AKC's vegetarianism. Reprinted in E189, pp. 317-19.

E210 WARNER, Langdon. [A letter on AKC]. *Homage to Ananda K. Coomaraswamy*, edited by S. Durai Raja Singam ([1948])—E188—pp. 125-7.

Reprinted, in part, in E189, p. xviii, and again in E191, p. 200. See also the references to AKC in *Langdon Warner Through His Letters*, edited by Theodore Bowie (Bloomington & London: Indiana University Press, 1966), pp. 165, 195-6, 220.

E211 WATSON, Ian K. Ananda Kentish Coomaraswamy and the Traditionalists. *Asian Studies Association of Australia Review*, Canberra, VII. 3 (Apr. 1984) 52-8.

An obloquy by a former adherent.

E212 WATTS, Alan Wilson. *In My Own Way: An Autobiography 1915-1965*. London: Jonathan Cape [1973], pp. 226-7.

These pages contain a tribute to AKC; other (brief) comments concerning AKC occur on pp. 94, 198, 215, 343. See also the references to AKC in Watts' *Myth and Ritual in Christianity* (London: Thames & Hudson [1953]), pp. 13-14, 20, and *passim*.

E213 WHITEHILL, Walter Muir. *Museum of Fine Arts Boston; a Centennial History*. Cambridge, Mass.: The Belknap Press of Harvard University, 1970, *Vol. One*, pp. 362-6, 368-71, 408; *Vol. Two*, pp. 792-3, 862-3.

Documents AKC's thirty years' association with the Museum, 1917-47.

E214 ——— People Who Helped Make the Museum Great . . . A.K. Coomaraswamy—"Art for Love's Sake". *Boston Globe*, Boston (17 Feb. 1970) 16.

Excerpted from E213, *Vol. One*, pp. 362-71, with omissions.

E214a ———Ananda Coomaraswamy. *Ananda Coomaraswamy:*

Remembering and Remembering Again and Again, edited by S. Durai Raja Singam (1974)—E191—pp. 328-30.

Reflections on AKC's curatorship at the Museum of Fine Arts, Boston, together with some personal reminiscences, incidental to the account given in E213.

E215 WICKRAMASURIYA, Sarathchandra. "A Generation of Spiritual Bastards and Intellectual Pariahs": A Study of Ananda Coomaraswamy's Attitudes to Colonial English Education in India and Sri Lanka. *Sri Lanka Journal of the Humanities*, Peradeniya, II. 1 (June 1976) [1]-31.

E216 WYMAN, Leland C. The Anthropological Approach to Art. *Homage to Ananda K. Coomaraswamy*, edited by S. Durai Raja Singam ([1948])—E188—pp. 151-4.

On AKC's claim for "the superiority of the anthropological to the psychological and aesthetic approaches to an unfamiliar art". Reprinted in E189, pp. 243-6, and E191, pp. 151-2.

Index

Titles of books or pamphlets by AKC or those with contributions by him are set in capital letters. Titles of essays, etc., by AKC, not separately published, are set within quotation marks. Titles of books by other authors reviewed by AKC or referred to by him or containing material about him are italicized. When titles are followed by two or more reference numbers, a main descriptive entry is indicated by the use of bold type. All references are to the serial numbers of the entries, not to page numbers. This index is, of course, an index to the bibliography, and not to the entire contents of AKC's writings themselves. Only historical persons have been indexed. The book reviews listed in Section A are not indexed.

J.S.C.